CHICKENHARE™

FIRE IN THE HOLE

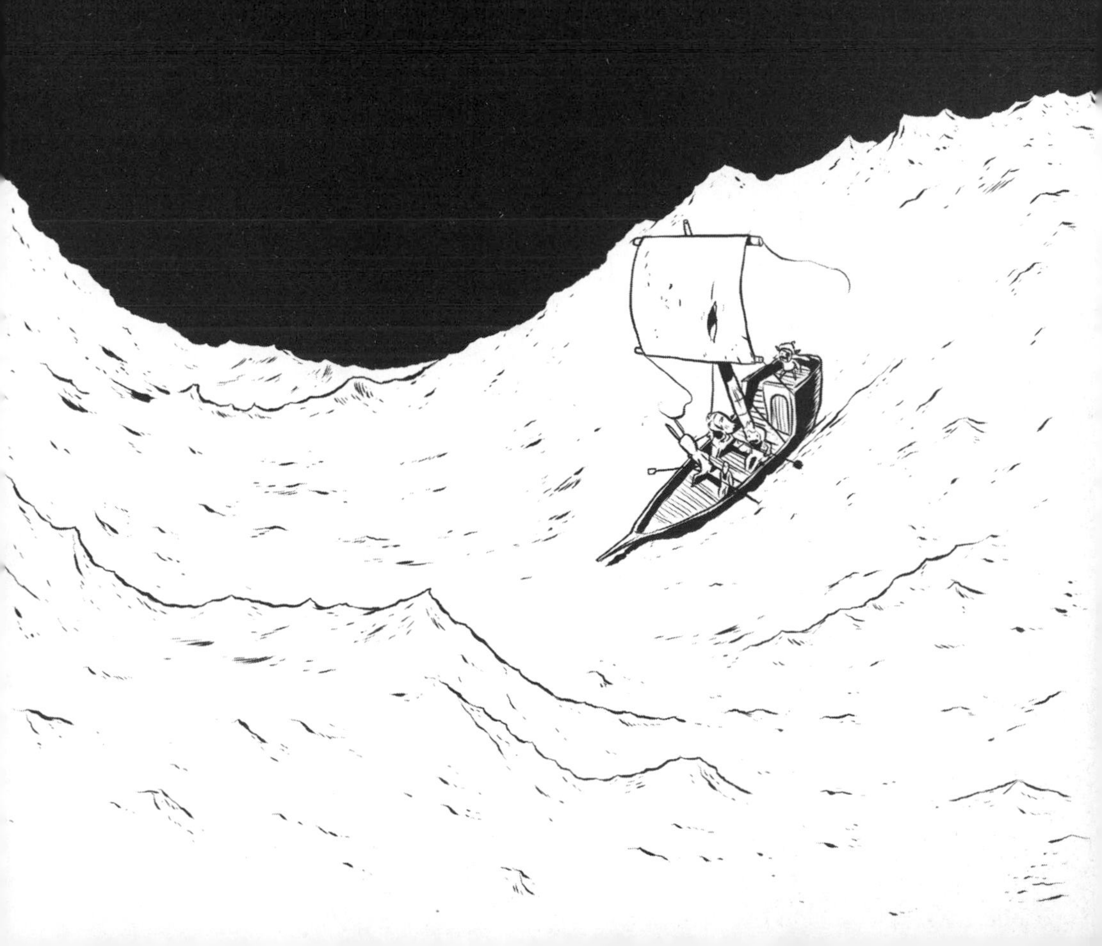

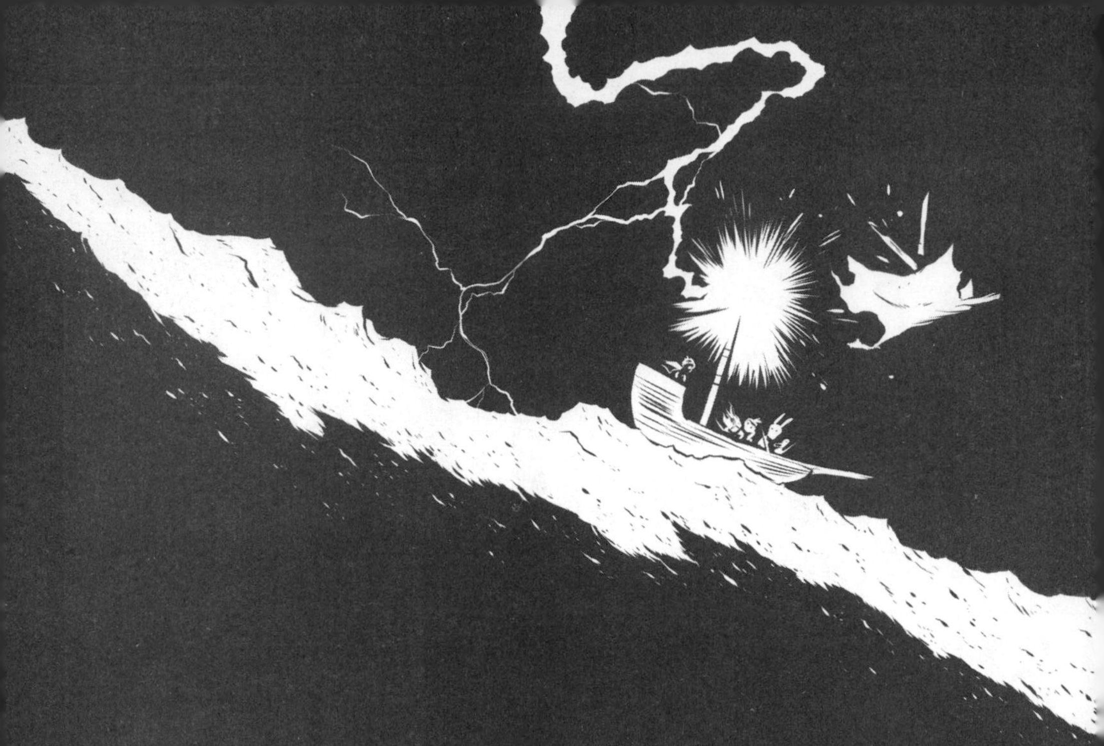

Designed by CHRIS GRINE
Edited by SHAWNA GORE
Assistant Editor JEMIAH JEFFERSON
Publisher MIKE RICHARDSON

Published by Dark Horse Books
A division of Dark Horse Comics, Inc.
10956 SE Main St.
Milwaukie, OR 97222

April 2008
First edition
ISBN 978-1-59307-907-9

1 3 5 7 9 10 8 6 4 2

CHICKENHARE™: FIRE IN THE HOLE.

Printed in the United States of America

CHICKENHARE™

FIRE IN THE HOLE

STORY & ARTWORK
BY
CHRIS GRINE

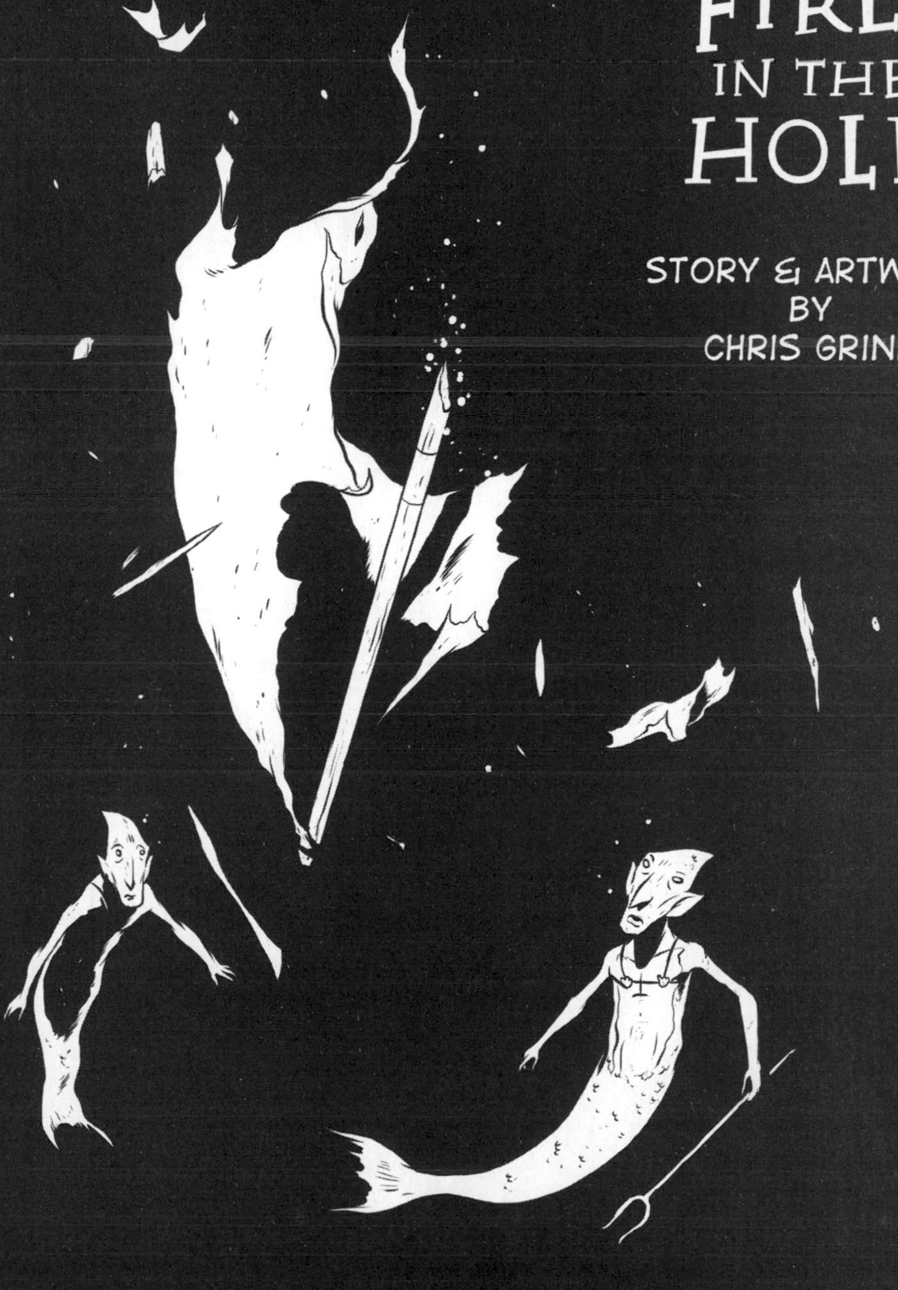

DEDICATED TO MY GRANDFATHER
ROBERT HALL

THE GREATEST ARTIST
I'LL EVER KNOW.

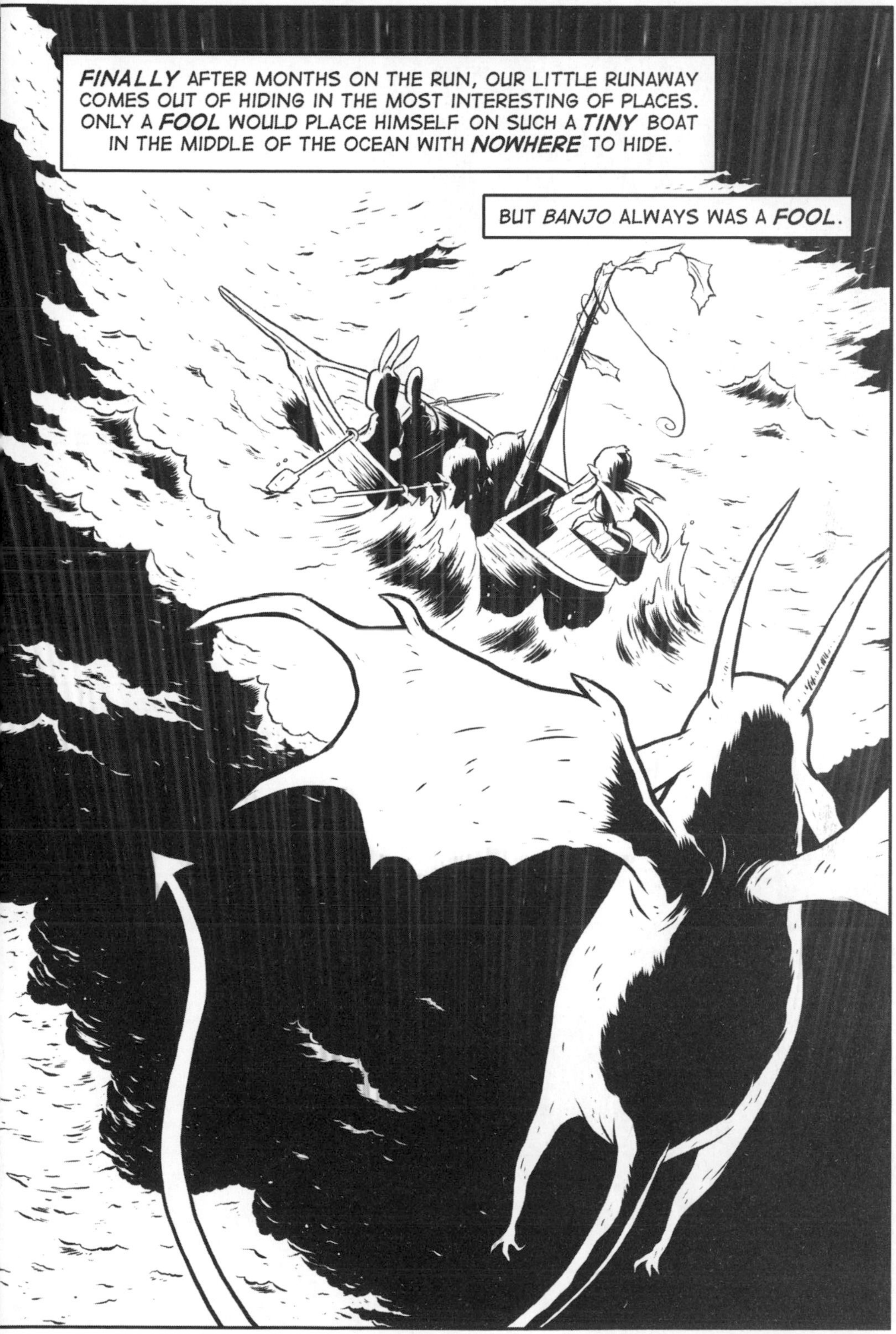
FINALLY AFTER MONTHS ON THE RUN, OUR LITTLE RUNAWAY COMES OUT OF HIDING IN THE MOST INTERESTING OF PLACES. ONLY A FOOL WOULD PLACE HIMSELF ON SUCH A TINY BOAT IN THE MIDDLE OF THE OCEAN WITH NOWHERE TO HIDE.
BUT BANJO ALWAYS WAS A FOOL.

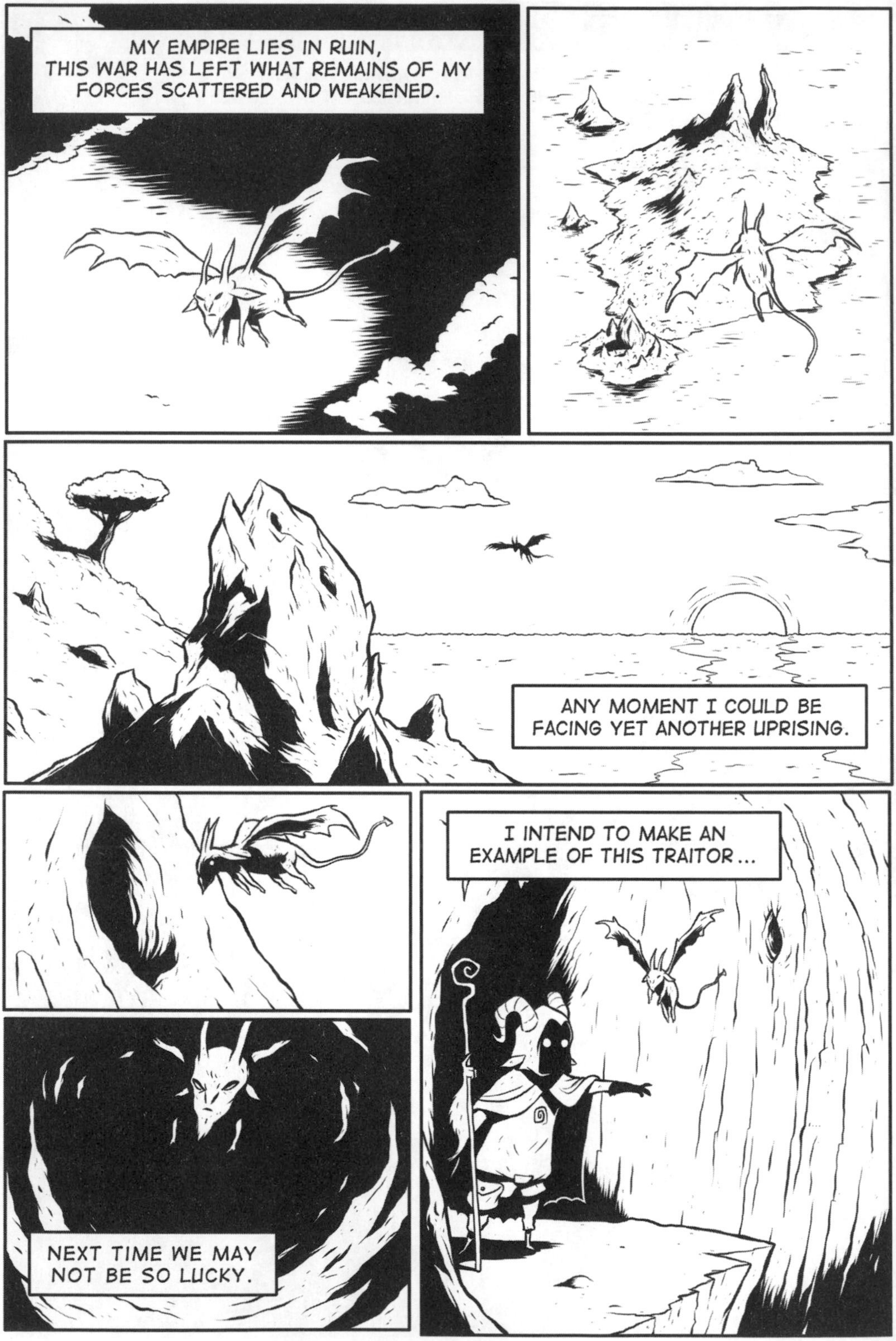
MY EMPIRE LIES IN RUIN, THIS WAR HAS LEFT WHAT REMAINS OF MY FORCES SCATTERED AND WEAKENED.
ANY MOMENT I COULD BE FACING YET ANOTHER UPRISING.
NEXT TIME WE MAY NOT BE SO LUCKY.
I INTEND TO MAKE AN EXAMPLE OF THIS TRAITOR...

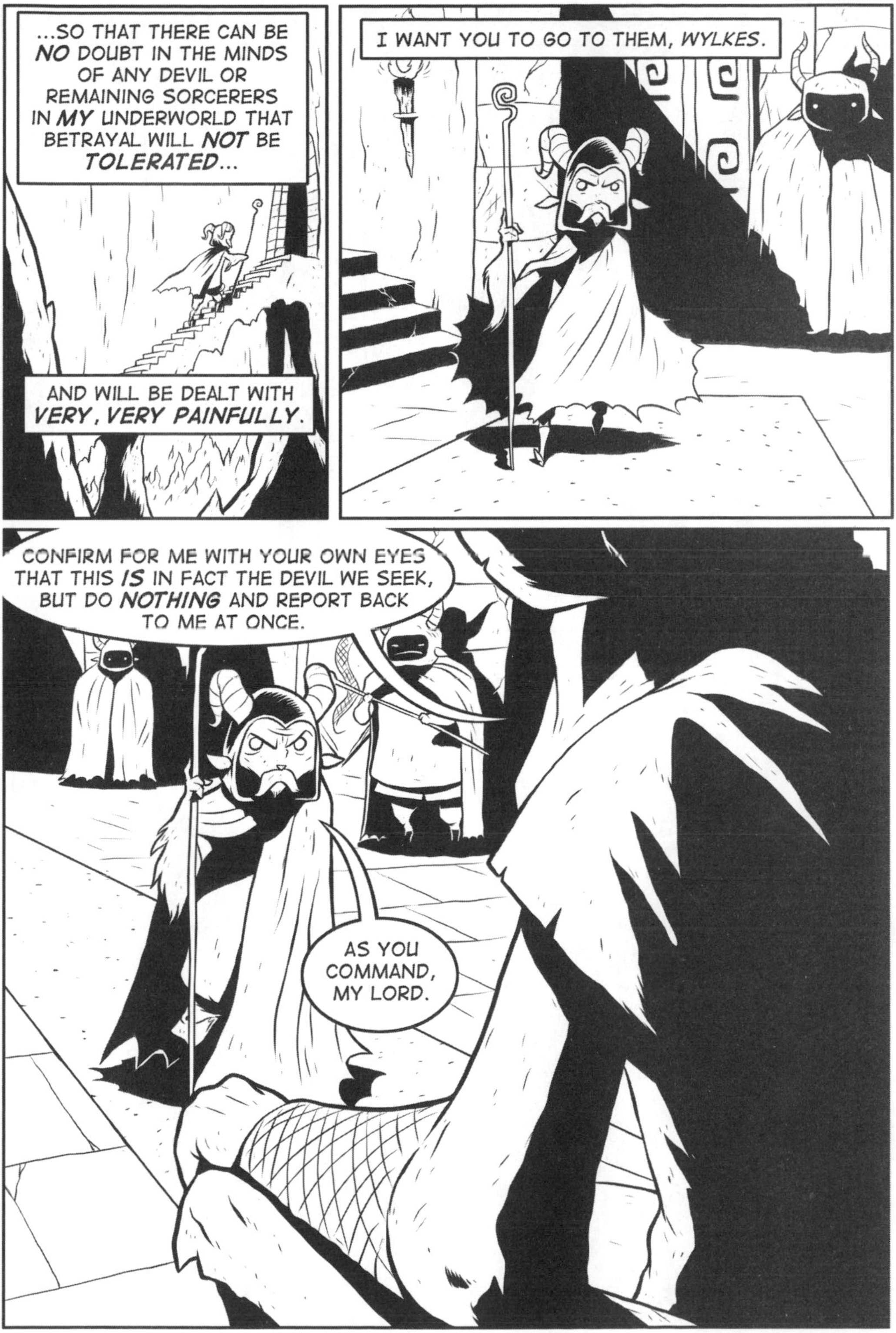
...SO THAT THERE CAN BE NO DOUBT IN THE MINDS OF ANY DEVIL OR REMAINING SORCERERS IN MY UNDERWORLD THAT BETRAYAL WILL NOT BE TOLERATED...
AND WILL BE DEALT WITH VERY, VERY PAINFULLY.
I WANT YOU TO GO TO THEM, WYLKES.
CONFIRM FOR ME WITH YOUR OWN EYES THAT THIS IS IN FACT THE DEVIL WE SEEK, BUT DO NOTHING AND REPORT BACK TO ME AT ONCE.
AS YOU COMMAND, MY LORD.

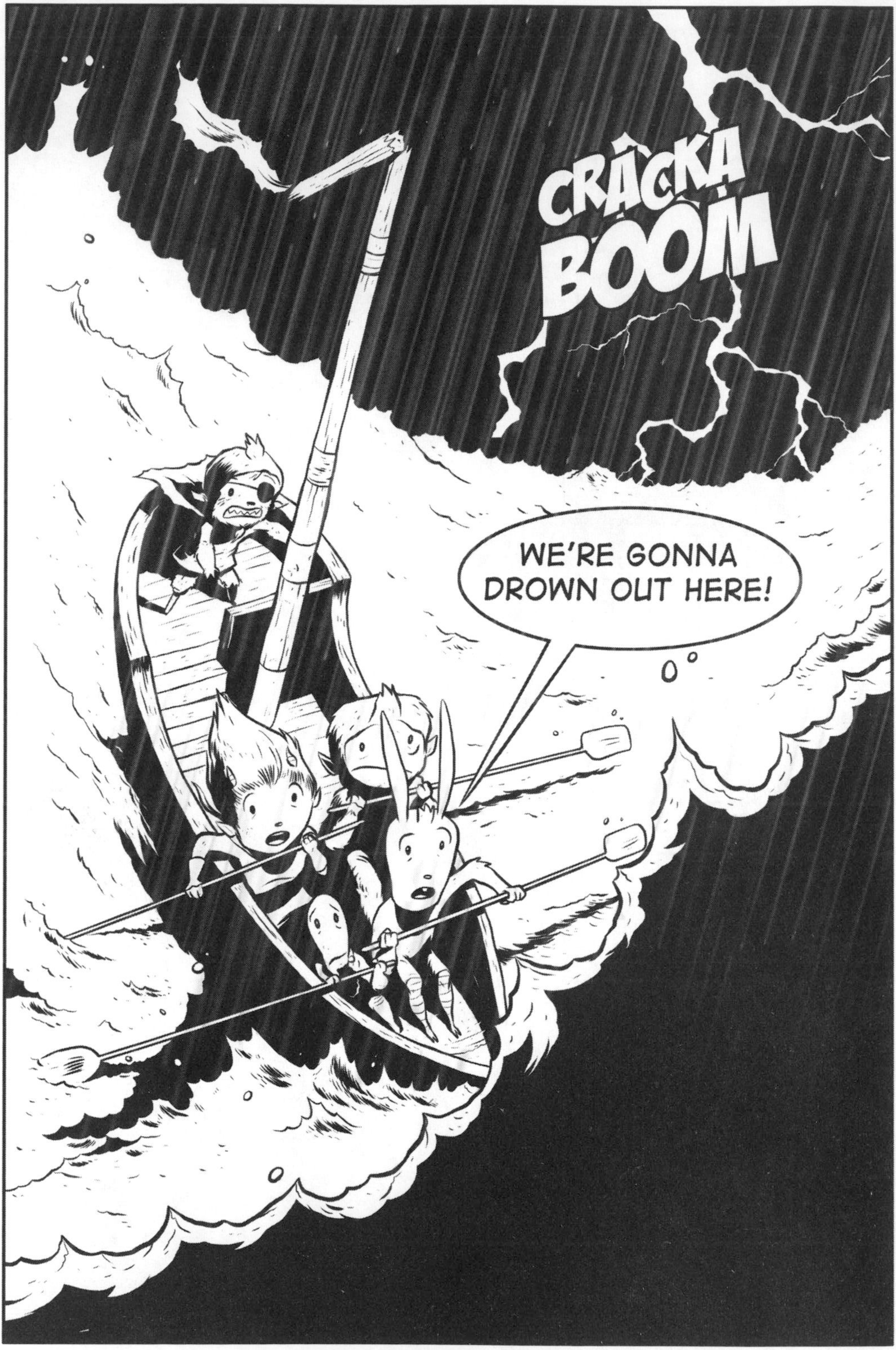
CRACKA
BOOM
WE'RE GONNA DROWN OUT HERE!

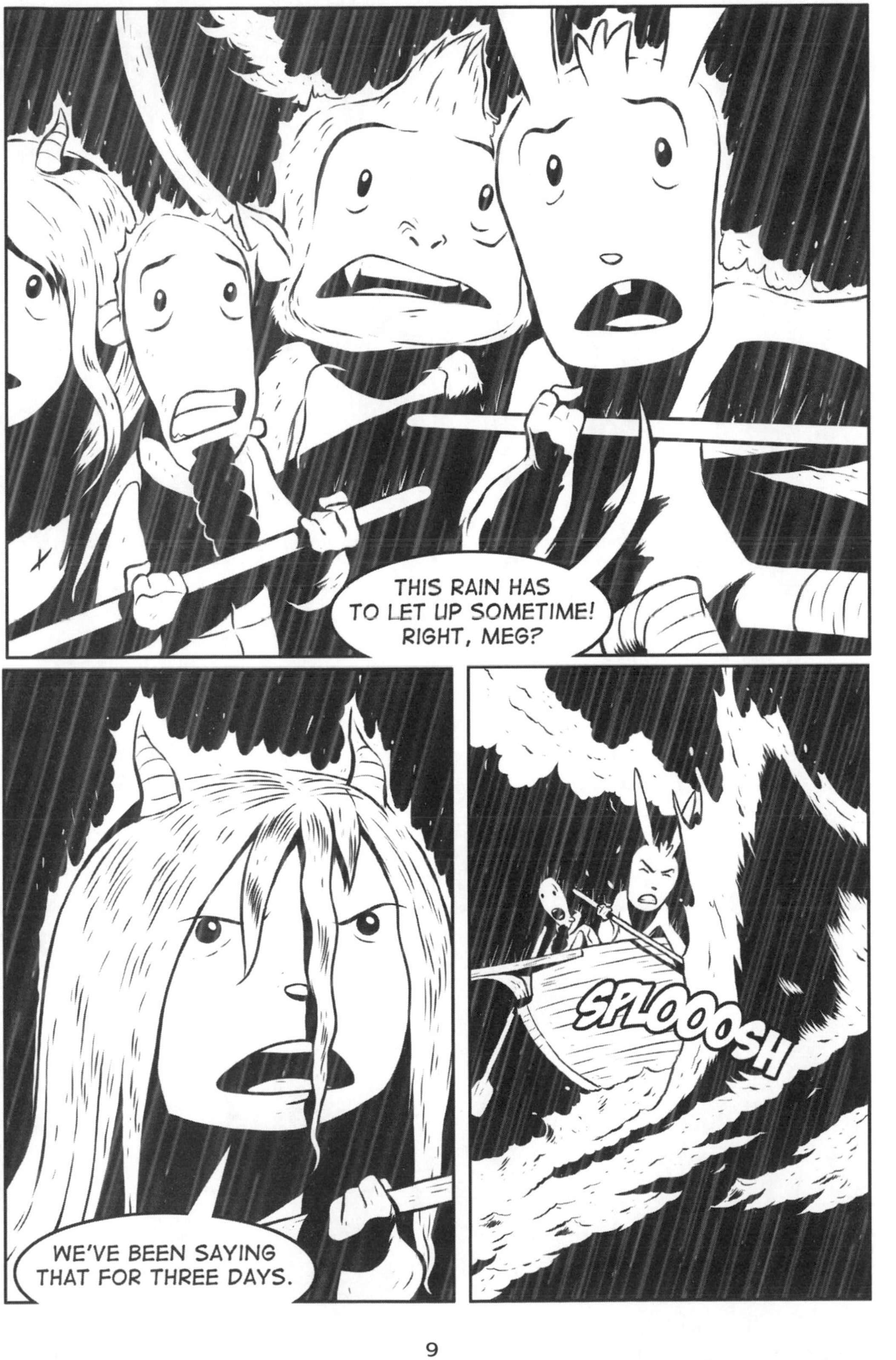
THIS RAIN HAS TO LET UP SOMETIME! RIGHT, MEG?
WE'VE BEEN SAYING THAT FOR THREE DAYS.
SPLOOOOSH

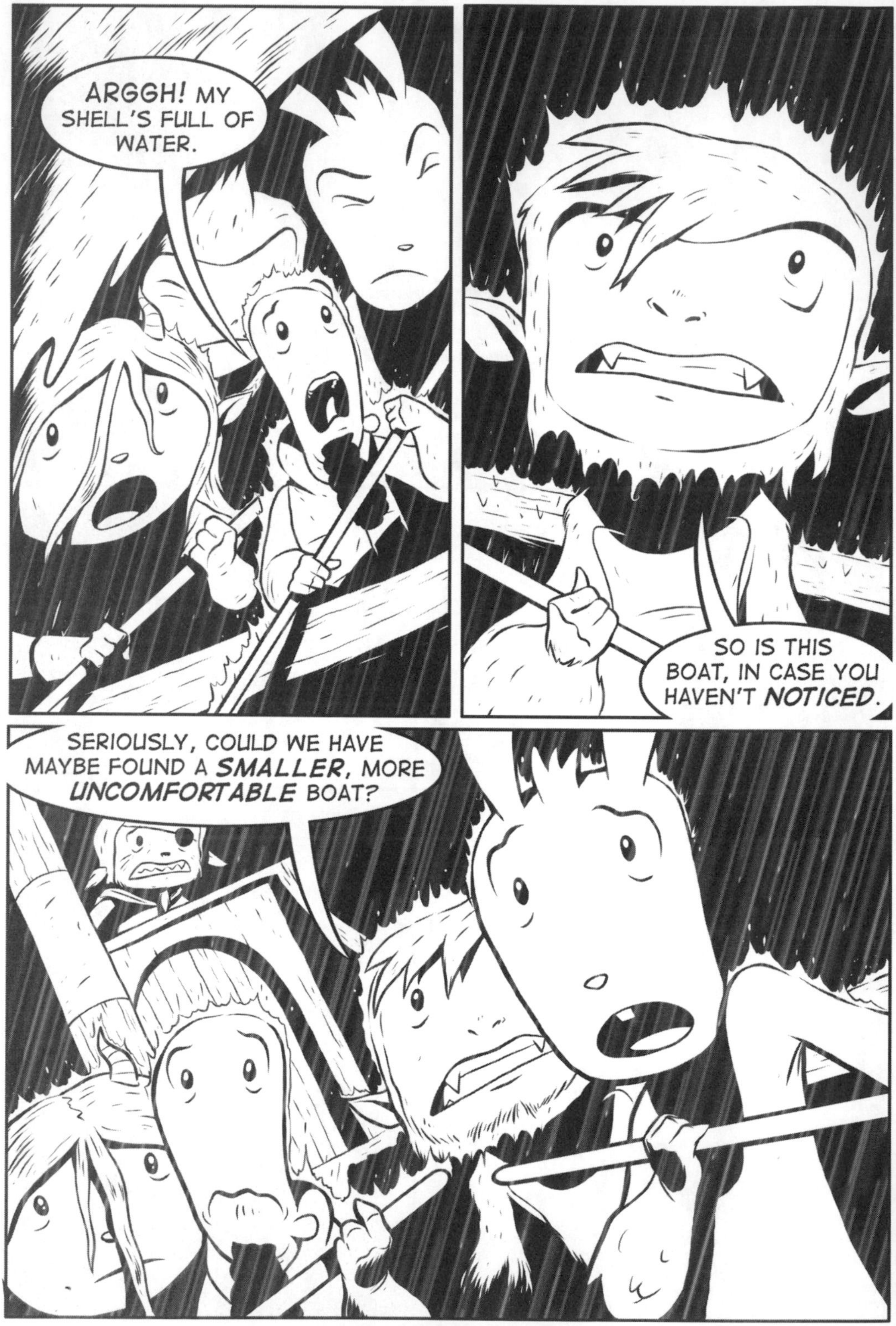
ARGGH! MY SHELL'S FULL OF WATER.
SO IS THIS BOAT, IN CASE YOU HAVEN'T *NOTICED*.
SERIOUSLY, COULD WE HAVE MAYBE FOUND A *SMALLER*, MORE *UNCOMFORTABLE* BOAT?

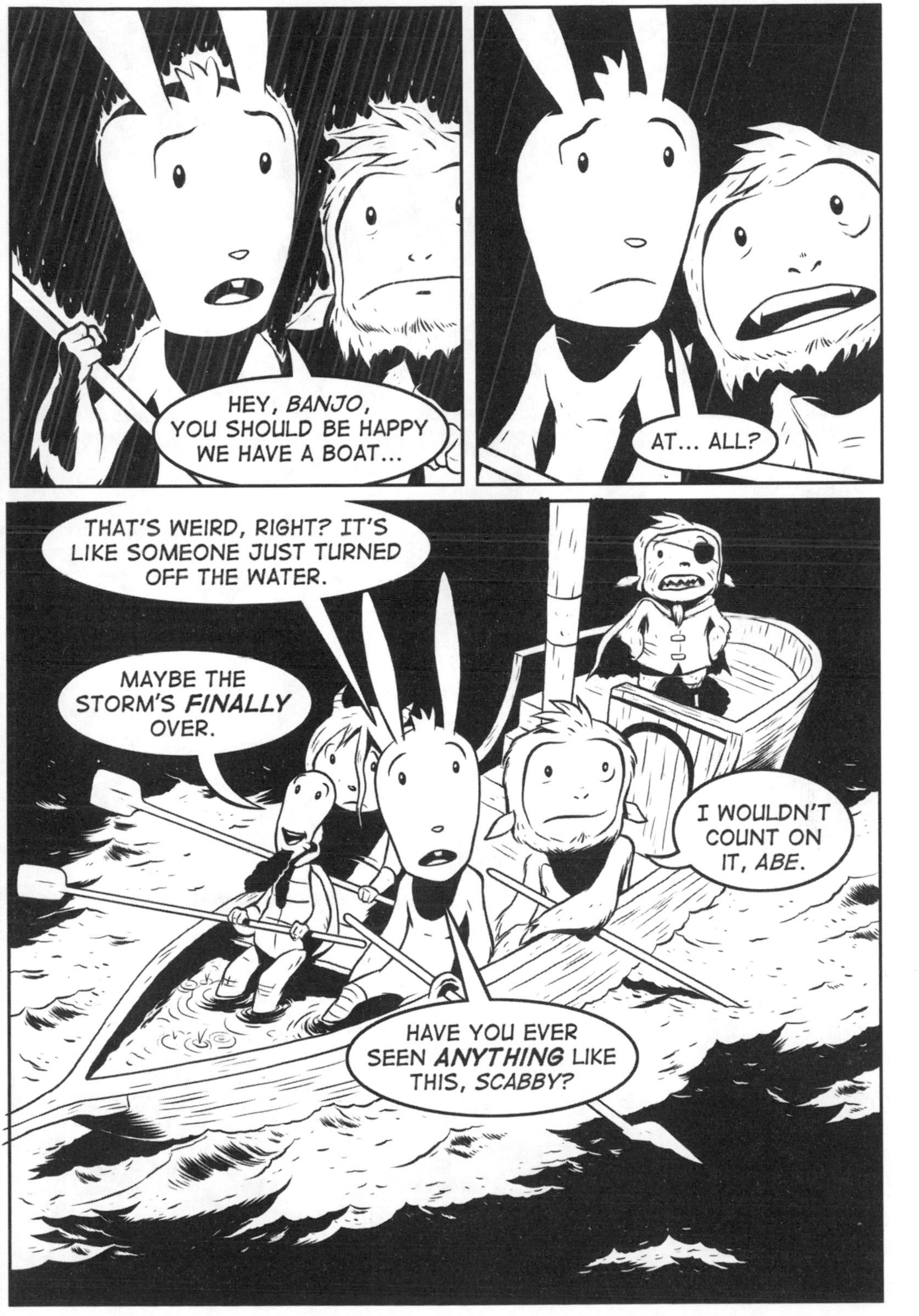
HEY, BANJO, YOU SHOULD BE HAPPY WE HAVE A BOAT...
AT... ALL?
THAT'S WEIRD, RIGHT? IT'S LIKE SOMEONE JUST TURNED OFF THE WATER.
MAYBE THE STORM'S FINALLY OVER.
I WOULDN'T COUNT ON IT, ABE.
HAVE YOU EVER SEEN ANYTHING LIKE THIS, SCABBY?

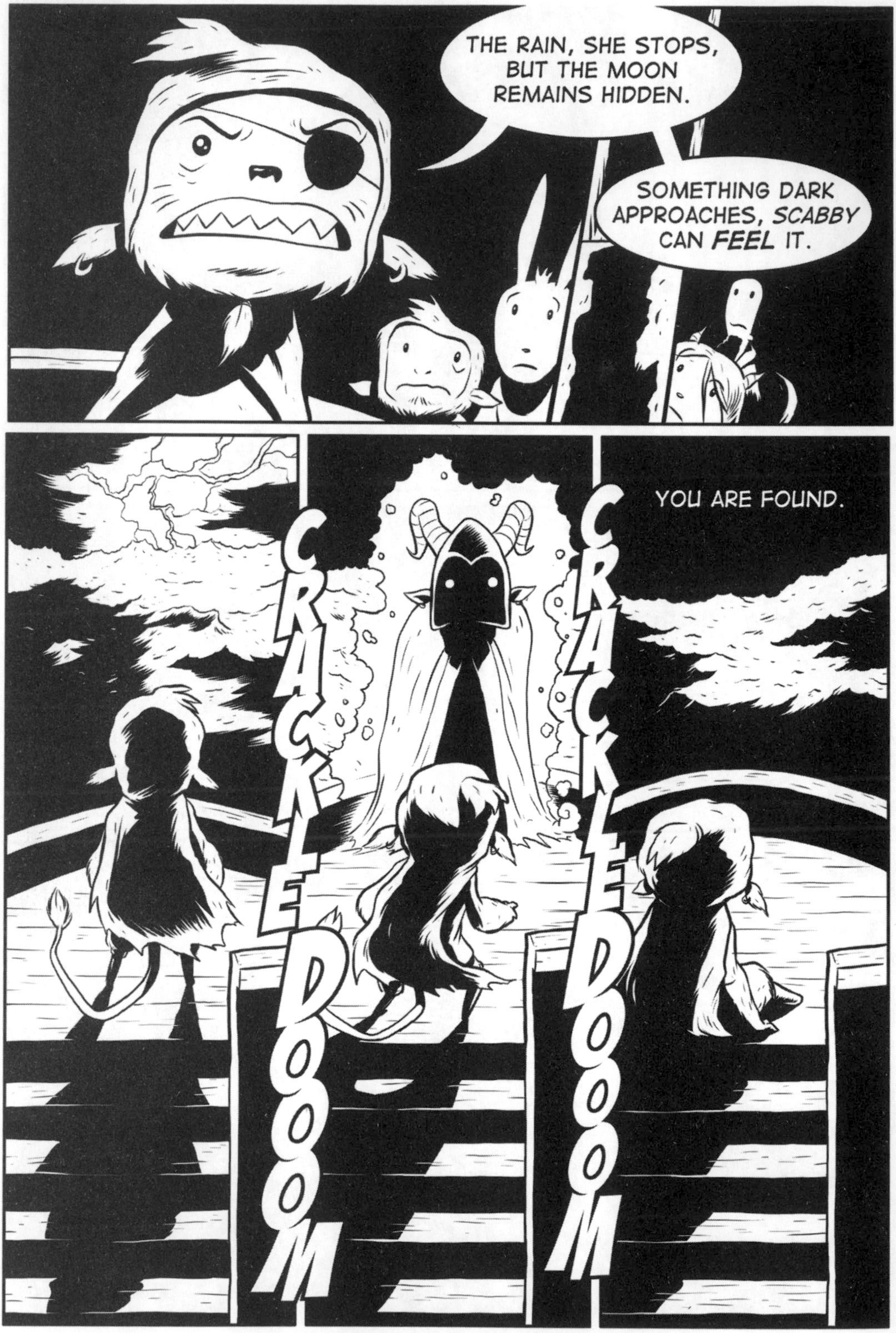
THE RAIN, SHE STOPS, BUT THE MOON REMAINS HIDDEN.
SOMETHING DARK APPROACHES, *SCABBY* CAN ***FEEL*** IT.
CRACKLEDOOOOM
YOU ARE FOUND.
CRACKLEDOOOOM

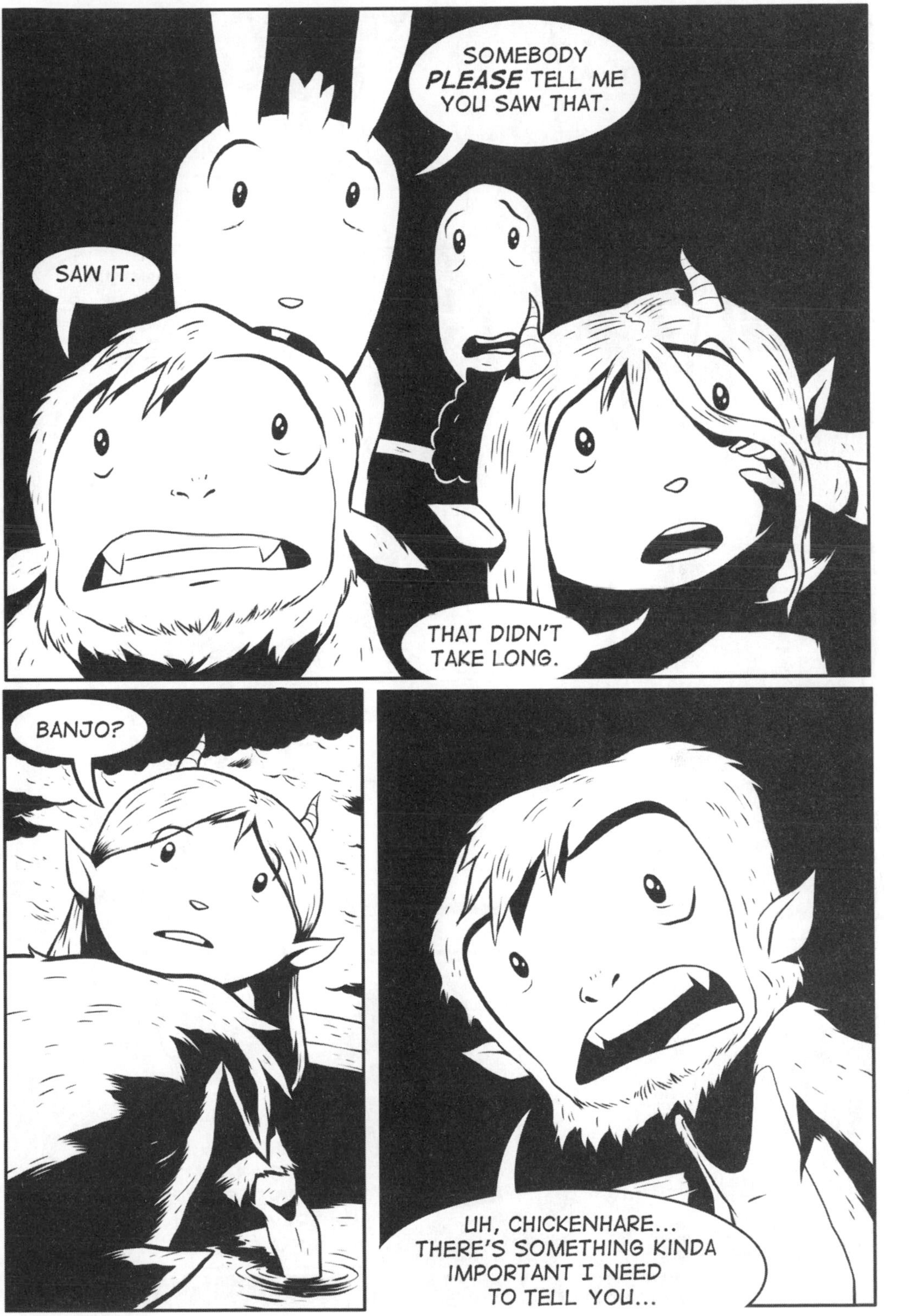
SOMEBODY *PLEASE* TELL ME YOU SAW THAT.
SAW IT.
THAT DIDN'T TAKE LONG.
BANJO?
UH, CHICKENHARE... THERE'S SOMETHING KINDA IMPORTANT I NEED TO TELL YOU...

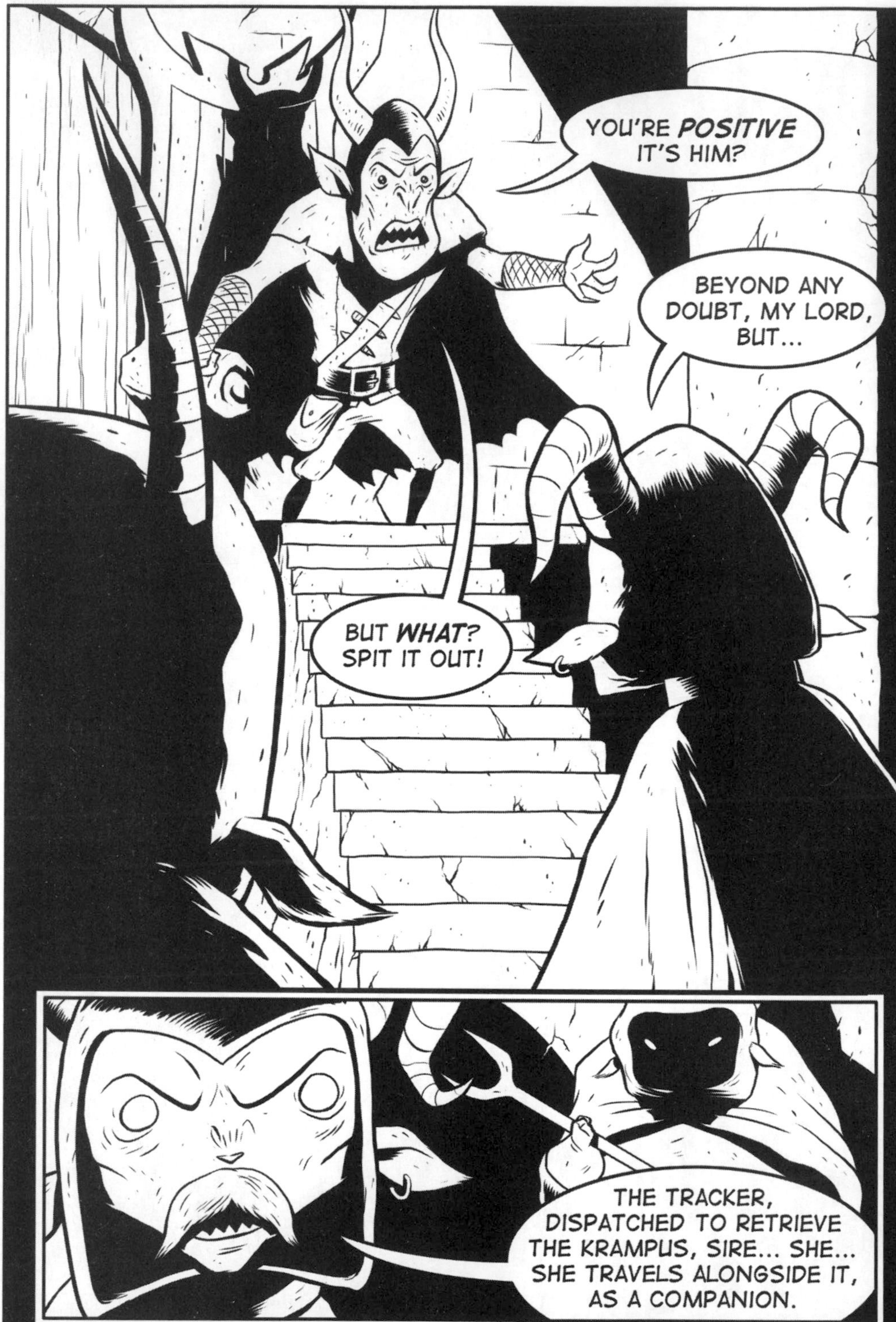
YOU'RE POSITIVE IT'S HIM?
BEYOND ANY DOUBT, MY LORD, BUT...
BUT WHAT? SPIT IT OUT!
THE TRACKER, DISPATCHED TO RETRIEVE THE KRAMPUS, SIRE... SHE... SHE TRAVELS ALONGSIDE IT, AS A COMPANION.

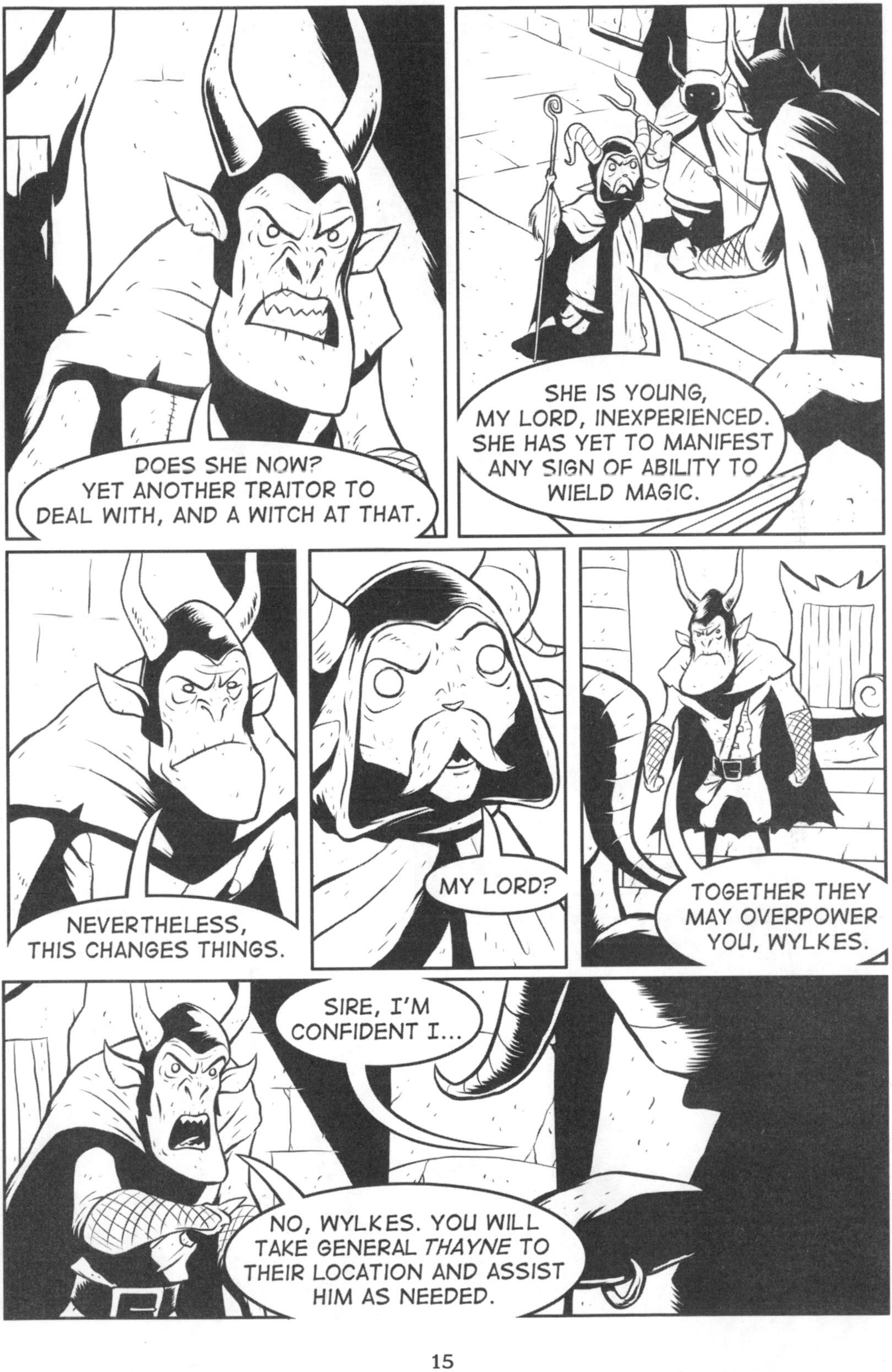
DOES SHE NOW? YET ANOTHER TRAITOR TO DEAL WITH, AND A WITCH AT THAT.
SHE IS YOUNG, MY LORD, INEXPERIENCED. SHE HAS YET TO MANIFEST ANY SIGN OF ABILITY TO WIELD MAGIC.
NEVERTHELESS, THIS CHANGES THINGS.
MY LORD?
TOGETHER THEY MAY OVERPOWER YOU, WYLKES.
SIRE, I'M CONFIDENT I...
NO, WYLKES. YOU WILL TAKE GENERAL *THAYNE* TO THEIR LOCATION AND ASSIST HIM AS NEEDED.

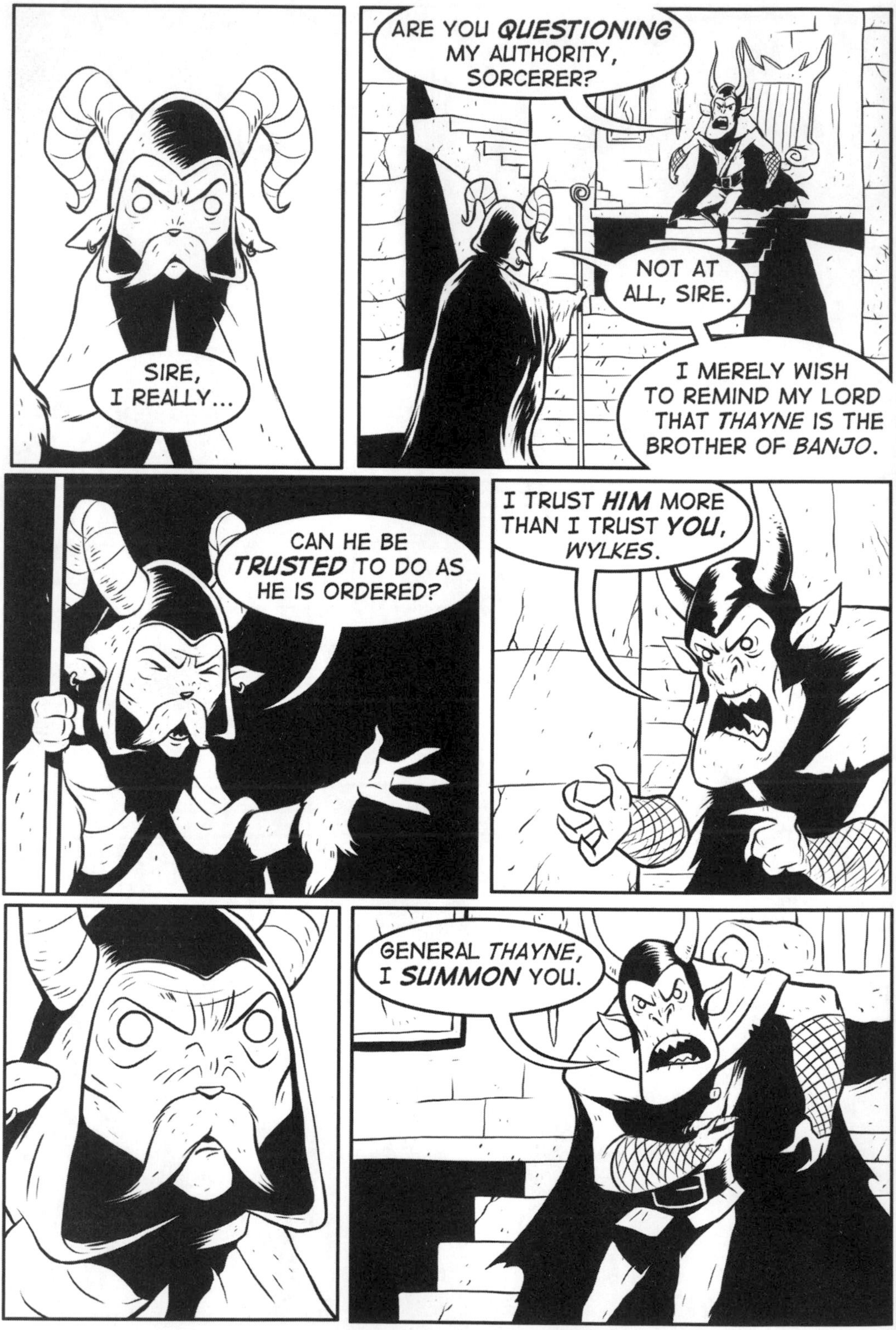
SIRE, I REALLY...
ARE YOU QUESTIONING MY AUTHORITY, SORCERER?
NOT AT ALL, SIRE.
I MERELY WISH TO REMIND MY LORD THAT THAYNE IS THE BROTHER OF BANJO.
CAN HE BE TRUSTED TO DO AS HE IS ORDERED?
I TRUST HIM MORE THAN I TRUST YOU, WYLKES.
GENERAL THAYNE, I SUMMON YOU.

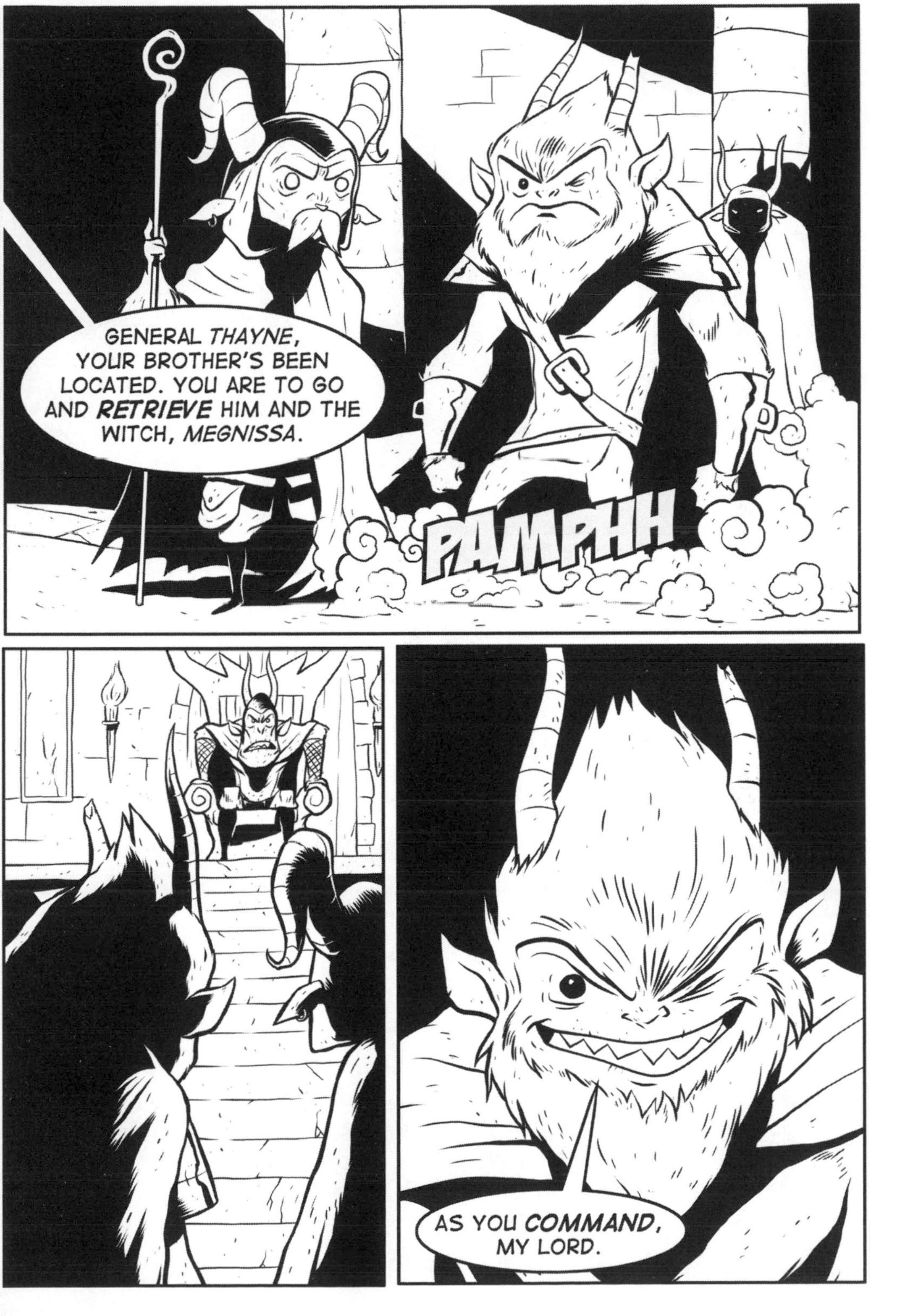

GENERAL THAYNE, YOUR BROTHER'S BEEN LOCATED. YOU ARE TO GO AND RETRIEVE HIM AND THE WITCH, MEGNISSA.
PAMPHH
AS YOU COMMAND, MY LORD.

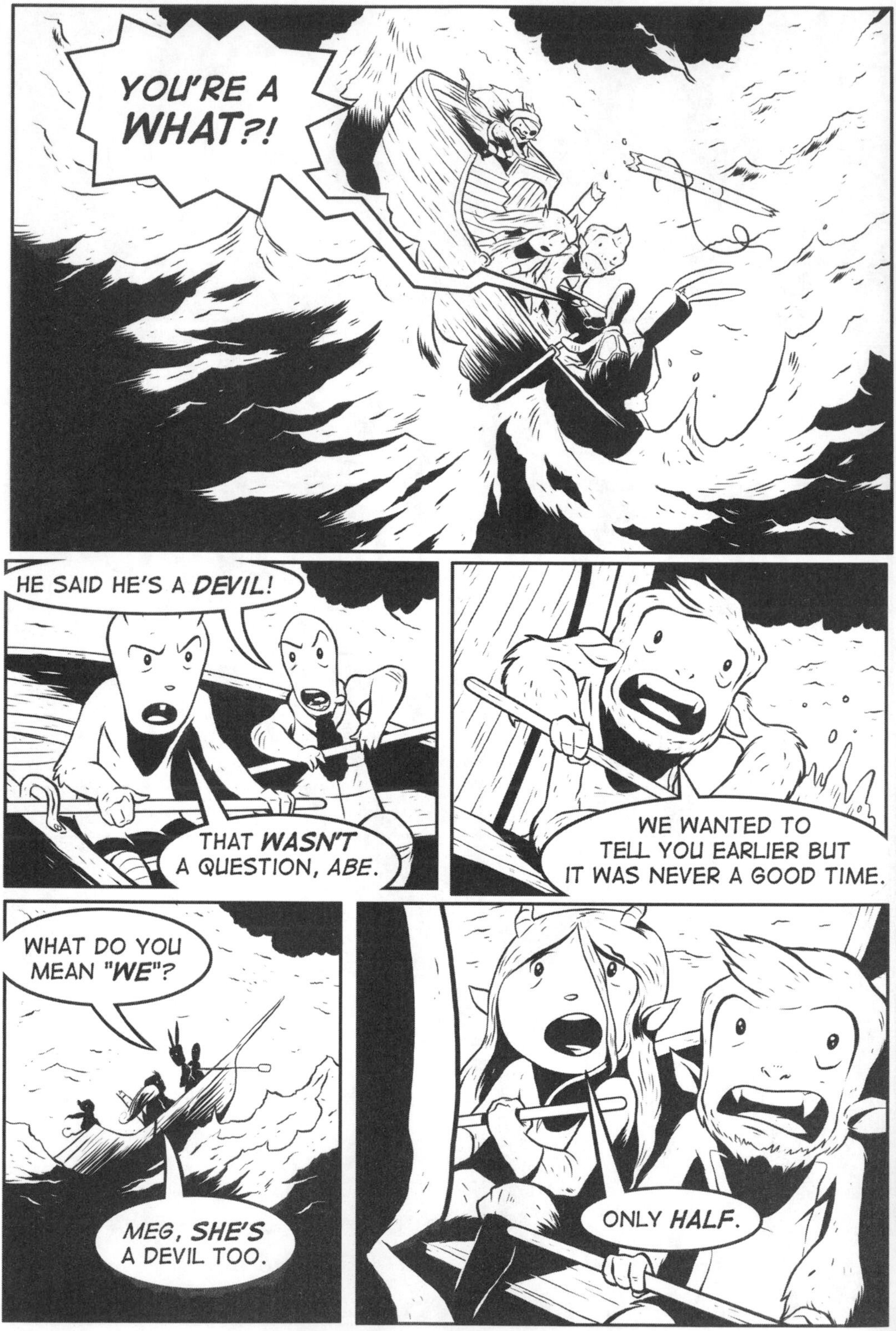
YOU'RE A WHAT?!
HE SAID HE'S A DEVIL!
THAT WASN'T A QUESTION, ABE.
WE WANTED TO TELL YOU EARLIER BUT IT WAS NEVER A GOOD TIME.
WHAT DO YOU MEAN "WE"?
MEG, SHE'S A DEVIL TOO.
ONLY HALF.

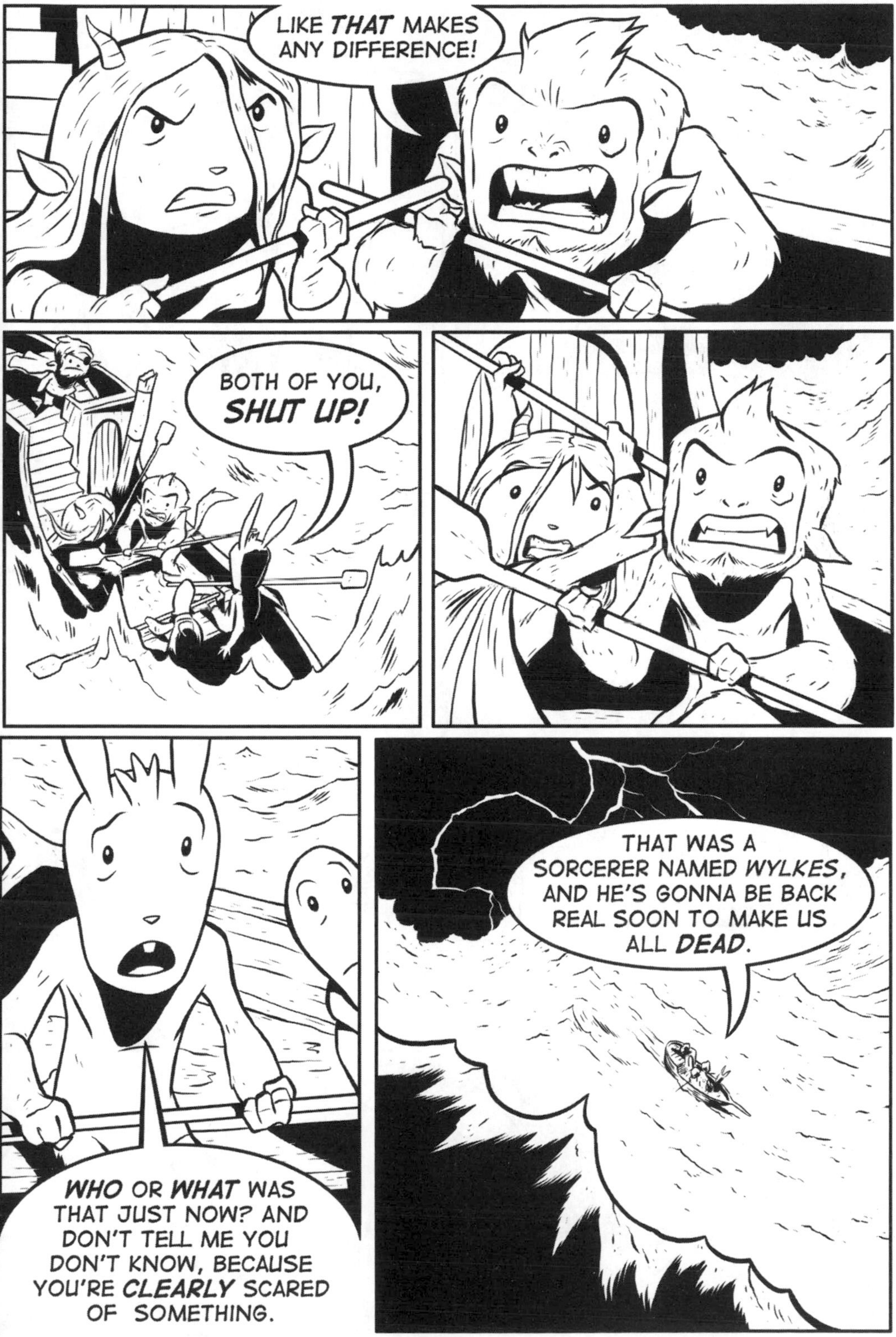
LIKE THAT MAKES ANY DIFFERENCE!
BOTH OF YOU, SHUT UP!
WHO OR WHAT WAS THAT JUST NOW? AND DON'T TELL ME YOU DON'T KNOW, BECAUSE YOU'RE CLEARLY SCARED OF SOMETHING.
THAT WAS A SORCERER NAMED WYLKES, AND HE'S GONNA BE BACK REAL SOON TO MAKE US ALL DEAD.

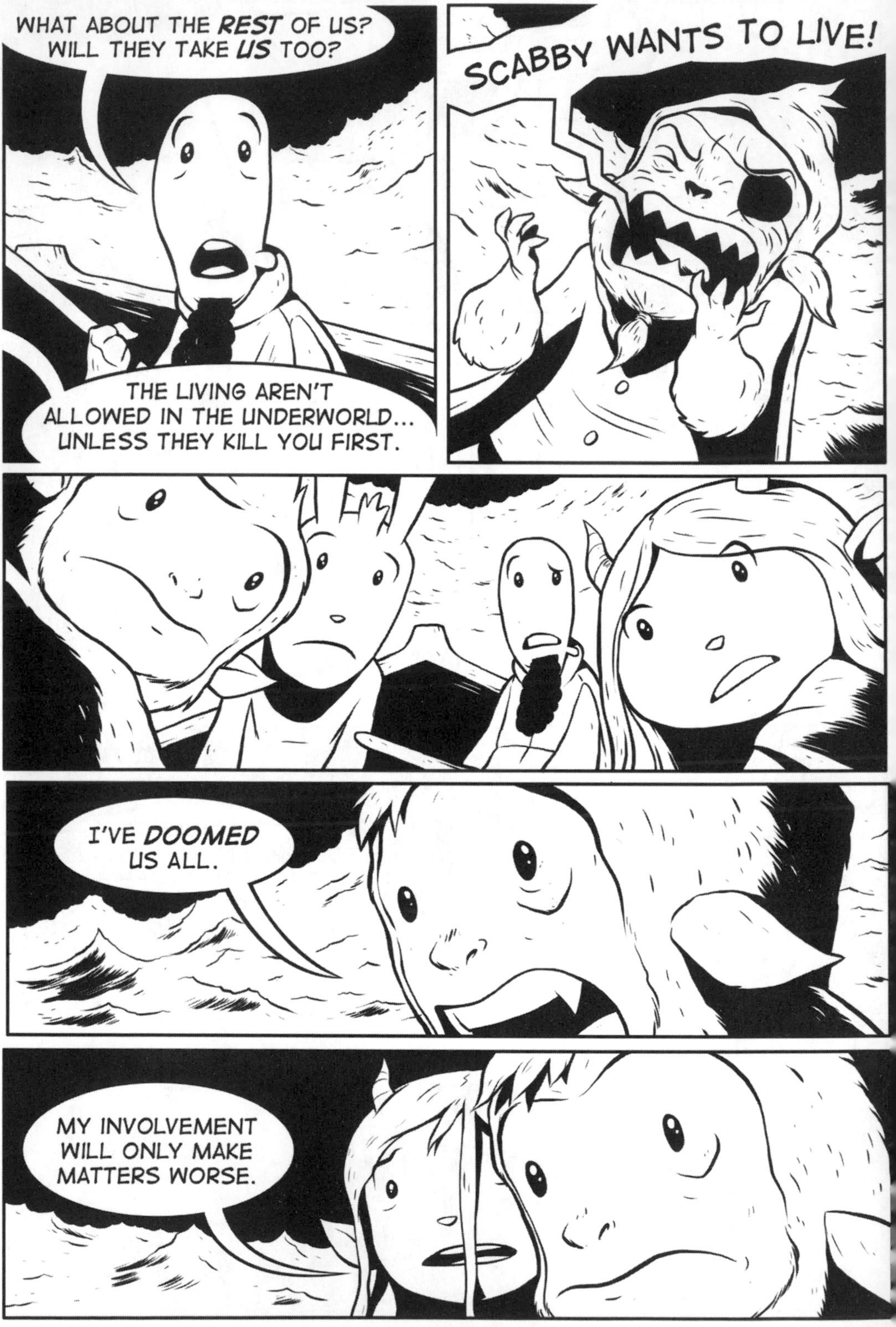
WHAT ABOUT THE REST OF US? WILL THEY TAKE US TOO?
THE LIVING AREN'T ALLOWED IN THE UNDERWORLD... UNLESS THEY KILL YOU FIRST.
SCABBY WANTS TO LIVE!
I'VE DOOMED US ALL.
MY INVOLVEMENT WILL ONLY MAKE MATTERS WORSE.

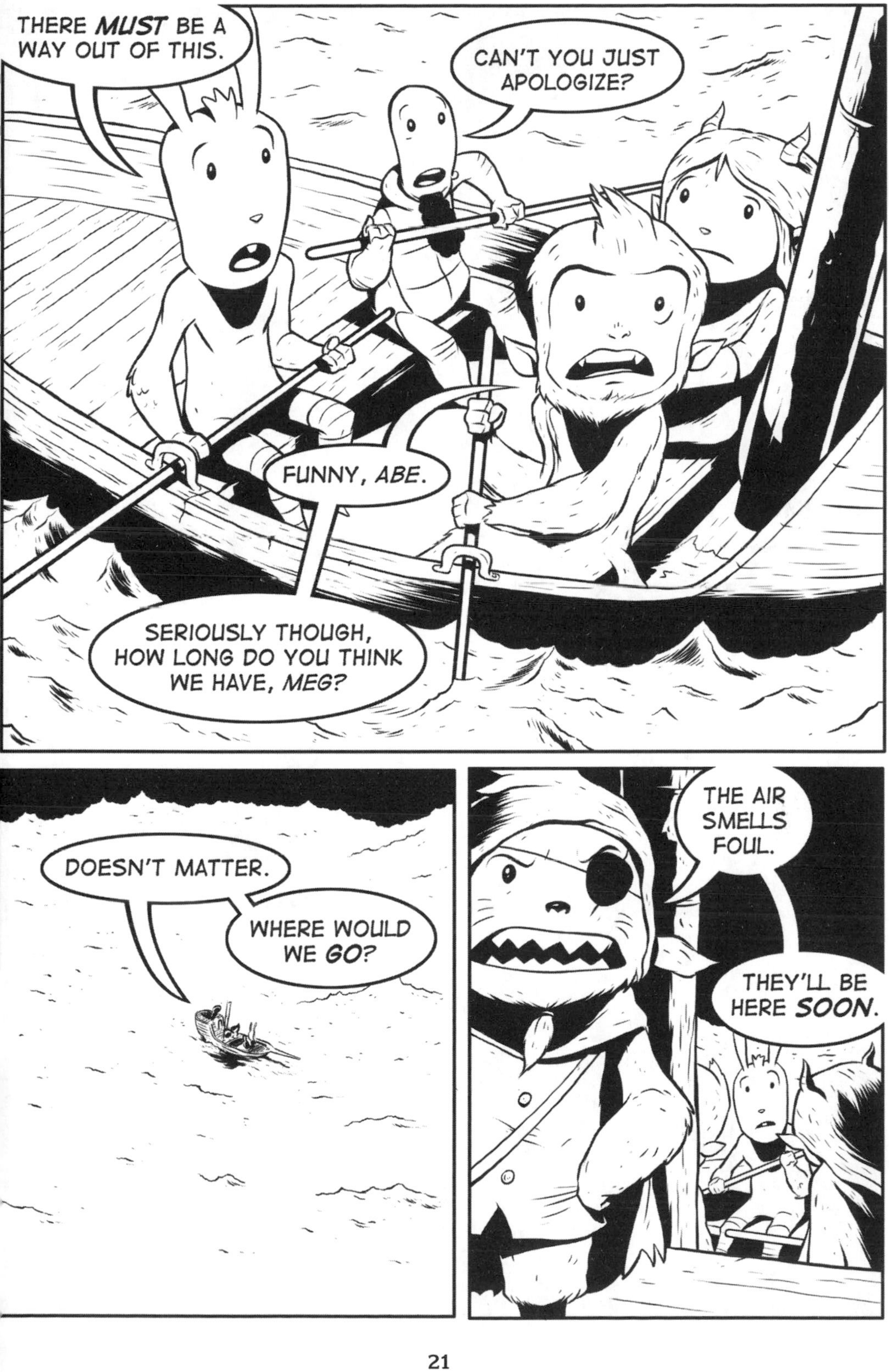
THERE *MUST* BE A WAY OUT OF THIS.
CAN'T YOU JUST APOLOGIZE?
FUNNY, *ABE*.
SERIOUSLY THOUGH, HOW LONG DO YOU THINK WE HAVE, *MEG*?
DOESN'T MATTER.
WHERE WOULD WE *GO*?
THE AIR SMELLS FOUL.
THEY'LL BE HERE ***SOON***.

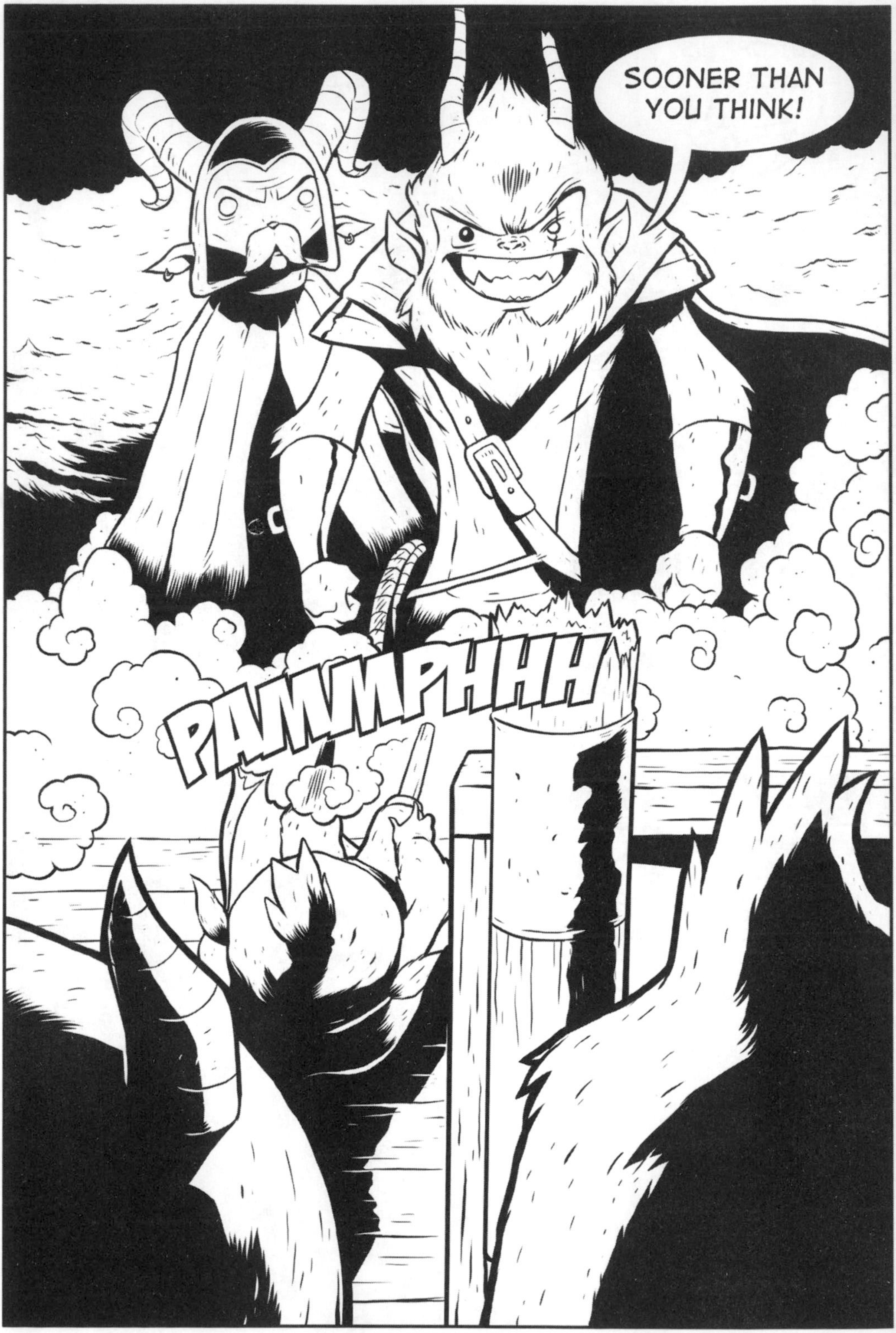
SOONER THAN YOU THINK!
PAMMPHHH

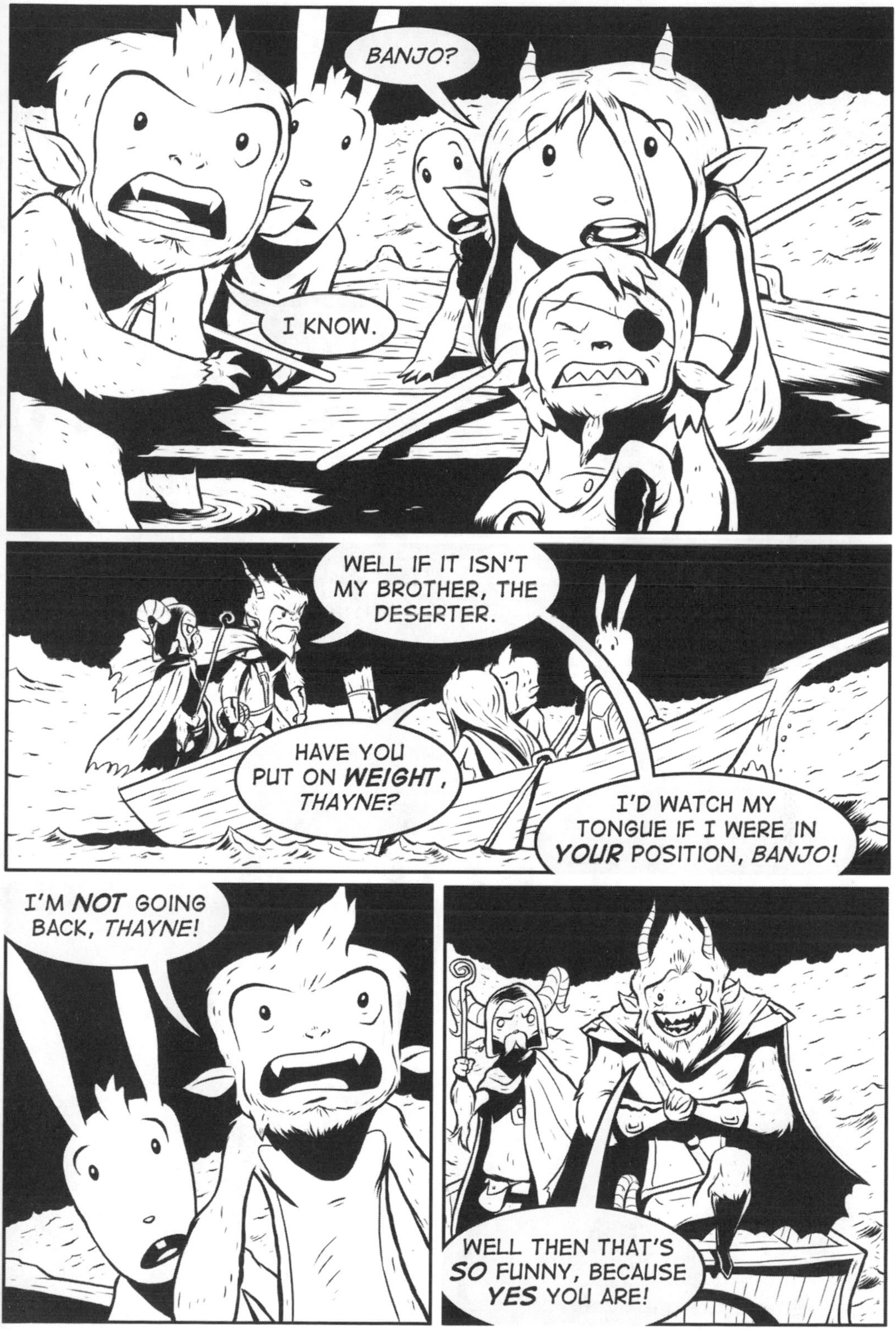
BANJO?
I KNOW.
WELL IF IT ISN'T MY BROTHER, THE DESERTER.
HAVE YOU PUT ON WEIGHT, THAYNE?
I'D WATCH MY TONGUE IF I WERE IN YOUR POSITION, BANJO!
I'M NOT GOING BACK, THAYNE!
WELL THEN THAT'S SO FUNNY, BECAUSE YES YOU ARE!

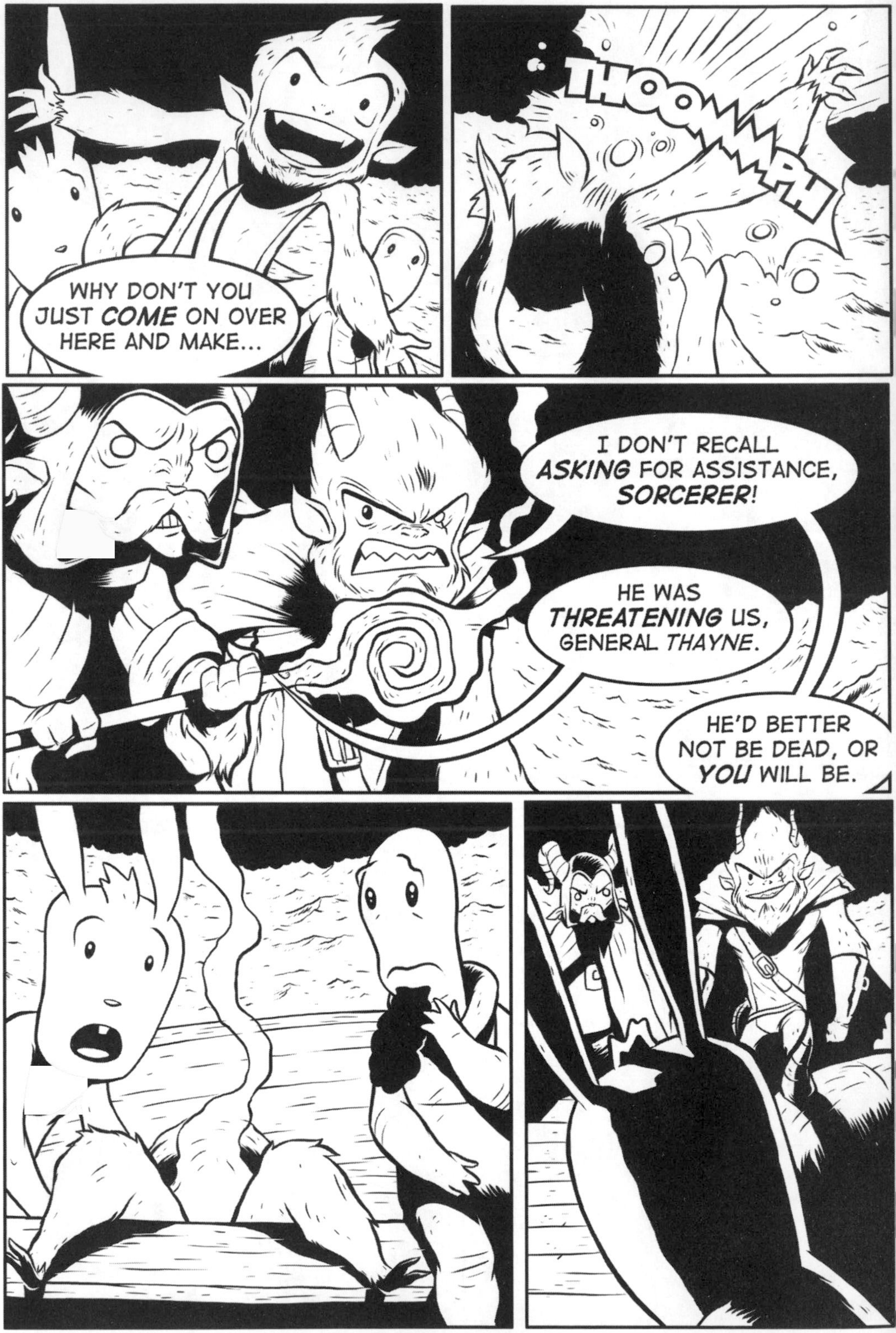
WHY DON'T YOU JUST COME ON OVER HERE AND MAKE...
THOOMPH
I DON'T RECALL ASKING FOR ASSISTANCE, SORCERER!
HE WAS THREATENING US, GENERAL THAYNE.
HE'D BETTER NOT BE DEAD, OR YOU WILL BE.

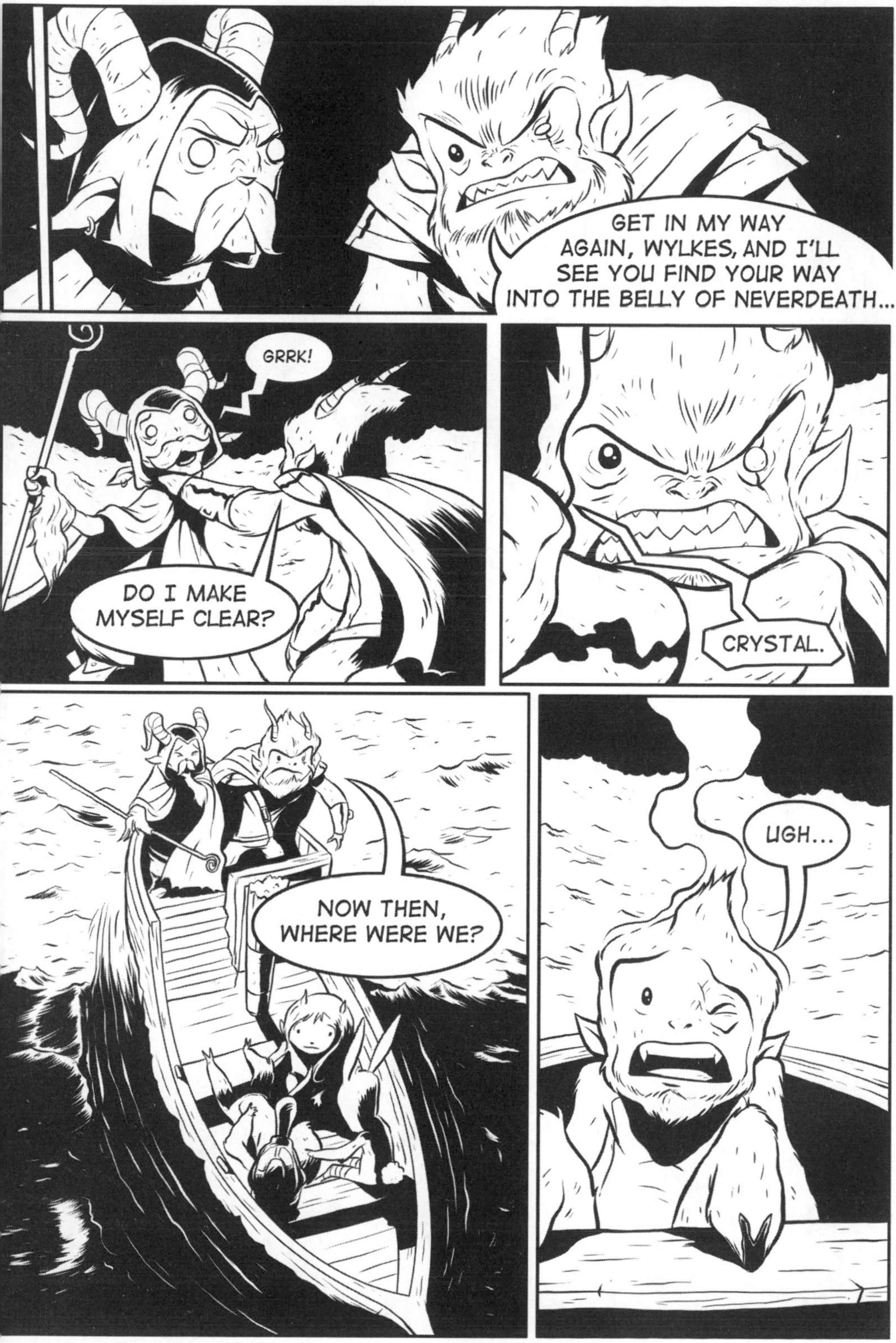
GET IN MY WAY AGAIN, WYLKES, AND I'LL SEE YOU FIND YOUR WAY INTO THE BELLY OF NEVERDEATH...
GRRK!
DO I MAKE MYSELF CLEAR?
CRYSTAL.
NOW THEN, WHERE WERE WE?
UGH...

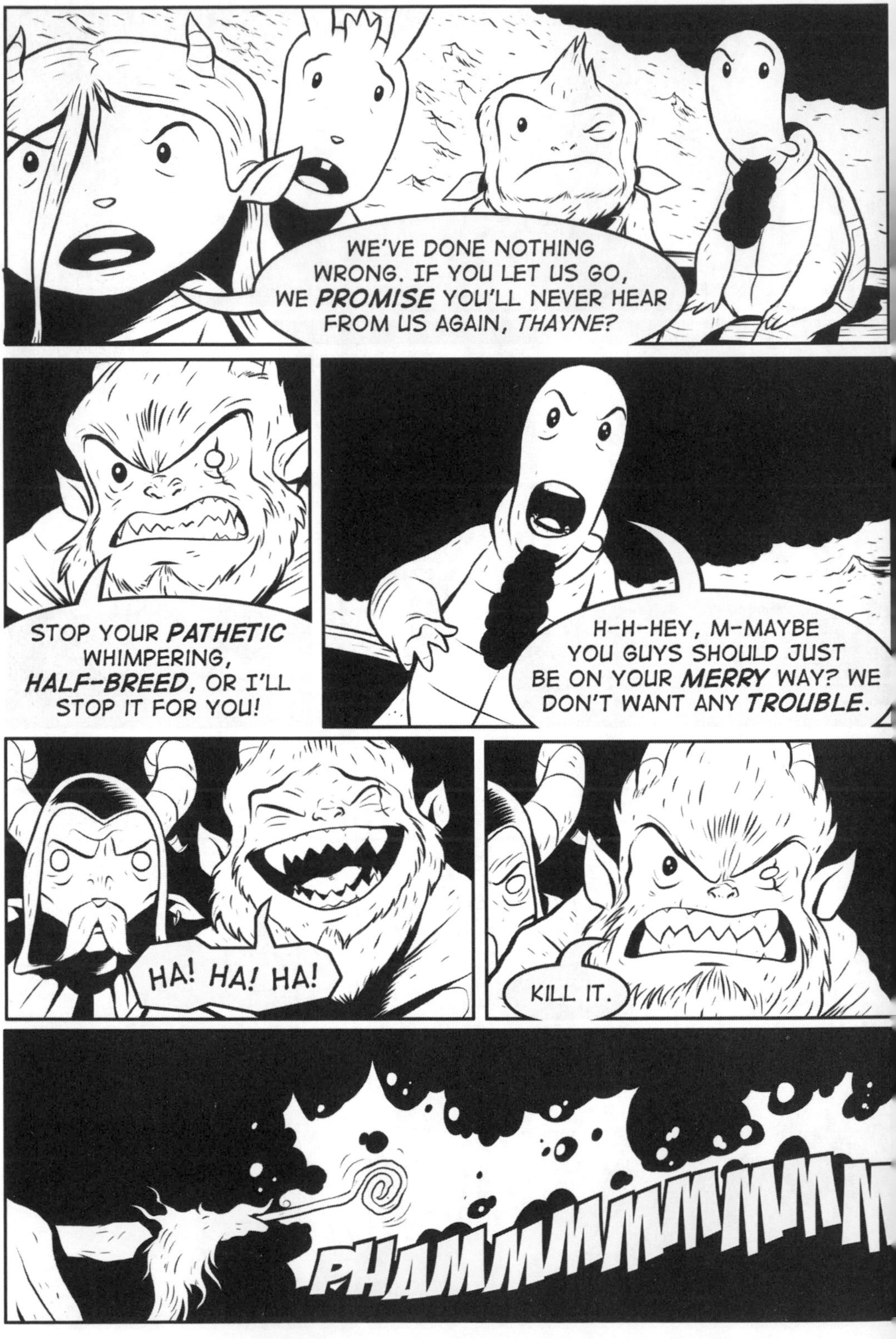
WE'VE DONE NOTHING WRONG. IF YOU LET US GO, WE *PROMISE* YOU'LL NEVER HEAR FROM US AGAIN, *THAYNE*?
STOP YOUR *PATHETIC* WHIMPERING, *HALF-BREED*, OR I'LL STOP IT FOR YOU!
H-H-HEY, M-MAYBE YOU GUYS SHOULD JUST BE ON YOUR *MERRY* WAY? WE DON'T WANT ANY *TROUBLE*.
HA! *HA!* HA!
KILL IT.
PHAMMMMMMMMMMM

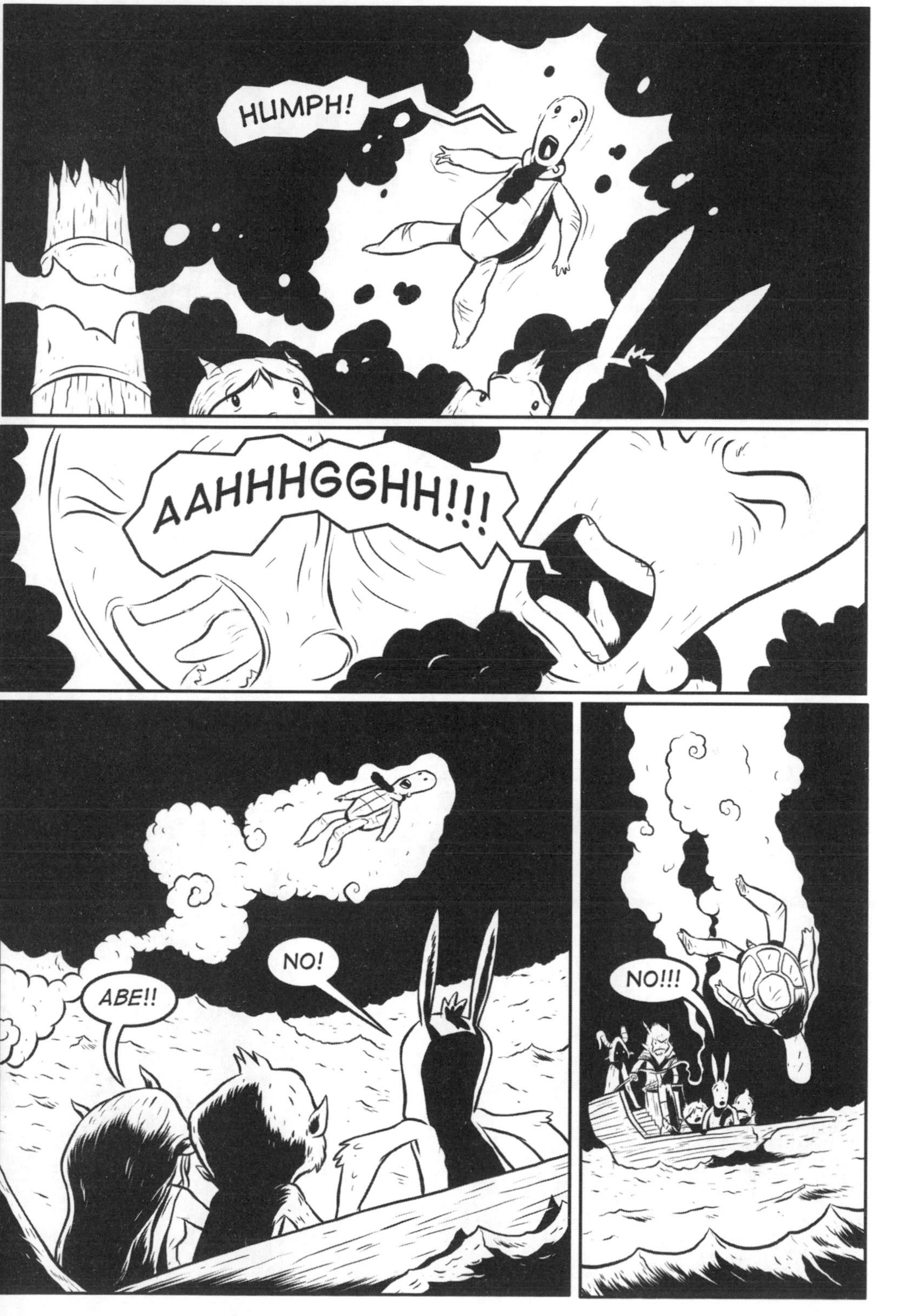
HUMPH!
AAHHHGGHH!!!
ABE!!
NO!
NO!!!

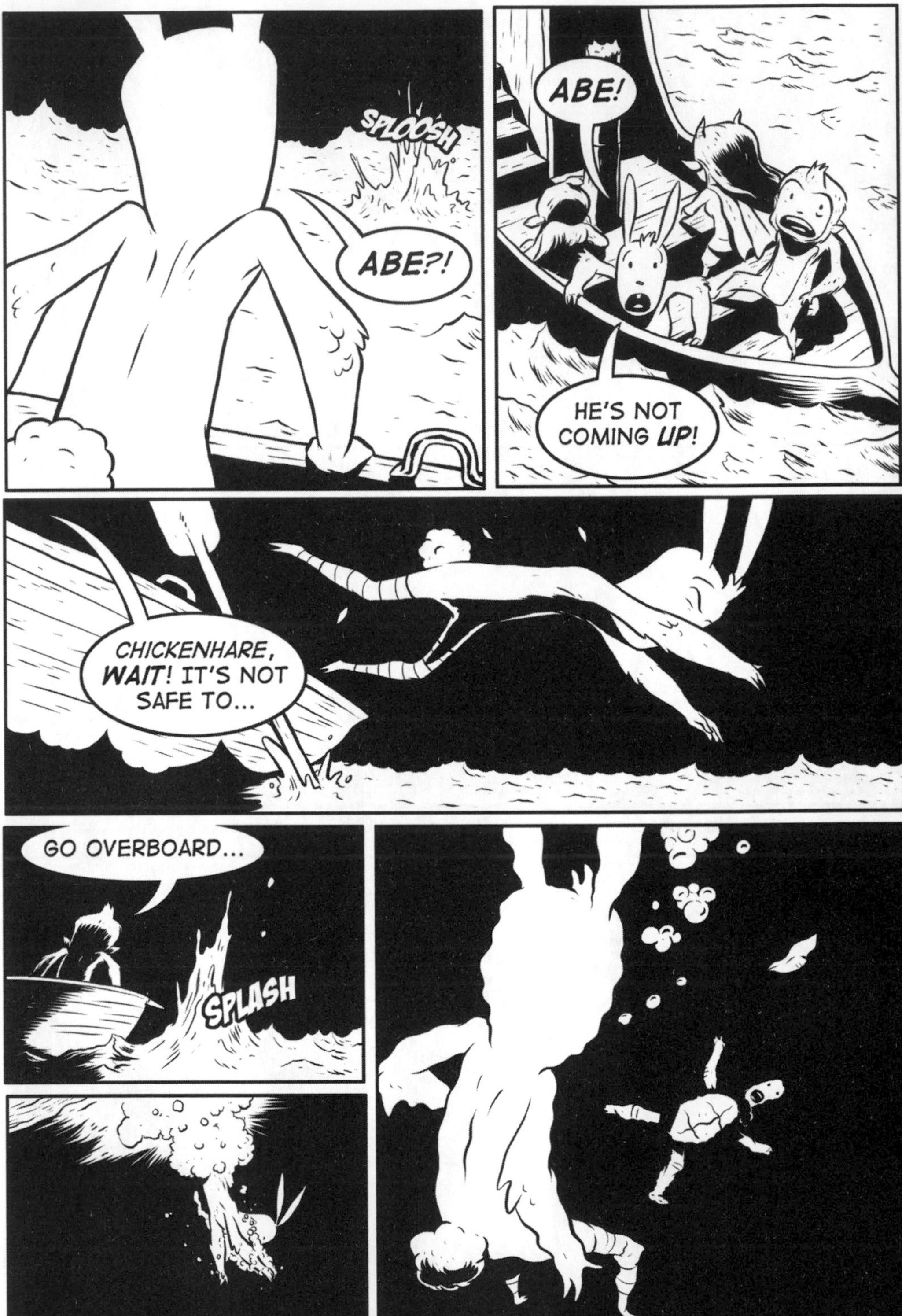
SPLOOSH
ABE?!
ABE!
HE'S NOT COMING UP!
CHICKENHARE, WAIT! IT'S NOT SAFE TO...
GO OVERBOARD...
SPLASH

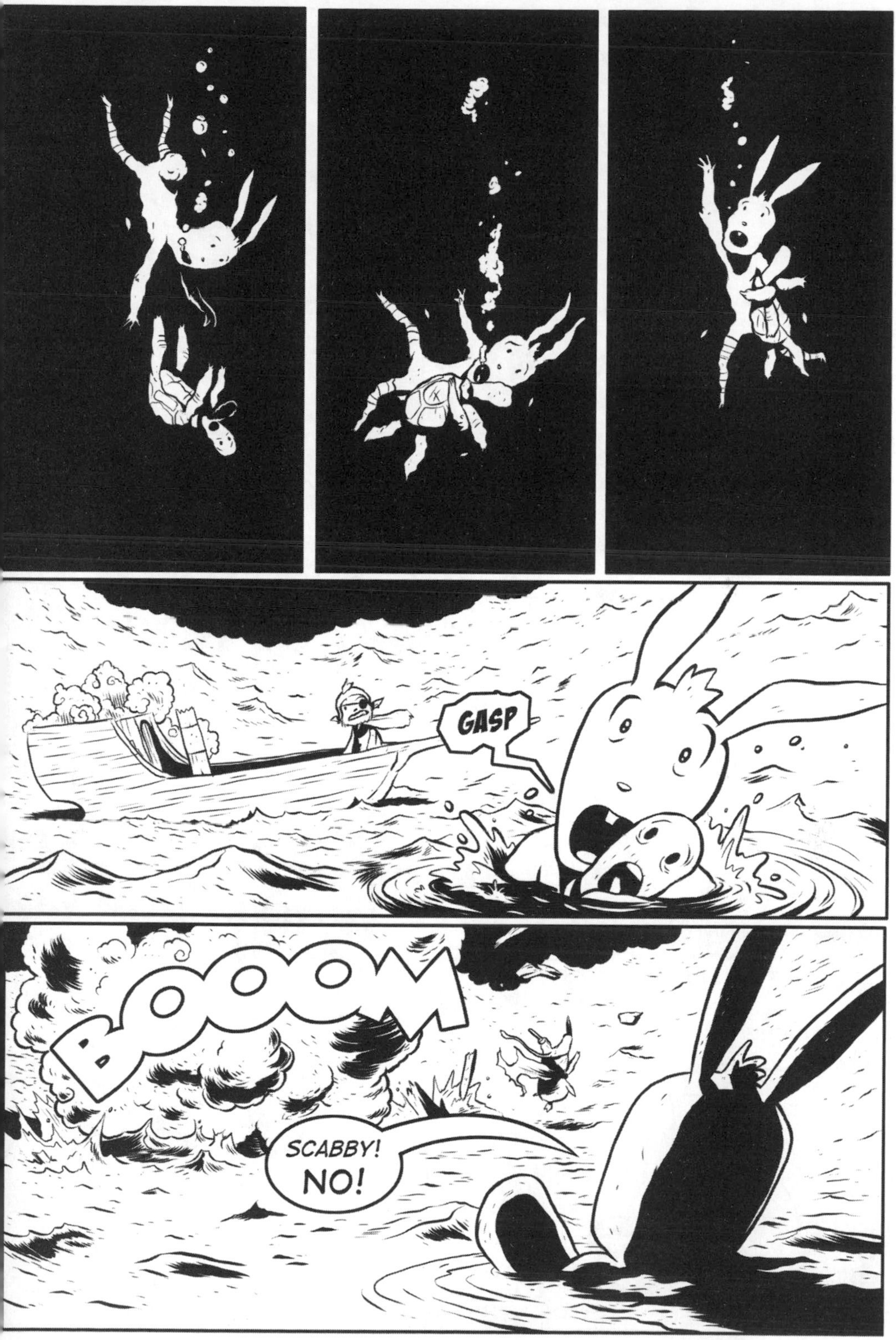
GASP
BOOOOM
SCABBY!
NO!

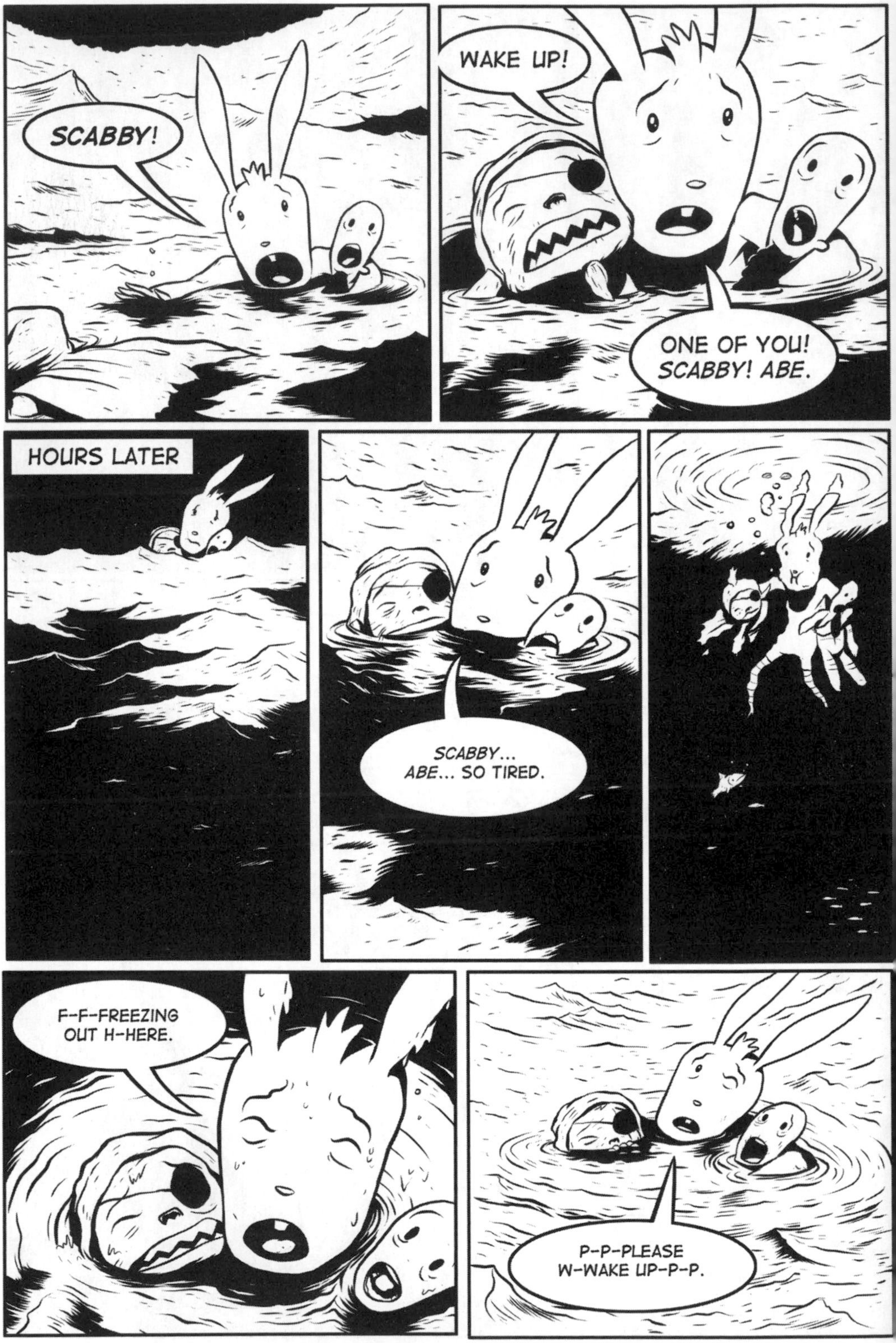
SCABBY!
WAKE UP!
ONE OF YOU! SCABBY! ABE.
HOURS LATER
SCABBY... ABE... SO TIRED.
F-F-FREEZING OUT H-HERE.
P-P-PLEASE W-WAKE UP-P-P.

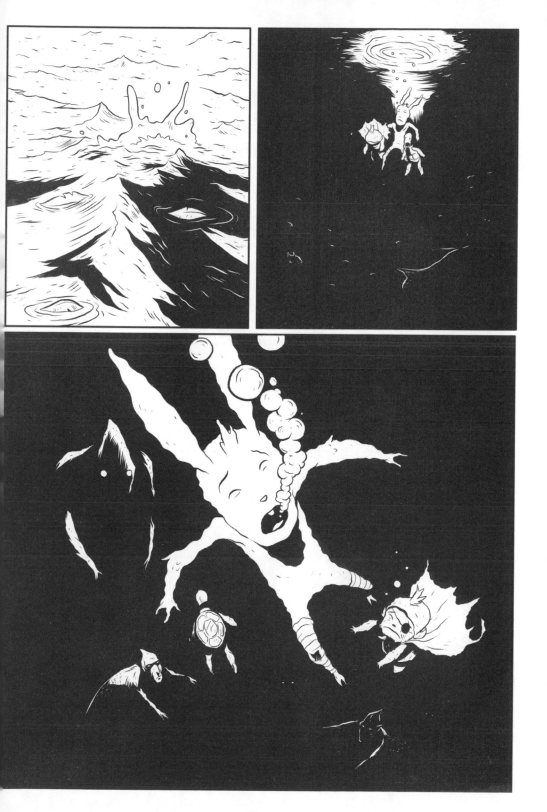

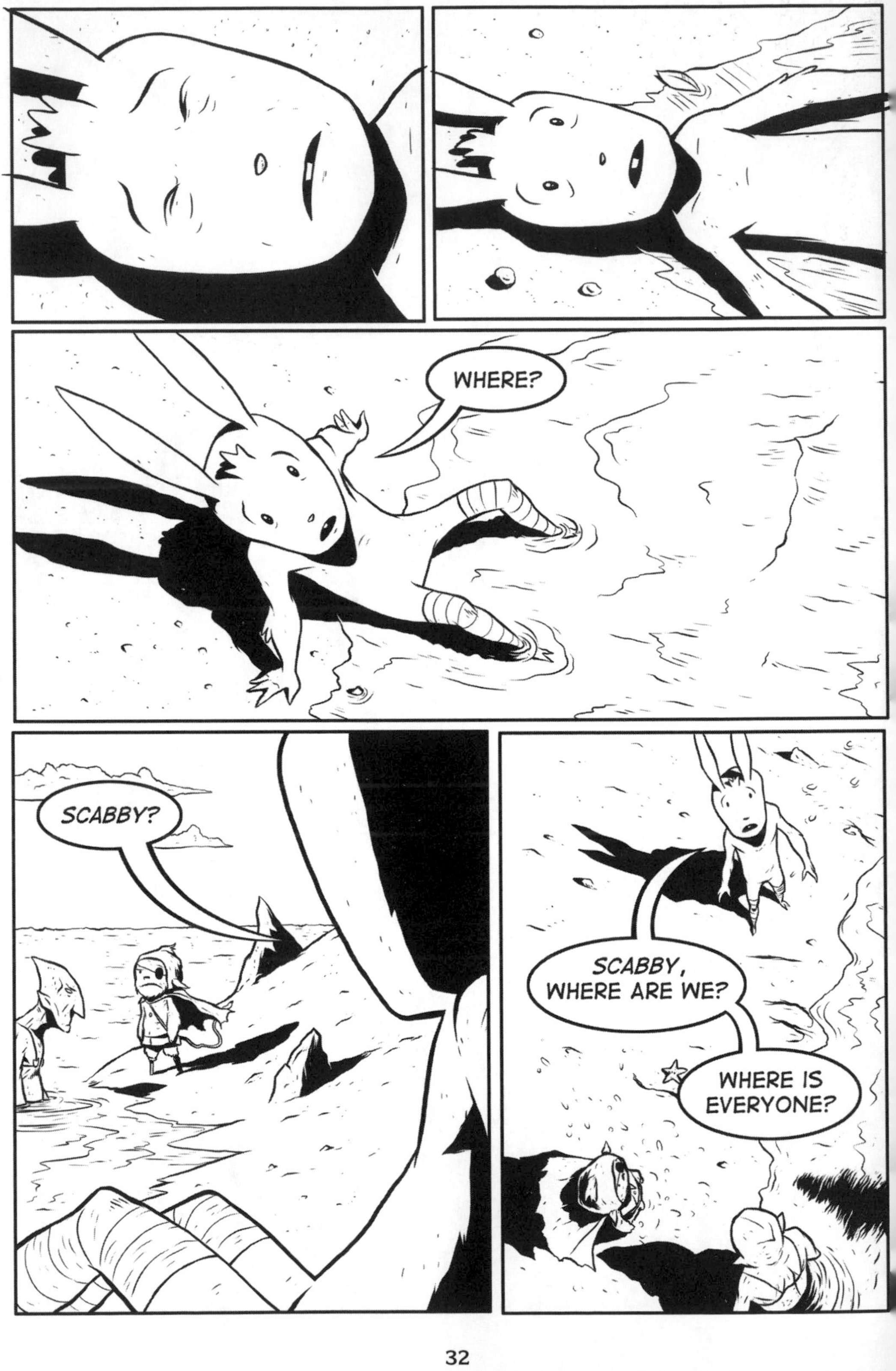
WHERE?
SCABBY?
SCABBY, WHERE ARE WE?
WHERE IS EVERYONE?

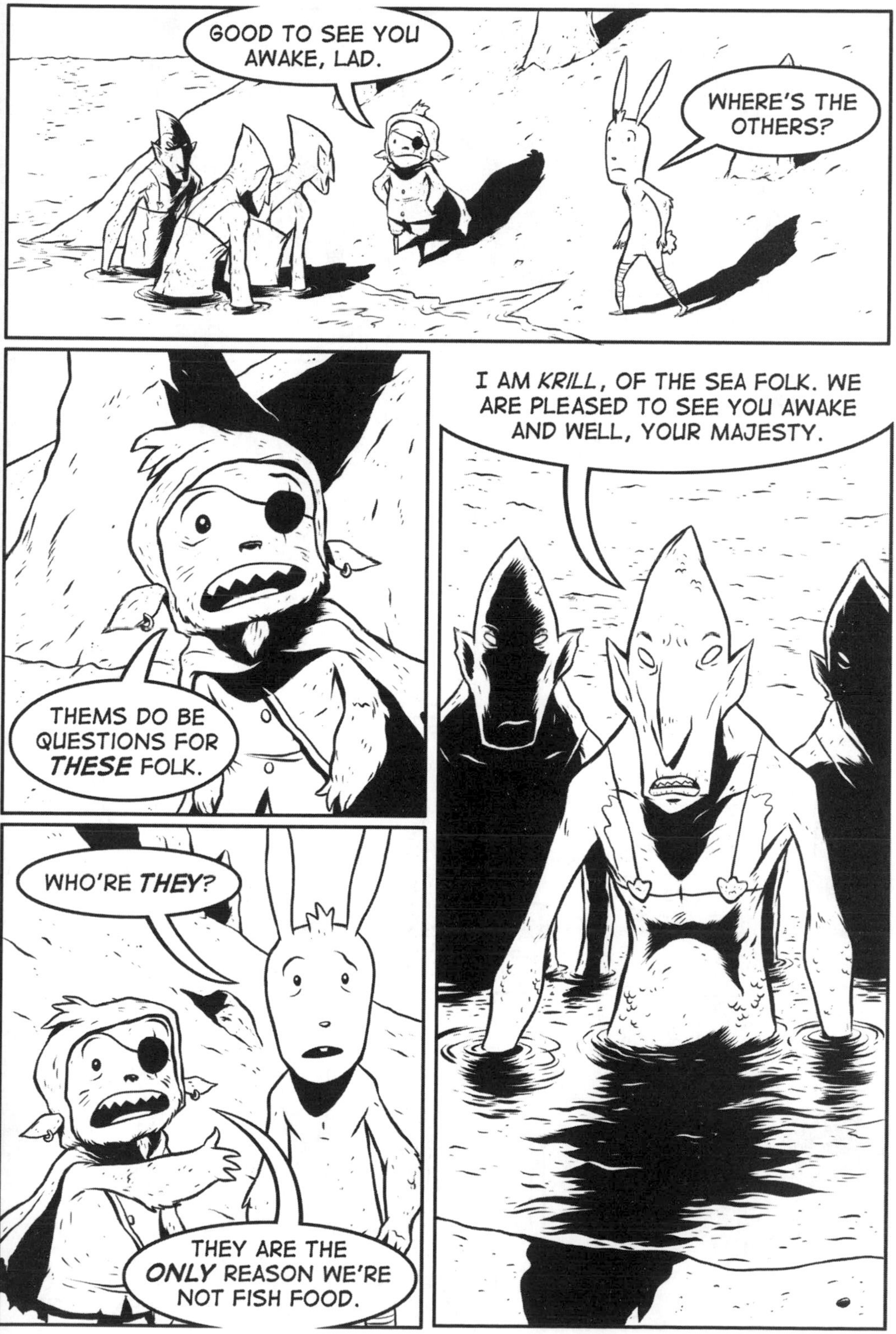
GOOD TO SEE YOU AWAKE, LAD.
WHERE'S THE OTHERS?
THEMS DO BE QUESTIONS FOR *THESE* FOLK.
I AM *KRILL*, OF THE SEA FOLK. WE ARE PLEASED TO SEE YOU AWAKE AND WELL, YOUR MAJESTY.
WHO'RE *THEY*?
THEY ARE THE *ONLY* REASON WE'RE NOT FISH FOOD.

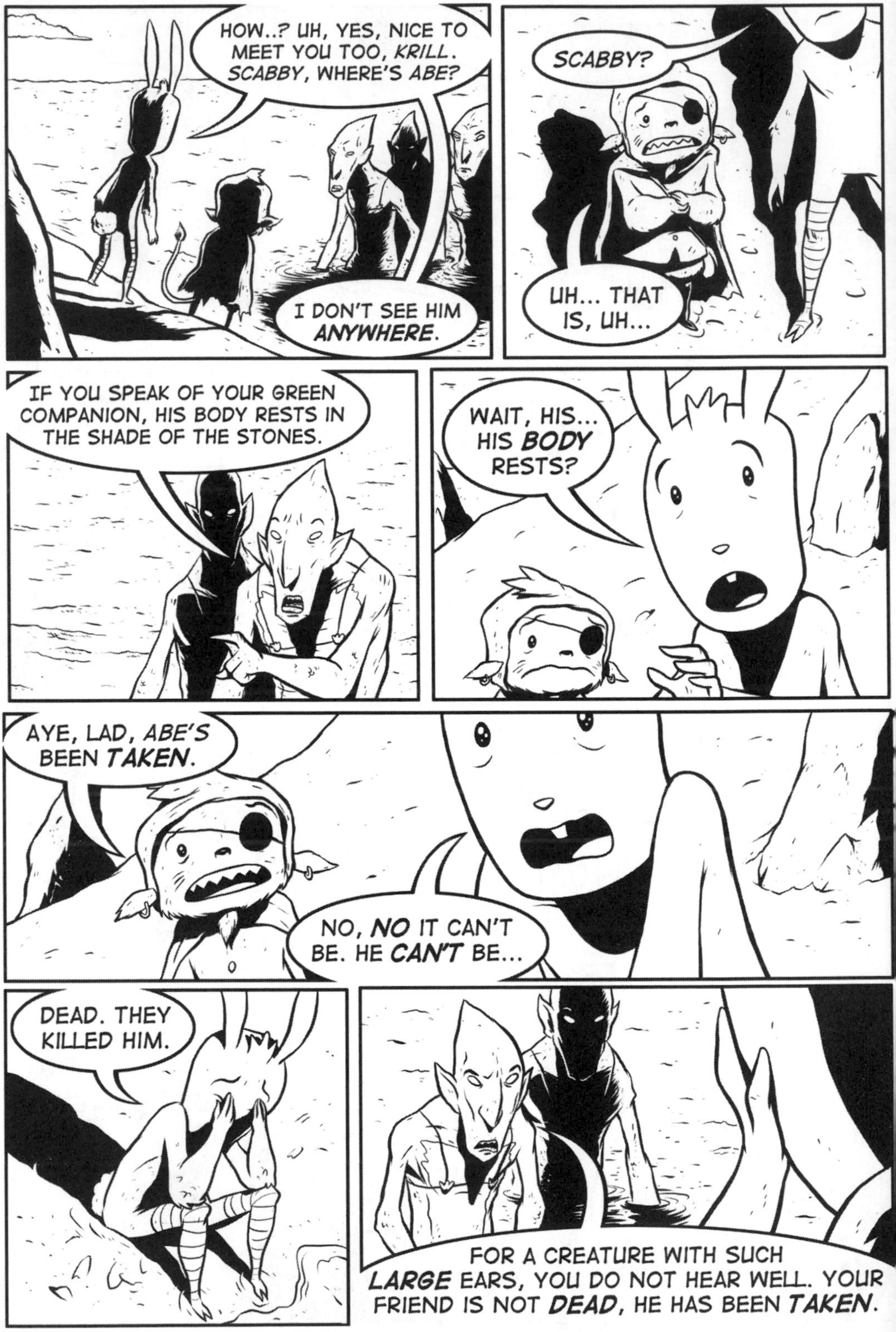
HOW..? UH, YES, NICE TO MEET YOU TOO, KRILL. SCABBY, WHERE'S ABE?
I DON'T SEE HIM ANYWHERE.
SCABBY?
UH... THAT IS, UH...
IF YOU SPEAK OF YOUR GREEN COMPANION, HIS BODY RESTS IN THE SHADE OF THE STONES.
WAIT, HIS... HIS BODY RESTS?
AYE, LAD, ABE'S BEEN TAKEN.
NO, NO IT CAN'T BE. HE CAN'T BE...
DEAD. THEY KILLED HIM.
FOR A CREATURE WITH SUCH LARGE EARS, YOU DO NOT HEAR WELL. YOUR FRIEND IS NOT DEAD, HE HAS BEEN TAKEN.

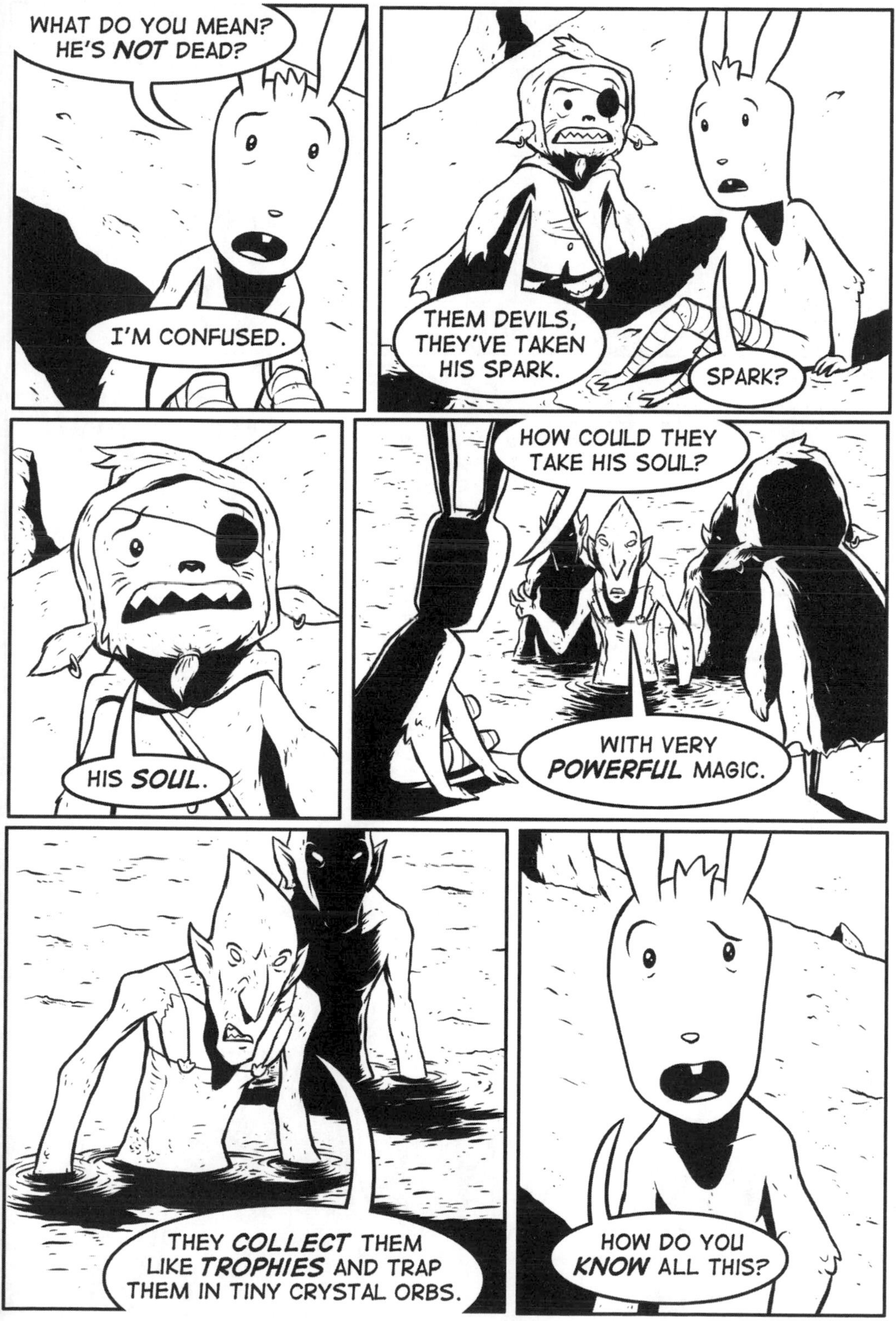
WHAT DO YOU MEAN? HE'S NOT DEAD?
I'M CONFUSED.
THEM DEVILS, THEY'VE TAKEN HIS SPARK.
SPARK?
HIS SOUL.
HOW COULD THEY TAKE HIS SOUL?
WITH VERY POWERFUL MAGIC.
THEY COLLECT THEM LIKE TROPHIES AND TRAP THEM IN TINY CRYSTAL ORBS.
HOW DO YOU KNOW ALL THIS?

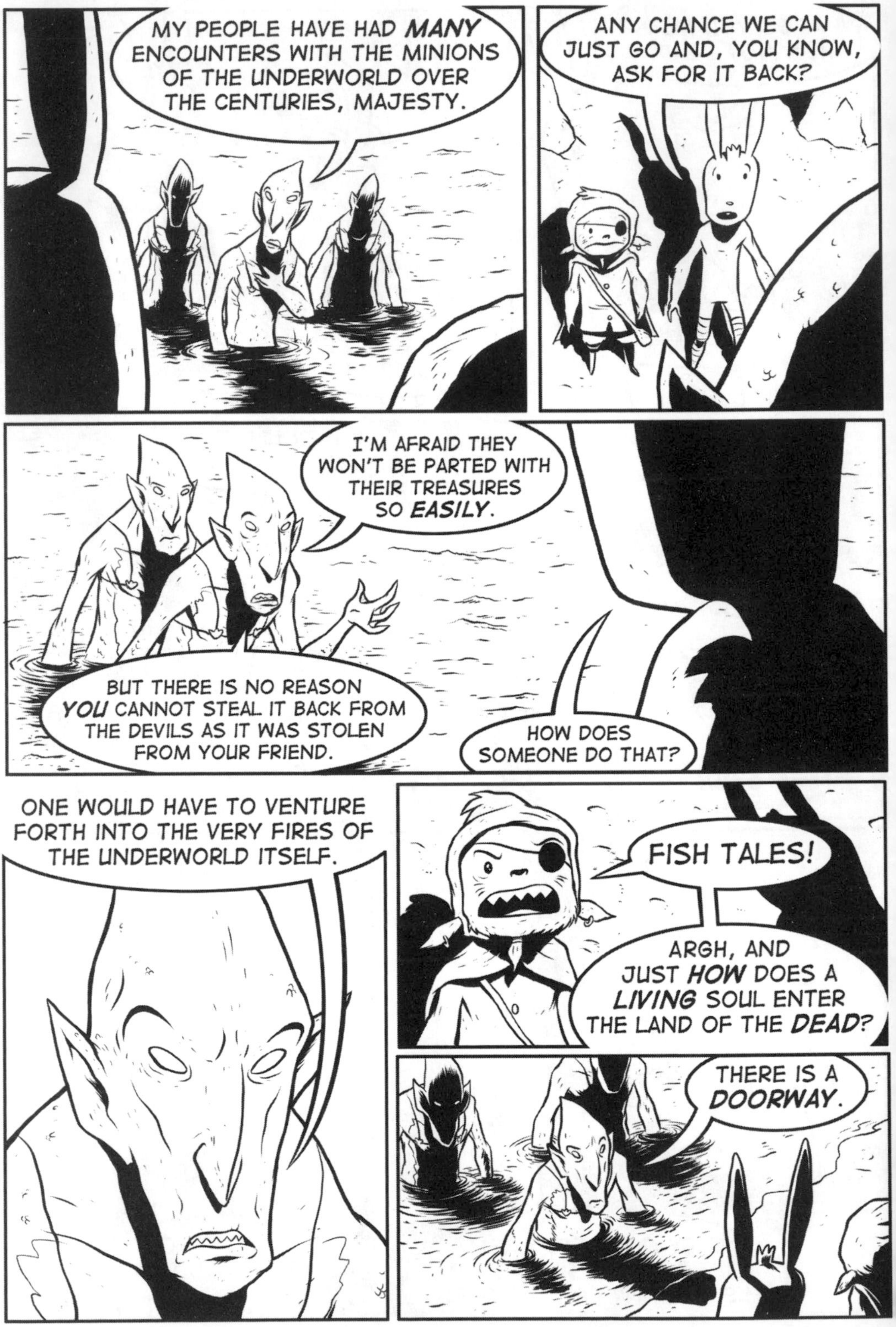
MY PEOPLE HAVE HAD MANY ENCOUNTERS WITH THE MINIONS OF THE UNDERWORLD OVER THE CENTURIES, MAJESTY.
ANY CHANCE WE CAN JUST GO AND, YOU KNOW, ASK FOR IT BACK?
I'M AFRAID THEY WON'T BE PARTED WITH THEIR TREASURES SO EASILY.
BUT THERE IS NO REASON YOU CANNOT STEAL IT BACK FROM THE DEVILS AS IT WAS STOLEN FROM YOUR FRIEND.
HOW DOES SOMEONE DO THAT?
ONE WOULD HAVE TO VENTURE FORTH INTO THE VERY FIRES OF THE UNDERWORLD ITSELF.
FISH TALES!
ARGH, AND JUST HOW DOES A LIVING SOUL ENTER THE LAND OF THE DEAD?
THERE IS A DOORWAY.

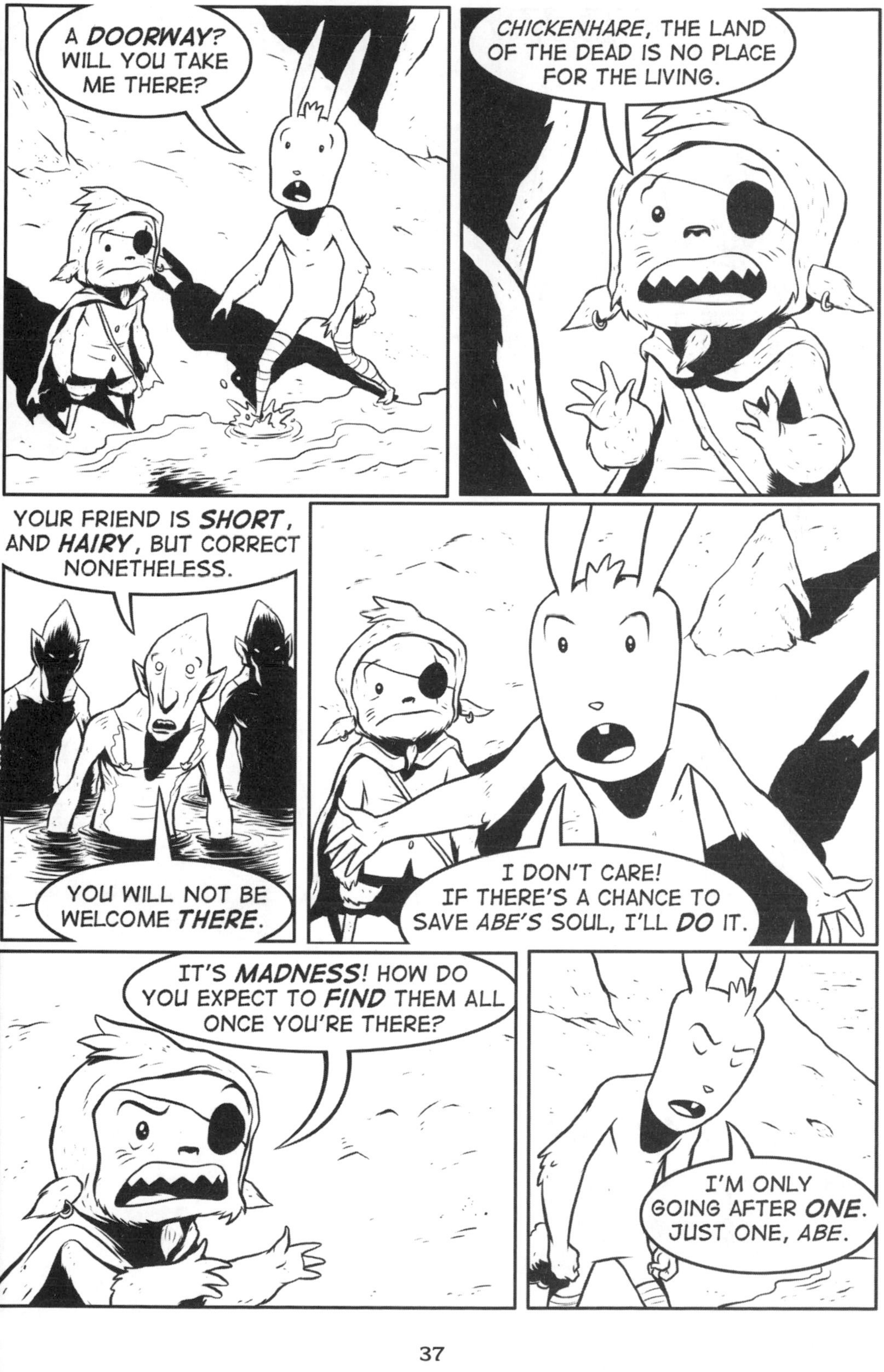
A DOORWAY? WILL YOU TAKE ME THERE?
CHICKENHARE, THE LAND OF THE DEAD IS NO PLACE FOR THE LIVING.
YOUR FRIEND IS SHORT, AND HAIRY, BUT CORRECT NONETHELESS.
YOU WILL NOT BE WELCOME THERE.
I DON'T CARE! IF THERE'S A CHANCE TO SAVE ABE'S SOUL, I'LL DO IT.
IT'S MADNESS! HOW DO YOU EXPECT TO FIND THEM ALL ONCE YOU'RE THERE?
I'M ONLY GOING AFTER ONE. JUST ONE, ABE.

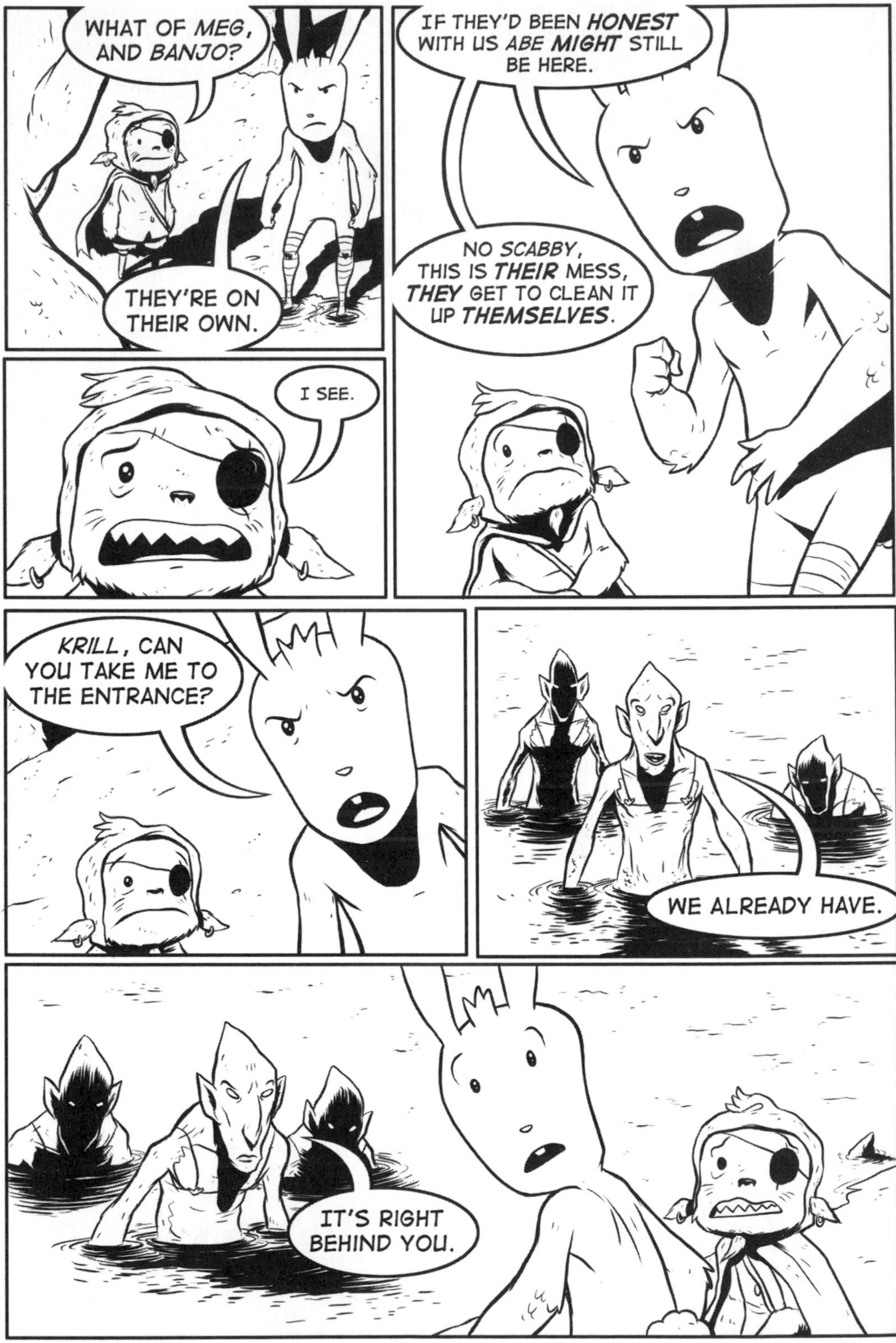
WHAT OF MEG, AND BANJO?
THEY'RE ON THEIR OWN.
IF THEY'D BEEN HONEST WITH US ABE MIGHT STILL BE HERE.
NO SCABBY, THIS IS THEIR MESS, THEY GET TO CLEAN IT UP THEMSELVES.
I SEE.
KRILL, CAN YOU TAKE ME TO THE ENTRANCE?
WE ALREADY HAVE.
IT'S RIGHT BEHIND YOU.

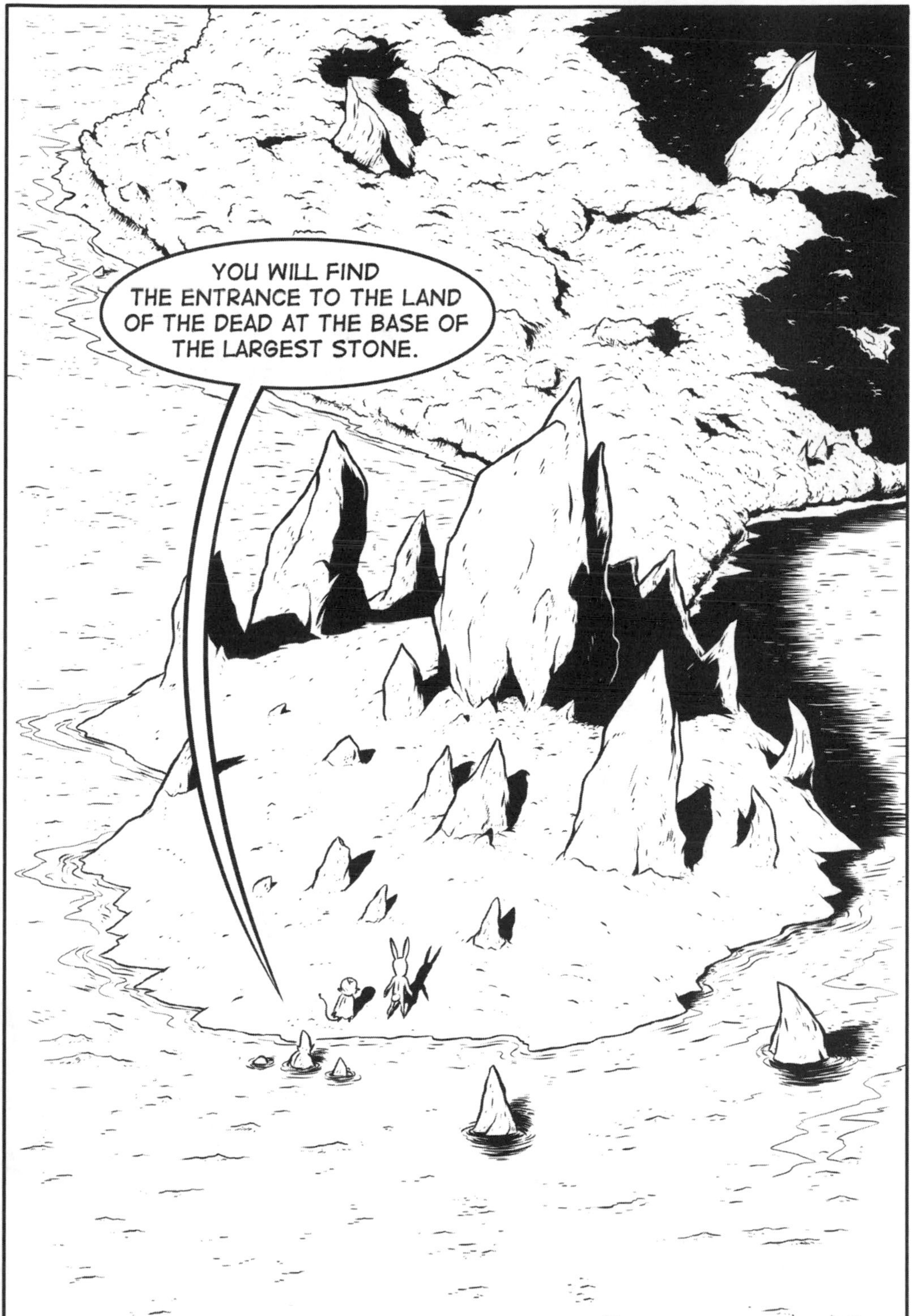
YOU WILL FIND THE ENTRANCE TO THE LAND OF THE DEAD AT THE BASE OF THE LARGEST STONE.

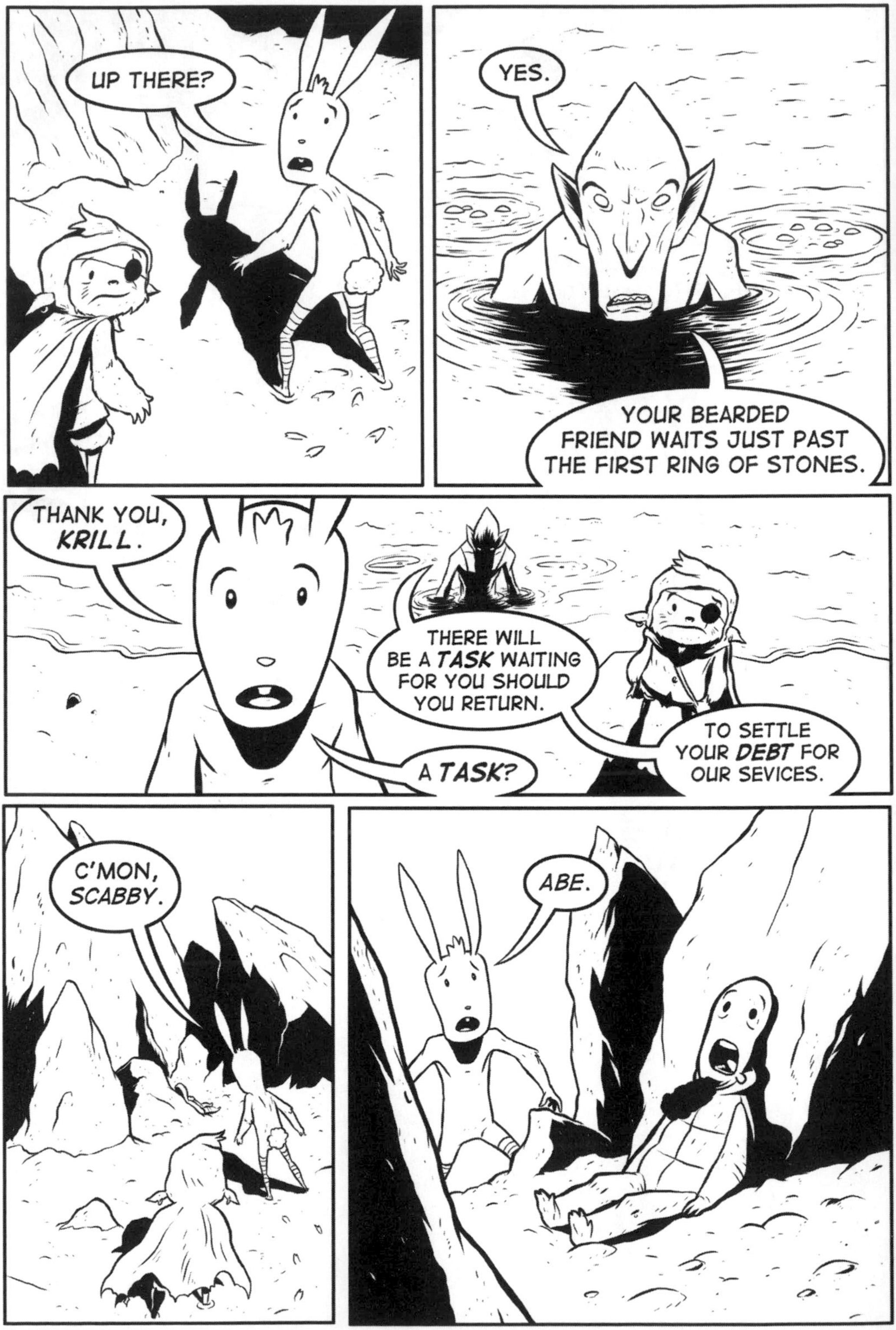
UP THERE?
YES.
YOUR BEARDED FRIEND WAITS JUST PAST THE FIRST RING OF STONES.
THANK YOU, KRILL.
THERE WILL BE A TASK WAITING FOR YOU SHOULD YOU RETURN.
A TASK?
TO SETTLE YOUR DEBT FOR OUR SEVICES.
C'MON, SCABBY.
ABE.

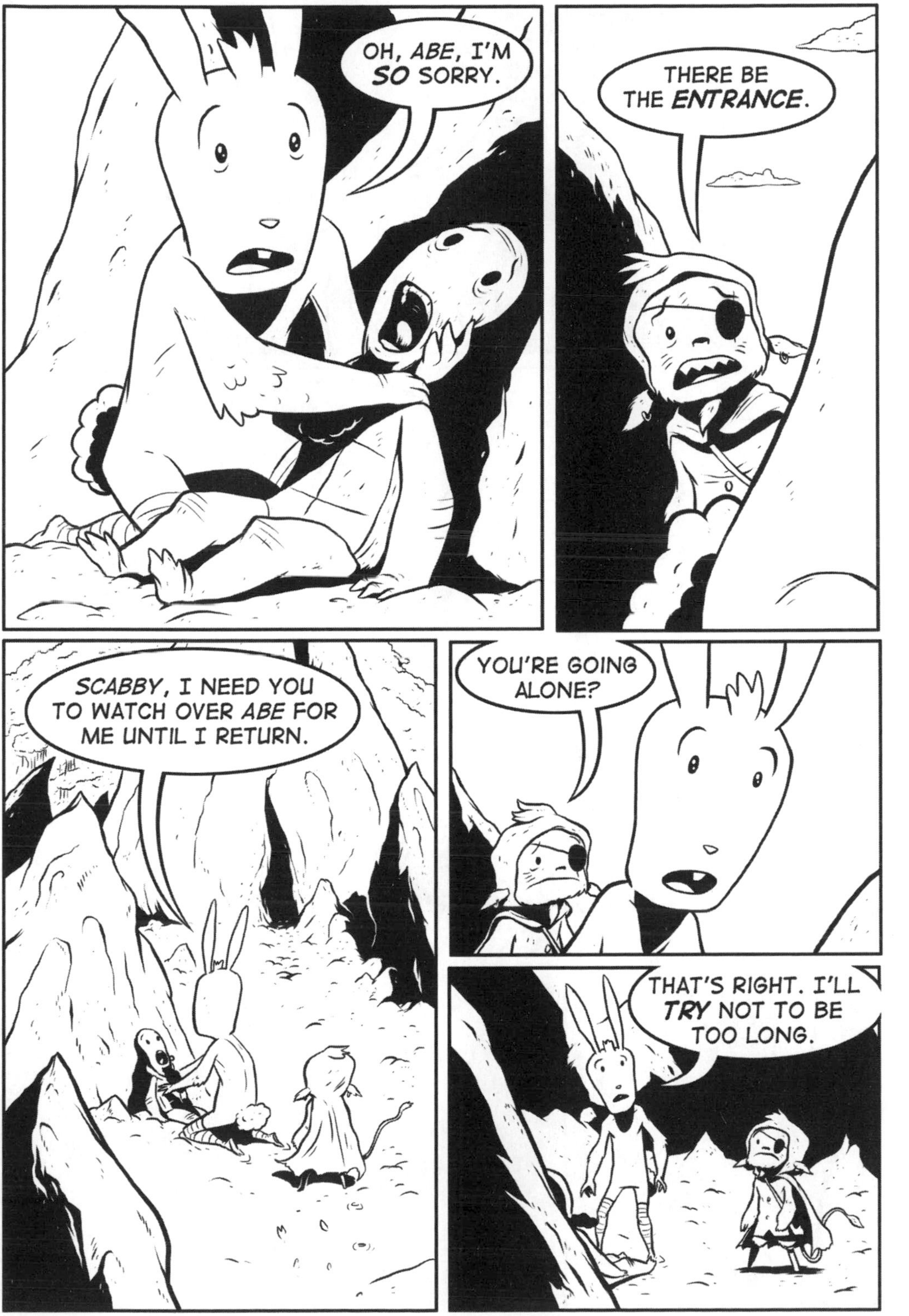

OH, ABE, I'M SO SORRY.
THERE BE THE ENTRANCE.
SCABBY, I NEED YOU TO WATCH OVER ABE FOR ME UNTIL I RETURN.
YOU'RE GOING ALONE?
THAT'S RIGHT. I'LL TRY NOT TO BE TOO LONG.

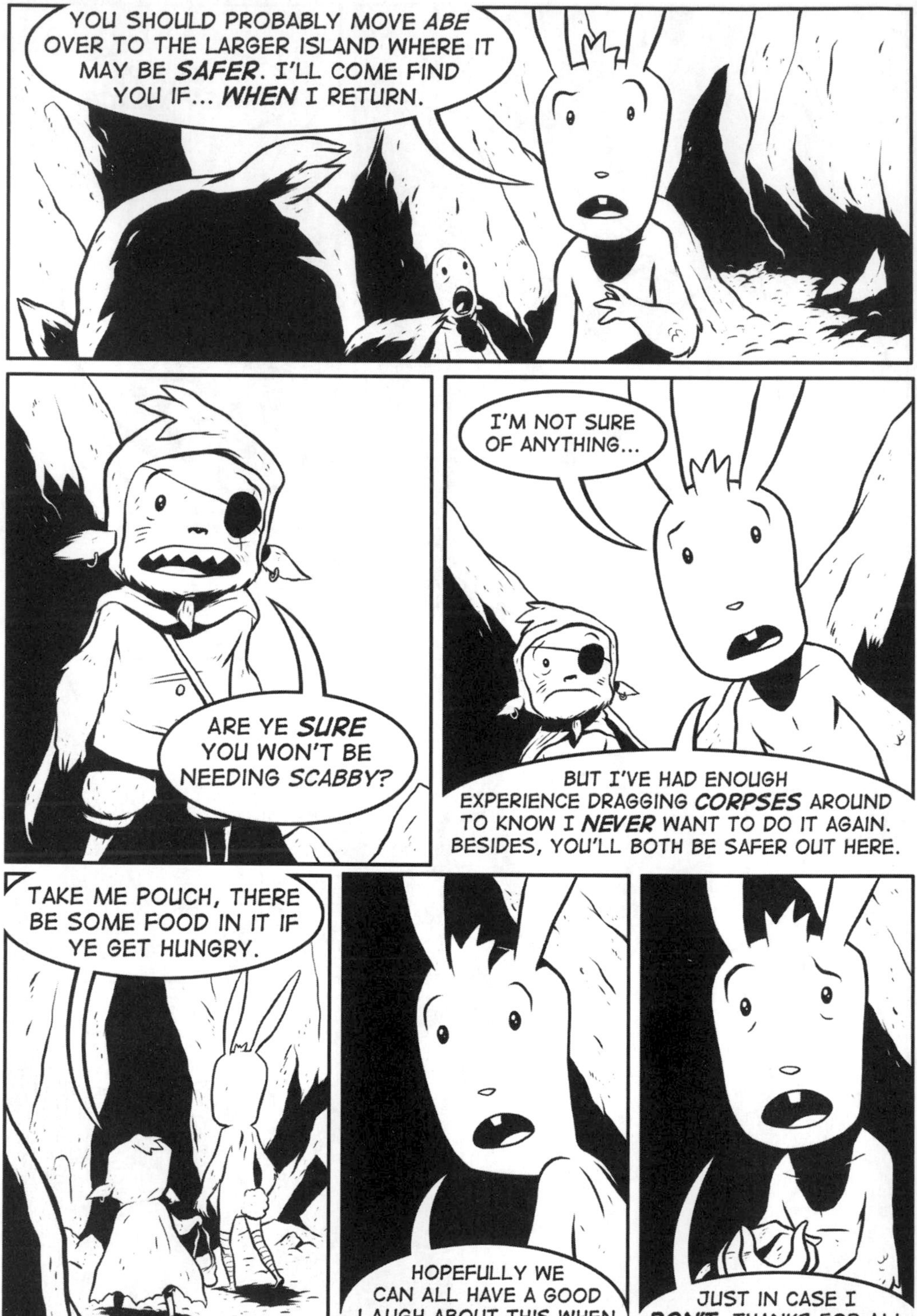
YOU SHOULD PROBABLY MOVE ABE OVER TO THE LARGER ISLAND WHERE IT MAY BE SAFER. I'LL COME FIND YOU IF... WHEN I RETURN.
ARE YE SURE YOU WON'T BE NEEDING SCABBY?
I'M NOT SURE OF ANYTHING...
BUT I'VE HAD ENOUGH EXPERIENCE DRAGGING CORPSES AROUND TO KNOW I NEVER WANT TO DO IT AGAIN. BESIDES, YOU'LL BOTH BE SAFER OUT HERE.
TAKE ME POUCH, THERE BE SOME FOOD IN IT IF YE GET HUNGRY.
HOPEFULLY WE CAN ALL HAVE A GOOD LAUGH ABOUT THIS WHEN I GET BACK, HUH?
JUST IN CASE I DON'T, THANKS FOR ALL YOUR HELP, SCABBY.

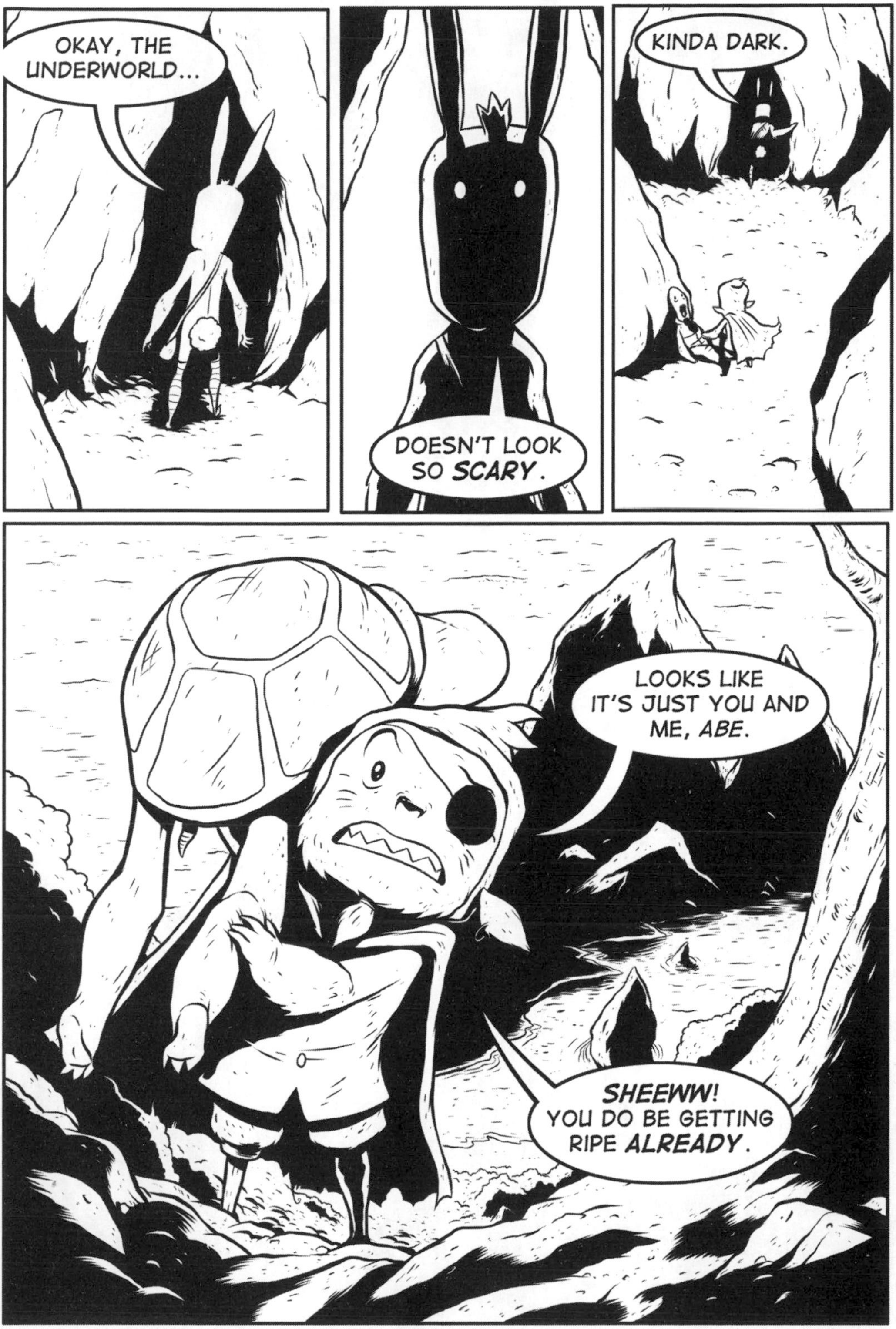
OKAY, THE UNDERWORLD...
DOESN'T LOOK SO SCARY.
KINDA DARK.
LOOKS LIKE IT'S JUST YOU AND ME, ABE.
SHEEWW! YOU DO BE GETTING RIPE ALREADY.

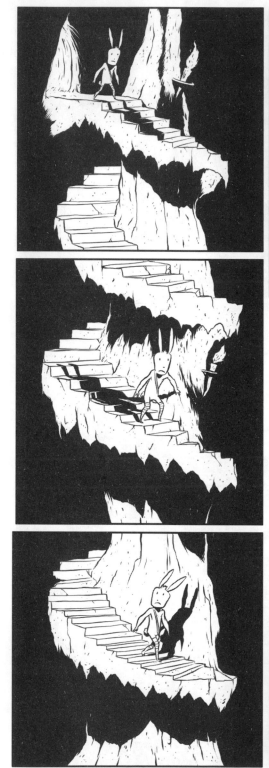

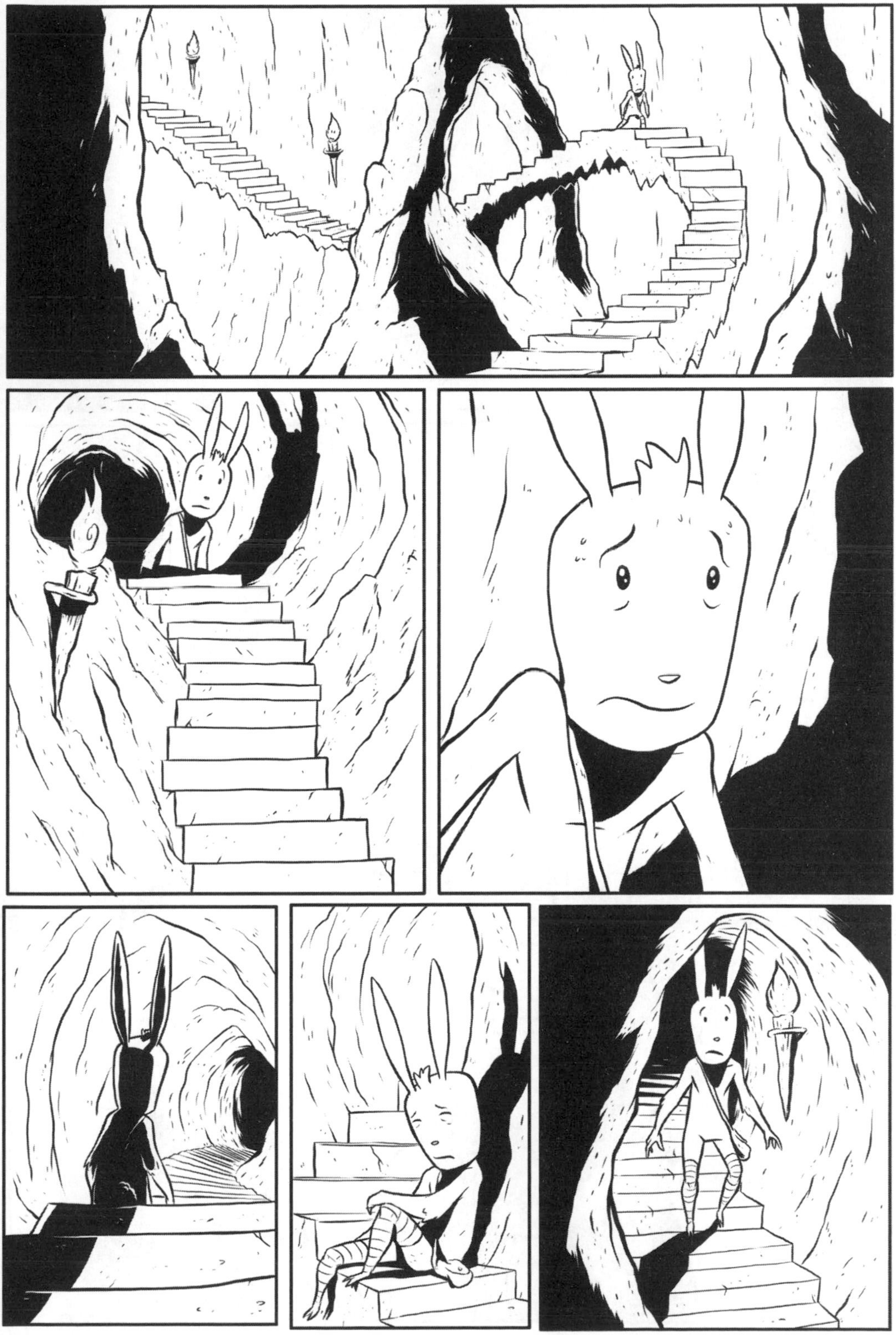

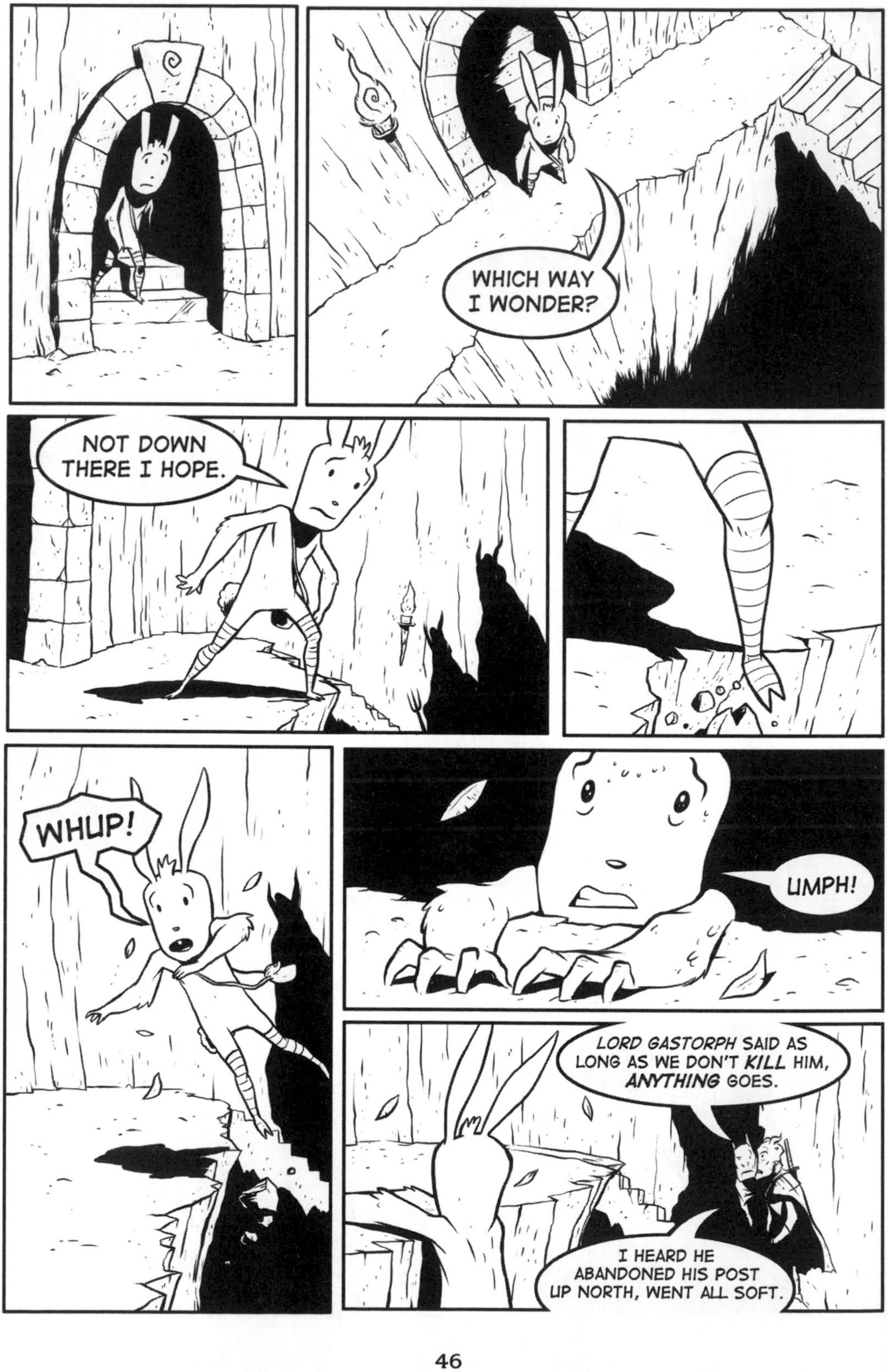
WHICH WAY I WONDER?
NOT DOWN THERE I HOPE.
WHUP!
UMPH!
LORD GASTORPH SAID AS LONG AS WE DON'T KILL HIM, ANYTHING GOES.
I HEARD HE ABANDONED HIS POST UP NORTH, WENT ALL SOFT.

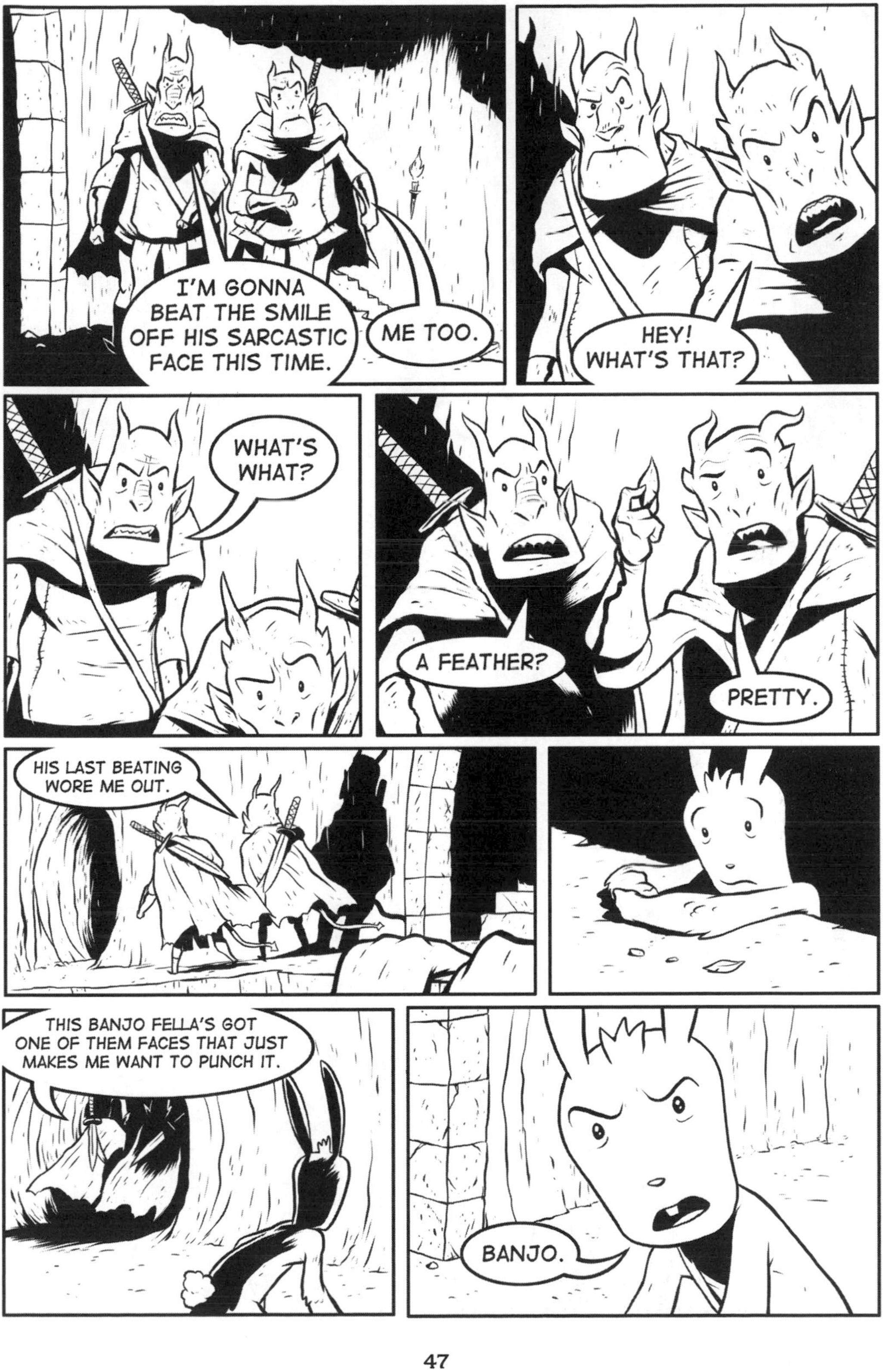
I'M GONNA BEAT THE SMILE OFF HIS SARCASTIC FACE THIS TIME.
ME TOO.
HEY! WHAT'S THAT?
WHAT'S WHAT?
A FEATHER?
PRETTY.
HIS LAST BEATING WORE ME OUT.
THIS BANJO FELLA'S GOT ONE OF THEM FACES THAT JUST MAKES ME WANT TO PUNCH IT.
BANJO.

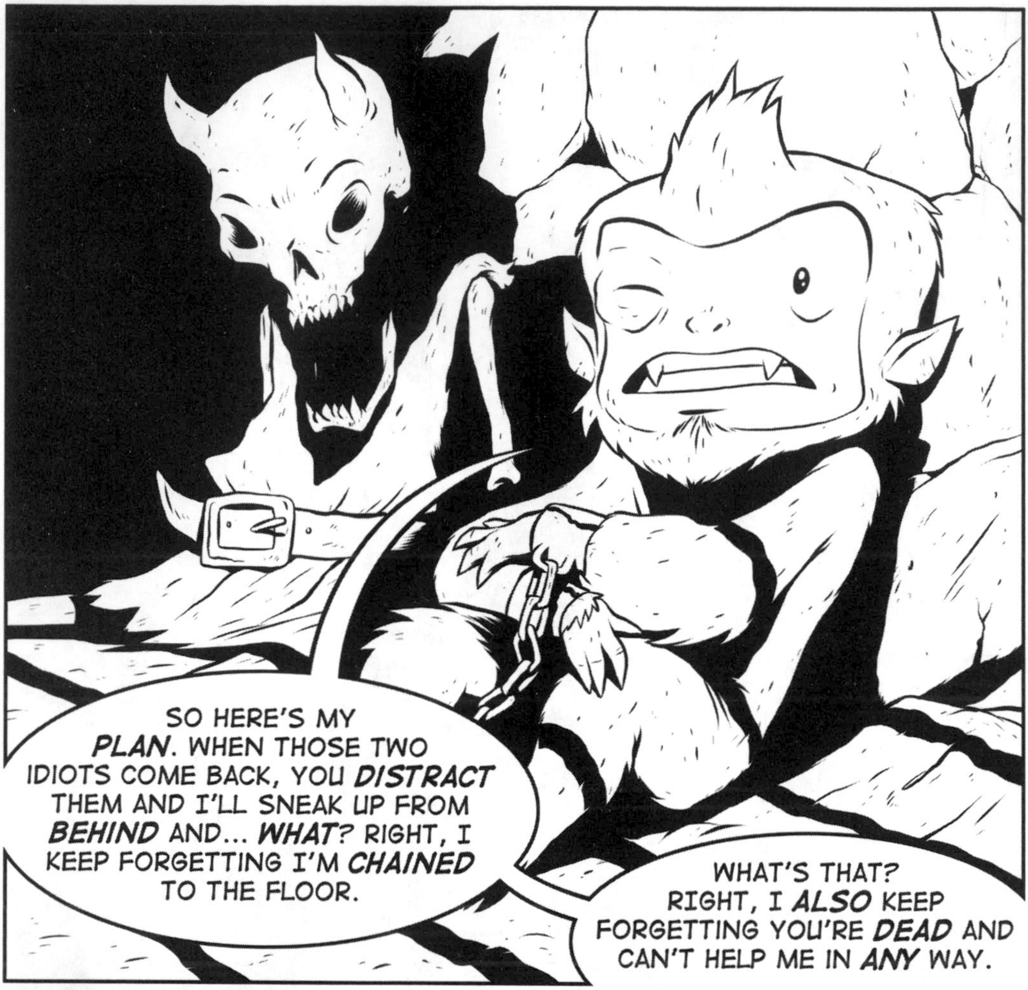
SO HERE'S MY PLAN. WHEN THOSE TWO IDIOTS COME BACK, YOU DISTRACT THEM AND I'LL SNEAK UP FROM BEHIND AND... WHAT? RIGHT, I KEEP FORGETTING I'M CHAINED TO THE FLOOR.
WHAT'S THAT? RIGHT, I ALSO KEEP FORGETTING YOU'RE DEAD AND CAN'T HELP ME IN ANY WAY.

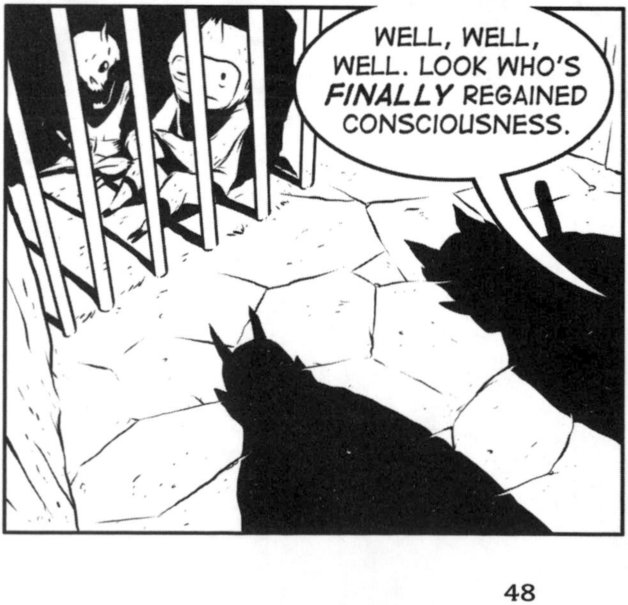
WELL, WELL, WELL. LOOK WHO'S FINALLY REGAINED CONSCIOUSNESS.

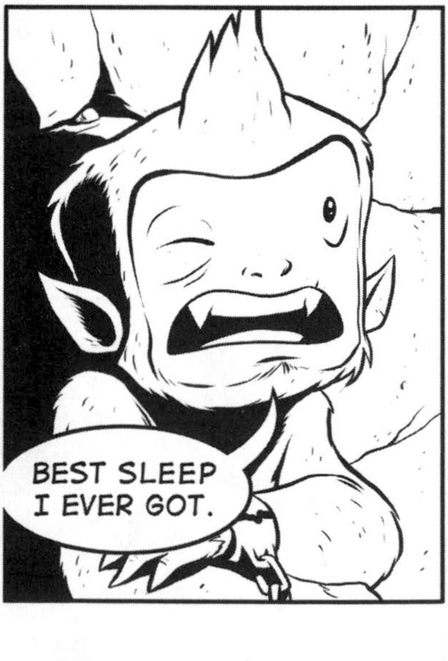
BEST SLEEP I EVER GOT.

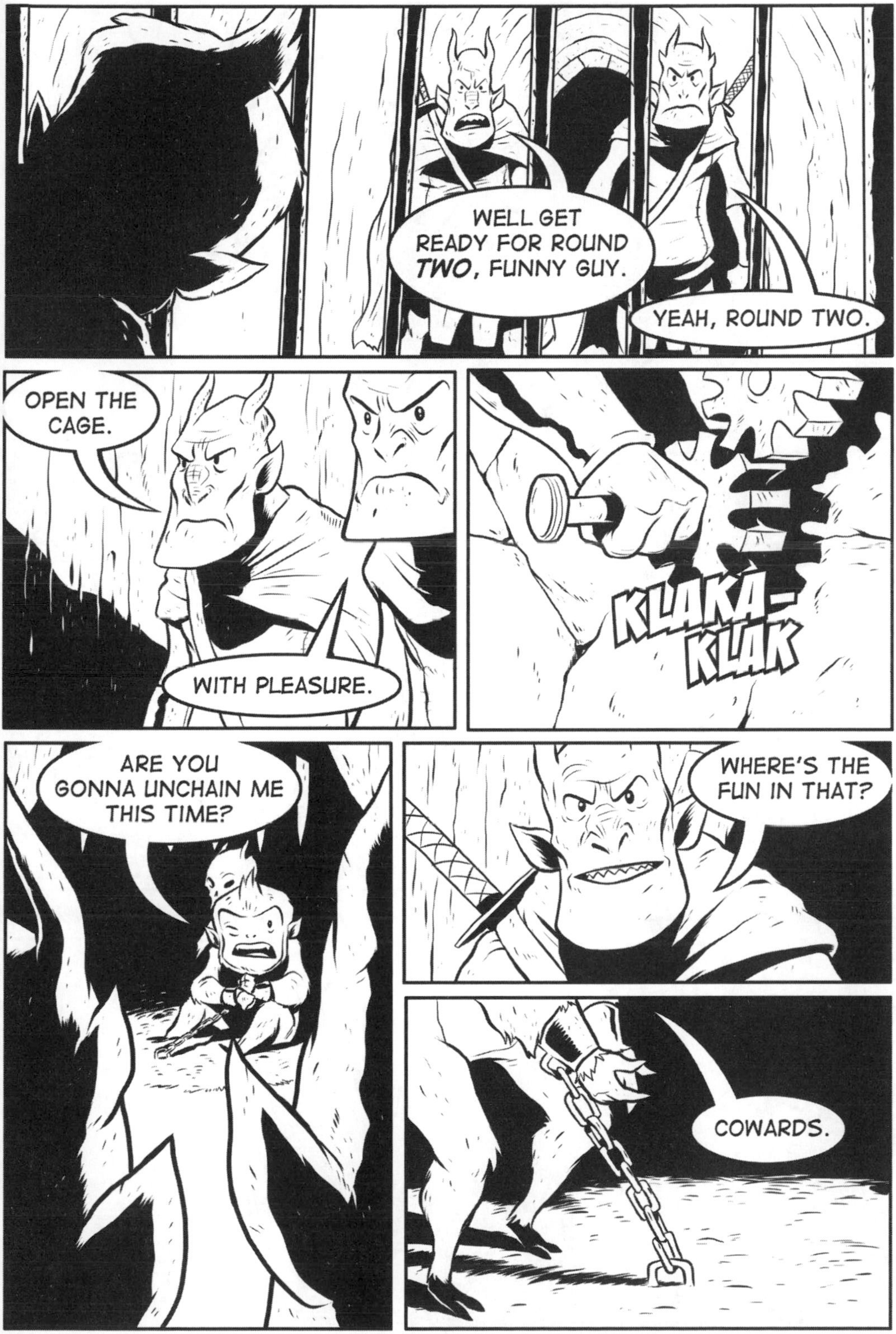
WELL GET READY FOR ROUND *TWO*, FUNNY GUY.
YEAH, ROUND TWO.
OPEN THE CAGE.
WITH PLEASURE.
KLAKA-KLAK
ARE YOU GONNA UNCHAIN ME THIS TIME?
WHERE'S THE FUN IN THAT?
COWARDS.

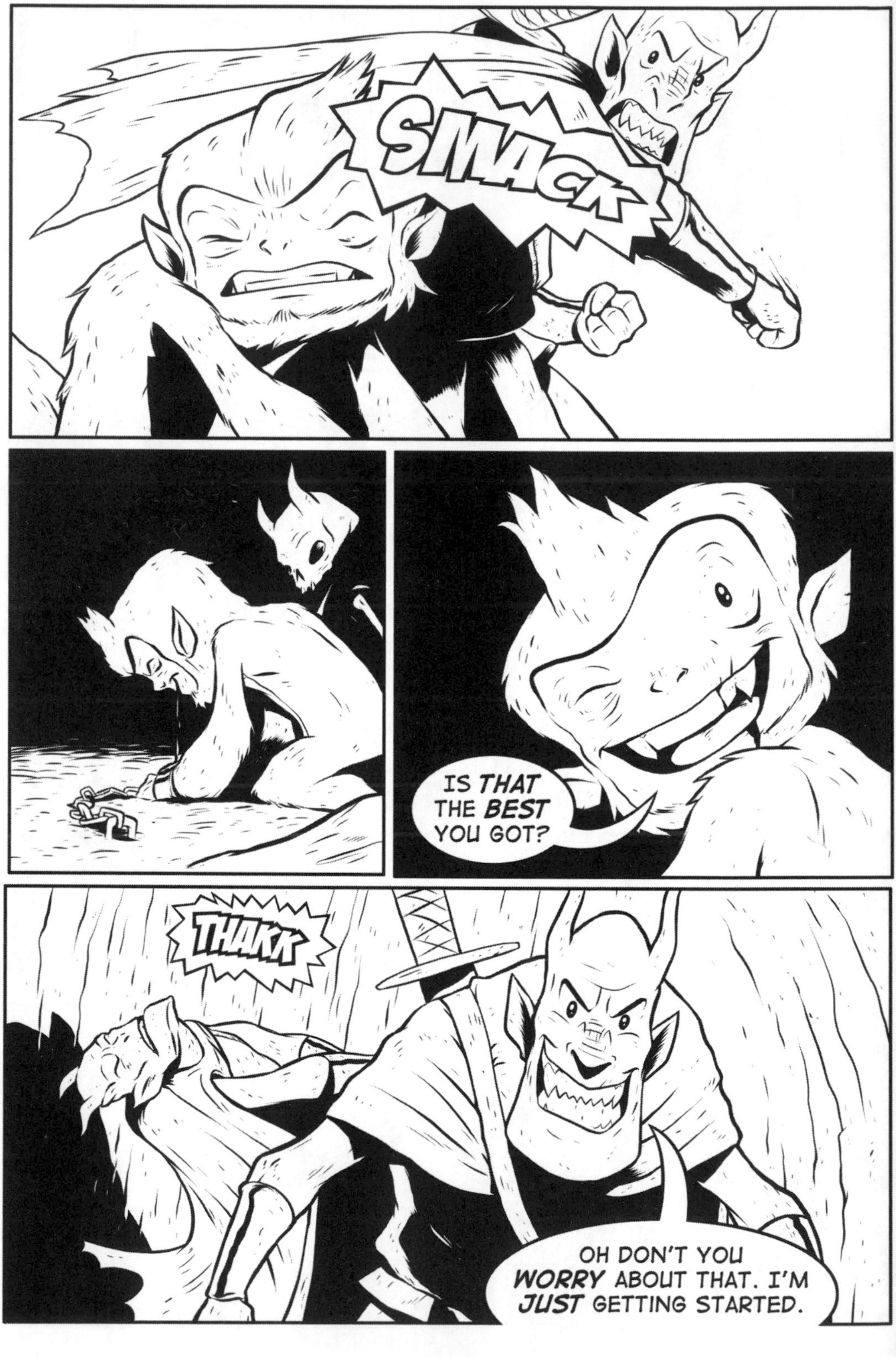
SMACK
IS THAT THE BEST YOU GOT?
THAKK
OH DON'T YOU WORRY ABOUT THAT. I'M JUST GETTING STARTED.

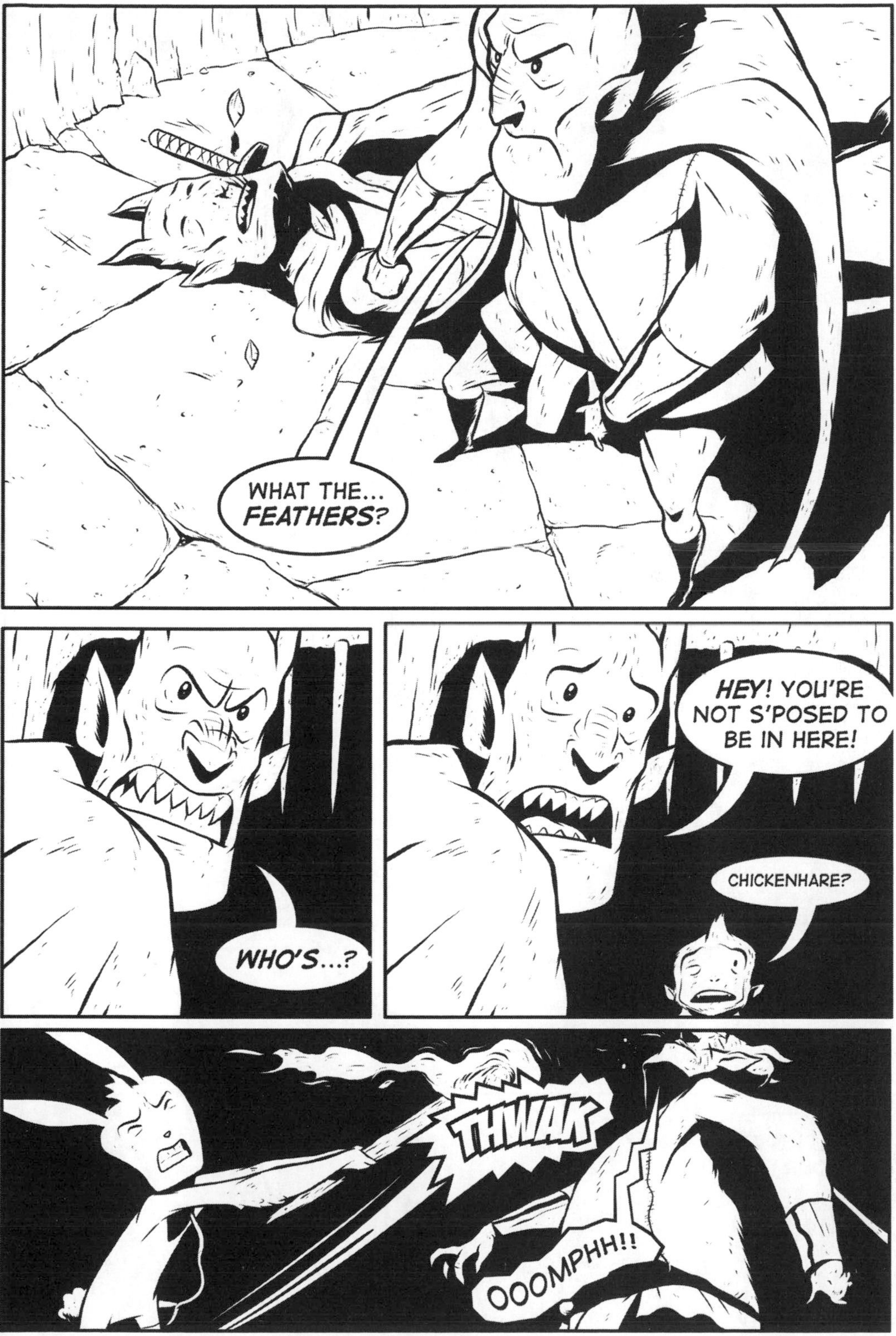
WHAT THE...
FEATHERS?
WHO'S...?
HEY! YOU'RE NOT S'POSED TO BE IN HERE!
CHICKENHARE?
THWAK
OOOMPHH!!

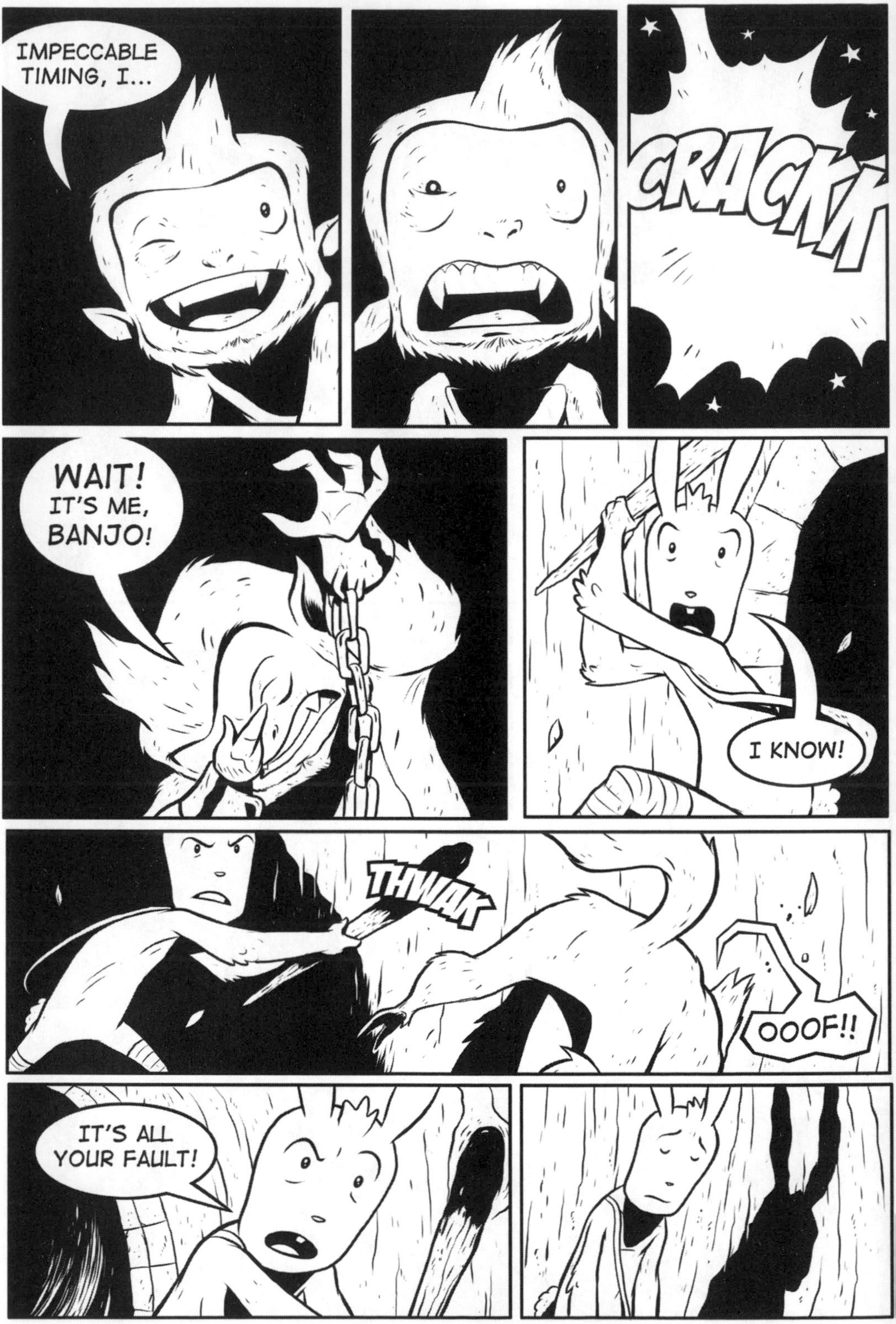
IMPECCABLE TIMING, I...
CRACKK
WAIT! IT'S ME, BANJO!
I KNOW!
THWAK
OOOF!!
IT'S ALL YOUR FAULT!

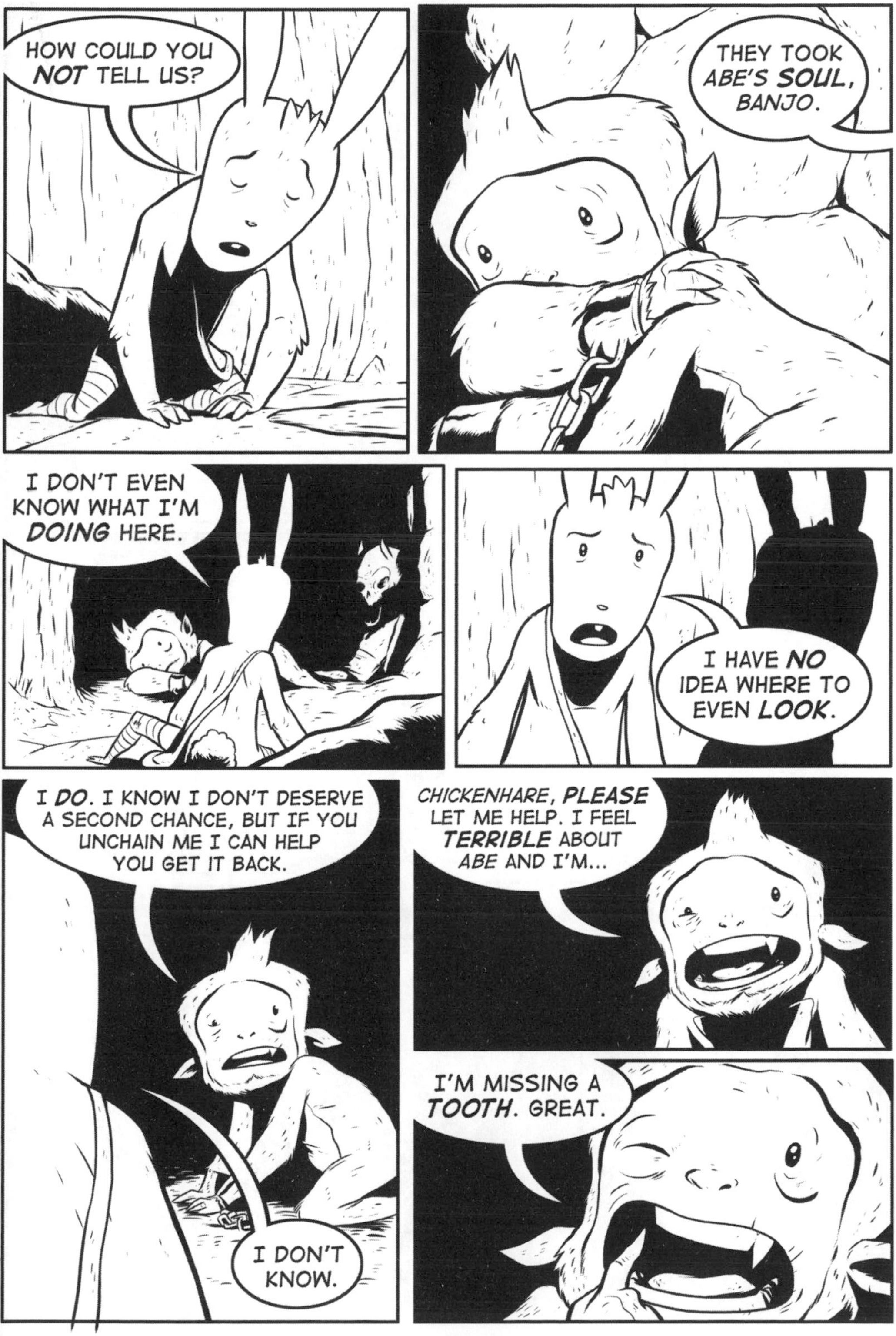
HOW COULD YOU NOT TELL US?
THEY TOOK ABE'S SOUL, BANJO.
I DON'T EVEN KNOW WHAT I'M DOING HERE.
I HAVE NO IDEA WHERE TO EVEN LOOK.
I DO. I KNOW I DON'T DESERVE A SECOND CHANCE, BUT IF YOU UNCHAIN ME I CAN HELP YOU GET IT BACK.
I DON'T KNOW.
CHICKENHARE, PLEASE LET ME HELP. I FEEL TERRIBLE ABOUT ABE AND I'M...
I'M MISSING A TOOTH. GREAT.

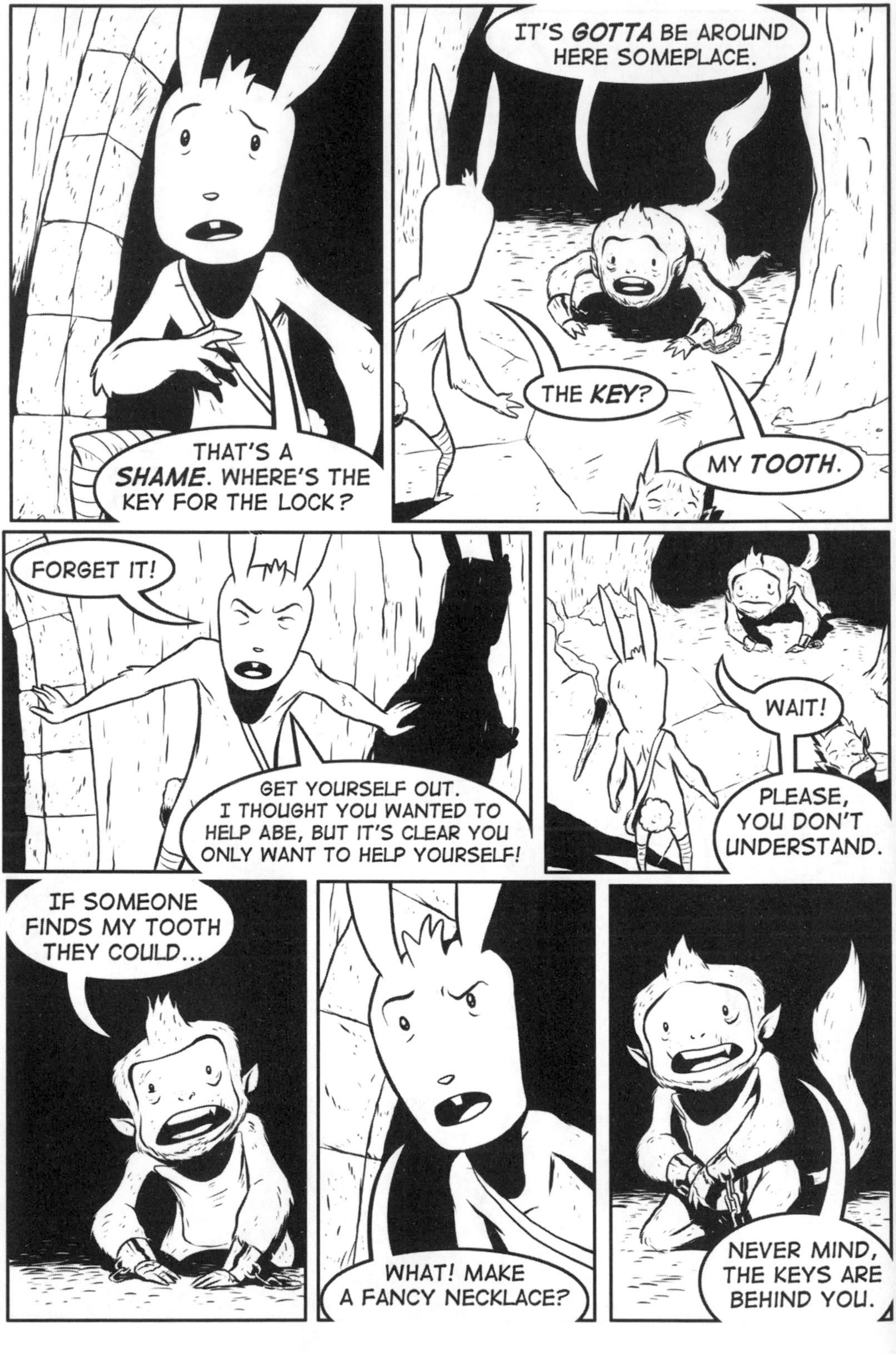
THAT'S A SHAME. WHERE'S THE KEY FOR THE LOCK?
IT'S GOTTA BE AROUND HERE SOMEPLACE.
THE KEY?
MY TOOTH.
FORGET IT!
GET YOURSELF OUT. I THOUGHT YOU WANTED TO HELP ABE, BUT IT'S CLEAR YOU ONLY WANT TO HELP YOURSELF!
WAIT!
PLEASE, YOU DON'T UNDERSTAND.
IF SOMEONE FINDS MY TOOTH THEY COULD...
WHAT! MAKE A FANCY NECKLACE?
NEVER MIND, THE KEYS ARE BEHIND YOU.

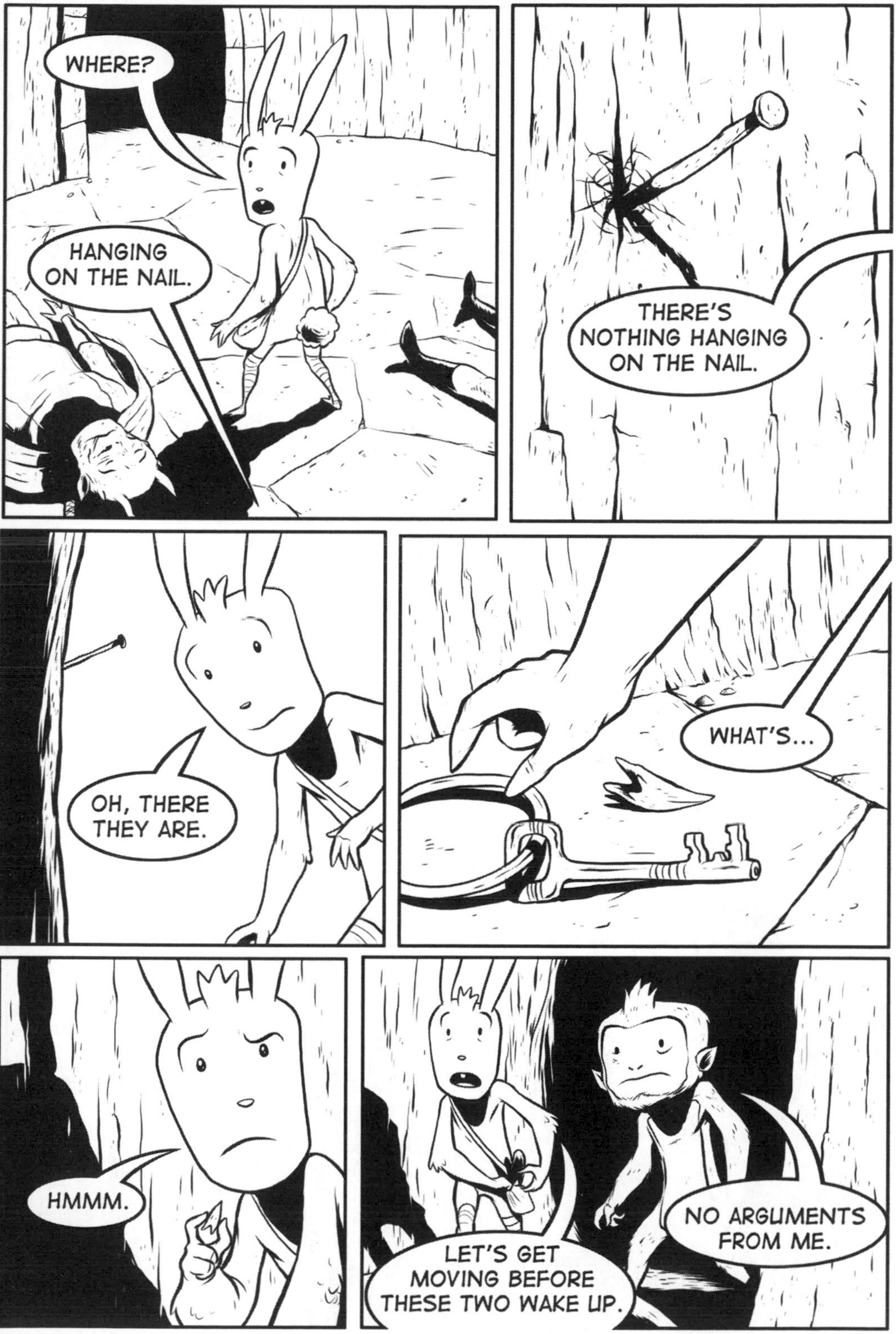
WHERE?
HANGING ON THE NAIL.
THERE'S NOTHING HANGING ON THE NAIL.
OH, THERE THEY ARE.
WHAT'S...
HMMM.
LET'S GET MOVING BEFORE THESE TWO WAKE UP.
NO ARGUMENTS FROM ME.

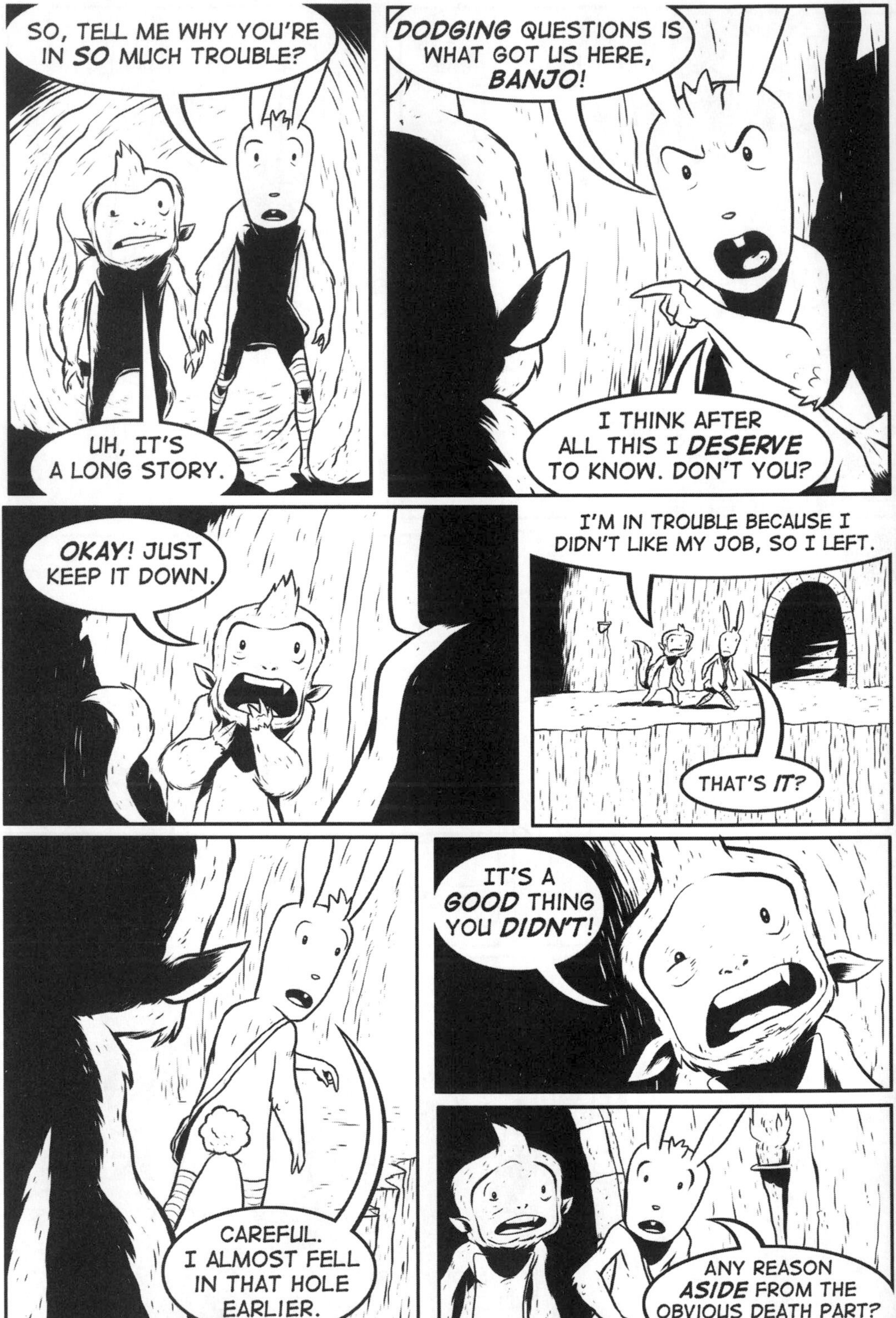
SO, TELL ME WHY YOU'RE IN SO MUCH TROUBLE?
UH, IT'S A LONG STORY.
DODGING QUESTIONS IS WHAT GOT US HERE, BANJO!
I THINK AFTER ALL THIS I DESERVE TO KNOW. DON'T YOU?
OKAY! JUST KEEP IT DOWN.
I'M IN TROUBLE BECAUSE I DIDN'T LIKE MY JOB, SO I LEFT.
THAT'S IT?
CAREFUL. I ALMOST FELL IN THAT HOLE EARLIER.
IT'S A GOOD THING YOU DIDN'T!
ANY REASON ASIDE FROM THE OBVIOUS DEATH PART?

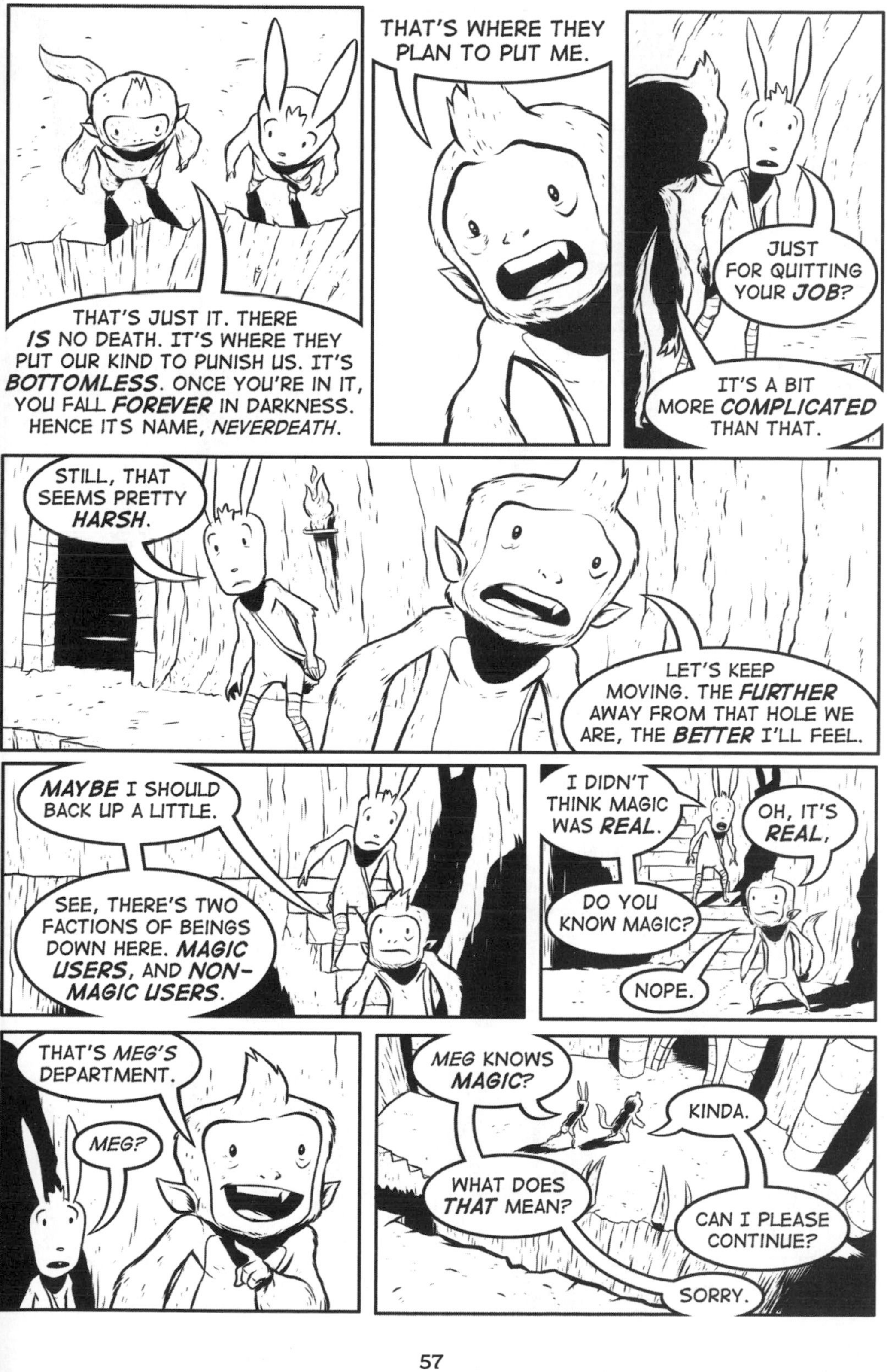
THAT'S JUST IT. THERE *IS* NO DEATH. IT'S WHERE THEY PUT OUR KIND TO PUNISH US. IT'S *BOTTOMLESS*. ONCE YOU'RE IN IT, YOU FALL *FOREVER* IN DARKNESS. HENCE ITS NAME, *NEVERDEATH*.
THAT'S WHERE THEY PLAN TO PUT ME.
JUST FOR QUITTING YOUR *JOB*?
IT'S A BIT MORE *COMPLICATED* THAN THAT.
STILL, THAT SEEMS PRETTY *HARSH*.
LET'S KEEP MOVING. THE *FURTHER* AWAY FROM THAT HOLE WE ARE, THE *BETTER* I'LL FEEL.
MAYBE I SHOULD BACK UP A LITTLE.
SEE, THERE'S TWO FACTIONS OF BEINGS DOWN HERE. *MAGIC USERS*, AND *NON-MAGIC USERS*.
I DIDN'T THINK MAGIC WAS *REAL*.
OH, IT'S *REAL*.
DO YOU KNOW MAGIC?
NOPE.
THAT'S *MEG'S* DEPARTMENT.
MEG?
MEG KNOWS *MAGIC*?
KINDA.
WHAT DOES *THAT* MEAN?
CAN I PLEASE CONTINUE?
SORRY.

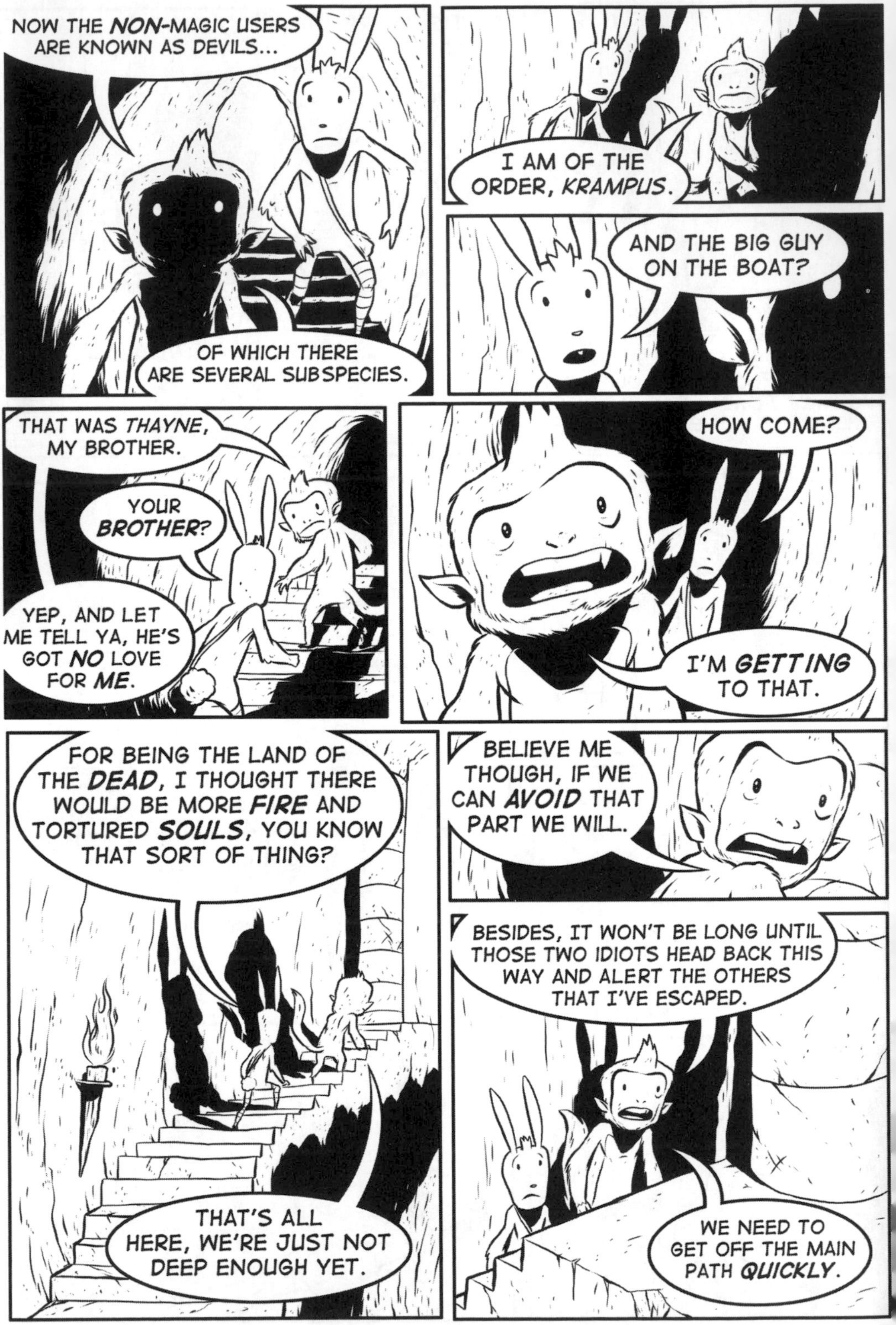
NOW THE NON-MAGIC USERS ARE KNOWN AS DEVILS...
OF WHICH THERE ARE SEVERAL SUBSPECIES.
I AM OF THE ORDER, KRAMPUS.
AND THE BIG GUY ON THE BOAT?
THAT WAS THAYNE, MY BROTHER.
YOUR BROTHER?
YEP, AND LET ME TELL YA, HE'S GOT NO LOVE FOR ME.
HOW COME?
I'M GETTING TO THAT.
FOR BEING THE LAND OF THE DEAD, I THOUGHT THERE WOULD BE MORE FIRE AND TORTURED SOULS, YOU KNOW THAT SORT OF THING?
THAT'S ALL HERE, WE'RE JUST NOT DEEP ENOUGH YET.
BELIEVE ME THOUGH, IF WE CAN AVOID THAT PART WE WILL.
BESIDES, IT WON'T BE LONG UNTIL THOSE TWO IDIOTS HEAD BACK THIS WAY AND ALERT THE OTHERS THAT I'VE ESCAPED.
WE NEED TO GET OFF THE MAIN PATH QUICKLY.

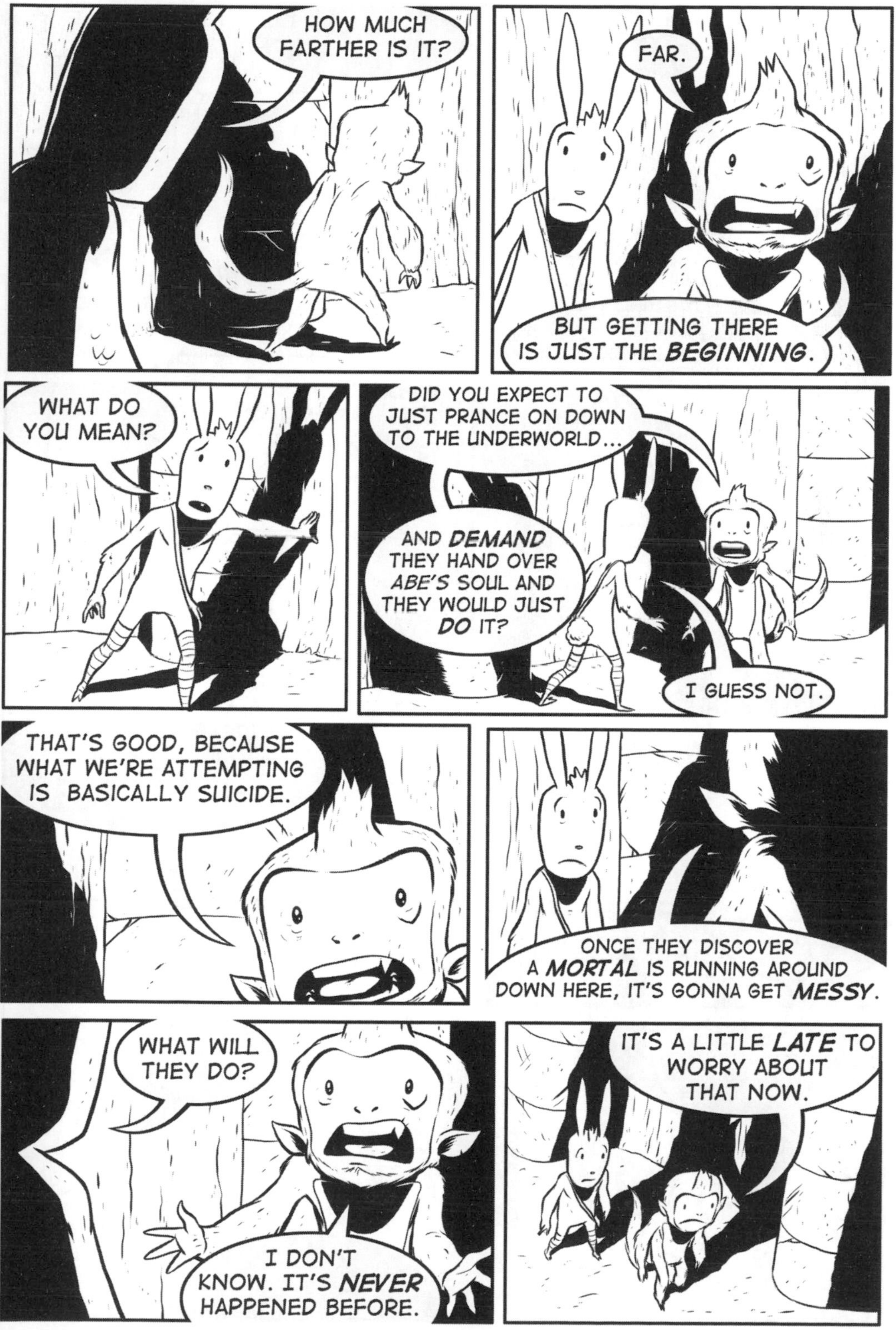
HOW MUCH FARTHER IS IT?
FAR.
BUT GETTING THERE IS JUST THE *BEGINNING*.
WHAT DO YOU MEAN?
DID YOU EXPECT TO JUST PRANCE ON DOWN TO THE UNDERWORLD...
AND *DEMAND* THEY HAND OVER *ABE'S* SOUL AND THEY WOULD JUST *DO* IT?
I GUESS NOT.
THAT'S GOOD, BECAUSE WHAT WE'RE ATTEMPTING IS BASICALLY SUICIDE.
ONCE THEY DISCOVER A *MORTAL* IS RUNNING AROUND DOWN HERE, IT'S GONNA GET *MESSY*.
WHAT WILL THEY DO?
I DON'T KNOW. IT'S *NEVER* HAPPENED BEFORE.
IT'S A LITTLE *LATE* TO WORRY ABOUT THAT NOW.

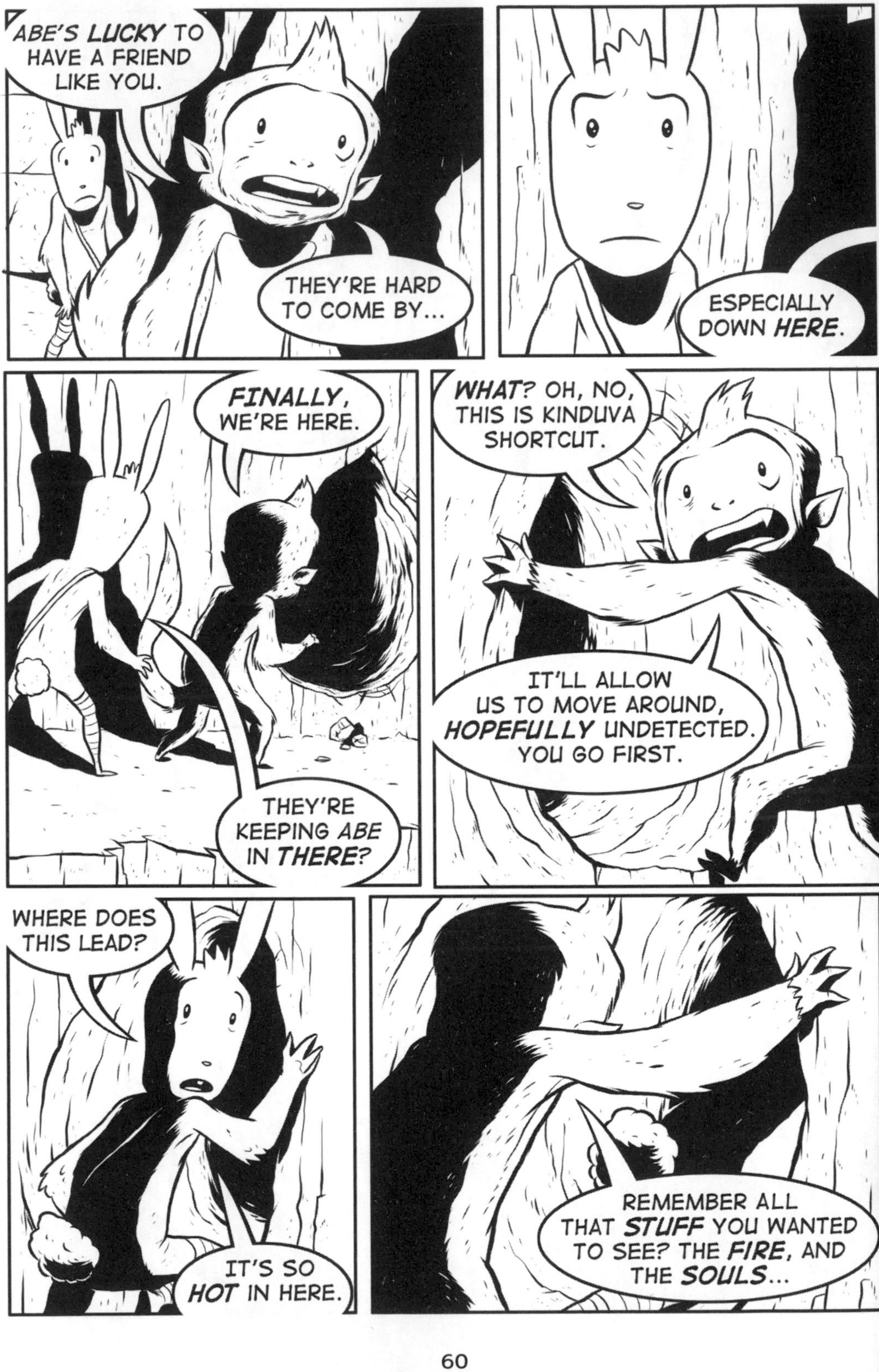
ABE'S **LUCKY** TO HAVE A FRIEND LIKE YOU.
THEY'RE HARD TO COME BY...
ESPECIALLY DOWN ***HERE***.
FINALLY, WE'RE HERE.
THEY'RE KEEPING *ABE* IN ***THERE***?
WHAT? OH, NO, THIS IS KINDUVA SHORTCUT.
IT'LL ALLOW US TO MOVE AROUND, ***HOPEFULLY*** UNDETECTED. YOU GO FIRST.
WHERE DOES THIS LEAD?
IT'S SO ***HOT*** IN HERE.
REMEMBER ALL THAT ***STUFF*** YOU WANTED TO SEE? THE ***FIRE***, AND THE ***SOULS***...

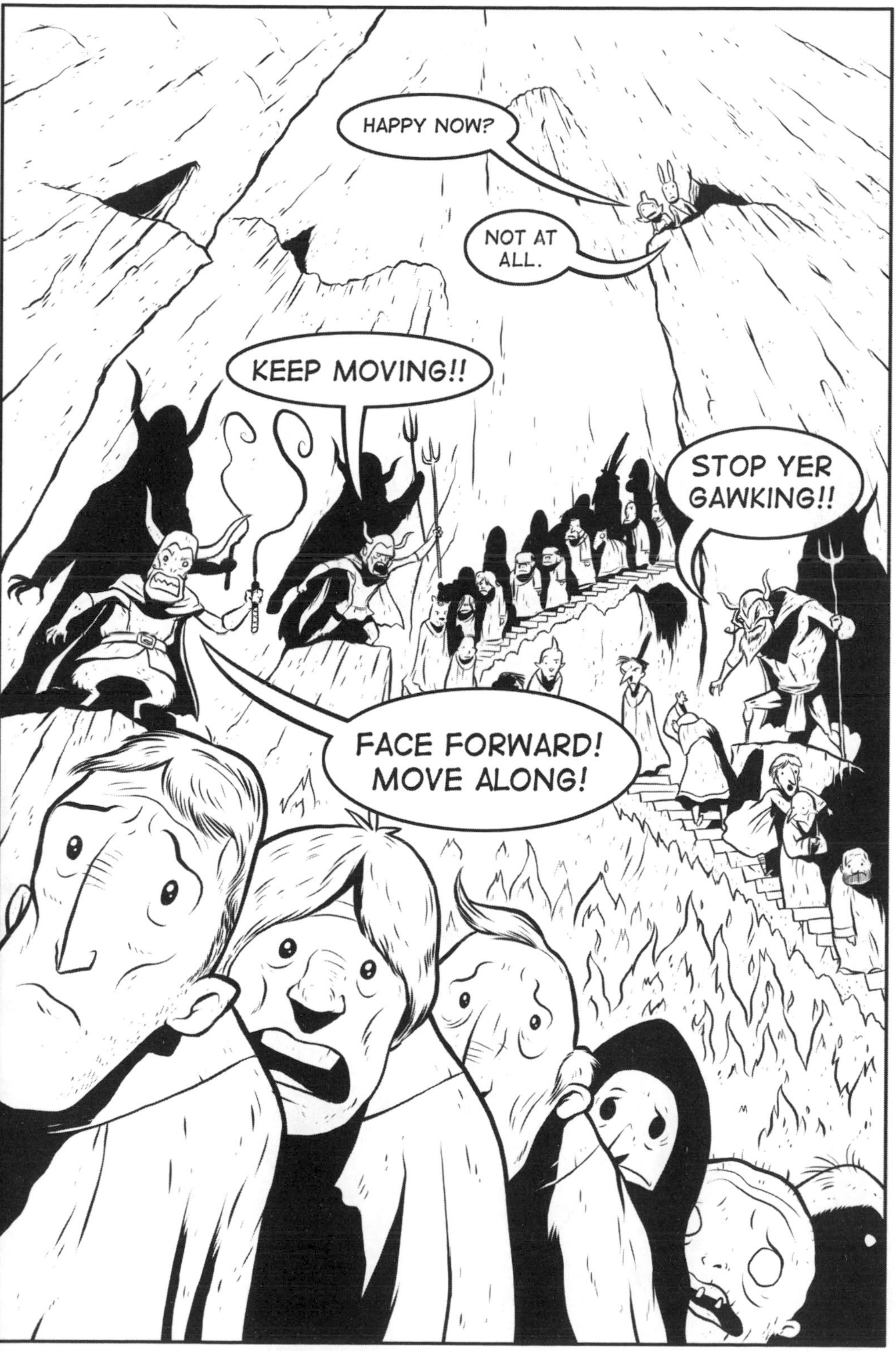
HAPPY NOW?
NOT AT ALL.
KEEP MOVING!!
STOP YER GAWKING!!
FACE FORWARD! MOVE ALONG!

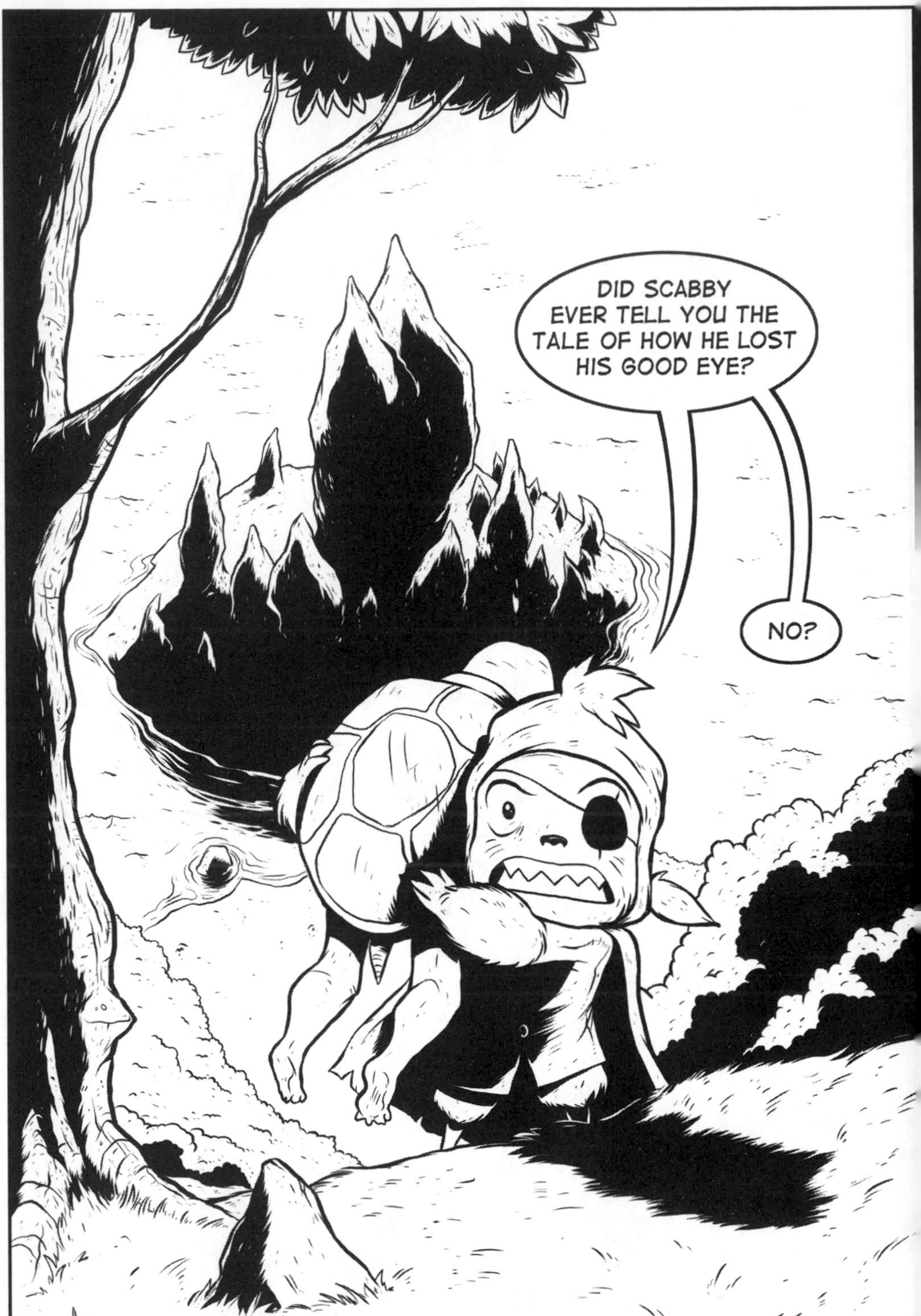
DID SCABBY EVER TELL YOU THE TALE OF HOW HE LOST HIS GOOD EYE?
NO?

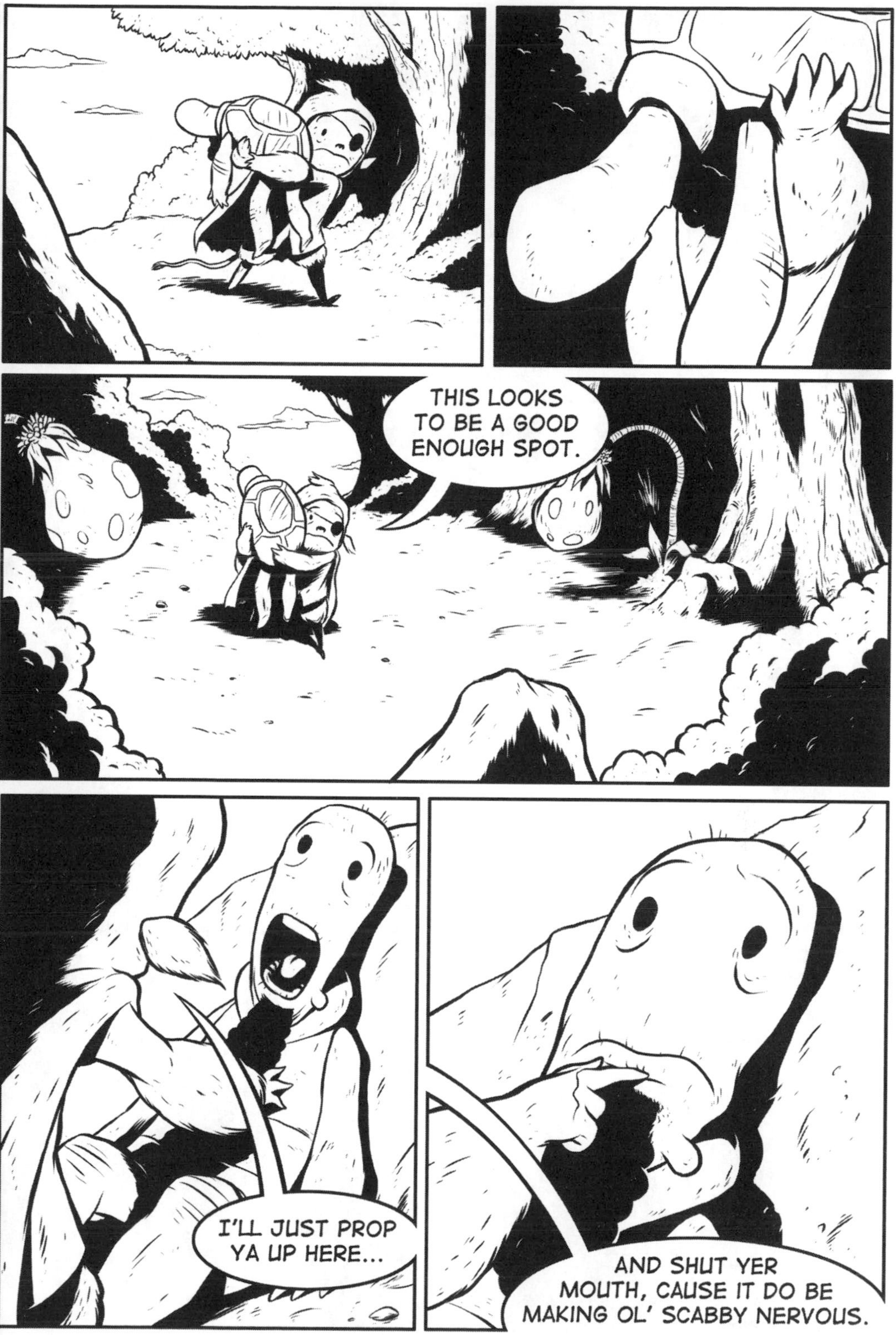
THIS LOOKS TO BE A GOOD ENOUGH SPOT.
I'LL JUST PROP YA UP HERE...
AND SHUT YER MOUTH, CAUSE IT DO BE MAKING OL' SCABBY NERVOUS.

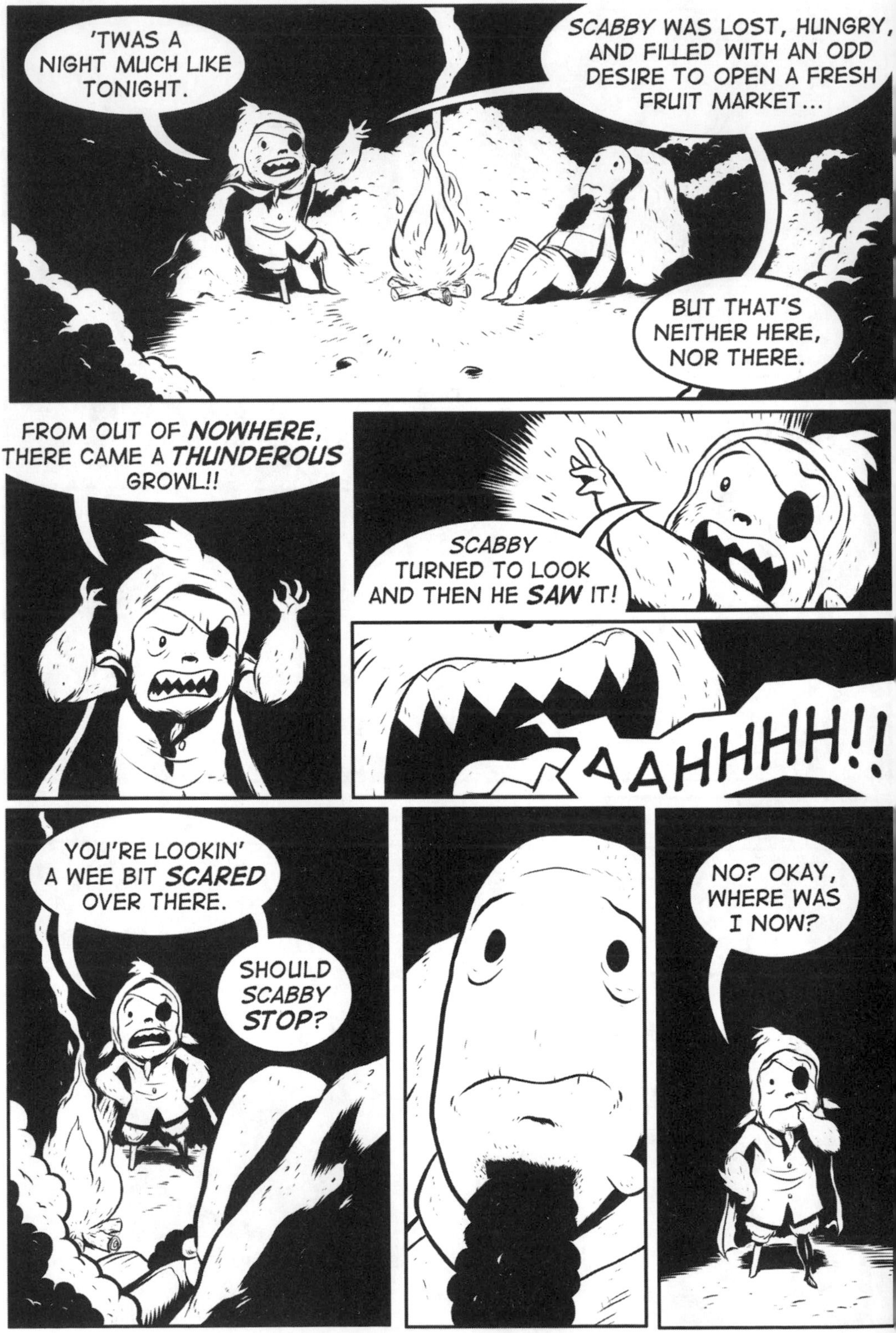
'TWAS A NIGHT MUCH LIKE TONIGHT.
SCABBY WAS LOST, HUNGRY, AND FILLED WITH AN ODD DESIRE TO OPEN A FRESH FRUIT MARKET...
BUT THAT'S NEITHER HERE, NOR THERE.
FROM OUT OF NOWHERE, THERE CAME A THUNDEROUS GROWL!!
SCABBY TURNED TO LOOK AND THEN HE SAW IT!
AAHHHH!!
YOU'RE LOOKIN' A WEE BIT SCARED OVER THERE.
SHOULD SCABBY STOP?
NO? OKAY, WHERE WAS I NOW?

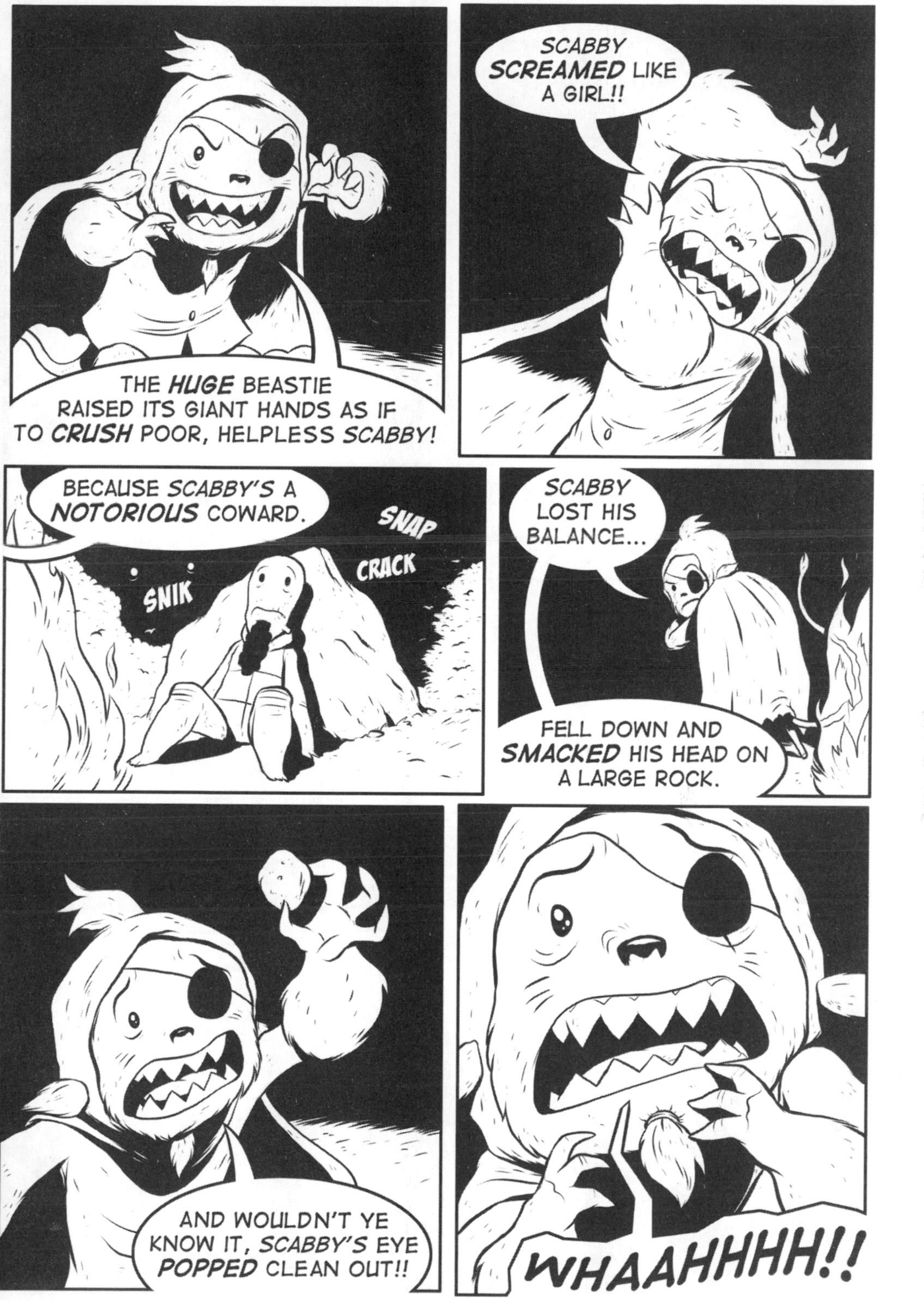
THE HUGE BEASTIE RAISED ITS GIANT HANDS AS IF TO CRUSH POOR, HELPLESS SCABBY!
SCABBY SCREAMED LIKE A GIRL!!
BECAUSE SCABBY'S A NOTORIOUS COWARD.
SNAP
CRACK
SNIK
SCABBY LOST HIS BALANCE...
FELL DOWN AND SMACKED HIS HEAD ON A LARGE ROCK.
AND WOULDN'T YE KNOW IT, SCABBY'S EYE POPPED CLEAN OUT!!
WHAAHHHH!!

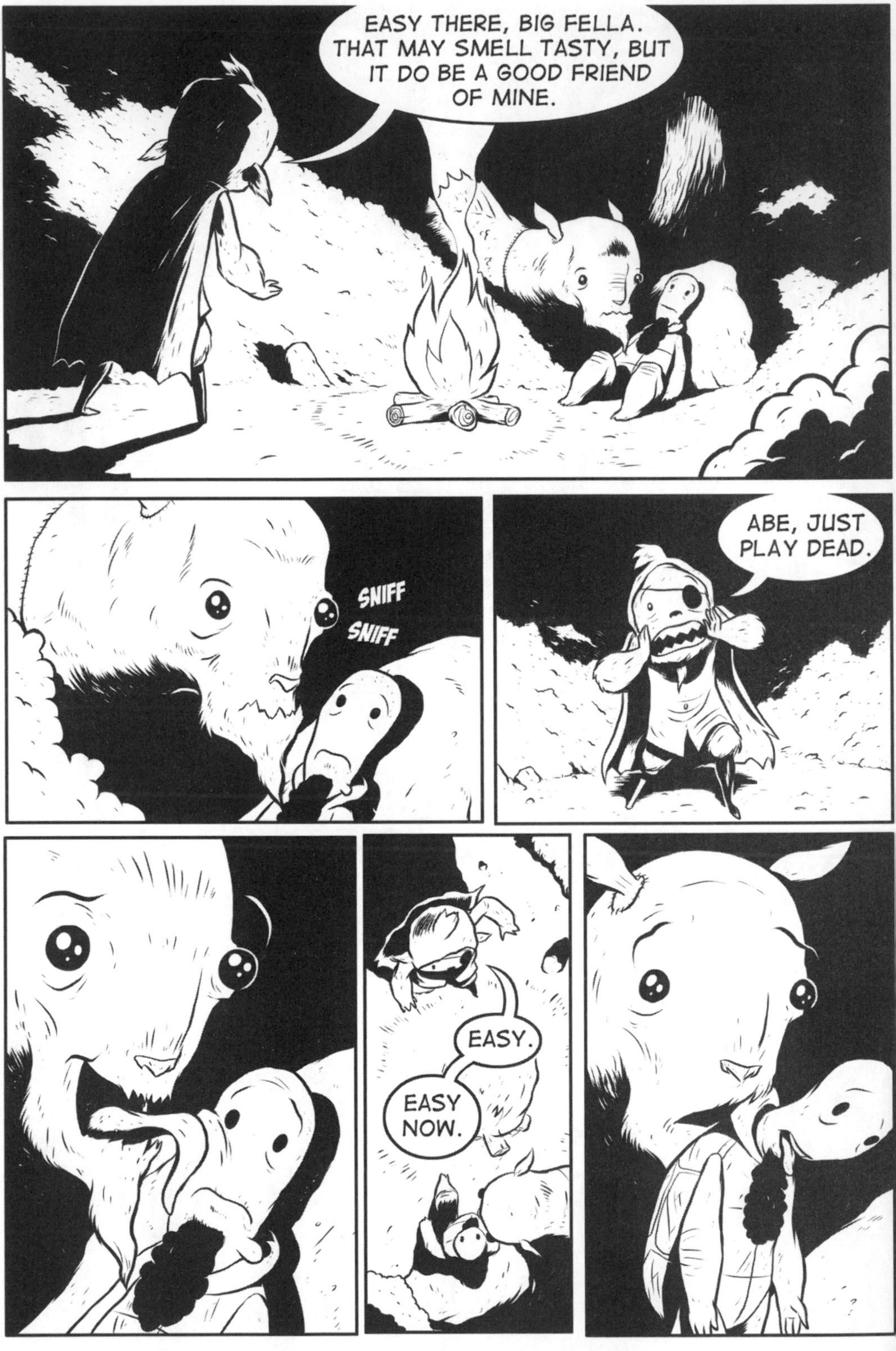
EASY THERE, BIG FELLA. THAT MAY SMELL TASTY, BUT IT DO BE A GOOD FRIEND OF MINE.
SNIFF
SNIFF
ABE, JUST PLAY DEAD.
EASY.
EASY NOW.

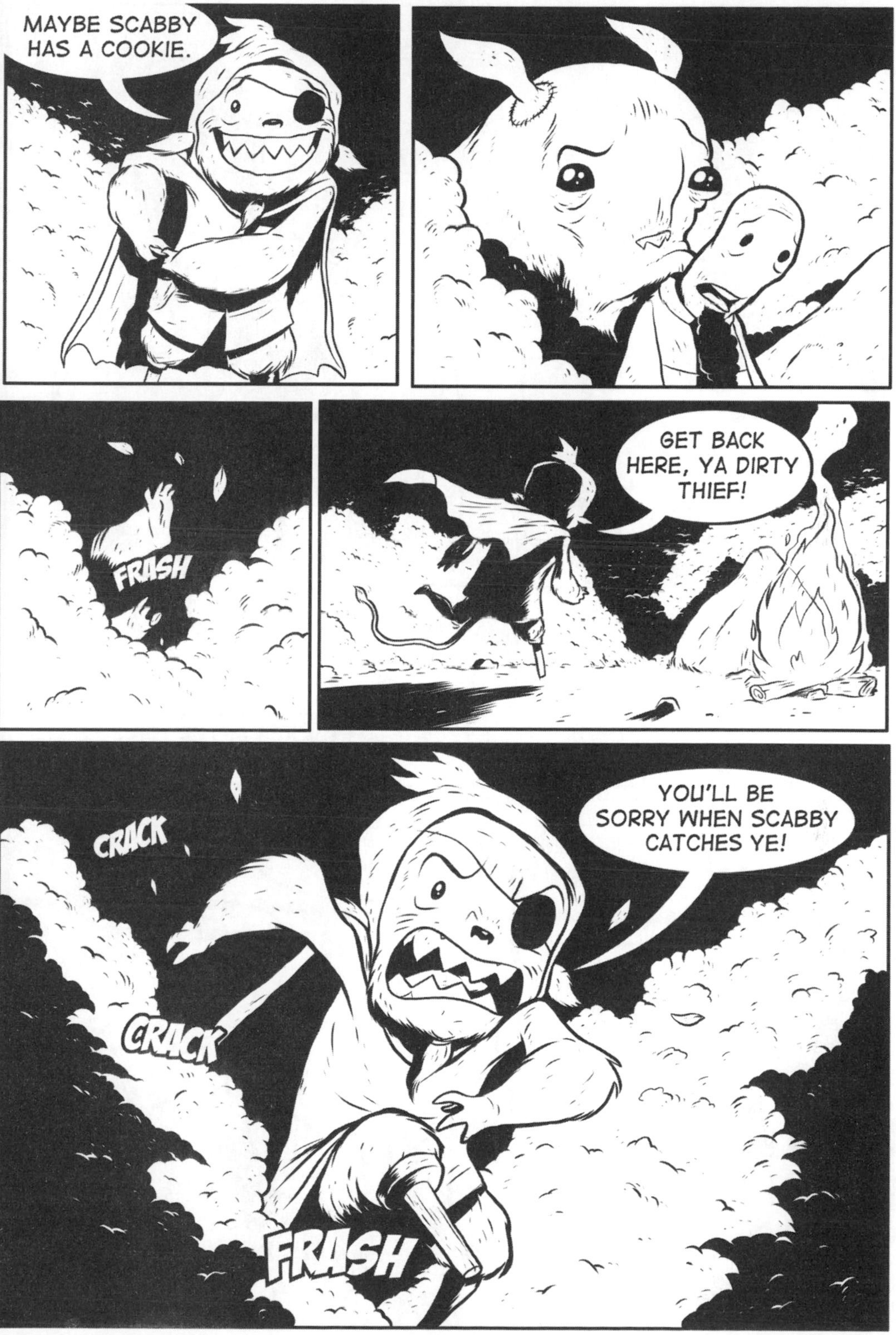
MAYBE SCABBY HAS A COOKIE.
FRASH
GET BACK HERE, YA DIRTY THIEF!
CRACK
YOU'LL BE SORRY WHEN SCABBY CATCHES YE!
CRACK
FRASH

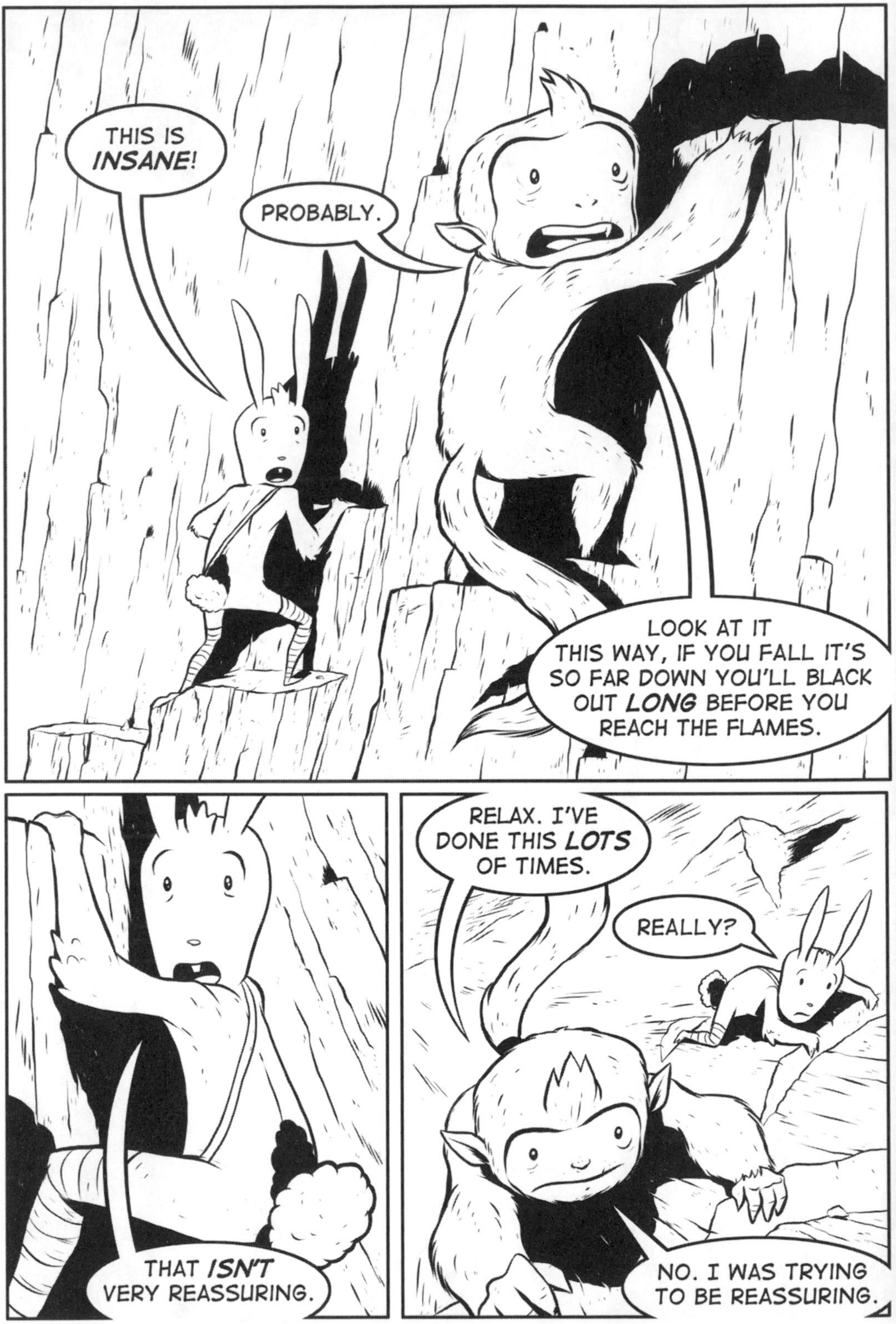
THIS IS INSANE!
PROBABLY.
LOOK AT IT THIS WAY, IF YOU FALL IT'S SO FAR DOWN YOU'LL BLACK OUT LONG BEFORE YOU REACH THE FLAMES.
THAT ISN'T VERY REASSURING.
RELAX. I'VE DONE THIS LOTS OF TIMES.
REALLY?
NO. I WAS TRYING TO BE REASSURING.

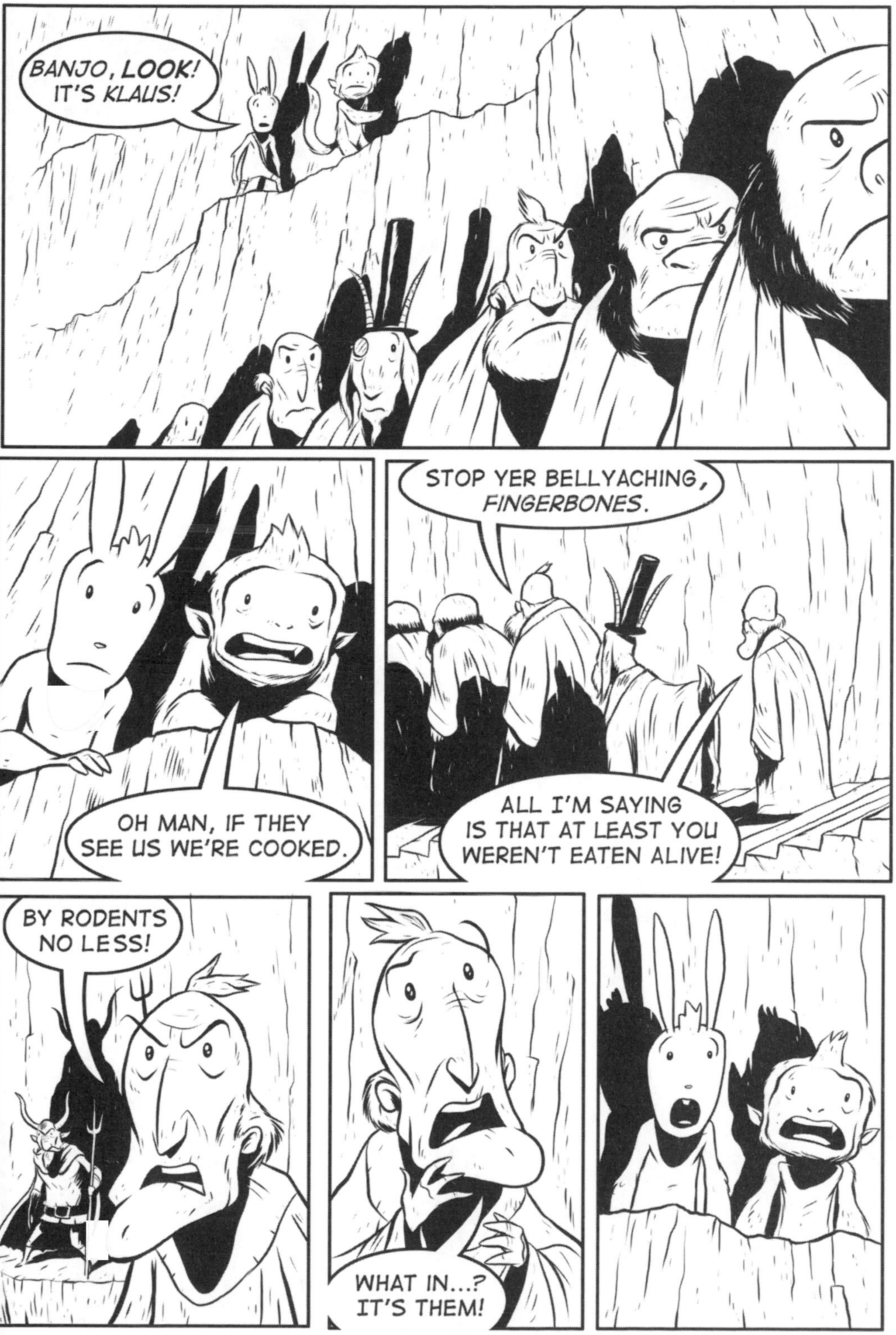
BANJO, LOOK! IT'S KLAUS!
OH MAN, IF THEY SEE US WE'RE COOKED.
STOP YER BELLYACHING, FINGERBONES.
ALL I'M SAYING IS THAT AT LEAST YOU WEREN'T EATEN ALIVE!
BY RODENTS NO LESS!
WHAT IN...? IT'S THEM!

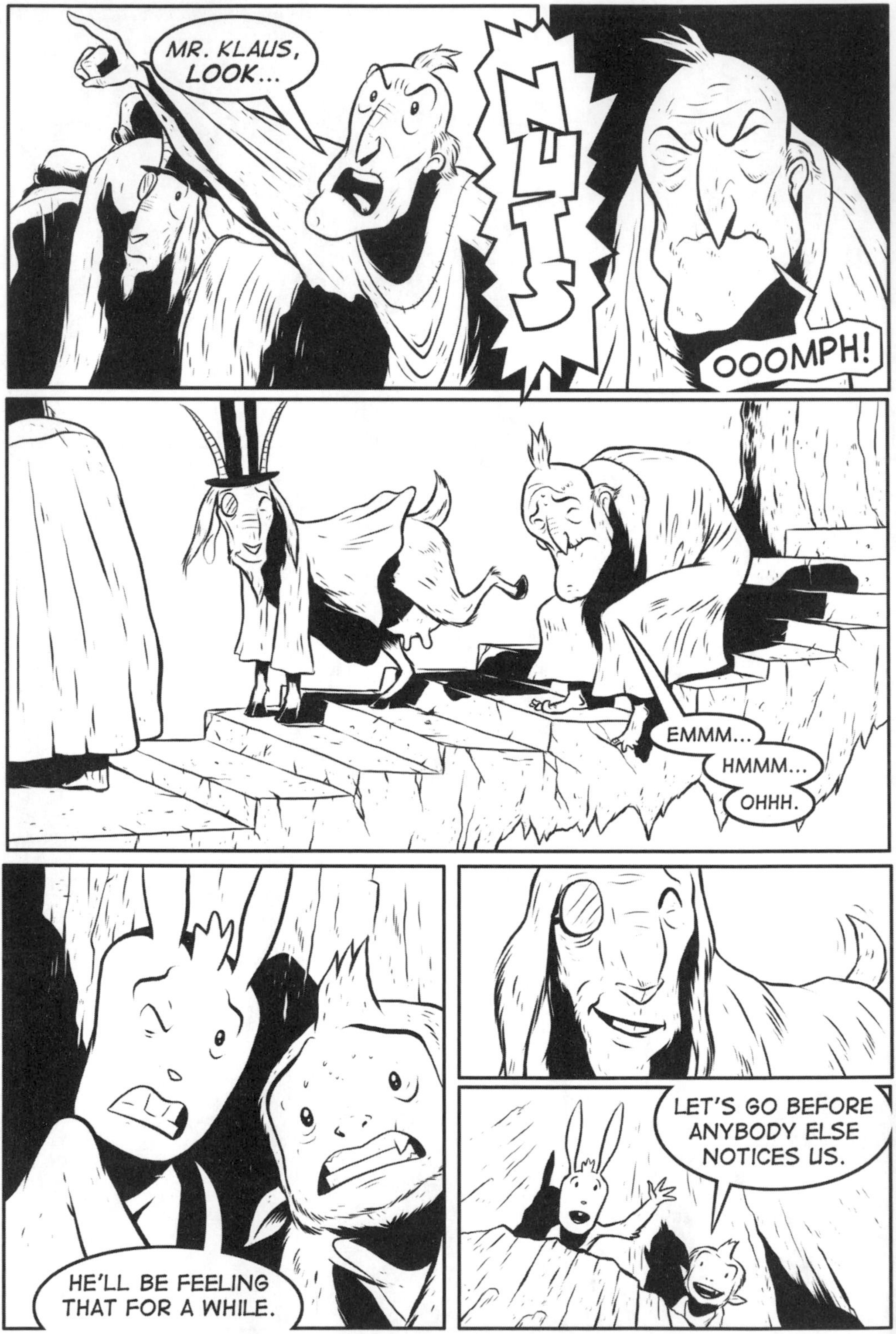
MR. KLAUS, LOOK...
NUTS
OOOMPH!
EMMM...
HMMM...
OHHH.
HE'LL BE FEELING THAT FOR A WHILE.
LET'S GO BEFORE ANYBODY ELSE NOTICES US.

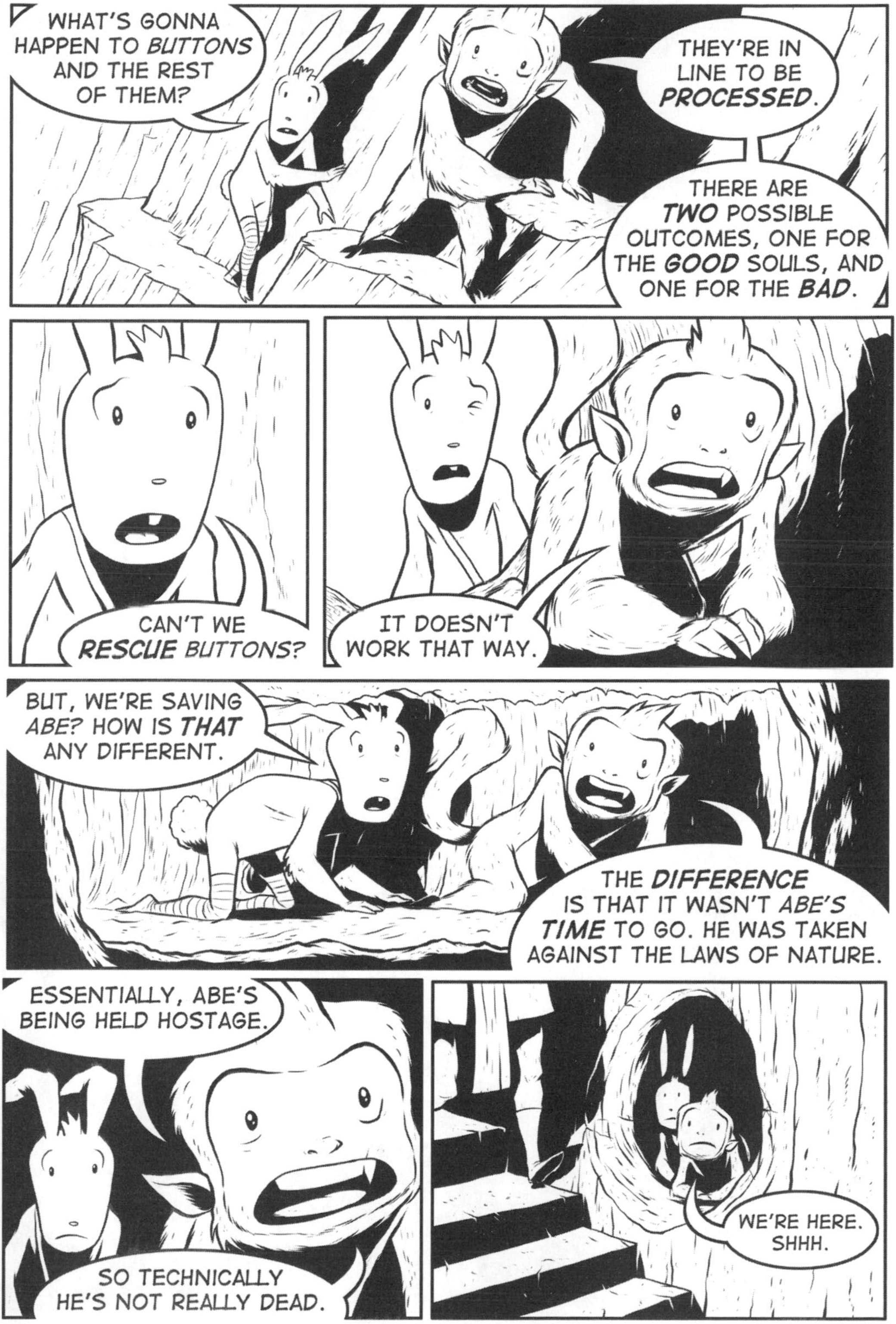
WHAT'S GONNA HAPPEN TO BUTTONS AND THE REST OF THEM?
THEY'RE IN LINE TO BE PROCESSED.
THERE ARE TWO POSSIBLE OUTCOMES, ONE FOR THE GOOD SOULS, AND ONE FOR THE BAD.
CAN'T WE RESCUE BUTTONS?
IT DOESN'T WORK THAT WAY.
BUT, WE'RE SAVING ABE? HOW IS THAT ANY DIFFERENT.
THE DIFFERENCE IS THAT IT WASN'T ABE'S TIME TO GO. HE WAS TAKEN AGAINST THE LAWS OF NATURE.
ESSENTIALLY, ABE'S BEING HELD HOSTAGE.
SO TECHNICALLY HE'S NOT REALLY DEAD.
WE'RE HERE. SHHH.

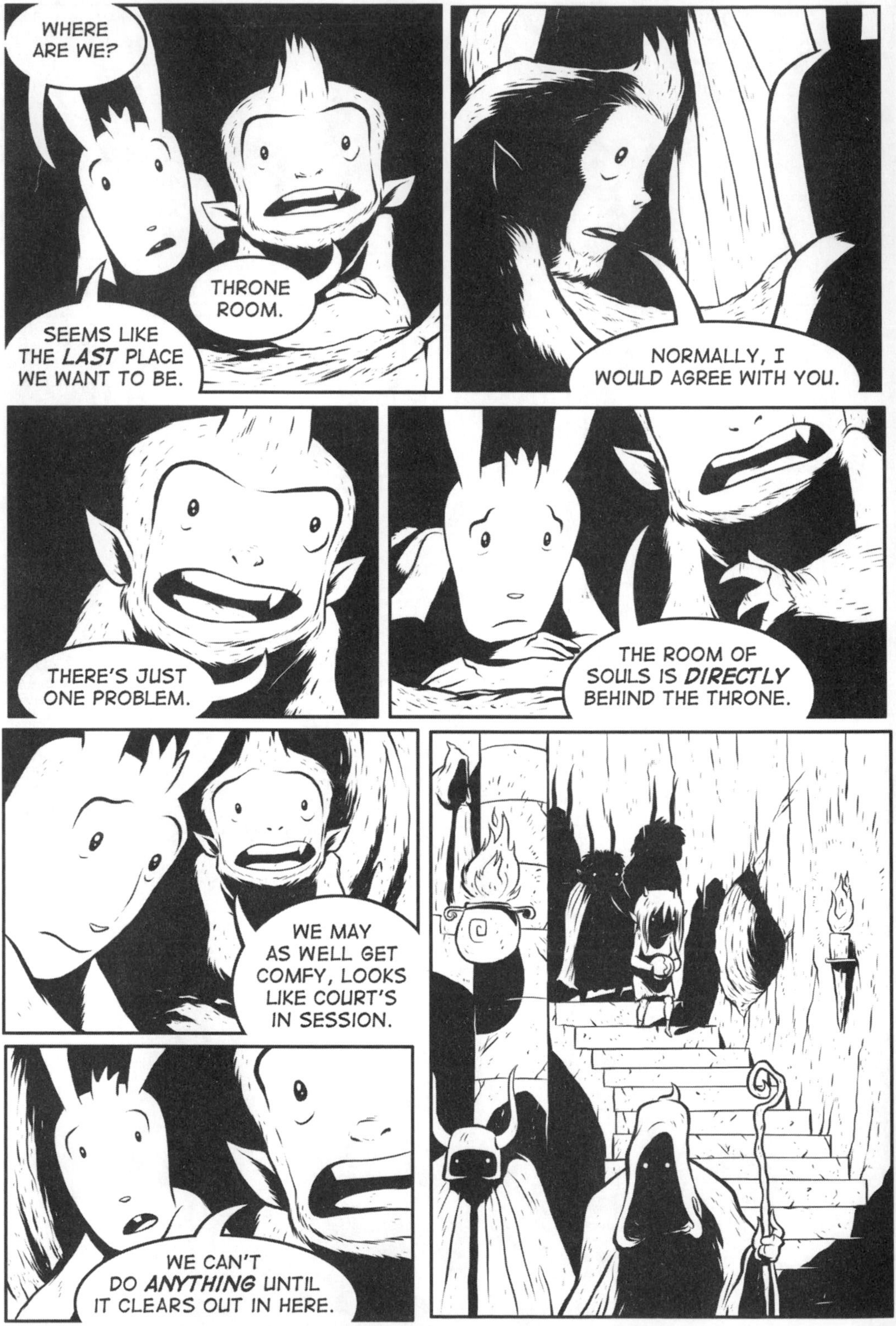
WHERE ARE WE?
THRONE ROOM.
SEEMS LIKE THE *LAST* PLACE WE WANT TO BE.
NORMALLY, I WOULD AGREE WITH YOU.
THERE'S JUST ONE PROBLEM.
THE ROOM OF SOULS IS *DIRECTLY* BEHIND THE THRONE.
WE MAY AS WELL GET COMFY, LOOKS LIKE COURT'S IN SESSION.
WE CAN'T DO *ANYTHING* UNTIL IT CLEARS OUT IN HERE.

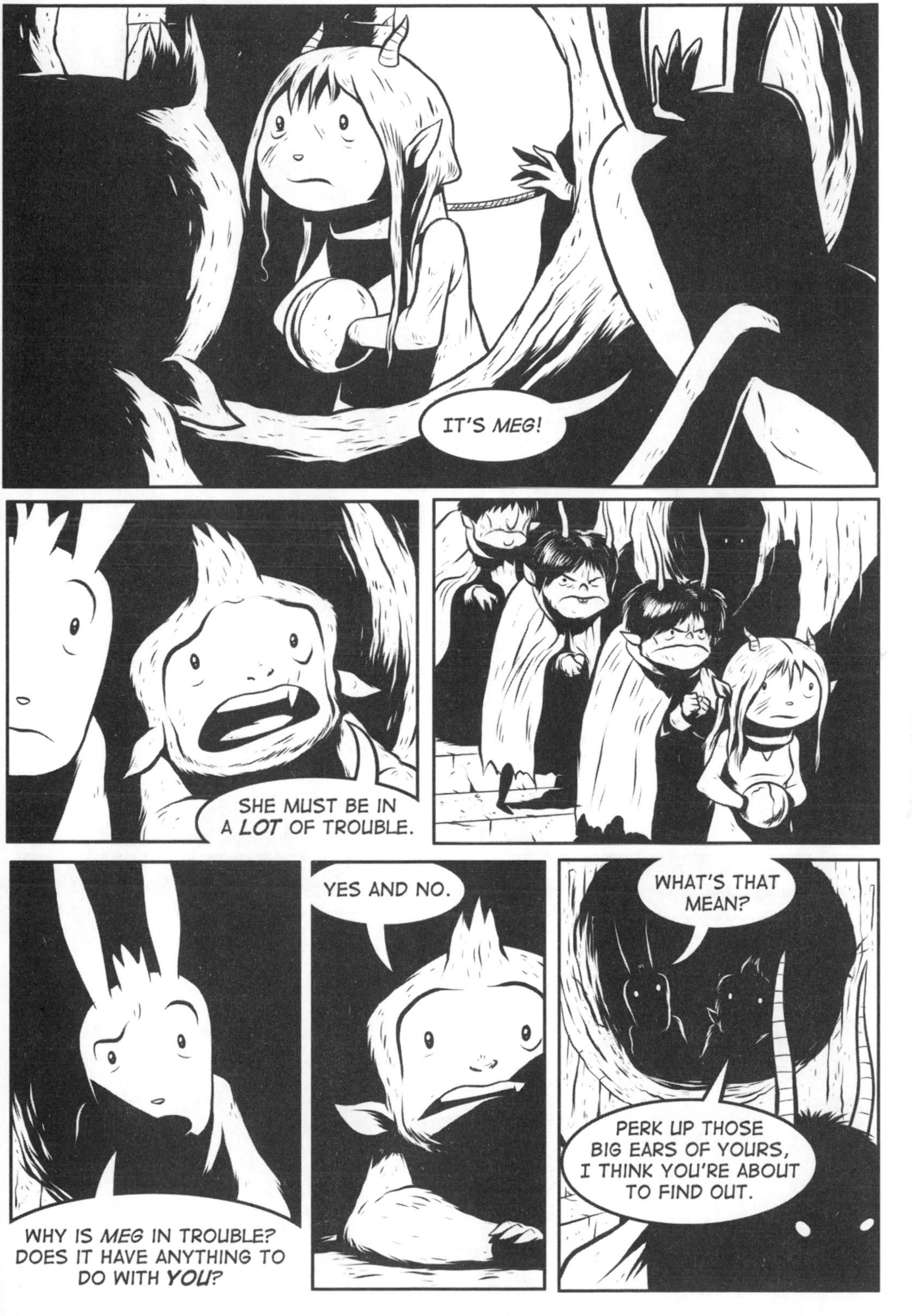
IT'S MEG!
SHE MUST BE IN A LOT OF TROUBLE.
WHY IS MEG IN TROUBLE? DOES IT HAVE ANYTHING TO DO WITH YOU?
YES AND NO.
WHAT'S THAT MEAN?
PERK UP THOSE BIG EARS OF YOURS, I THINK YOU'RE ABOUT TO FIND OUT.

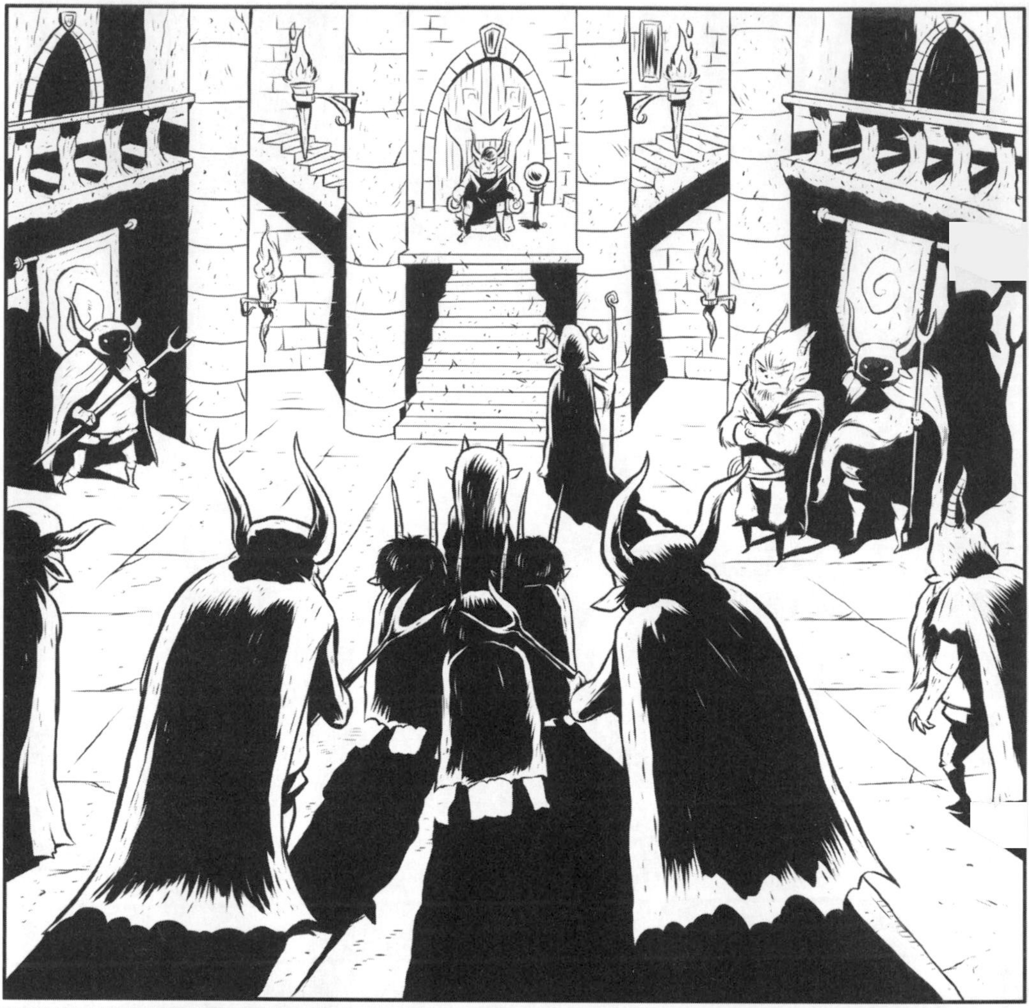

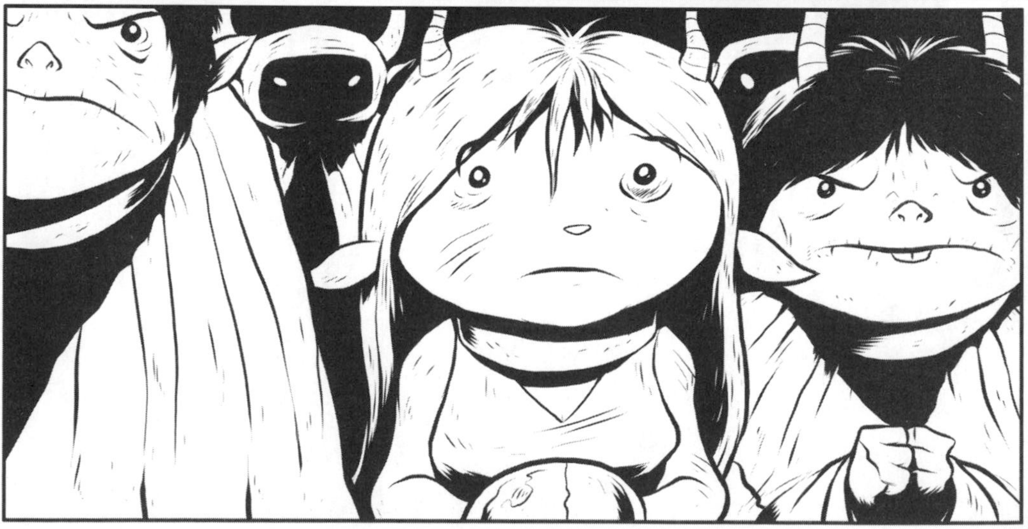

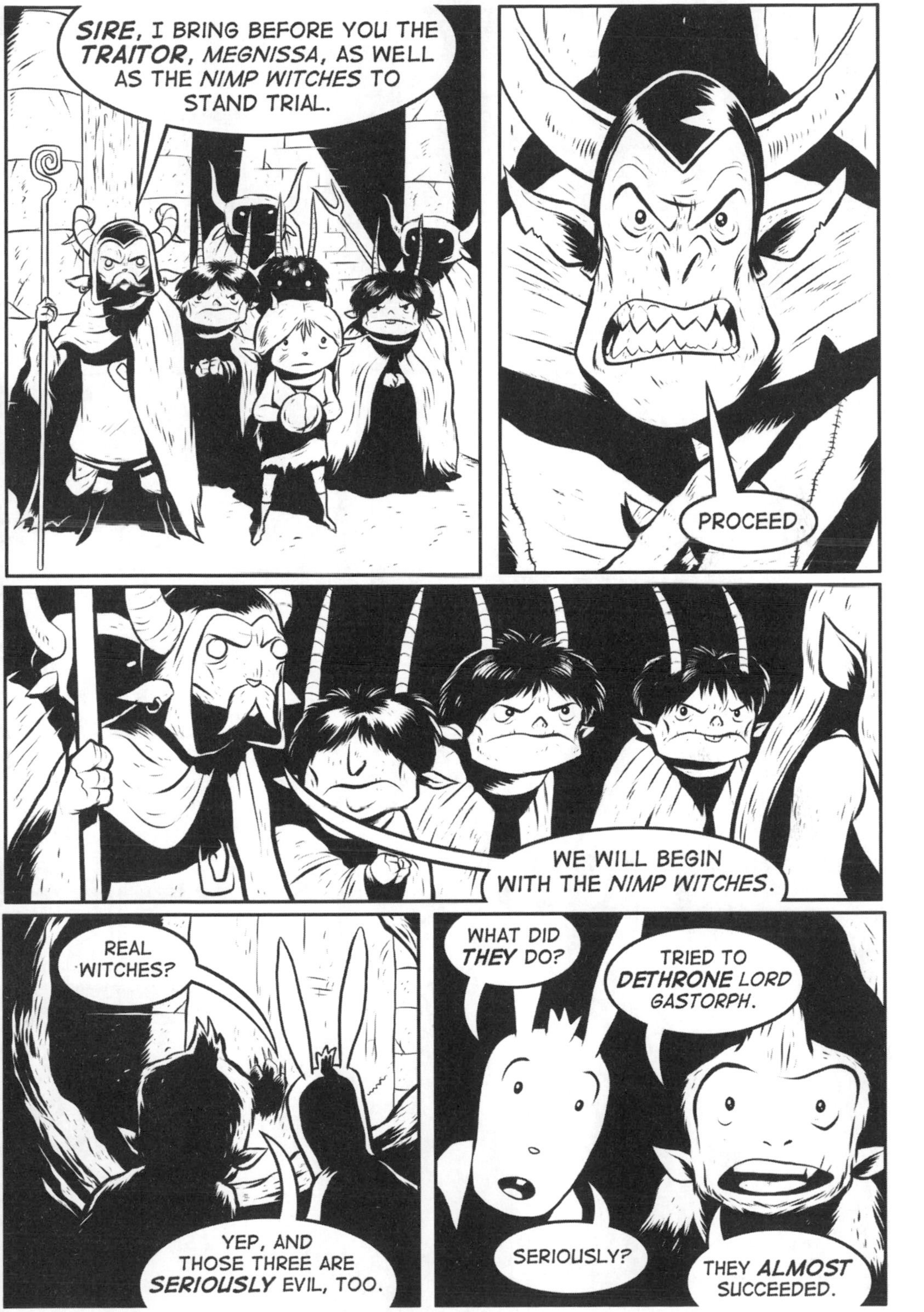
SIRE, I BRING BEFORE YOU THE TRAITOR, MEGNISSA, AS WELL AS THE NIMP WITCHES TO STAND TRIAL.
PROCEED.
WE WILL BEGIN WITH THE NIMP WITCHES.
REAL WITCHES?
YEP, AND THOSE THREE ARE SERIOUSLY EVIL, TOO.
WHAT DID THEY DO?
TRIED TO DETHRONE LORD GASTORPH.
SERIOUSLY?
THEY ALMOST SUCCEEDED.

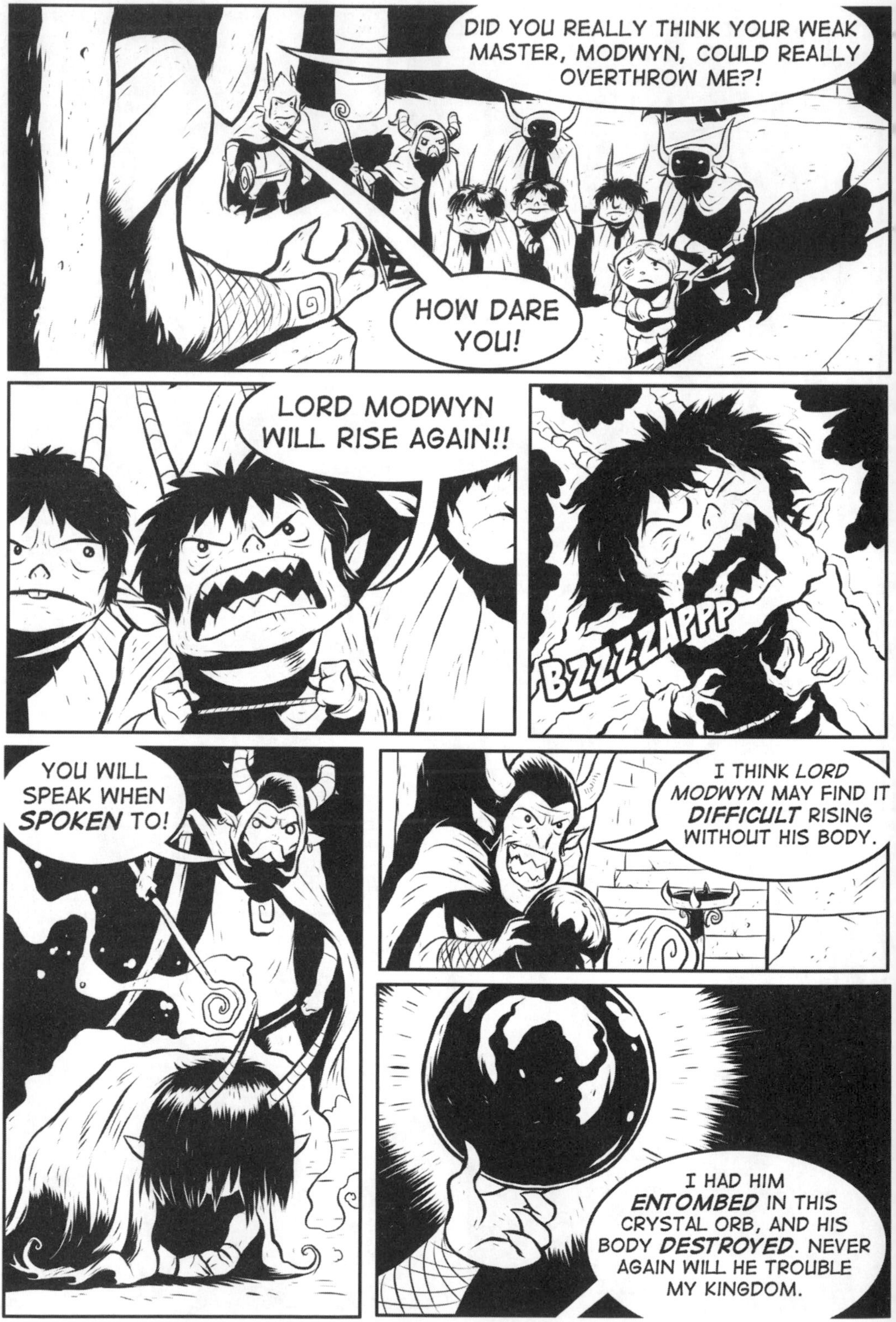
DID YOU REALLY THINK YOUR WEAK MASTER, MODWYN, COULD REALLY OVERTHROW ME?!
HOW DARE YOU!
LORD MODWYN WILL RISE AGAIN!!
BZZZZAPPP
YOU WILL SPEAK WHEN *SPOKEN* TO!
I THINK *LORD MODWYN* MAY FIND IT *DIFFICULT* RISING WITHOUT HIS BODY.
I HAD HIM *ENTOMBED* IN THIS CRYSTAL ORB, AND HIS BODY *DESTROYED*. NEVER AGAIN WILL HE TROUBLE MY KINGDOM.

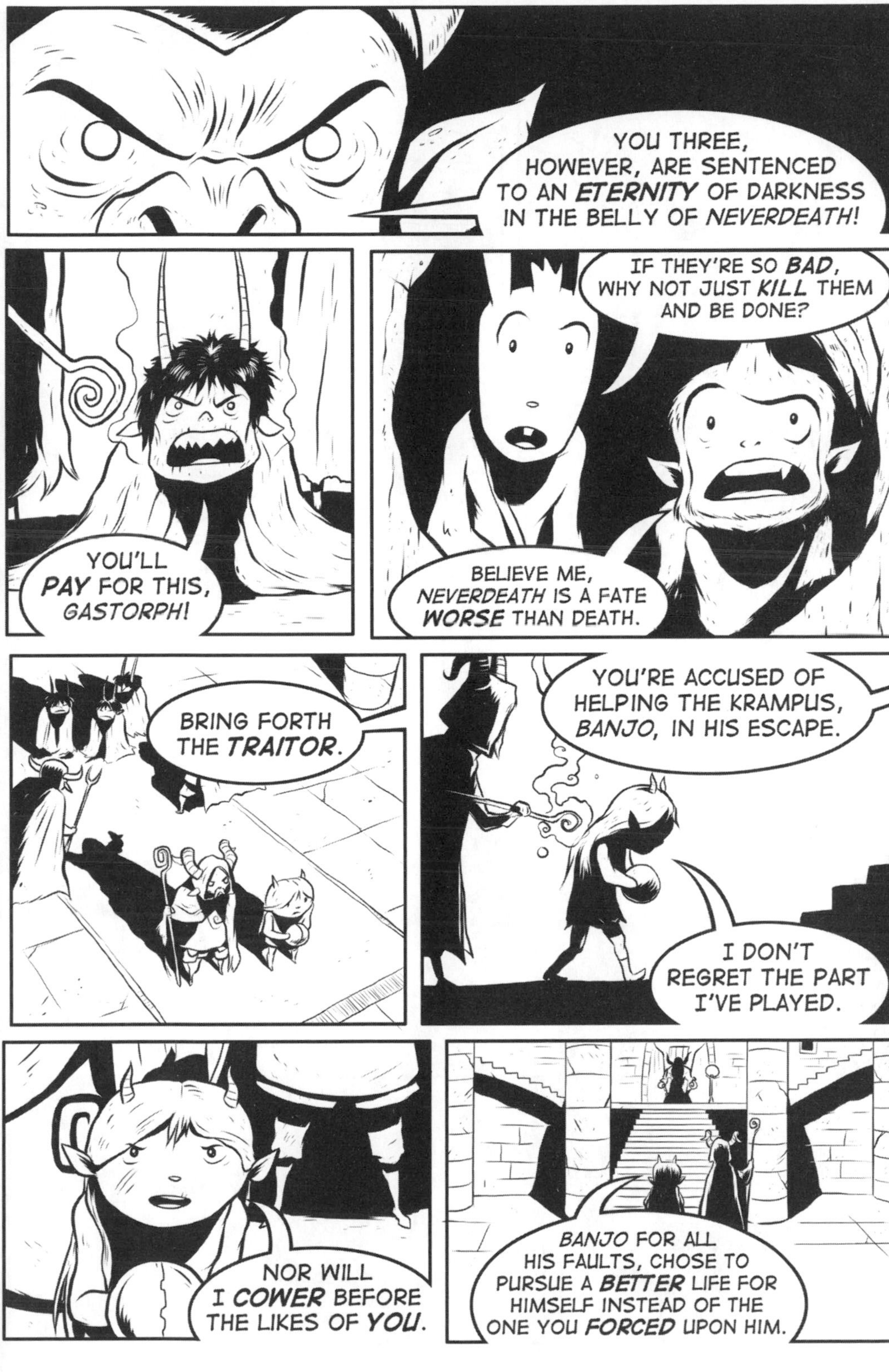
YOU THREE, HOWEVER, ARE SENTENCED TO AN *ETERNITY* OF DARKNESS IN THE BELLY OF *NEVERDEATH*!
YOU'LL *PAY* FOR THIS, *GASTORPH*!
IF THEY'RE SO *BAD*, WHY NOT JUST *KILL* THEM AND BE DONE?
BELIEVE ME, *NEVERDEATH* IS A FATE *WORSE* THAN DEATH.
BRING FORTH THE *TRAITOR*.
YOU'RE ACCUSED OF HELPING THE KRAMPUS, *BANJO*, IN HIS ESCAPE.
I DON'T REGRET THE PART I'VE PLAYED.
NOR WILL I *COWER* BEFORE THE LIKES OF *YOU*.
BANJO FOR ALL HIS FAULTS, CHOSE TO PURSUE A *BETTER* LIFE FOR HIMSELF INSTEAD OF THE ONE YOU *FORCED* UPON HIM.

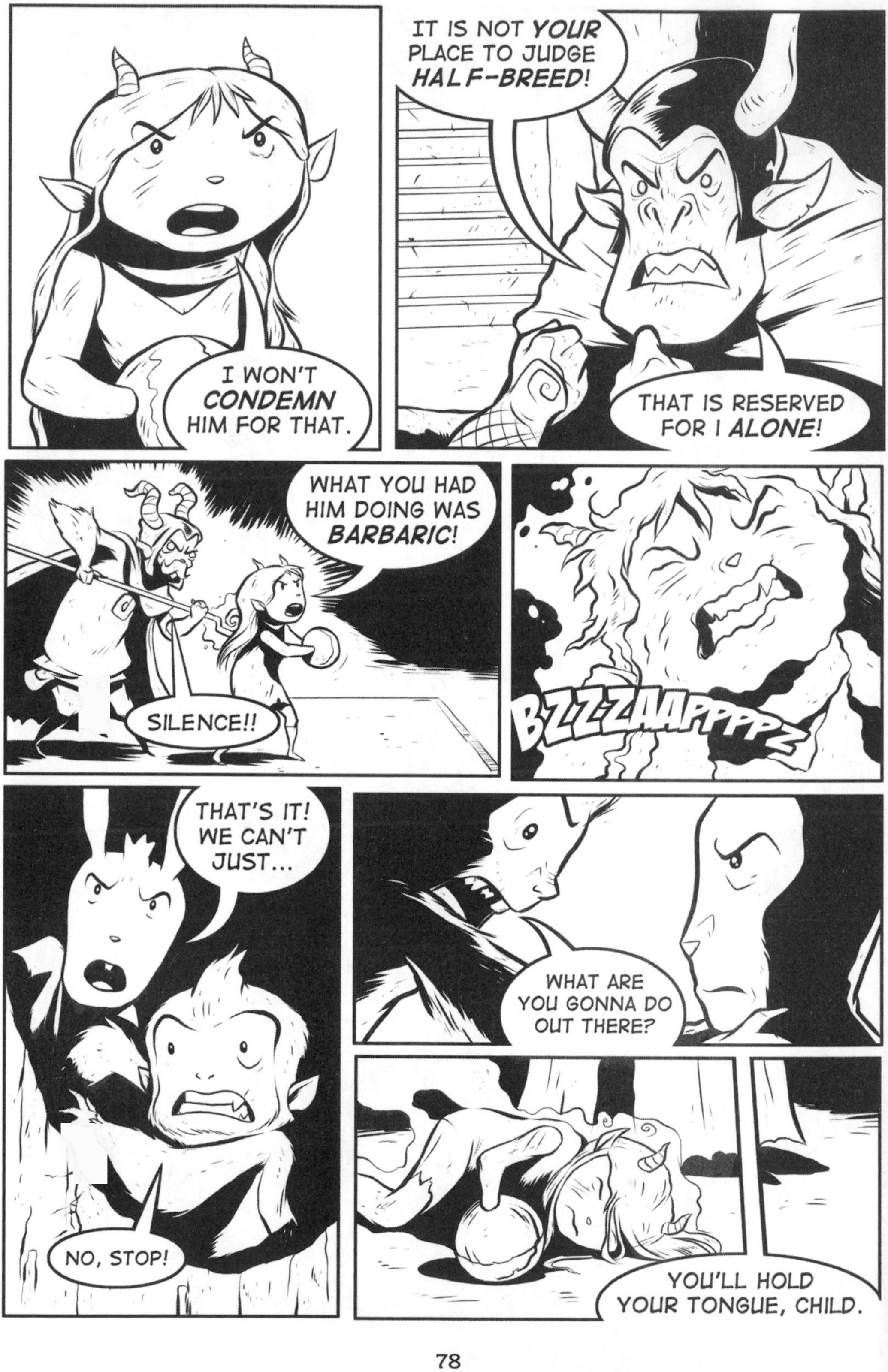
I WON'T CONDEMN HIM FOR THAT.
IT IS NOT YOUR PLACE TO JUDGE HALF-BREED!
THAT IS RESERVED FOR I ALONE!
WHAT YOU HAD HIM DOING WAS BARBARIC!
SILENCE!!
BZZZAAPPPPZ
THAT'S IT! WE CAN'T JUST...
NO, STOP!
WHAT ARE YOU GONNA DO OUT THERE?
YOU'LL HOLD YOUR TONGUE, CHILD.

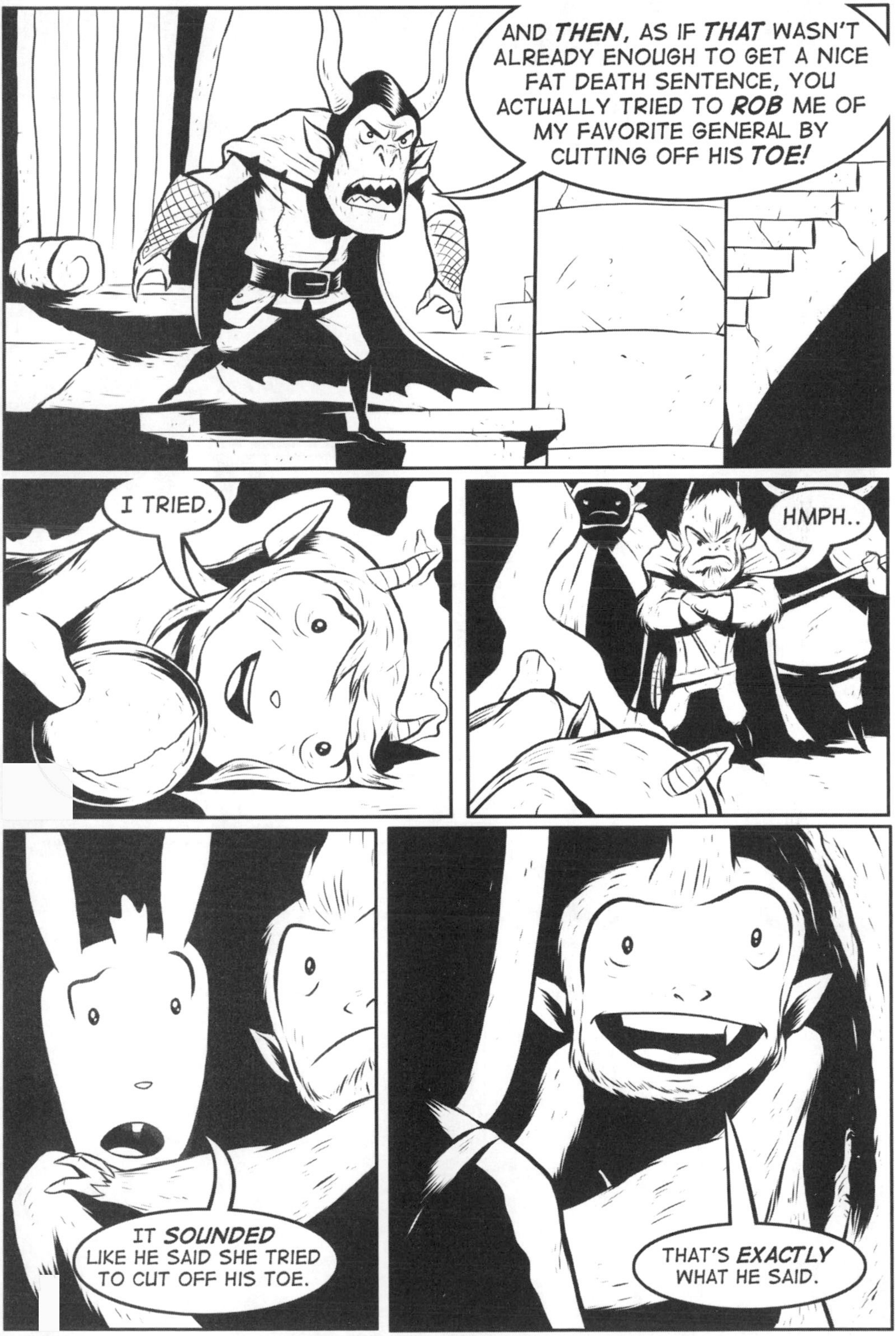
AND THEN, AS IF THAT WASN'T ALREADY ENOUGH TO GET A NICE FAT DEATH SENTENCE, YOU ACTUALLY TRIED TO ROB ME OF MY FAVORITE GENERAL BY CUTTING OFF HIS TOE!
I TRIED.
HMPH..
IT SOUNDED LIKE HE SAID SHE TRIED TO CUT OFF HIS TOE.
THAT'S EXACTLY WHAT HE SAID.

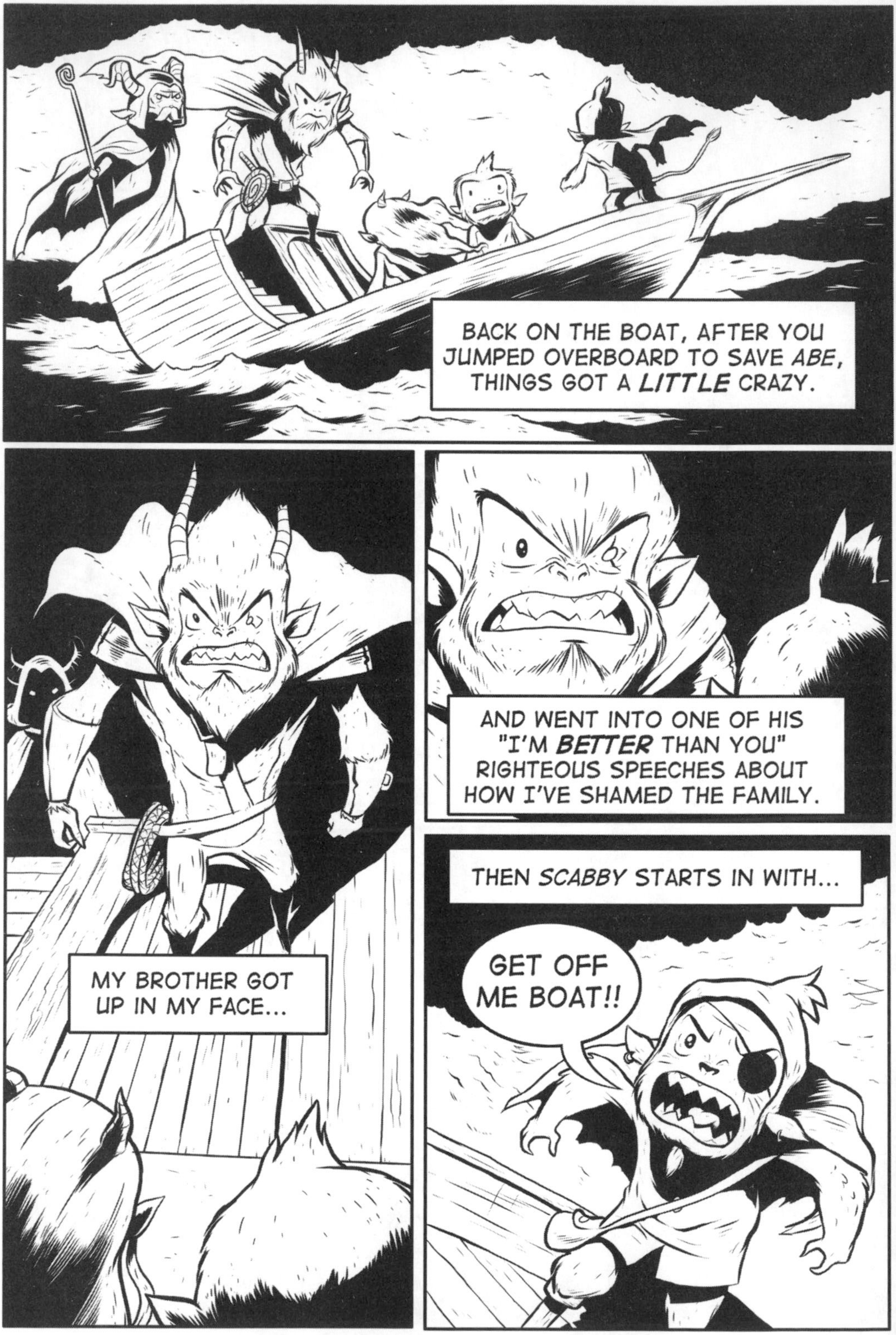
BACK ON THE BOAT, AFTER YOU JUMPED OVERBOARD TO SAVE *ABE*, THINGS GOT A *LITTLE* CRAZY.
MY BROTHER GOT UP IN MY FACE...
AND WENT INTO ONE OF HIS "I'M ***BETTER*** THAN YOU" RIGHTEOUS SPEECHES ABOUT HOW I'VE SHAMED THE FAMILY.
THEN *SCABBY* STARTS IN WITH...
GET OFF ME BOAT!!

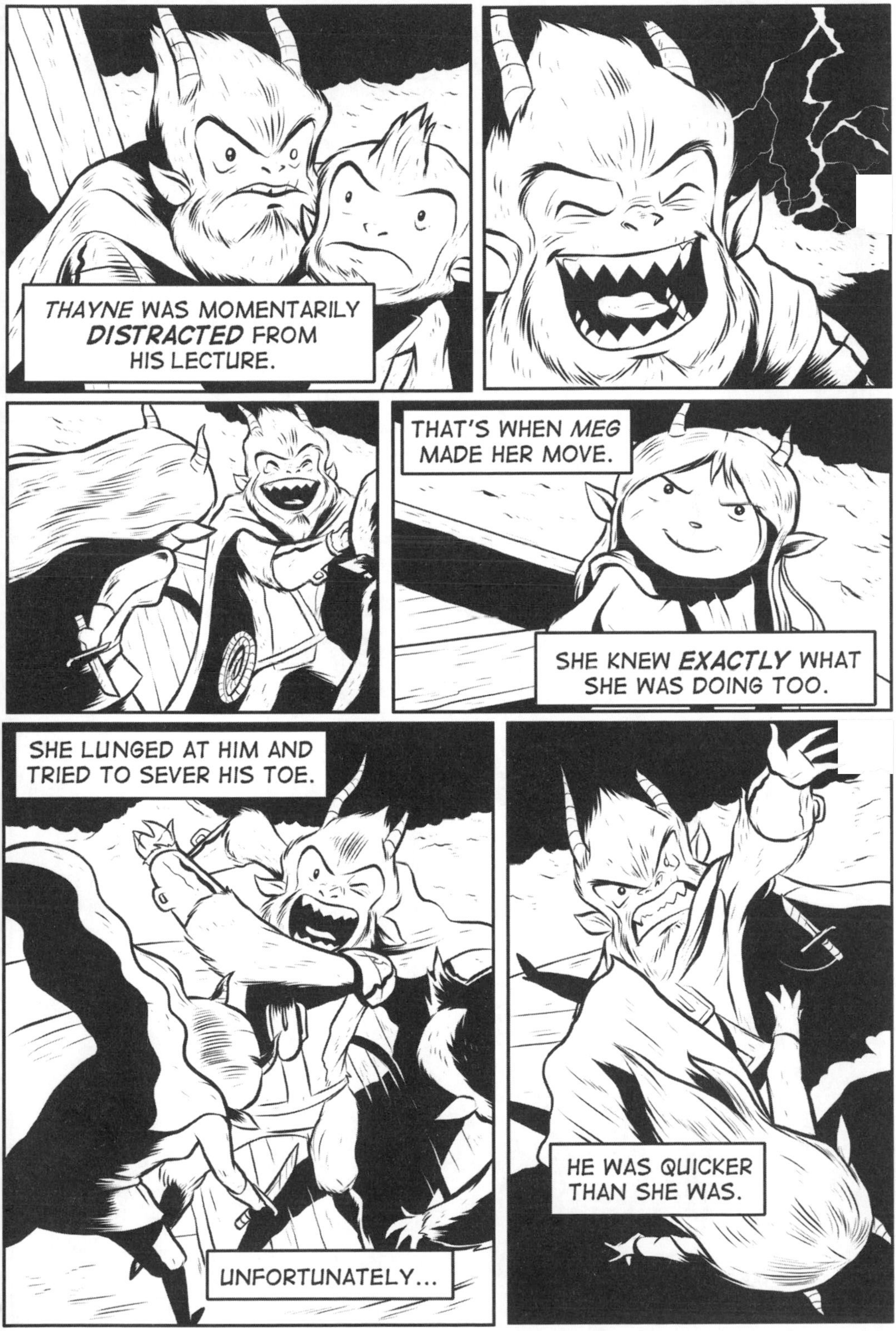
THAYNE WAS MOMENTARILY DISTRACTED FROM HIS LECTURE.
THAT'S WHEN MEG MADE HER MOVE.
SHE KNEW EXACTLY WHAT SHE WAS DOING TOO.
SHE LUNGED AT HIM AND TRIED TO SEVER HIS TOE.
UNFORTUNATELY...
HE WAS QUICKER THAN SHE WAS.

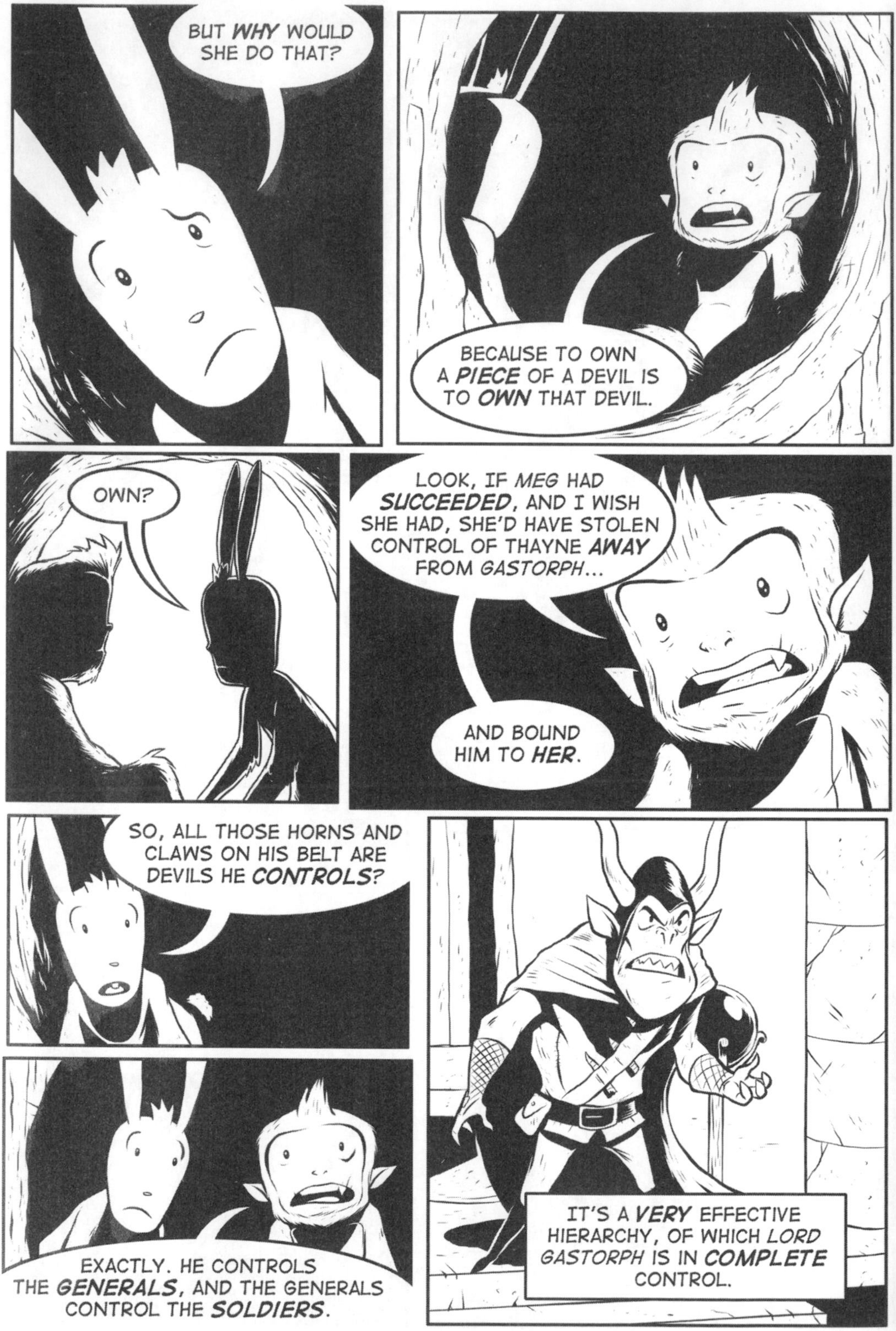

BUT WHY WOULD SHE DO THAT?
BECAUSE TO OWN A PIECE OF A DEVIL IS TO OWN THAT DEVIL.
OWN?
LOOK, IF MEG HAD SUCCEEDED, AND I WISH SHE HAD, SHE'D HAVE STOLEN CONTROL OF THAYNE AWAY FROM GASTORPH...
AND BOUND HIM TO HER.
SO, ALL THOSE HORNS AND CLAWS ON HIS BELT ARE DEVILS HE CONTROLS?
EXACTLY. HE CONTROLS THE GENERALS, AND THE GENERALS CONTROL THE SOLDIERS.
IT'S A VERY EFFECTIVE HIERARCHY, OF WHICH LORD GASTORPH IS IN COMPLETE CONTROL.

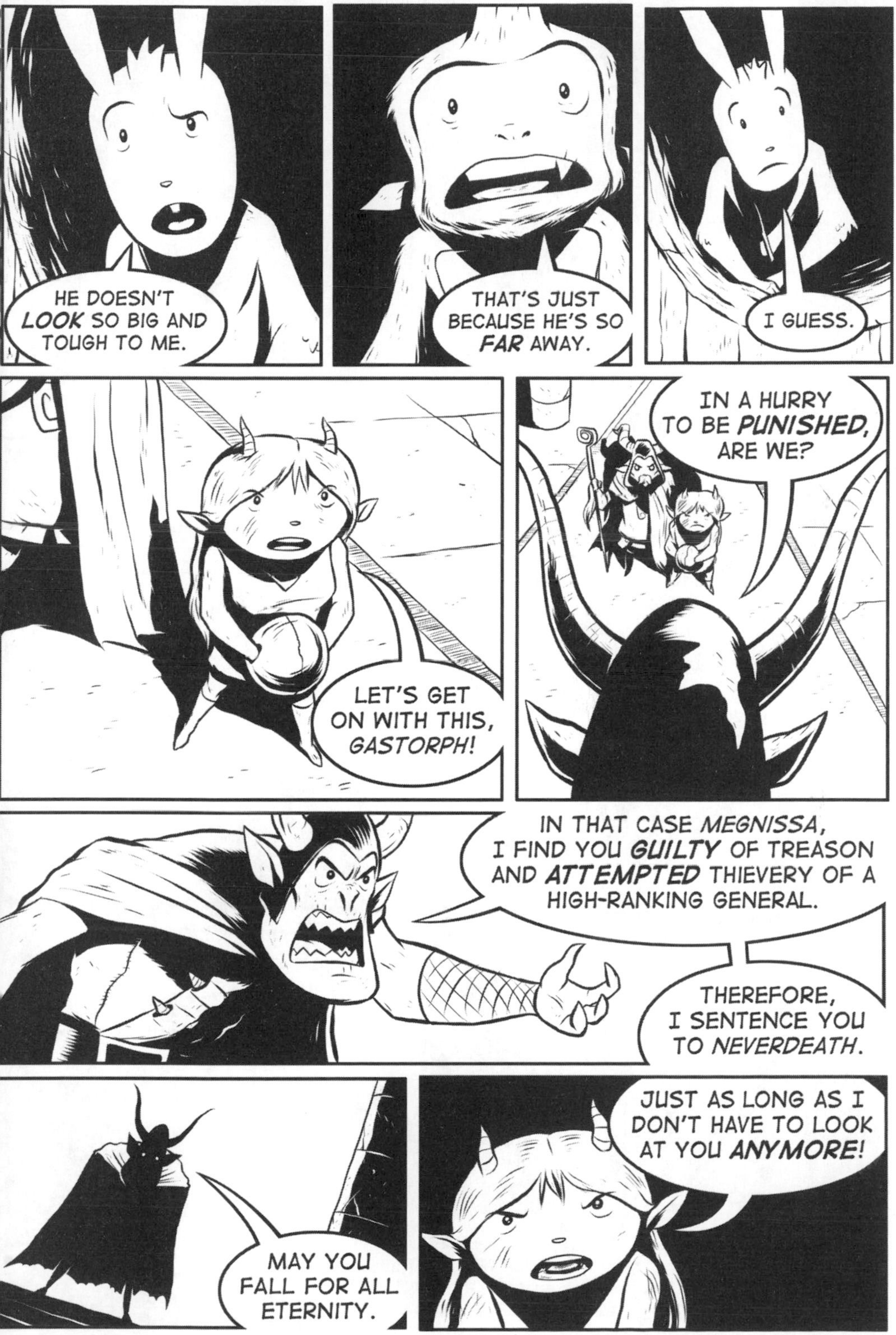
HE DOESN'T *LOOK* SO BIG AND TOUGH TO ME.
THAT'S JUST BECAUSE HE'S SO *FAR* AWAY.
I GUESS.
LET'S GET ON WITH THIS, *GASTORPH*!
IN A HURRY TO BE *PUNISHED*, ARE WE?
IN THAT CASE *MEGNISSA*, I FIND YOU *GUILTY* OF TREASON AND *ATTEMPTED* THIEVERY OF A HIGH-RANKING GENERAL.
THEREFORE, I SENTENCE YOU TO *NEVERDEATH*.
MAY YOU FALL FOR ALL ETERNITY.
JUST AS LONG AS I DON'T HAVE TO LOOK AT YOU *ANYMORE*!

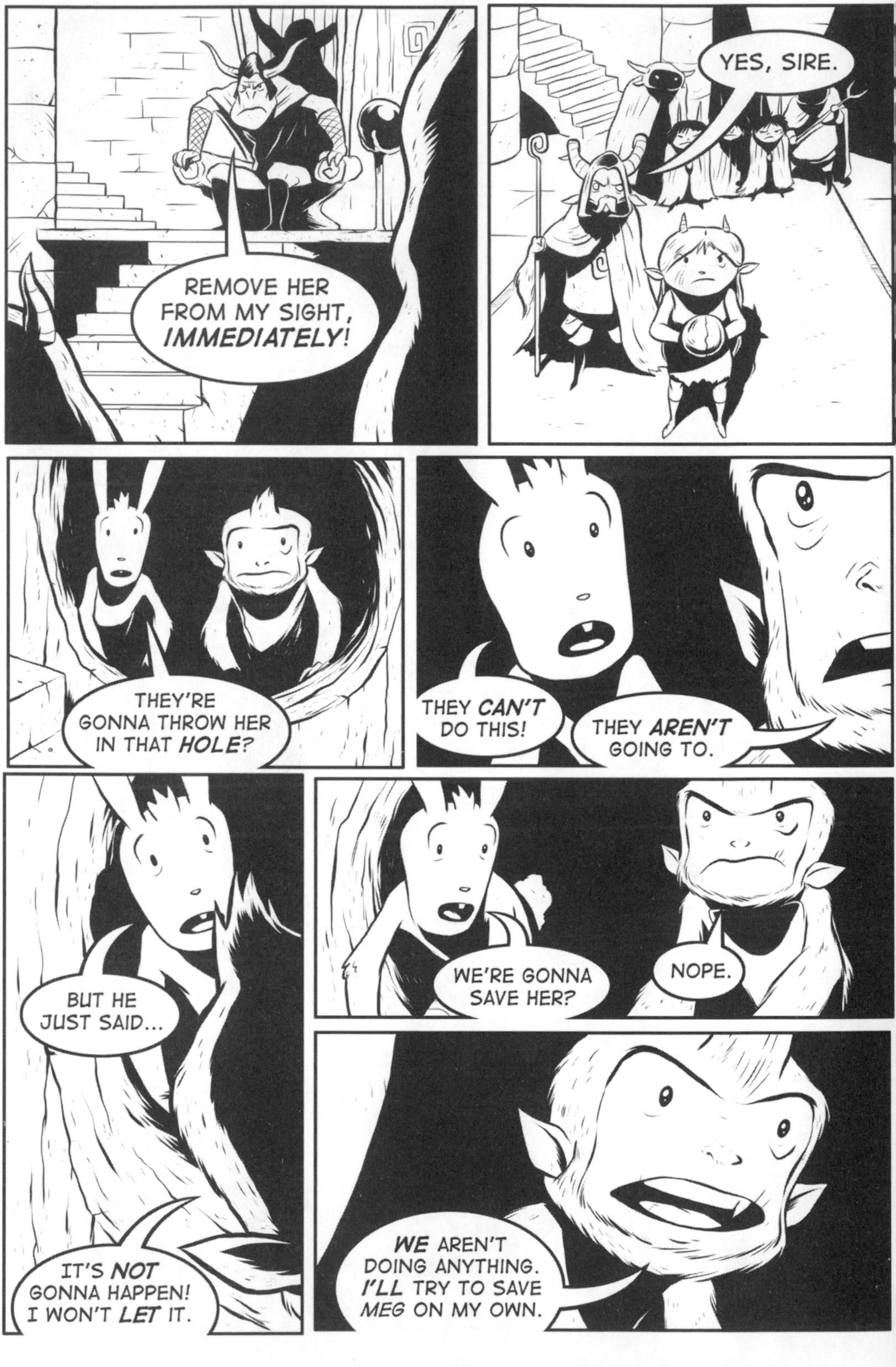
REMOVE HER FROM MY SIGHT, *IMMEDIATELY*!
YES, SIRE.
THEY'RE GONNA THROW HER IN THAT *HOLE*?
THEY *CAN'T* DO THIS!
THEY *AREN'T* GOING TO.
BUT HE JUST SAID...
IT'S *NOT* GONNA HAPPEN! I WON'T *LET* IT.
WE'RE GONNA SAVE HER?
NOPE.
WE AREN'T DOING ANYTHING. *I'LL* TRY TO SAVE *MEG* ON MY OWN.

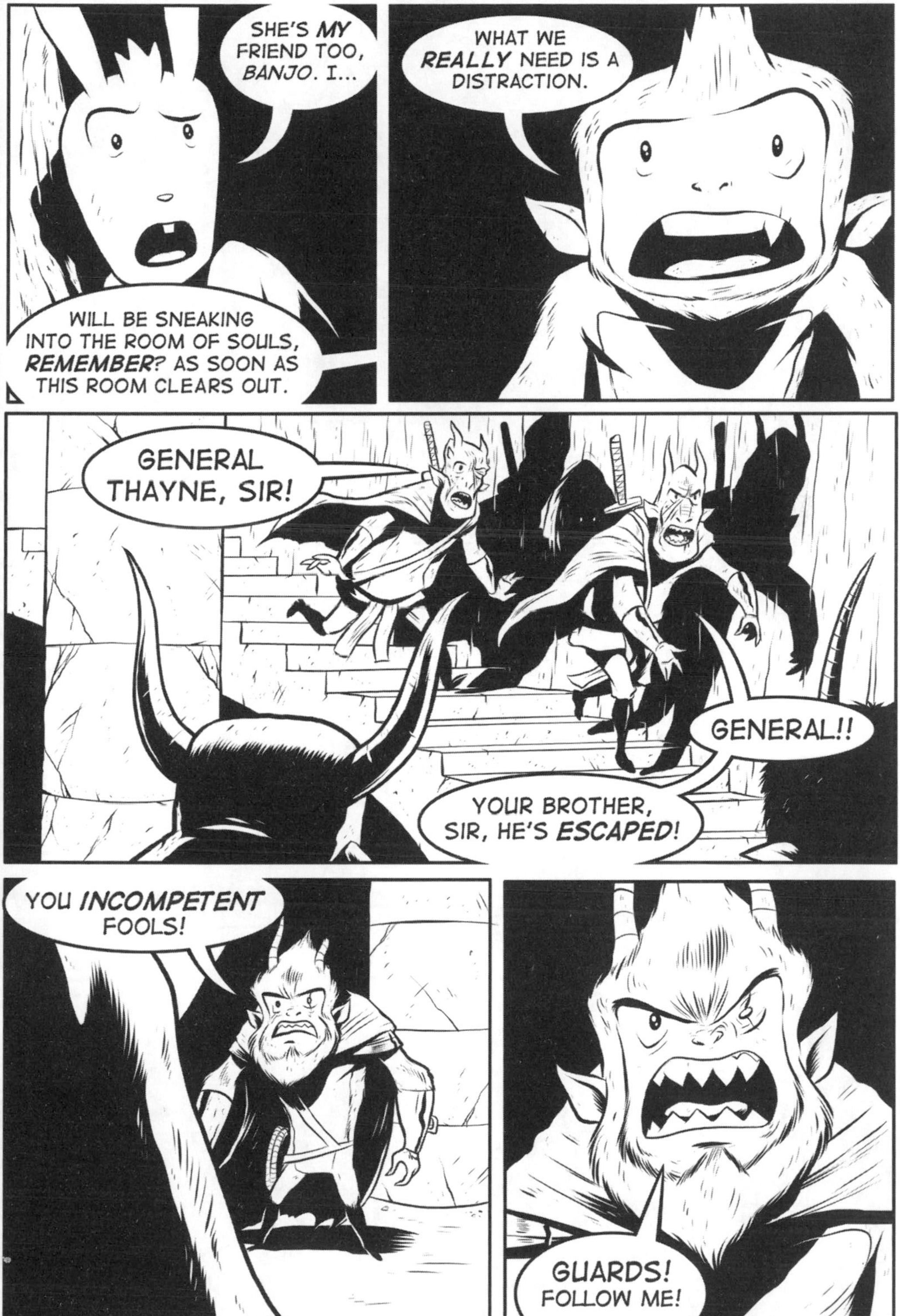
SHE'S MY FRIEND TOO, BANJO. I...
WILL BE SNEAKING INTO THE ROOM OF SOULS, REMEMBER? AS SOON AS THIS ROOM CLEARS OUT.
WHAT WE REALLY NEED IS A DISTRACTION.
GENERAL THAYNE, SIR!
GENERAL!!
YOUR BROTHER, SIR, HE'S ESCAPED!
YOU INCOMPETENT FOOLS!
GUARDS! FOLLOW ME!

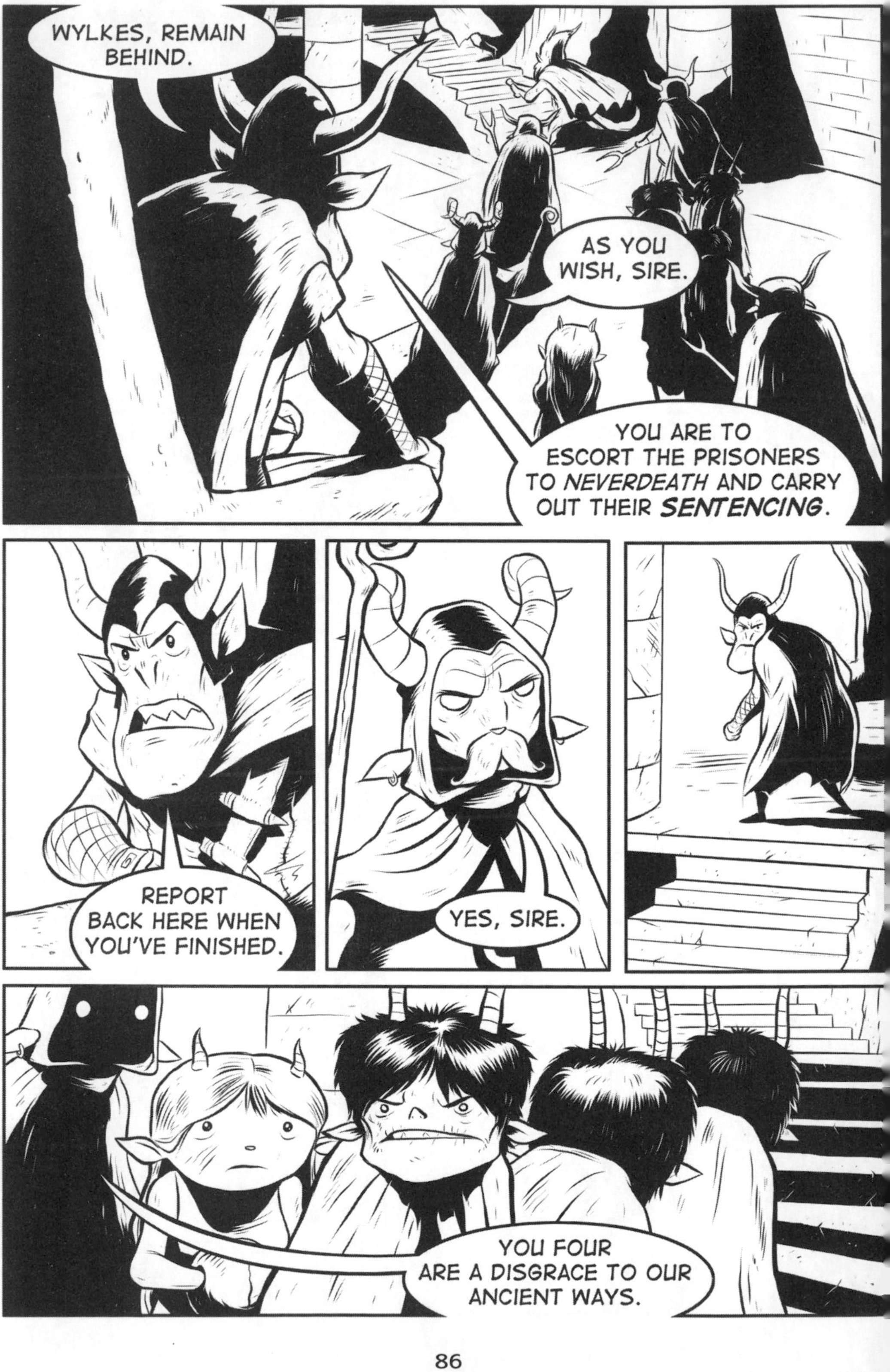
WYLKES, REMAIN BEHIND.
AS YOU WISH, SIRE.
YOU ARE TO ESCORT THE PRISONERS TO *NEVERDEATH* AND CARRY OUT THEIR ***SENTENCING***.
REPORT BACK HERE WHEN YOU'VE FINISHED.
YES, SIRE.
YOU FOUR ARE A DISGRACE TO OUR ANCIENT WAYS.

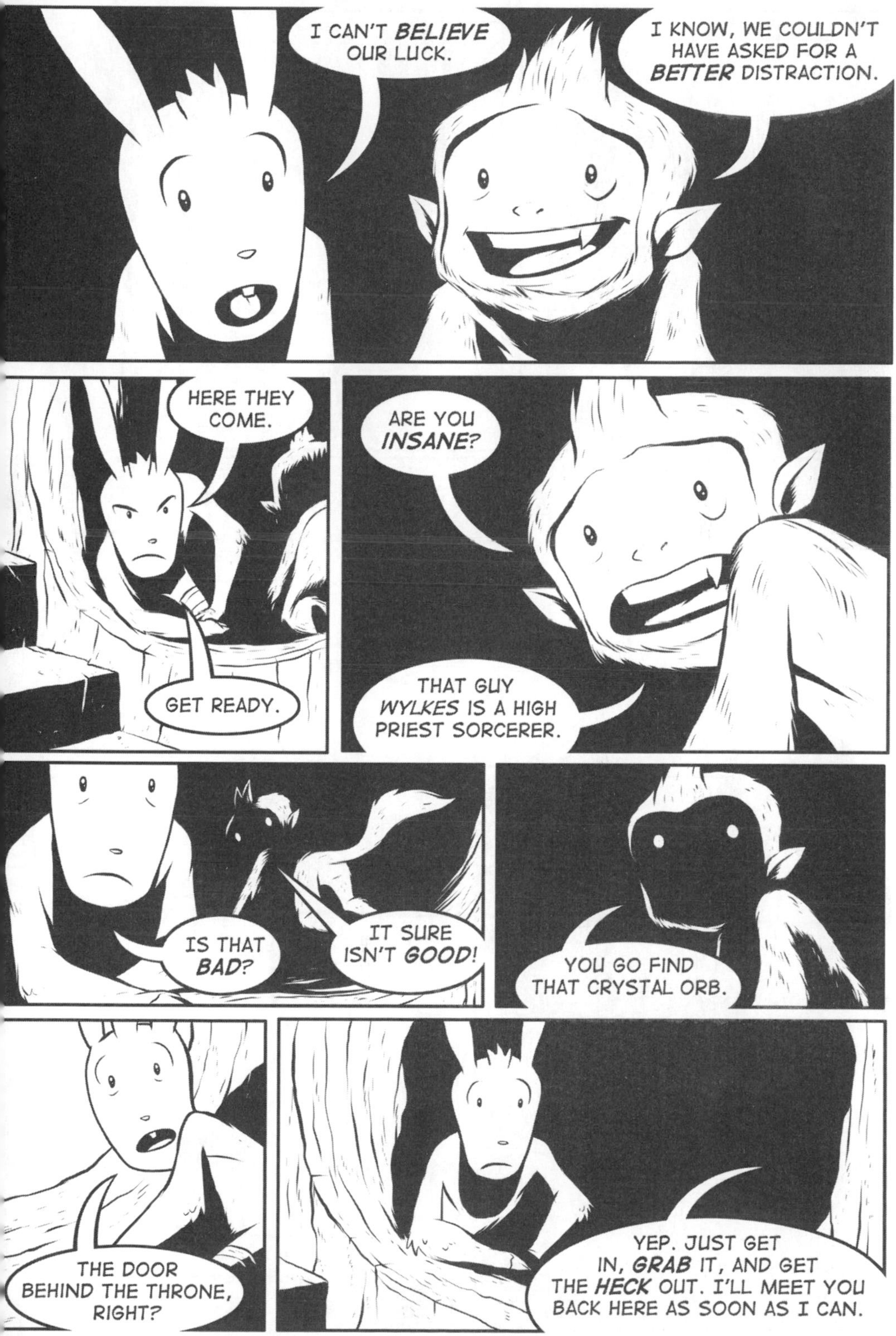
I CAN'T **BELIEVE** OUR LUCK.
I KNOW, WE COULDN'T HAVE ASKED FOR A **BETTER** DISTRACTION.
HERE THEY COME.
GET READY.
ARE YOU **INSANE?**
THAT GUY **WYLKES** IS A HIGH PRIEST SORCERER.
IS THAT **BAD?**
IT SURE ISN'T **GOOD!**
YOU GO FIND THAT CRYSTAL ORB.
THE DOOR BEHIND THE THRONE, RIGHT?
YEP. JUST GET IN, **GRAB** IT, AND GET THE **HECK** OUT. I'LL MEET YOU BACK HERE AS SOON AS I CAN.

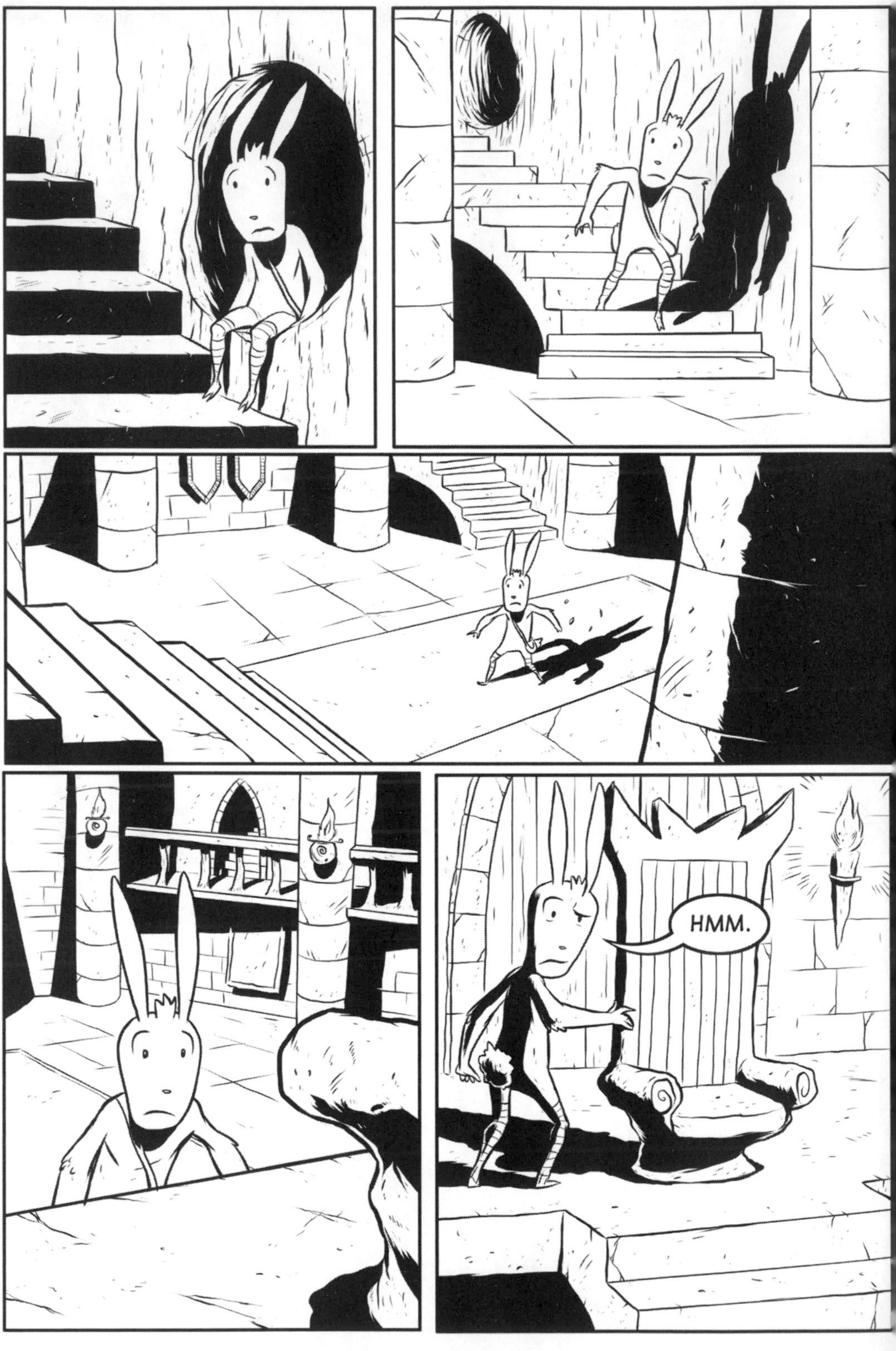
HMM.

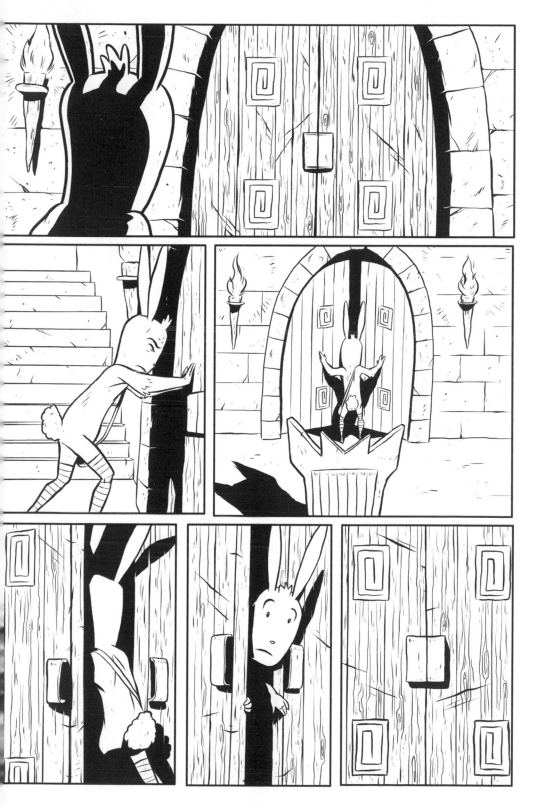

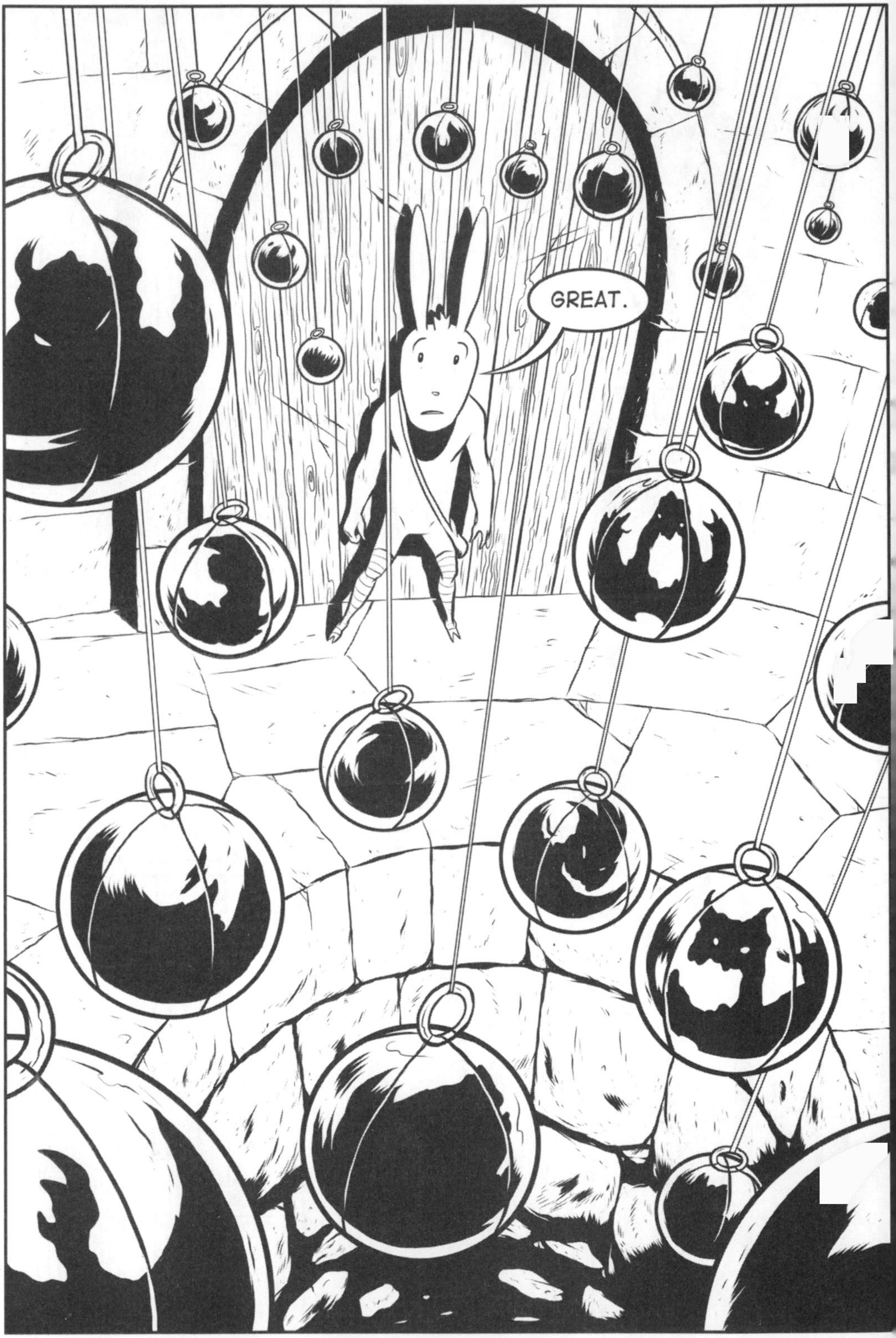
GREAT.

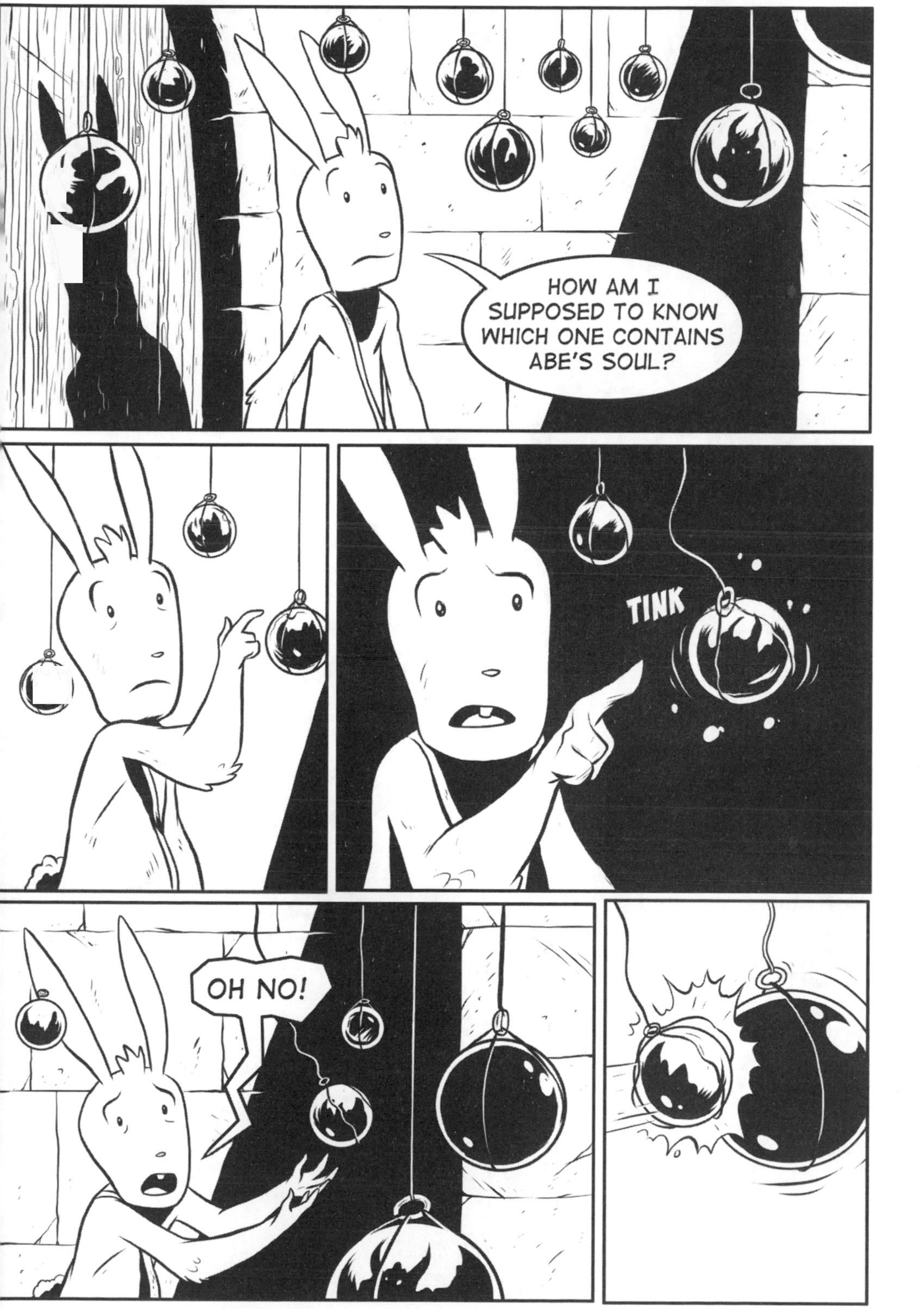
HOW AM I SUPPOSED TO KNOW WHICH ONE CONTAINS ABE'S SOUL?
TINK
OH NO!

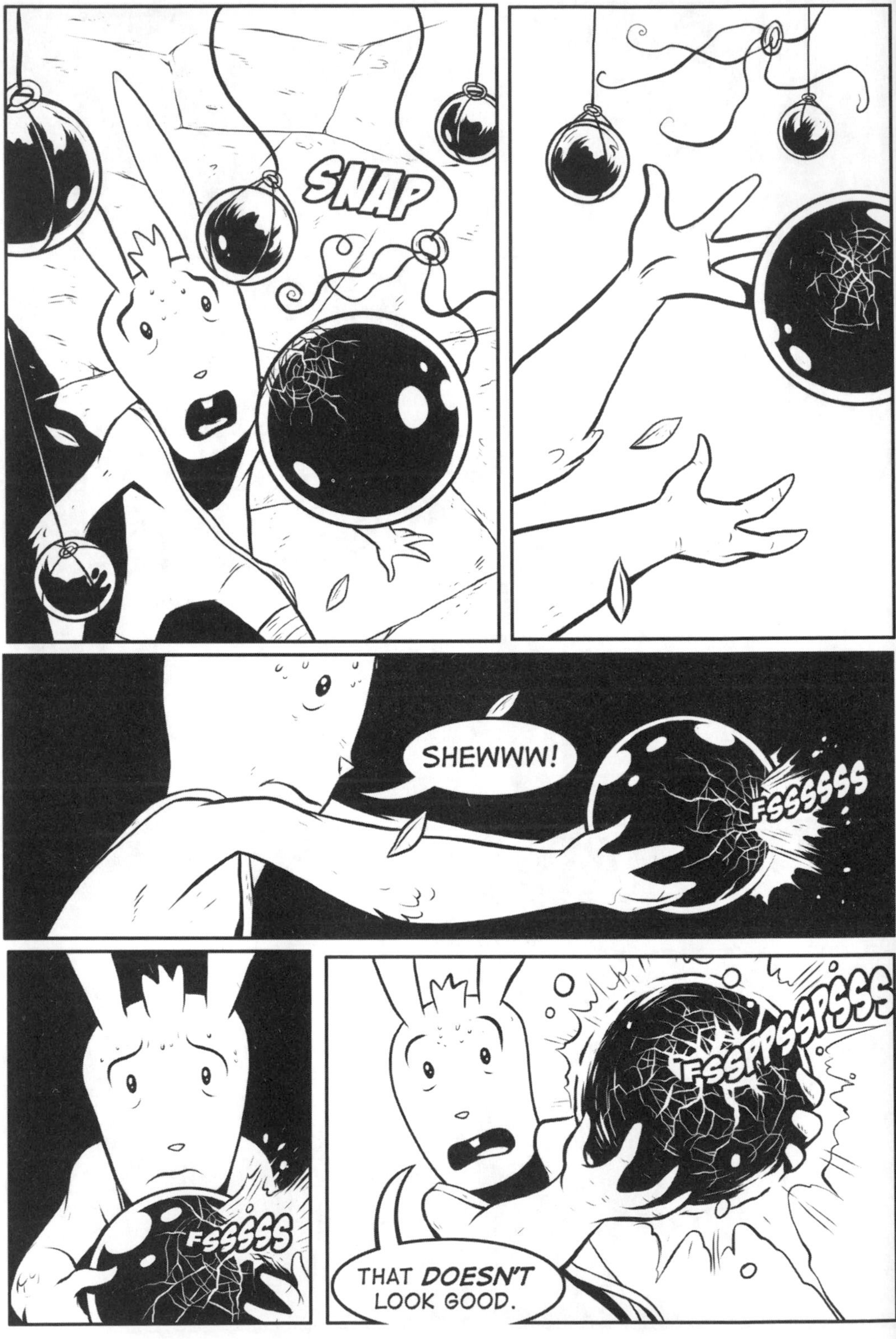
SNAP
SHEWWW!
FSSSSSS
FSSSSS
FSSPPSSSPSSS
THAT DOESN'T LOOK GOOD.

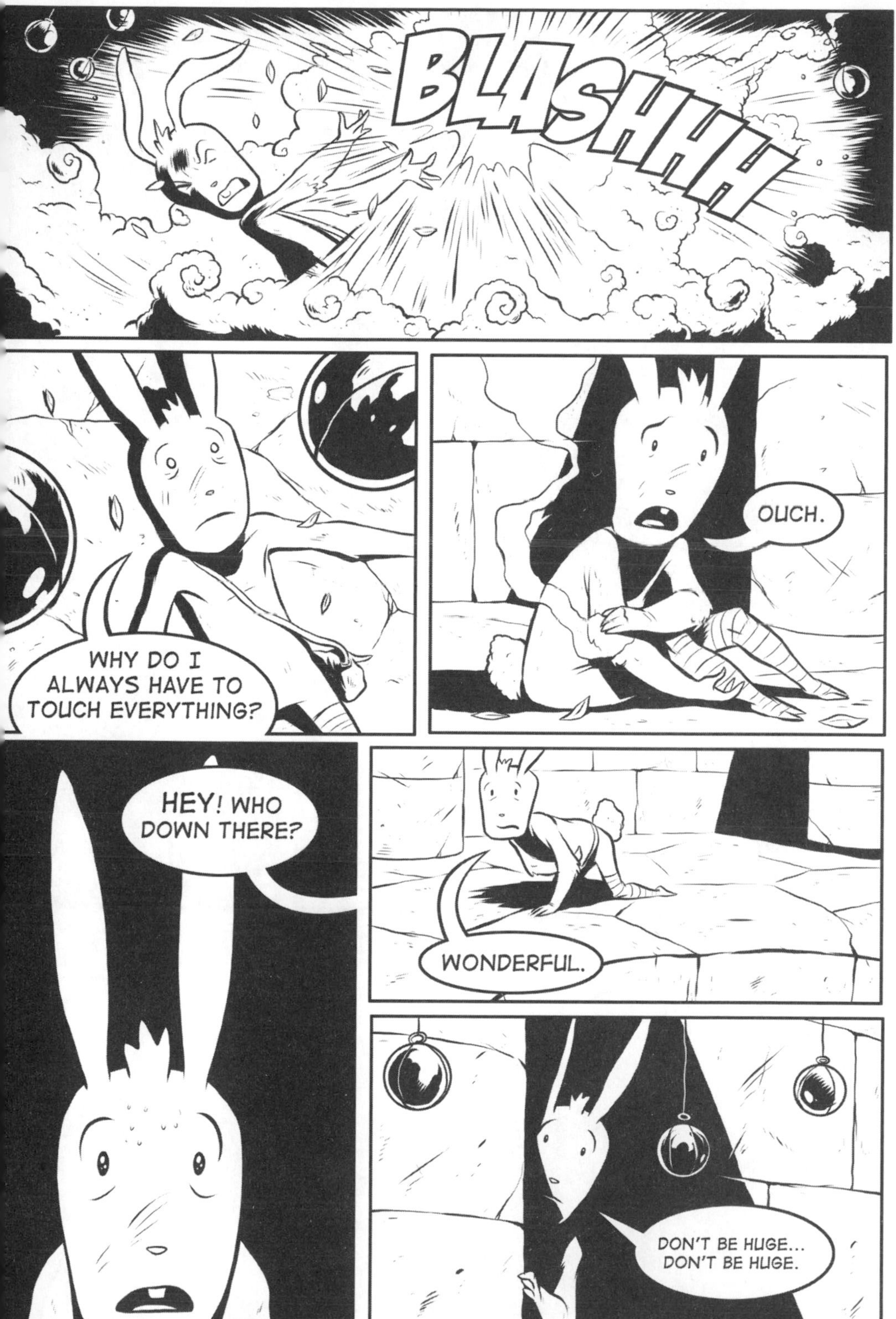
BLASHHH
WHY DO I ALWAYS HAVE TO TOUCH EVERYTHING?
OUCH.
HEY! WHO DOWN THERE?
WONDERFUL.
DON'T BE HUGE... DON'T BE HUGE.

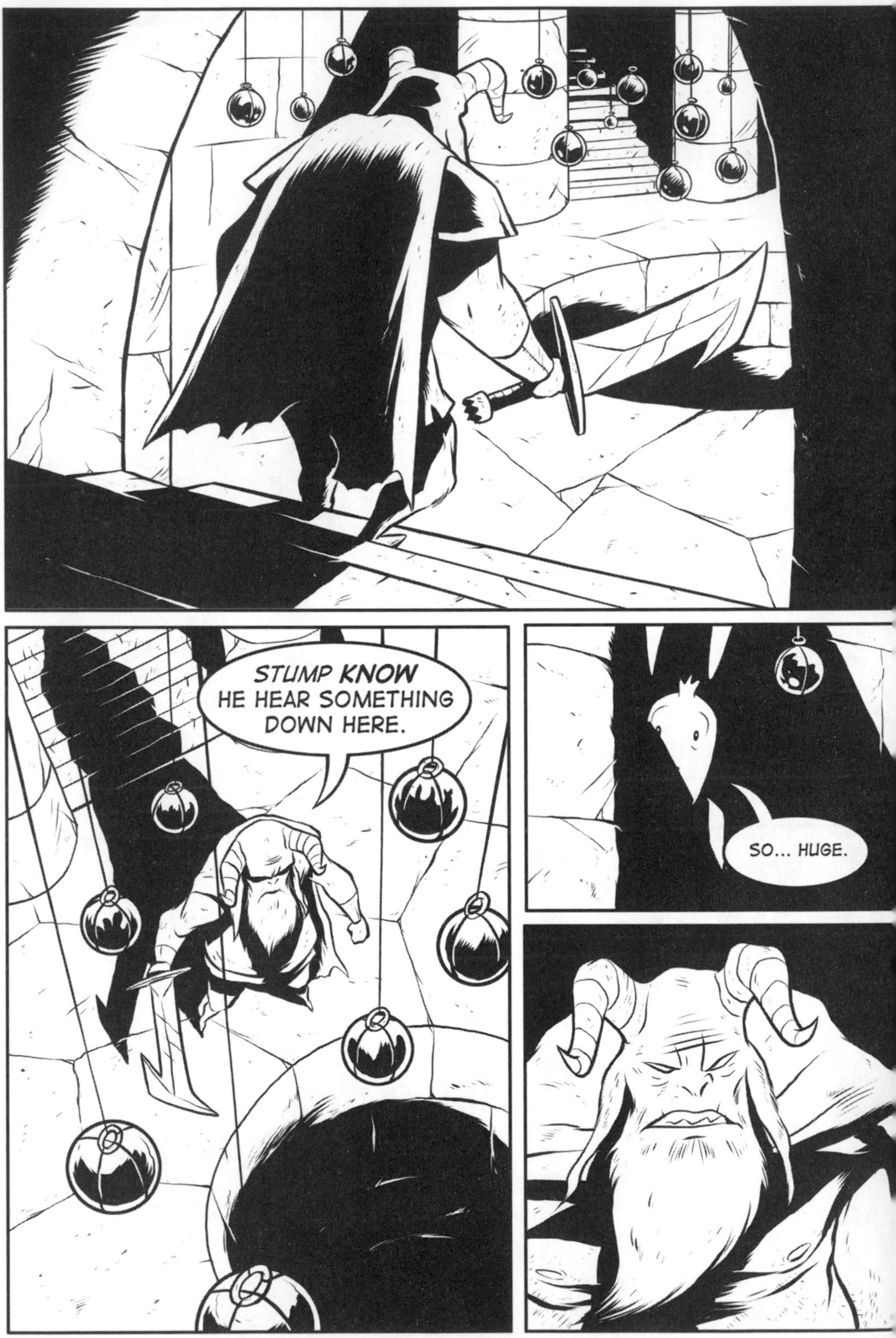
STUMP KNOW HE HEAR SOMETHING DOWN HERE.
SO... HUGE.

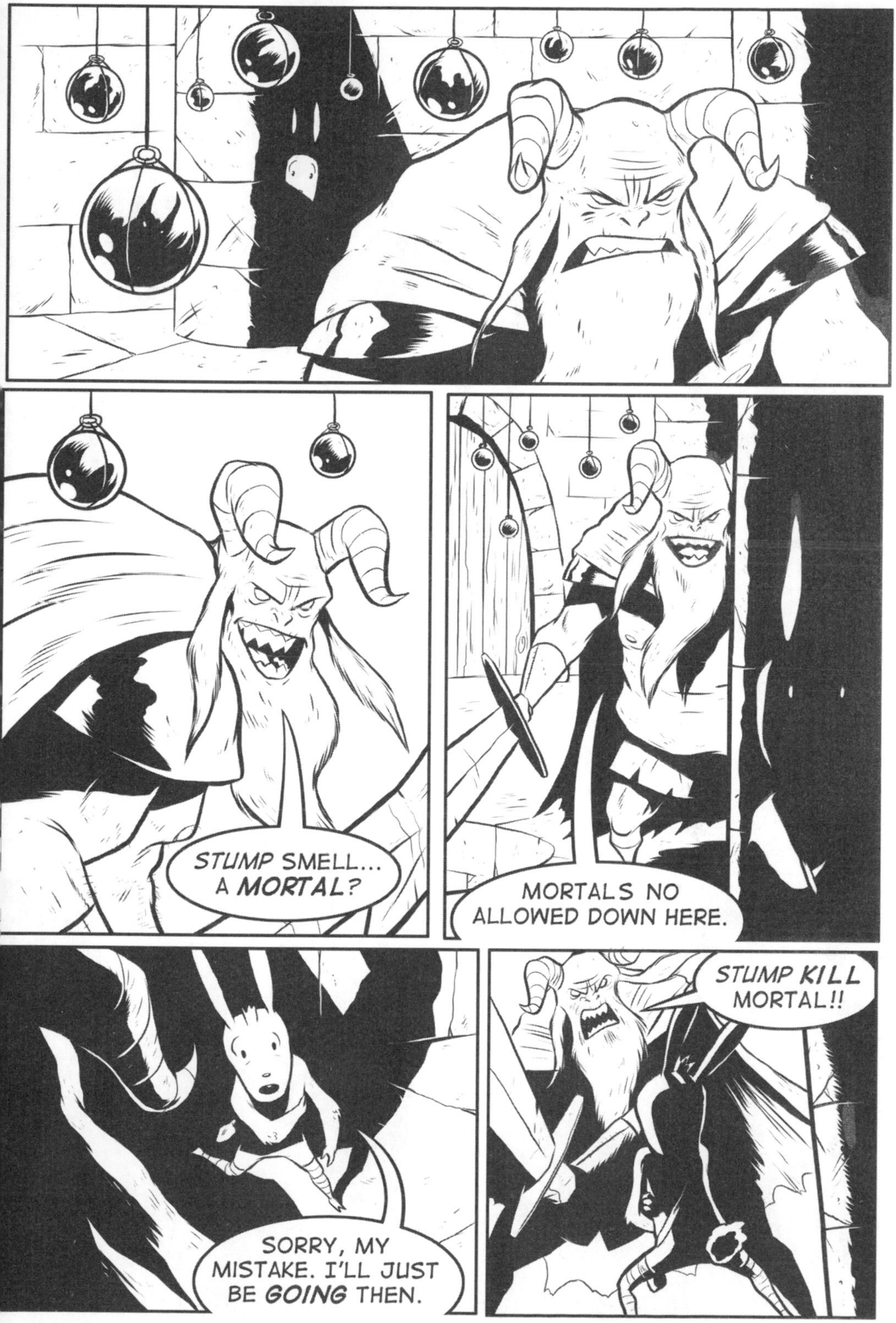
STUMP SMELL... A MORTAL?
MORTALS NO ALLOWED DOWN HERE.
SORRY, MY MISTAKE. I'LL JUST BE GOING THEN.
STUMP KILL MORTAL!!

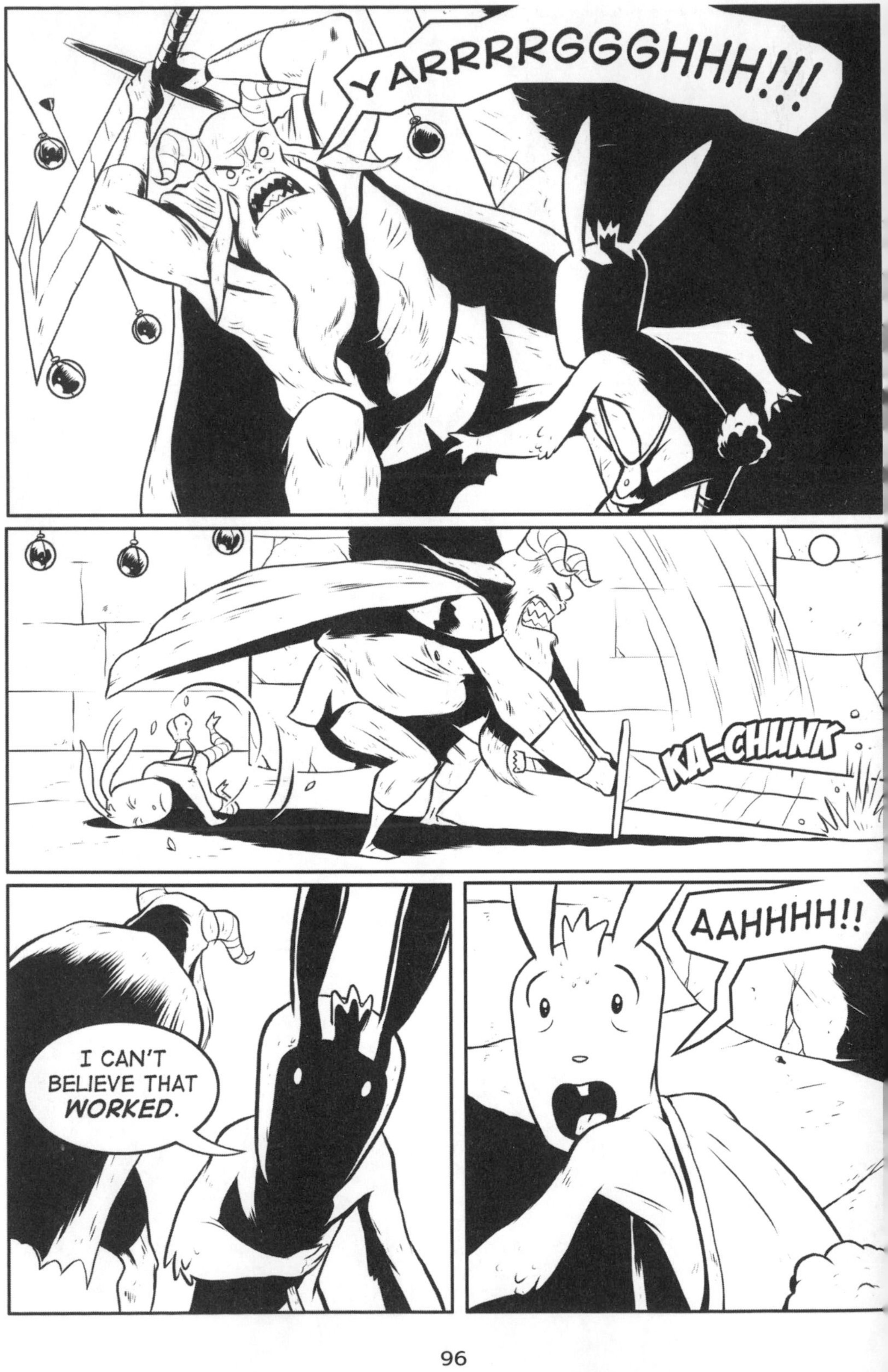
YARRRRGGGHHH!!!
KA-CHUNK
I CAN'T BELIEVE THAT WORKED.
AAHHHH!!

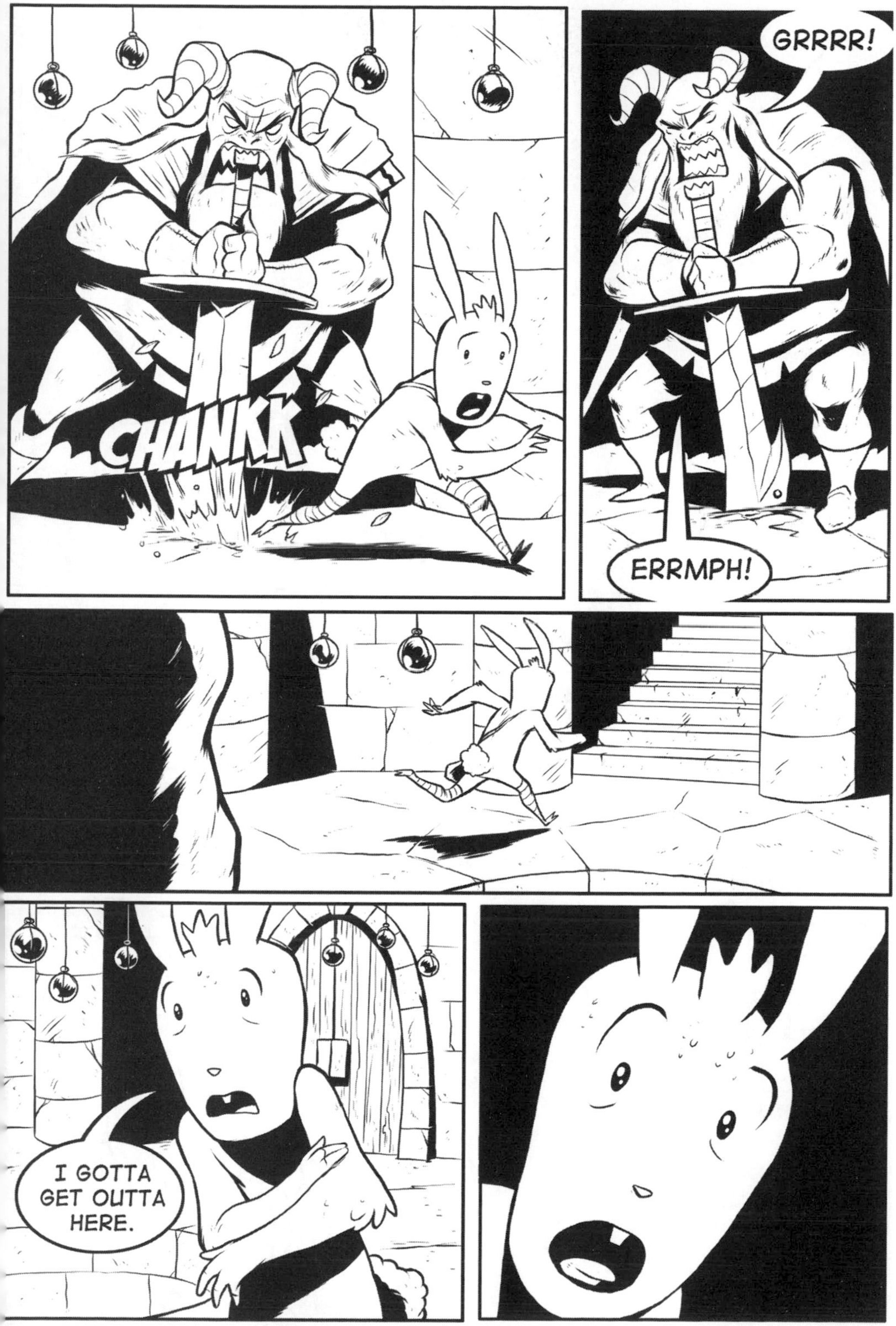
CHANKK
GRRRR!
ERRMPH!
I GOTTA GET OUTTA HERE.

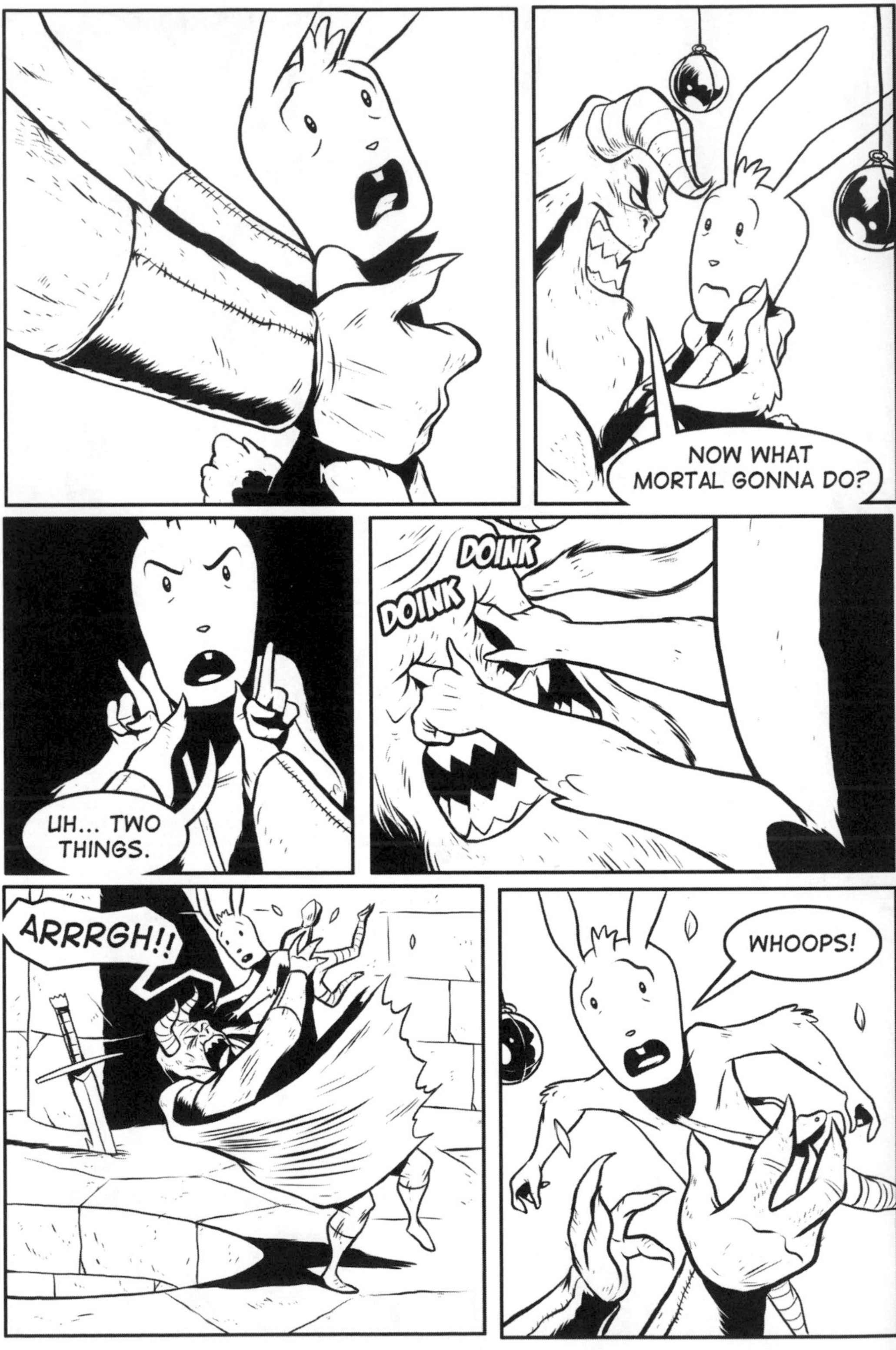
NOW WHAT
MORTAL GONNA DO?
UH... TWO
THINGS.
DOINK
DOINK
ARRRGH!!
WHOOPS!

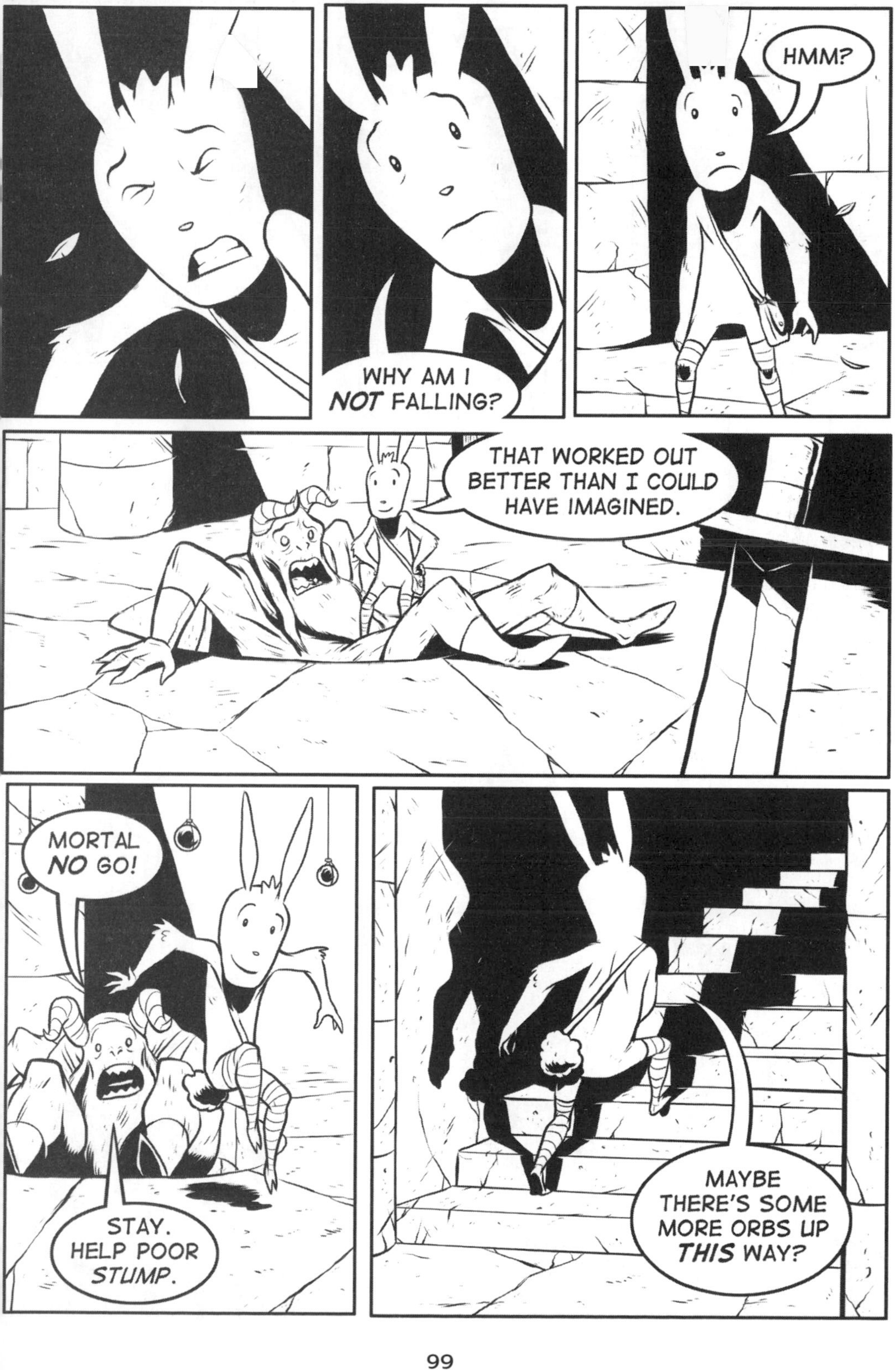
WHY AM I *NOT* FALLING?
HMM?
THAT WORKED OUT BETTER THAN I COULD HAVE IMAGINED.
MORTAL *NO* GO!
STAY. HELP POOR *STUMP*.
MAYBE THERE'S SOME MORE ORBS UP *THIS* WAY?

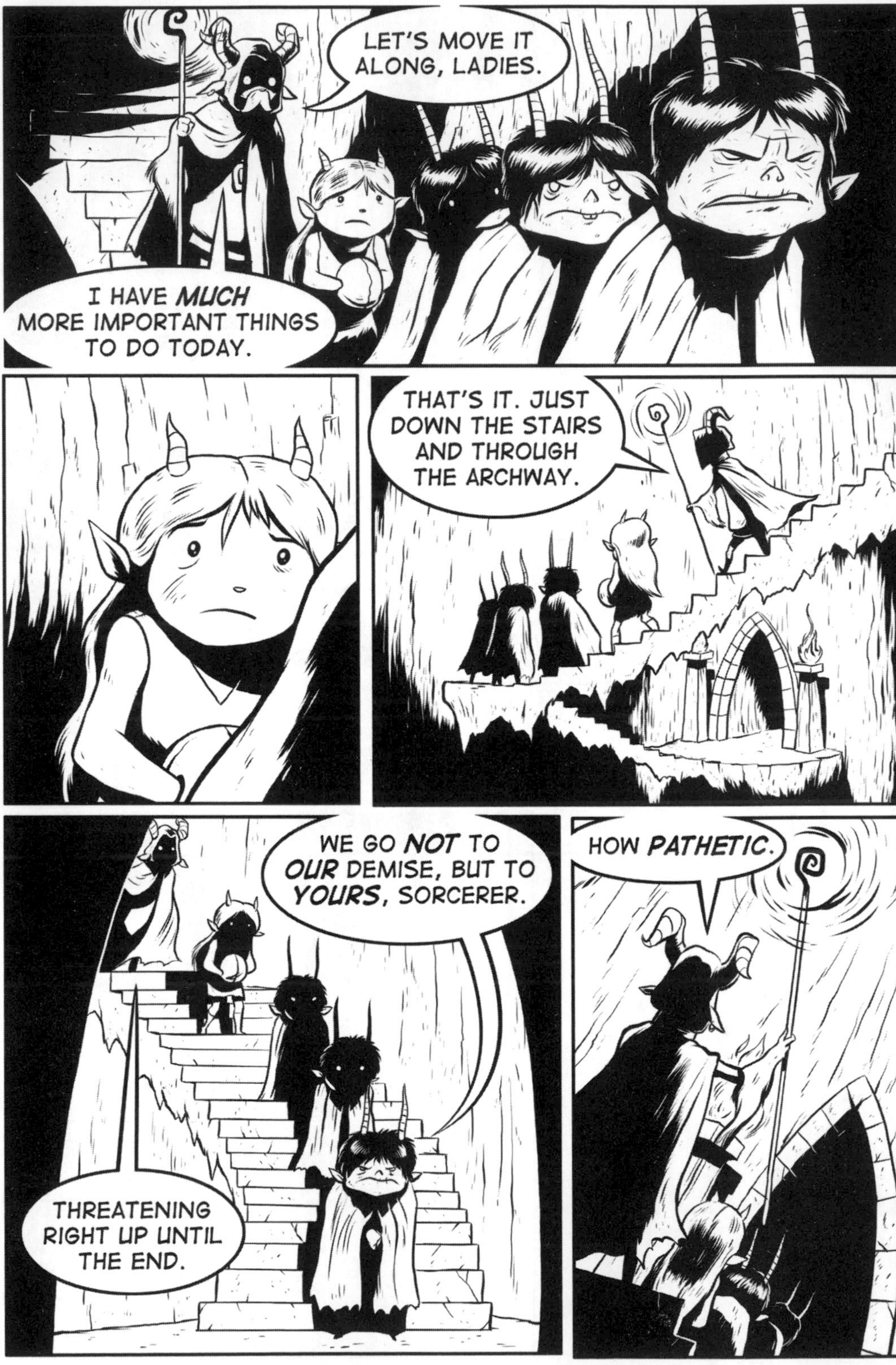
LET'S MOVE IT ALONG, LADIES.
I HAVE MUCH MORE IMPORTANT THINGS TO DO TODAY.
THAT'S IT. JUST DOWN THE STAIRS AND THROUGH THE ARCHWAY.
WE GO NOT TO OUR DEMISE, BUT TO YOURS, SORCERER.
THREATENING RIGHT UP UNTIL THE END.
HOW PATHETIC.

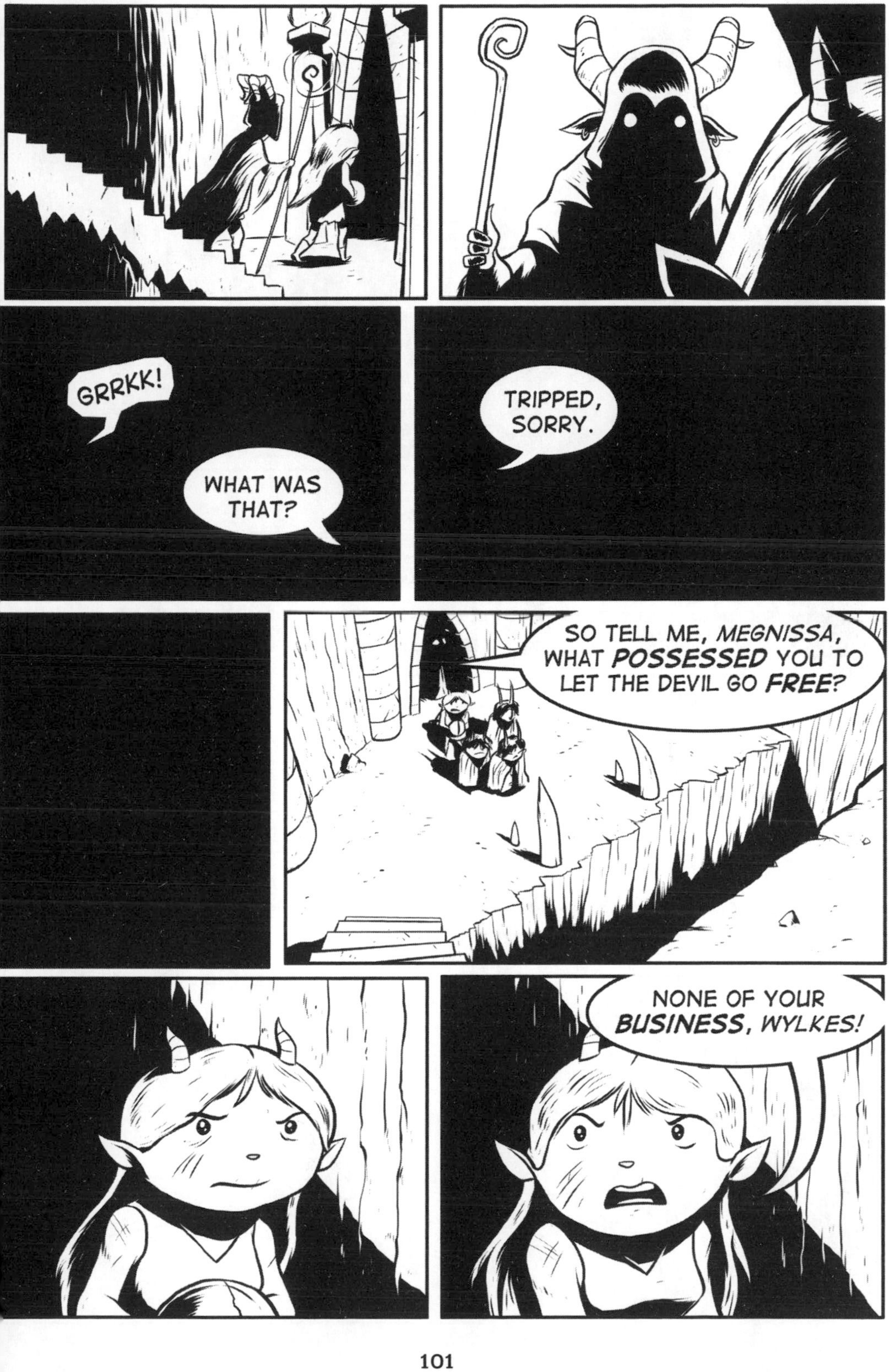
GRRKK!
WHAT WAS THAT?
TRIPPED, SORRY.
SO TELL ME, MEGNISSA, WHAT POSSESSED YOU TO LET THE DEVIL GO FREE?
NONE OF YOUR BUSINESS, WYLKES!

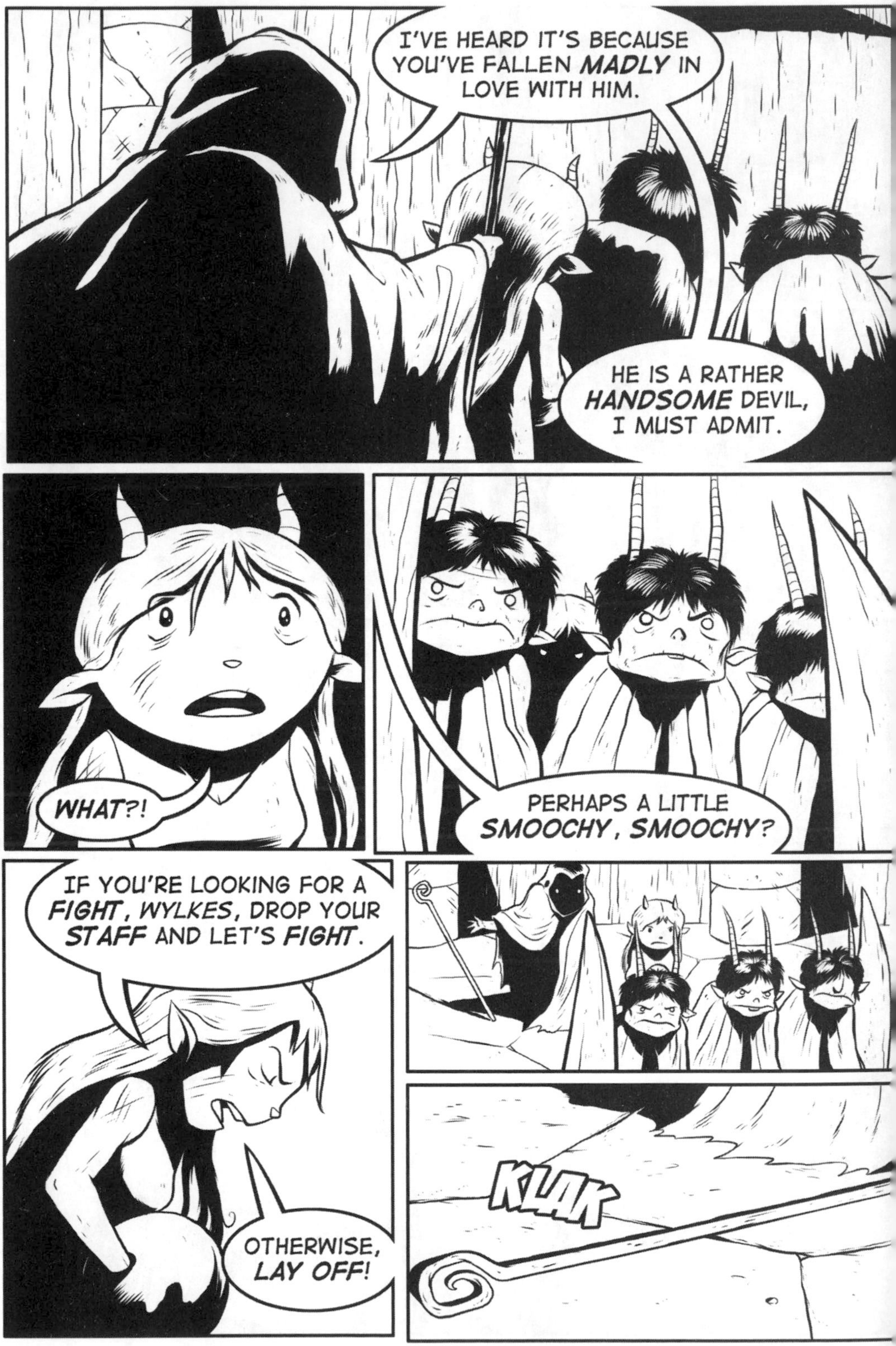
I'VE HEARD IT'S BECAUSE YOU'VE FALLEN MADLY IN LOVE WITH HIM.
HE IS A RATHER HANDSOME DEVIL, I MUST ADMIT.
WHAT?!
PERHAPS A LITTLE SMOOCHY, SMOOCHY?
IF YOU'RE LOOKING FOR A FIGHT, WYLKES, DROP YOUR STAFF AND LET'S FIGHT.
OTHERWISE, LAY OFF!
KLAK

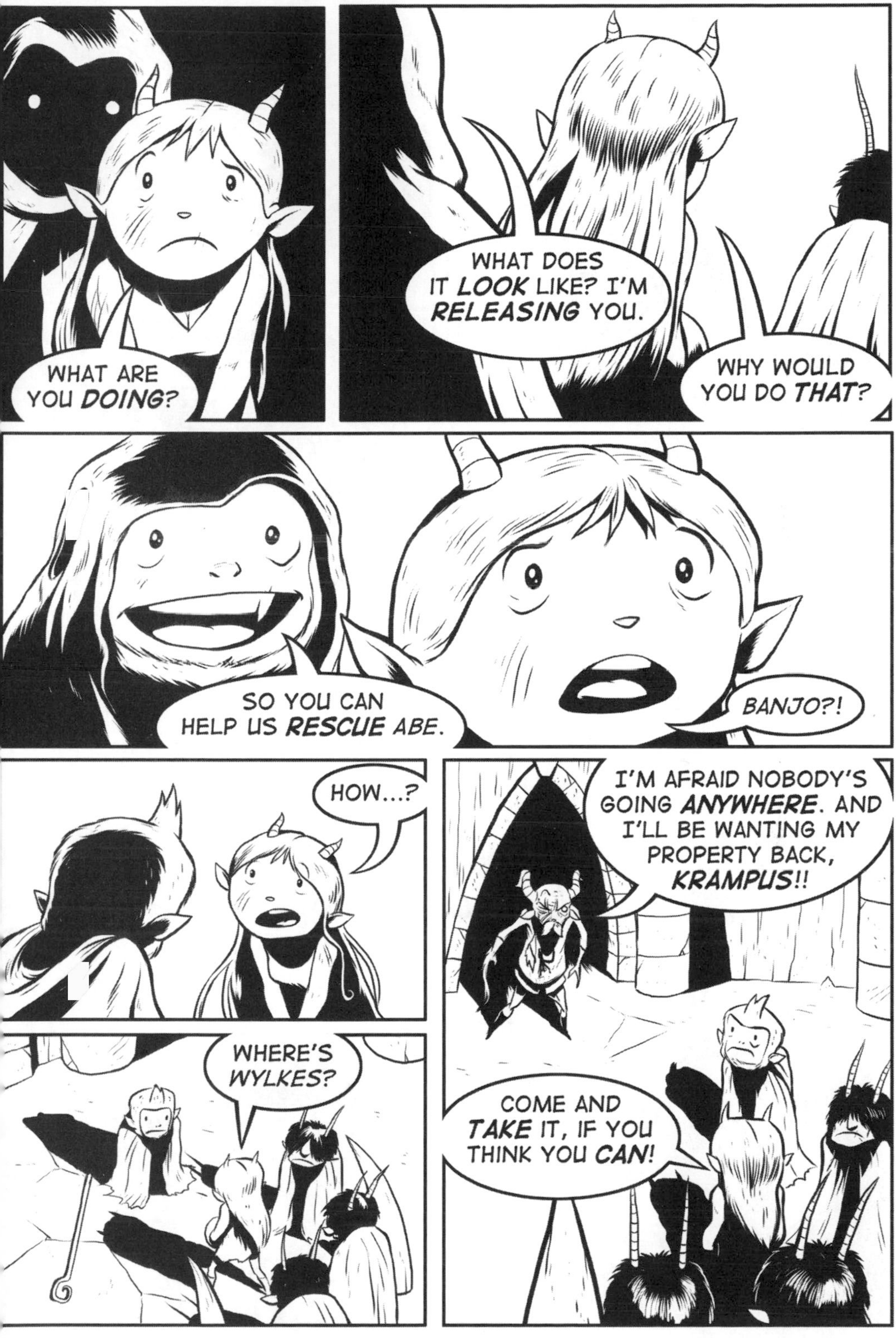
WHAT ARE YOU *DOING*?
WHAT DOES IT *LOOK* LIKE? I'M *RELEASING* YOU.
WHY WOULD YOU DO *THAT*?
SO YOU CAN HELP US *RESCUE* ABE.
BANJO?!
HOW...?
WHERE'S *WYLKES*?
I'M AFRAID NOBODY'S GOING *ANYWHERE*. AND I'LL BE WANTING MY PROPERTY BACK, *KRAMPUS*!!
COME AND *TAKE* IT, IF YOU THINK YOU *CAN*!

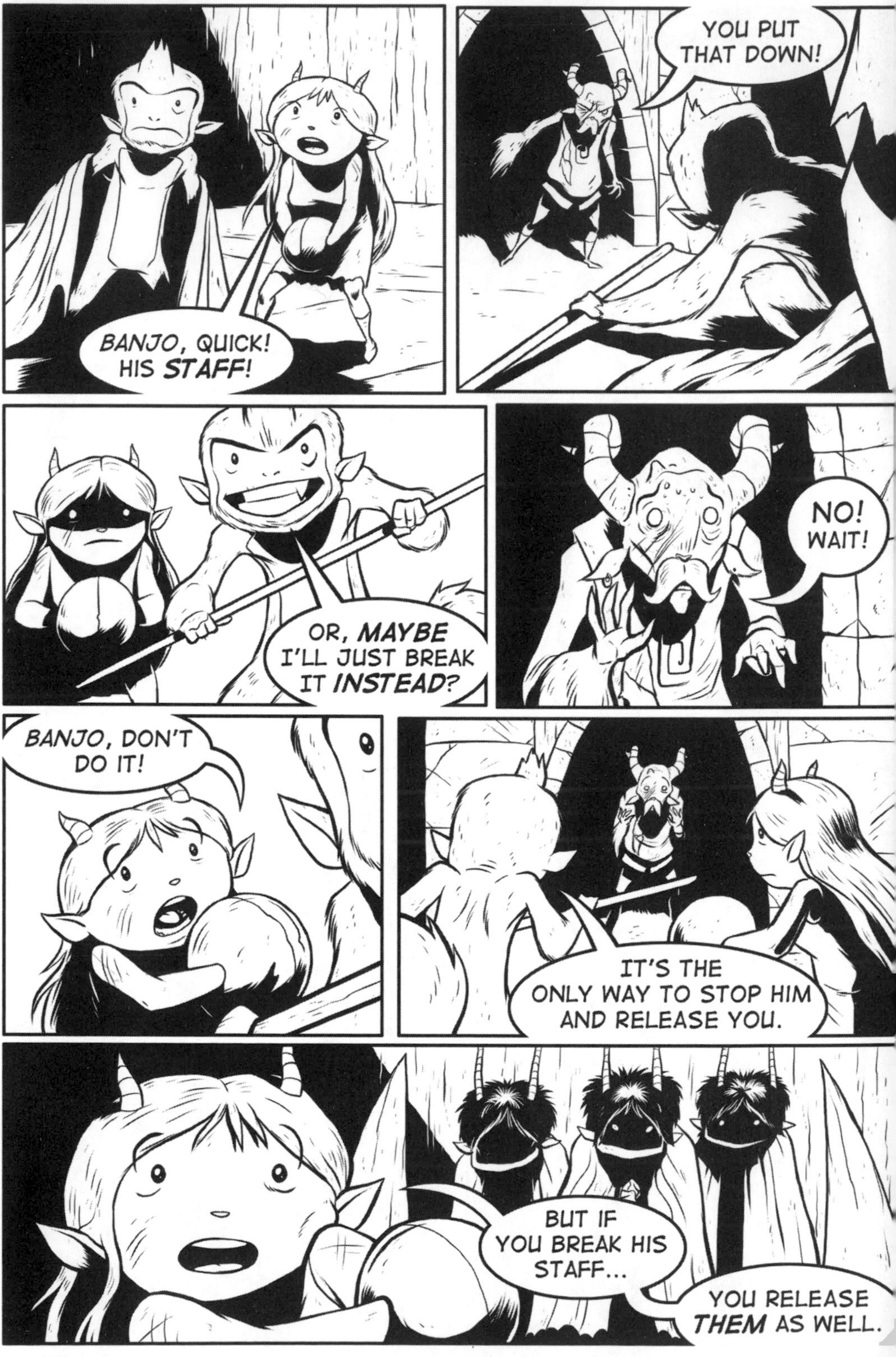
BANJO, QUICK! HIS STAFF!
YOU PUT THAT DOWN!
OR, MAYBE I'LL JUST BREAK IT INSTEAD?
NO! WAIT!
BANJO, DON'T DO IT!
IT'S THE ONLY WAY TO STOP HIM AND RELEASE YOU.
BUT IF YOU BREAK HIS STAFF...
YOU RELEASE THEM AS WELL.

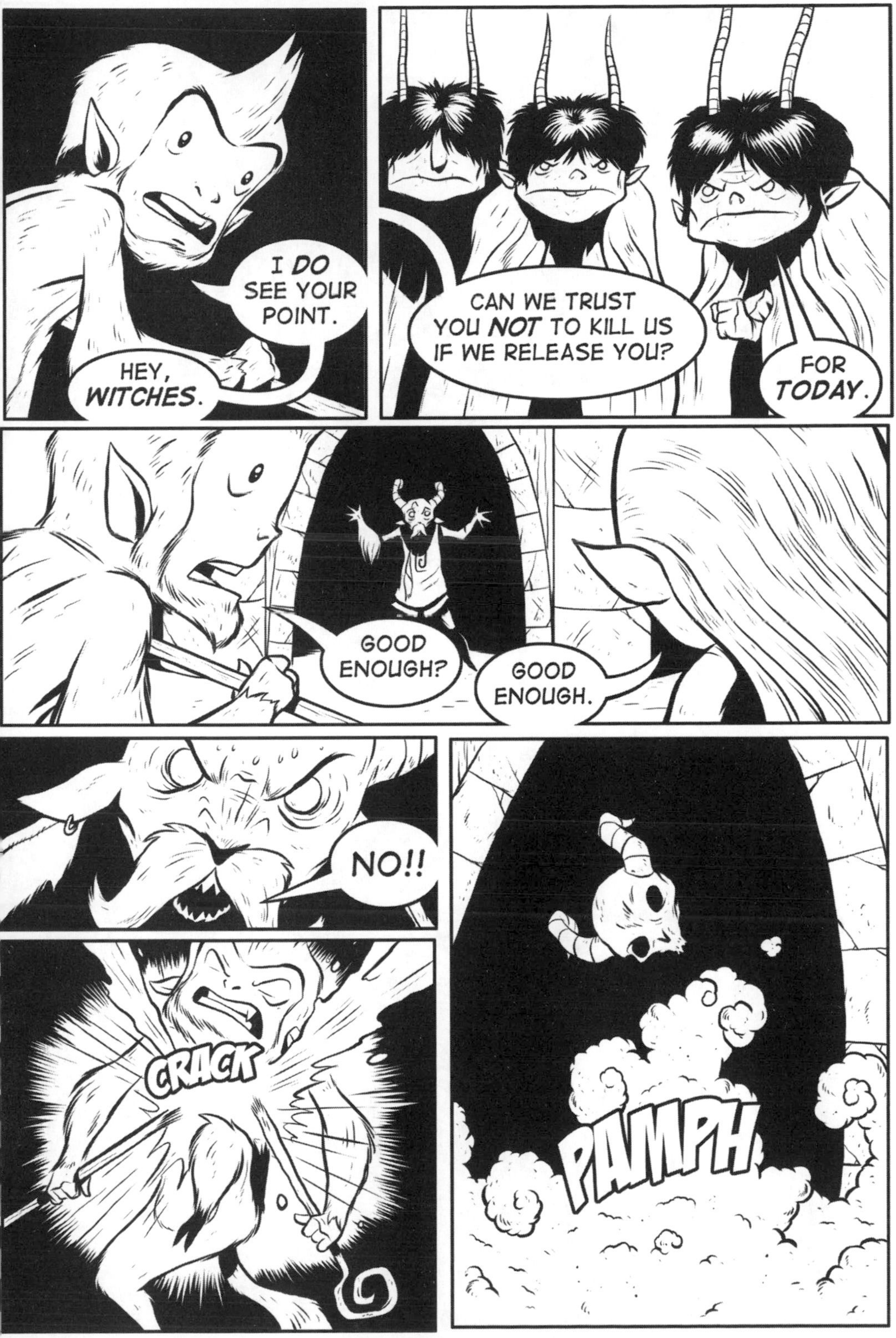
I DO SEE YOUR POINT.
HEY, WITCHES.
CAN WE TRUST YOU NOT TO KILL US IF WE RELEASE YOU?
FOR TODAY.
GOOD ENOUGH?
GOOD ENOUGH.
NO!!
CRACK
PAMPH

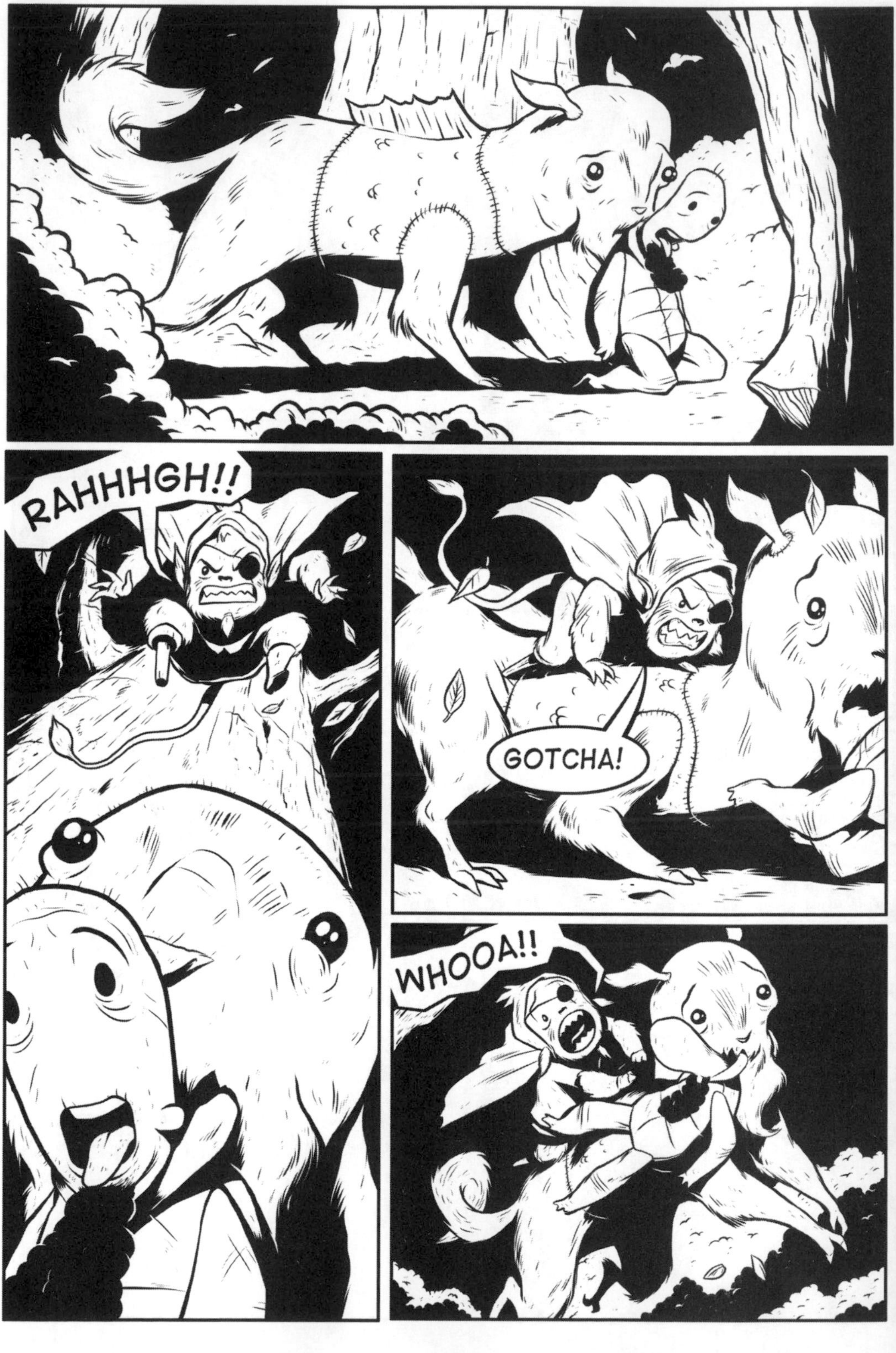
RAHHHGH!!
GOTCHA!
WHOOA!!

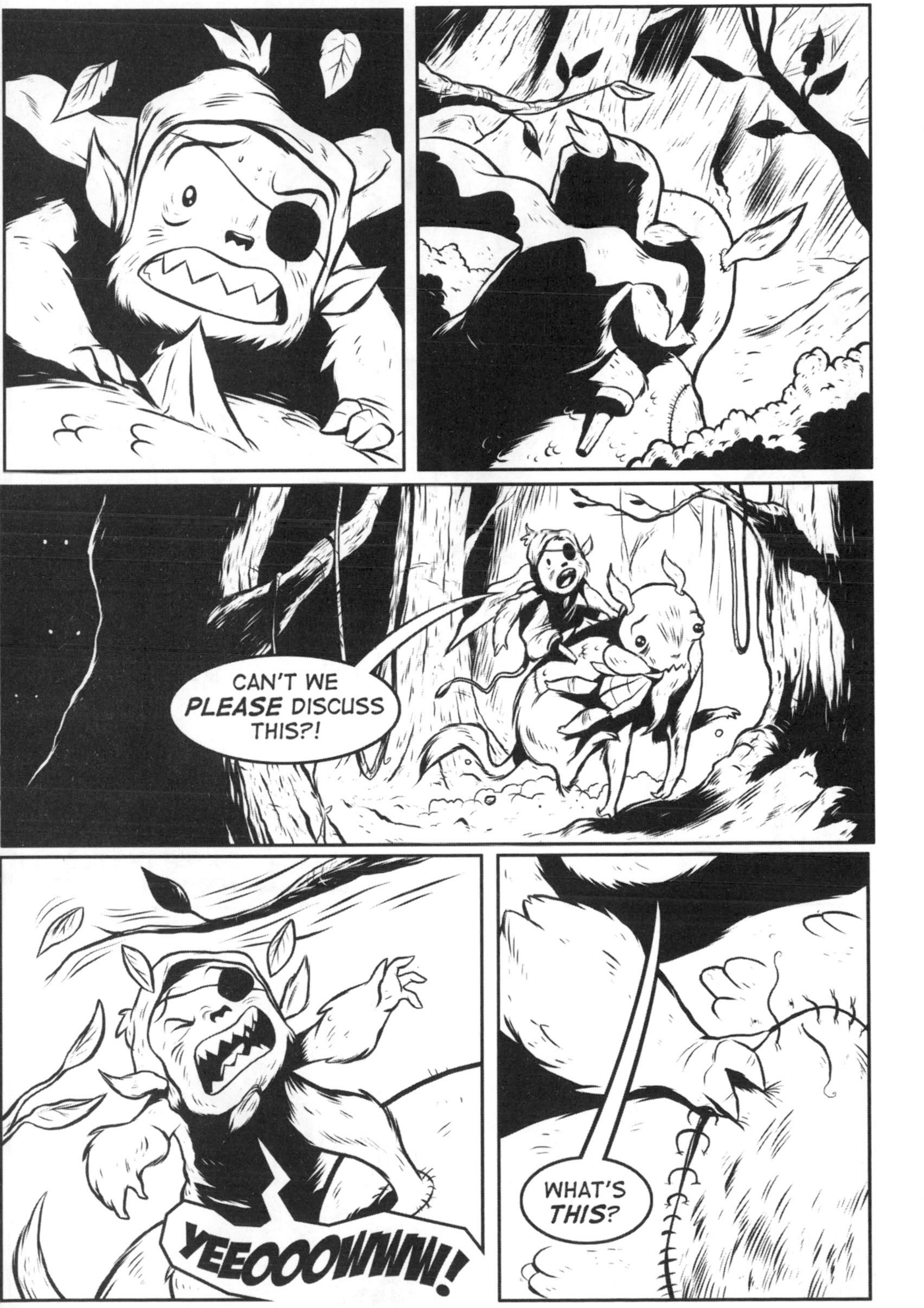
CAN'T WE *PLEASE* DISCUSS THIS?!
YEEOOOWWW!
WHAT'S *THIS*?

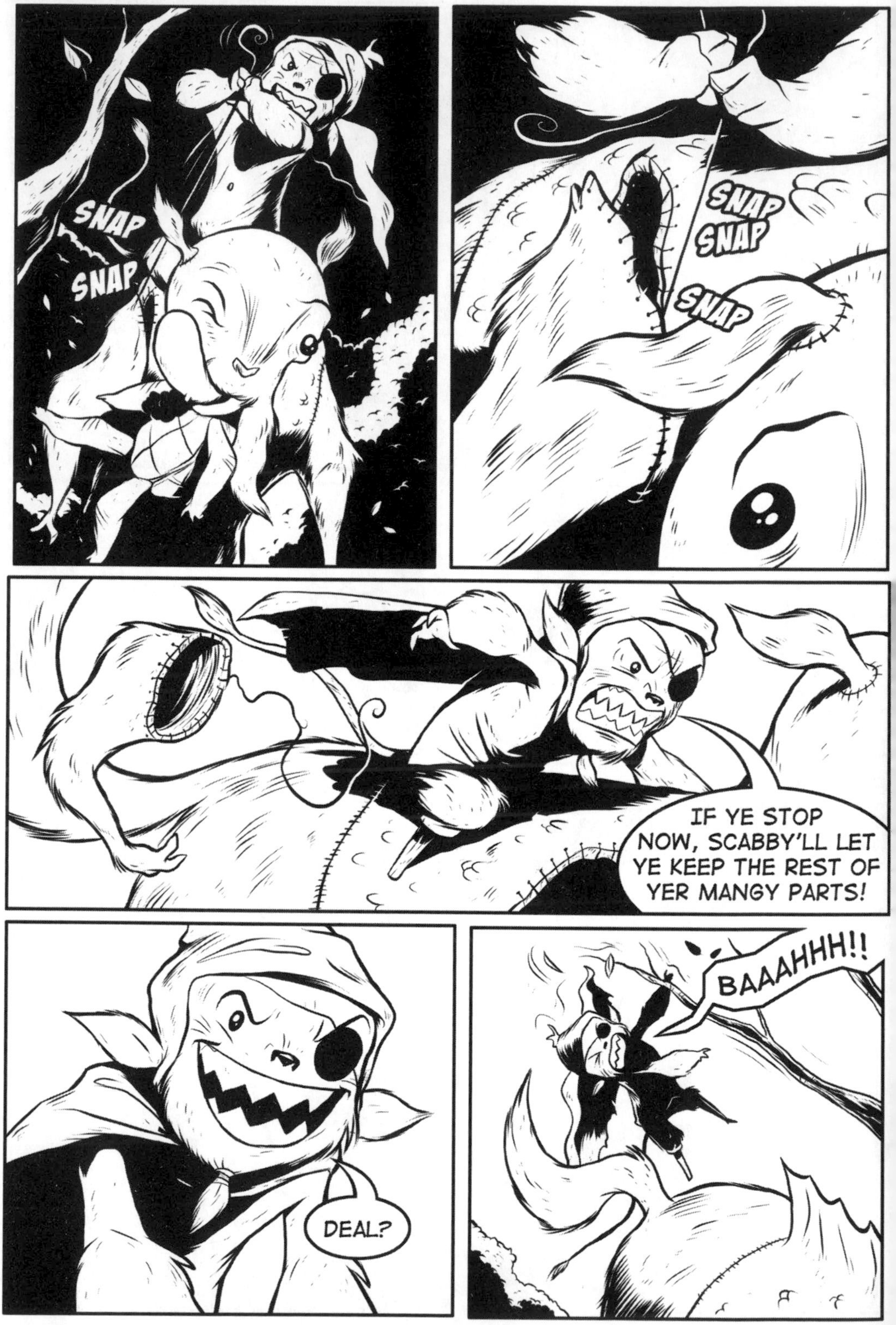
SNAP
SNAP
SNAP
SNAP
SNAP
IF YE STOP NOW, SCABBY'LL LET YE KEEP THE REST OF YER MANGY PARTS!
DEAL?
BAAAHHH!!

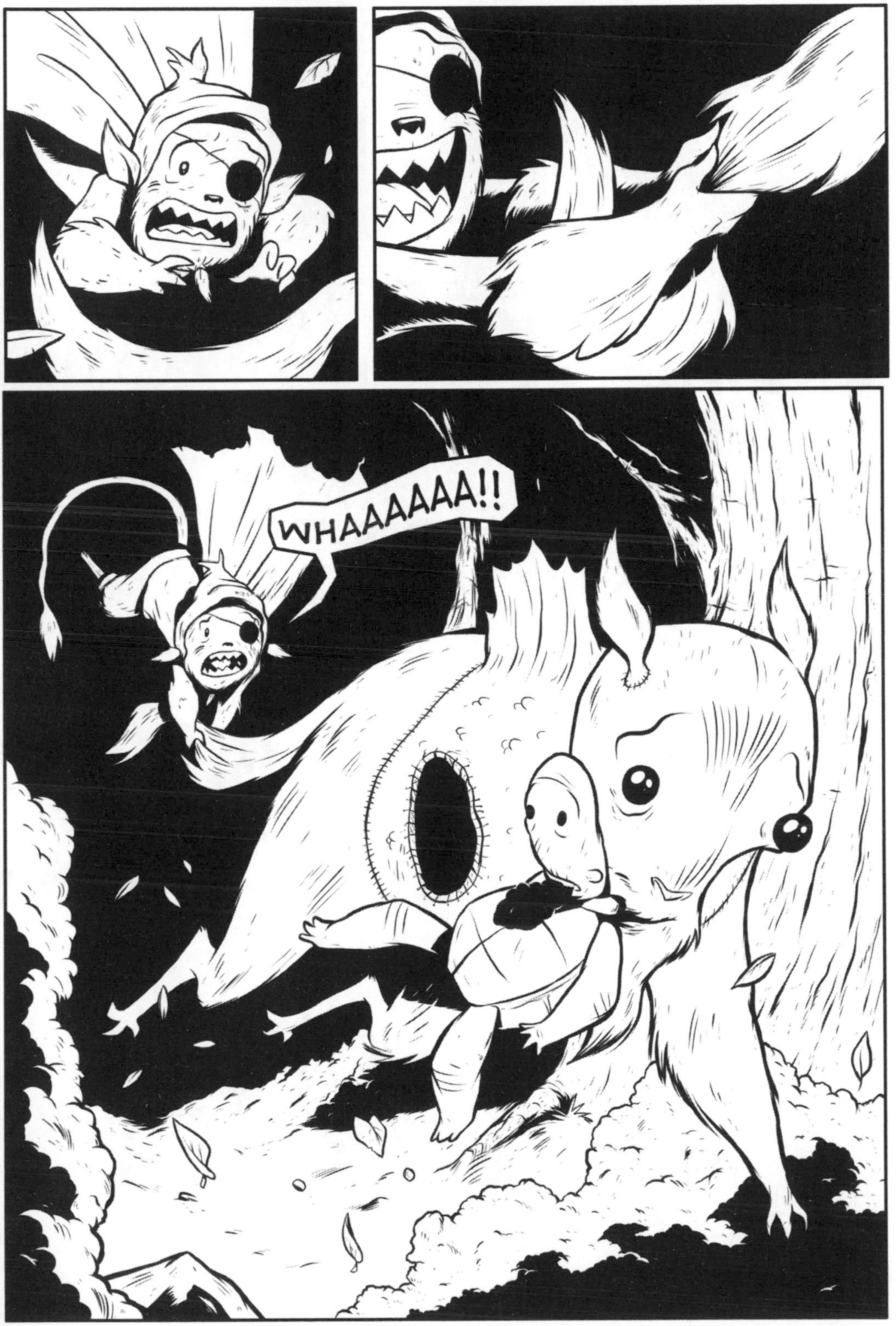
WHAAAAAA!!

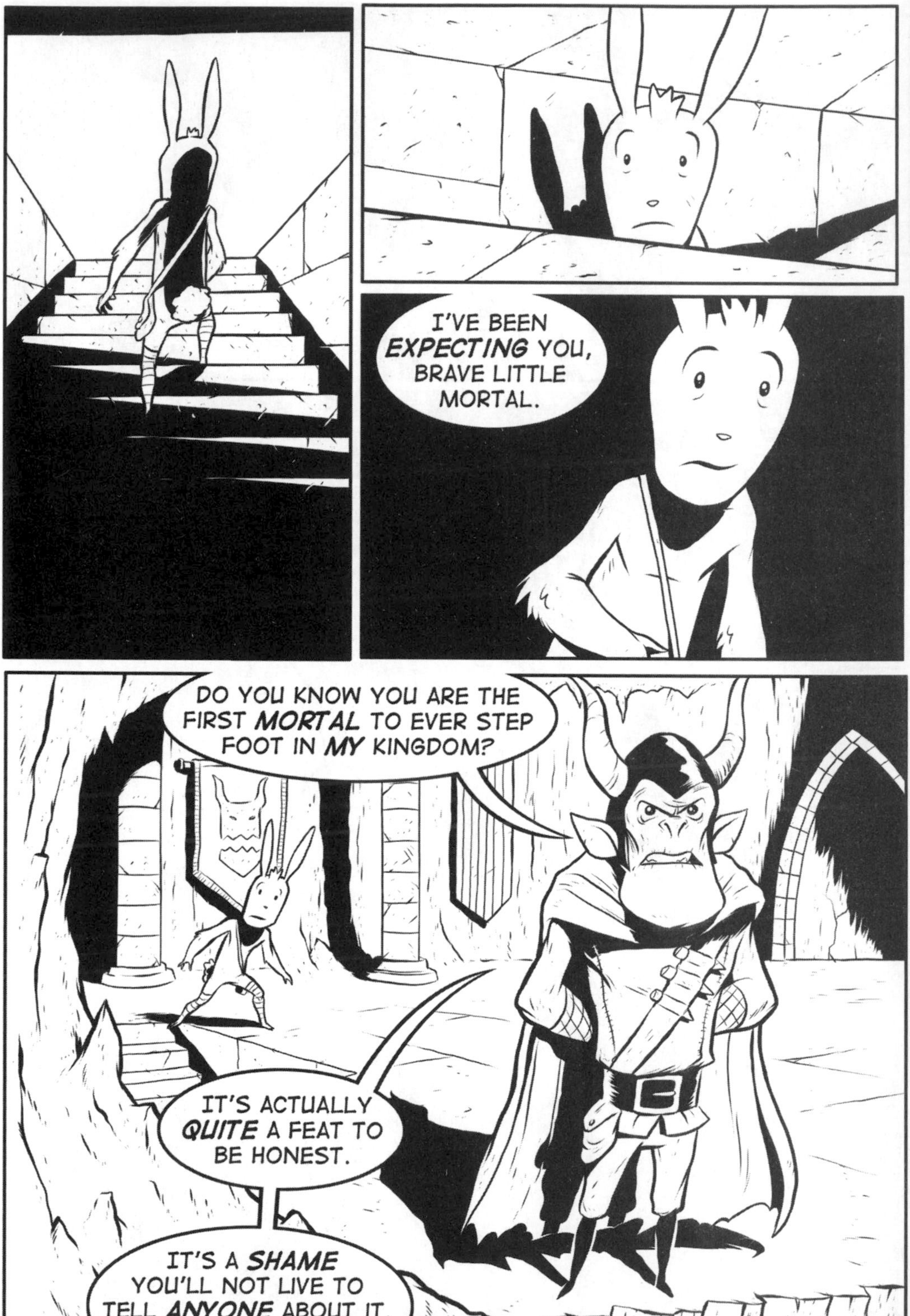
I'VE BEEN EXPECTING YOU, BRAVE LITTLE MORTAL.
DO YOU KNOW YOU ARE THE FIRST MORTAL TO EVER STEP FOOT IN MY KINGDOM?
IT'S ACTUALLY QUITE A FEAT TO BE HONEST.
IT'S A SHAME YOU'LL NOT LIVE TO TELL ANYONE ABOUT IT.

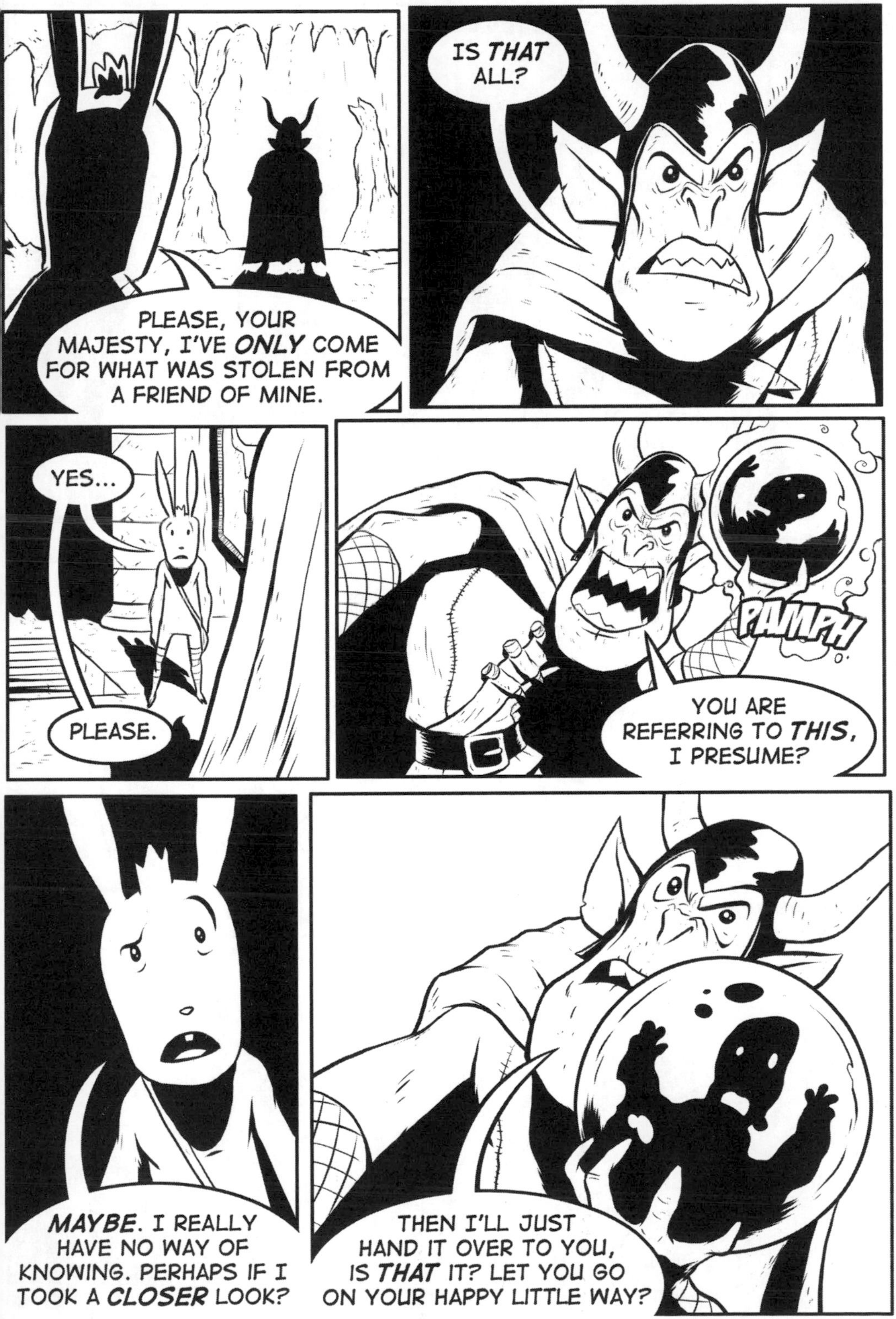
PLEASE, YOUR MAJESTY, I'VE ONLY COME FOR WHAT WAS STOLEN FROM A FRIEND OF MINE.
IS THAT ALL?
YES...
PLEASE.
PAMPH
YOU ARE REFERRING TO THIS, I PRESUME?
MAYBE. I REALLY HAVE NO WAY OF KNOWING. PERHAPS IF I TOOK A CLOSER LOOK?
THEN I'LL JUST HAND IT OVER TO YOU, IS THAT IT? LET YOU GO ON YOUR HAPPY LITTLE WAY?

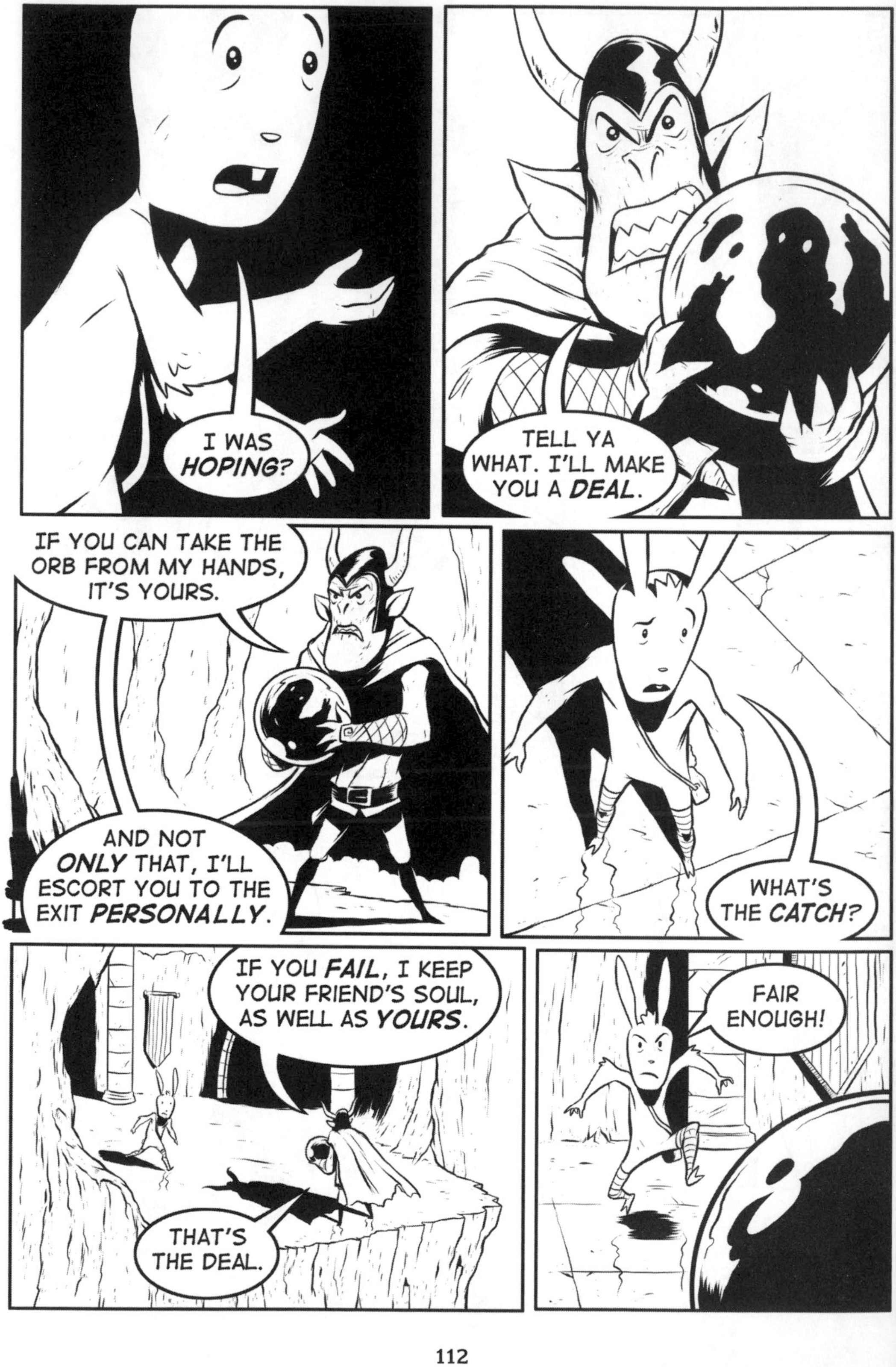
I WAS *HOPING*?
TELL YA WHAT. I'LL MAKE YOU A *DEAL*.
IF YOU CAN TAKE THE ORB FROM MY HANDS, IT'S YOURS.
AND NOT *ONLY* THAT, I'LL ESCORT YOU TO THE EXIT *PERSONALLY*.
WHAT'S THE *CATCH*?
IF YOU *FAIL*, I KEEP YOUR FRIEND'S SOUL, AS WELL AS *YOURS*.
THAT'S THE DEAL.
FAIR ENOUGH!

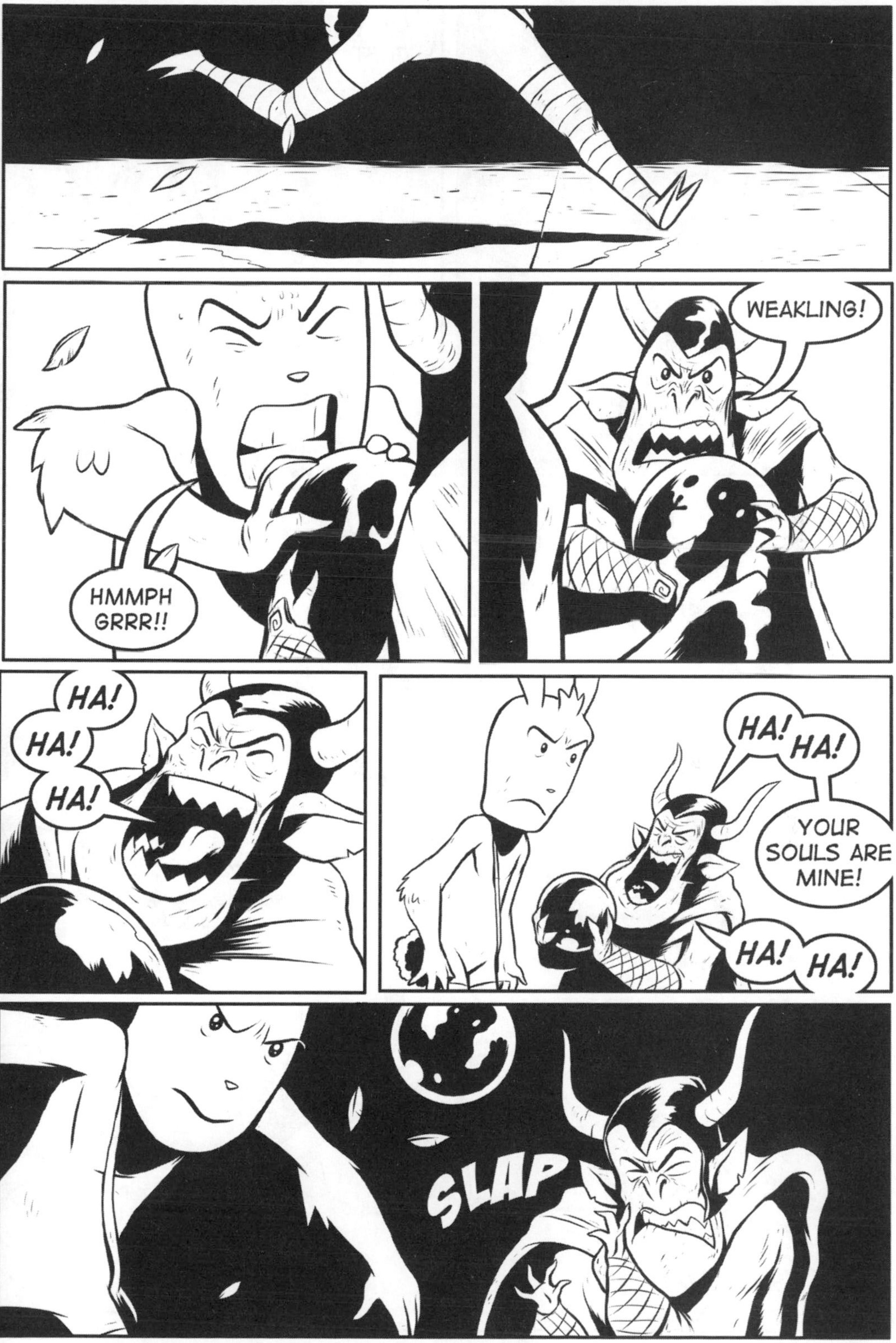
HMMPH
GRRR!!
WEAKLING!
HA!
HA!
HA!
HA!
HA!
YOUR SOULS ARE MINE!
HA!
HA!
SLAP

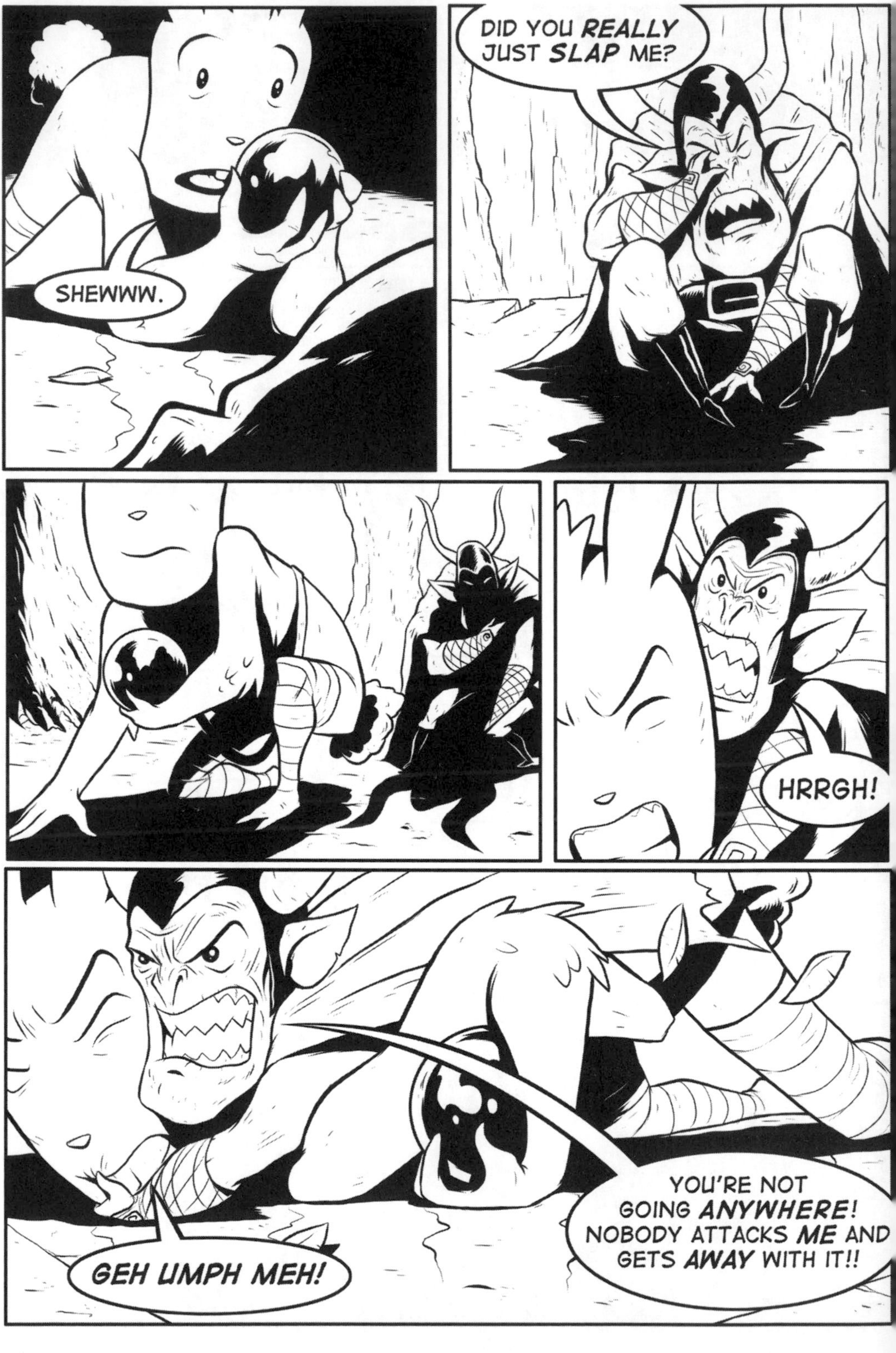
SHEWWW.
DID YOU REALLY JUST SLAP ME?
HRRGH!
GEH UMPH MEH!
YOU'RE NOT GOING ANYWHERE! NOBODY ATTACKS ME AND GETS AWAY WITH IT!!

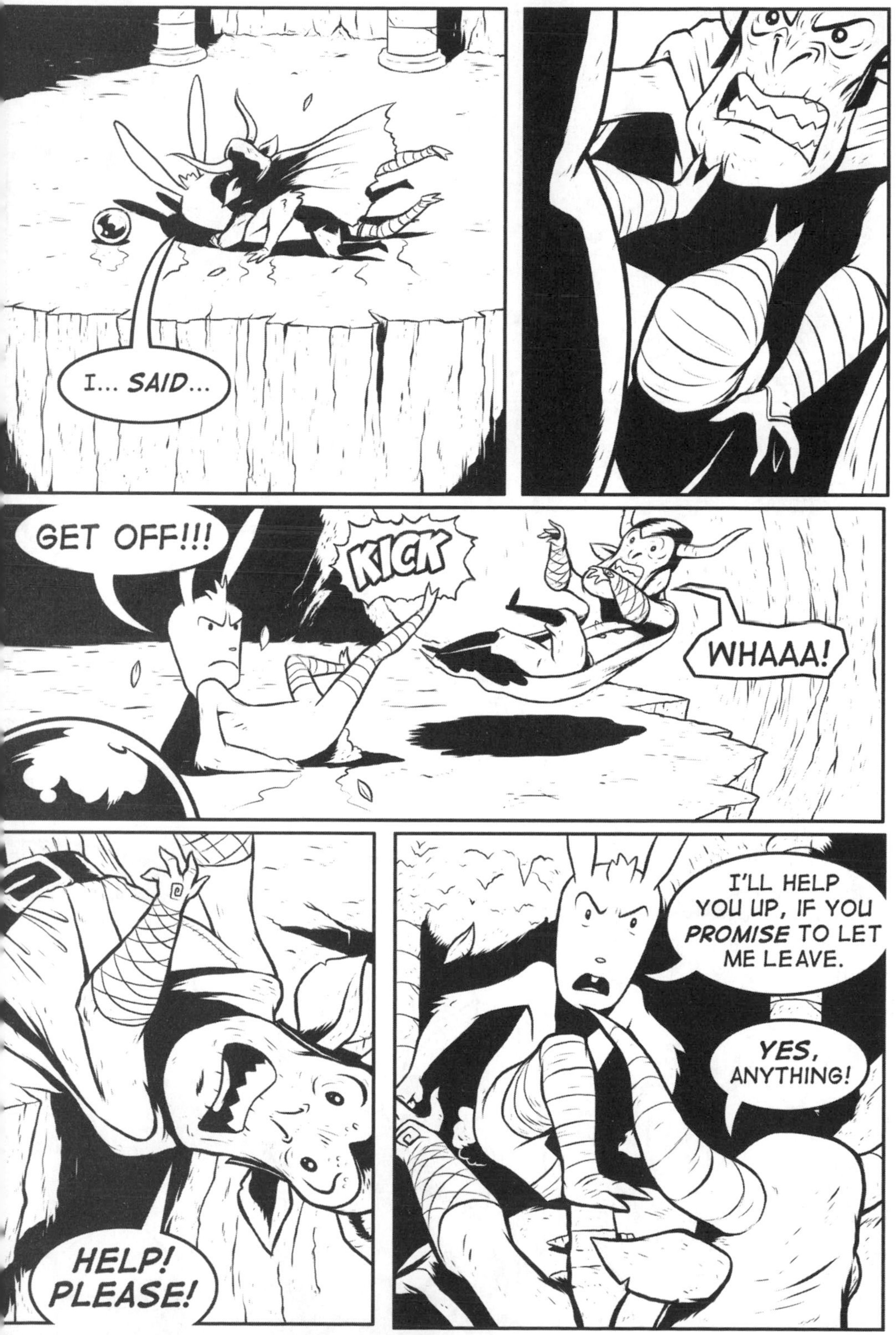

I... SAID...
GET OFF!!!
KICK
WHAAA!
HELP! PLEASE!
I'LL HELP YOU UP, IF YOU PROMISE TO LET ME LEAVE.
YES, ANYTHING!

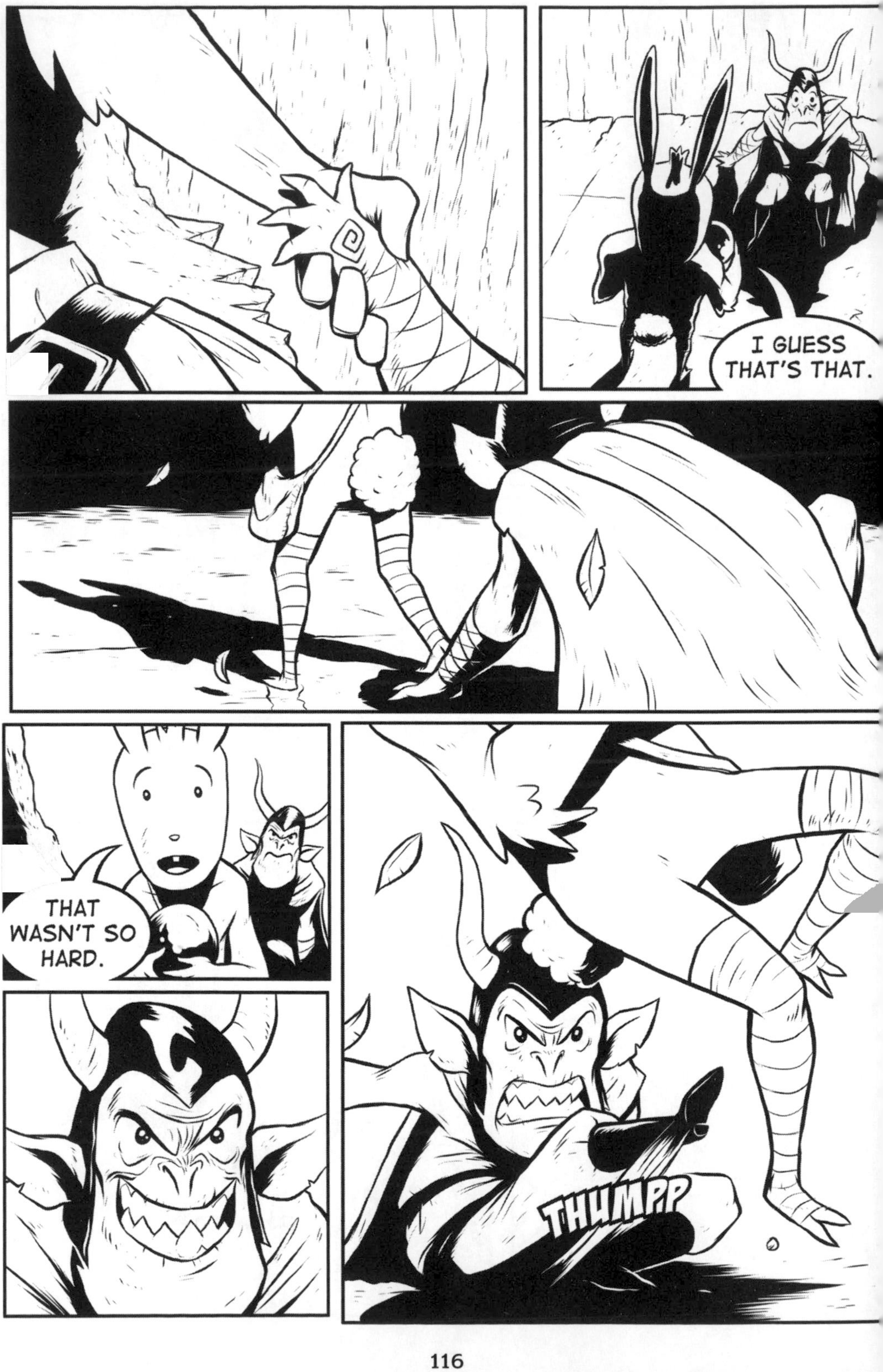
I GUESS THAT'S THAT.
THAT WASN'T SO HARD.
THUMPP

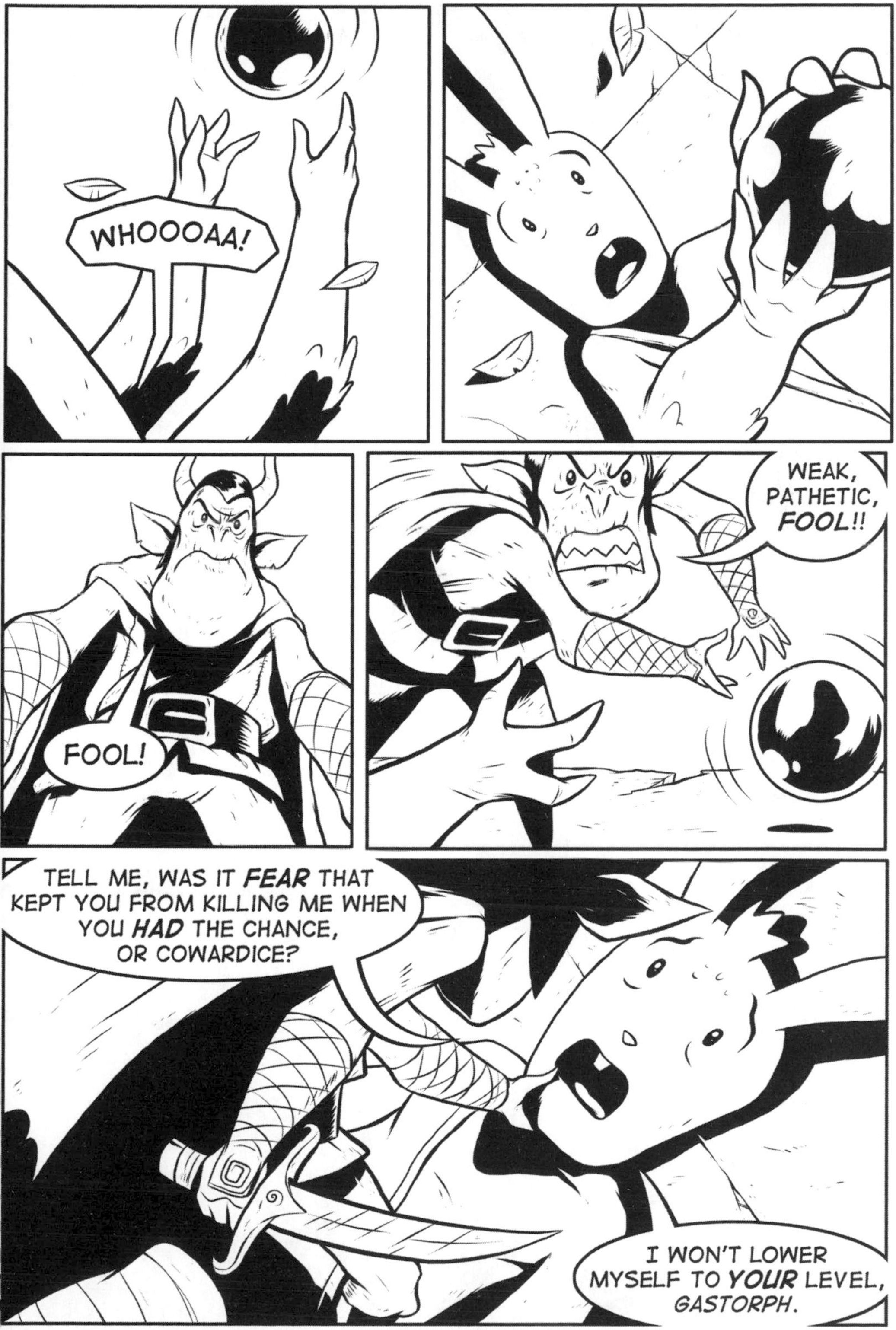
WHOOOAA!
FOOL!
WEAK, PATHETIC, FOOL!!
TELL ME, WAS IT FEAR THAT KEPT YOU FROM KILLING ME WHEN YOU HAD THE CHANCE, OR COWARDICE?
I WON'T LOWER MYSELF TO YOUR LEVEL, GASTORPH.

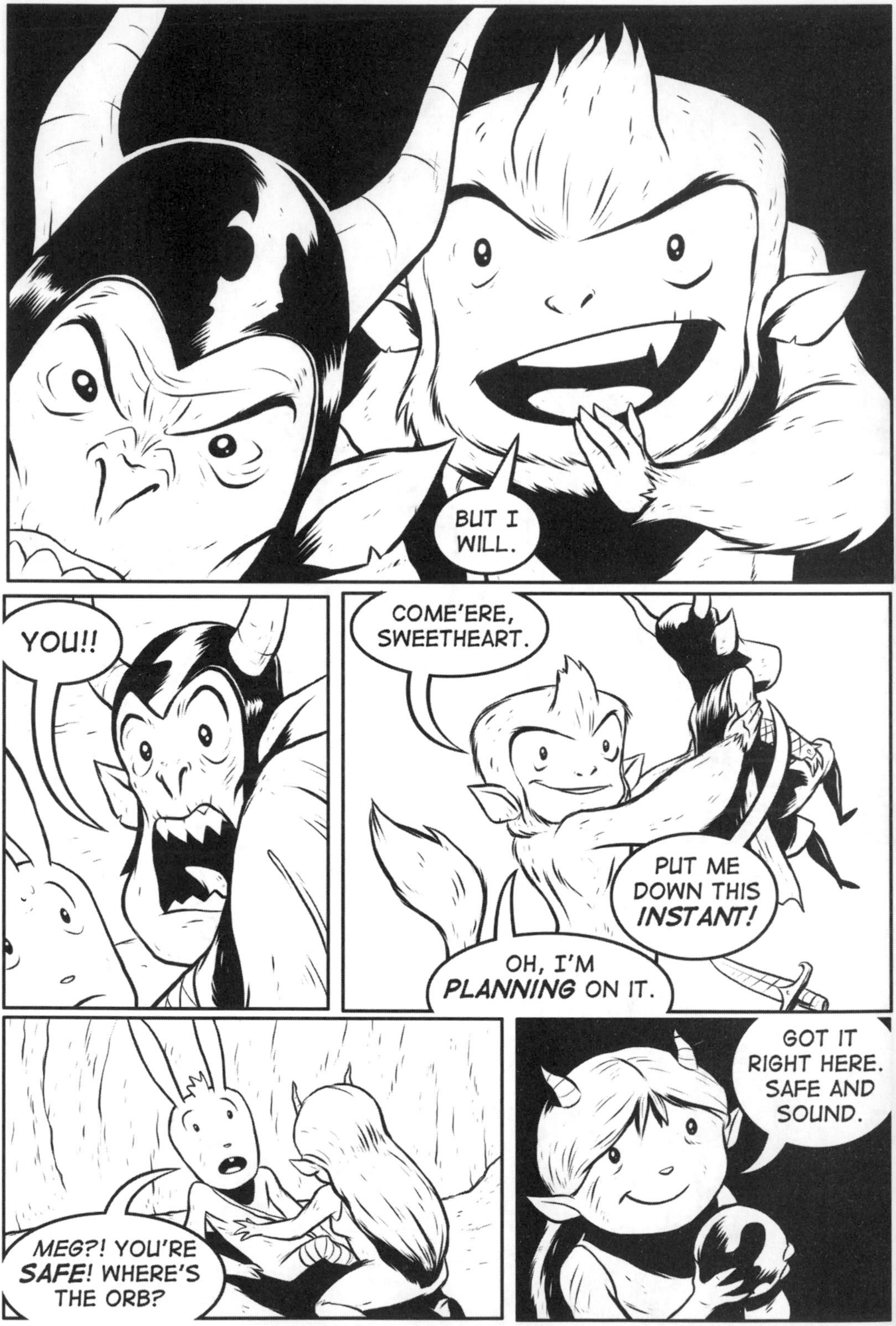
BUT I WILL.
YOU!!
COME'ERE, SWEETHEART.
PUT ME DOWN THIS *INSTANT!*
OH, I'M *PLANNING* ON IT.
MEG?! YOU'RE ***SAFE!*** *WHERE'S THE ORB?*
GOT IT RIGHT HERE. SAFE AND SOUND.

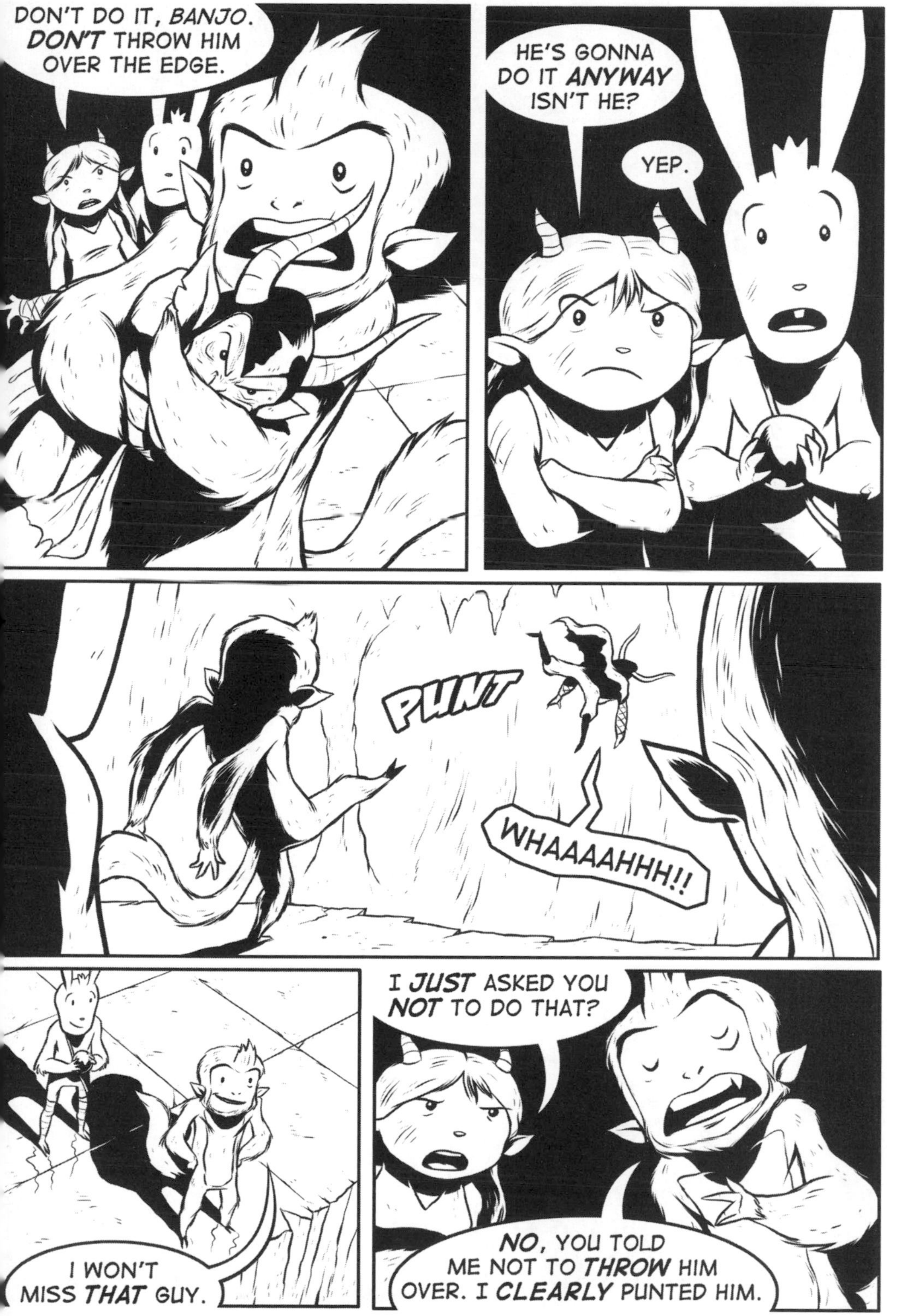
DON'T DO IT, BANJO. DON'T THROW HIM OVER THE EDGE.
HE'S GONNA DO IT ANYWAY ISN'T HE?
YEP.
PUNT
WHAAAAHHH!!
I WON'T MISS THAT GUY.
I JUST ASKED YOU NOT TO DO THAT?
NO, YOU TOLD ME NOT TO THROW HIM OVER. I CLEARLY PUNTED HIM.

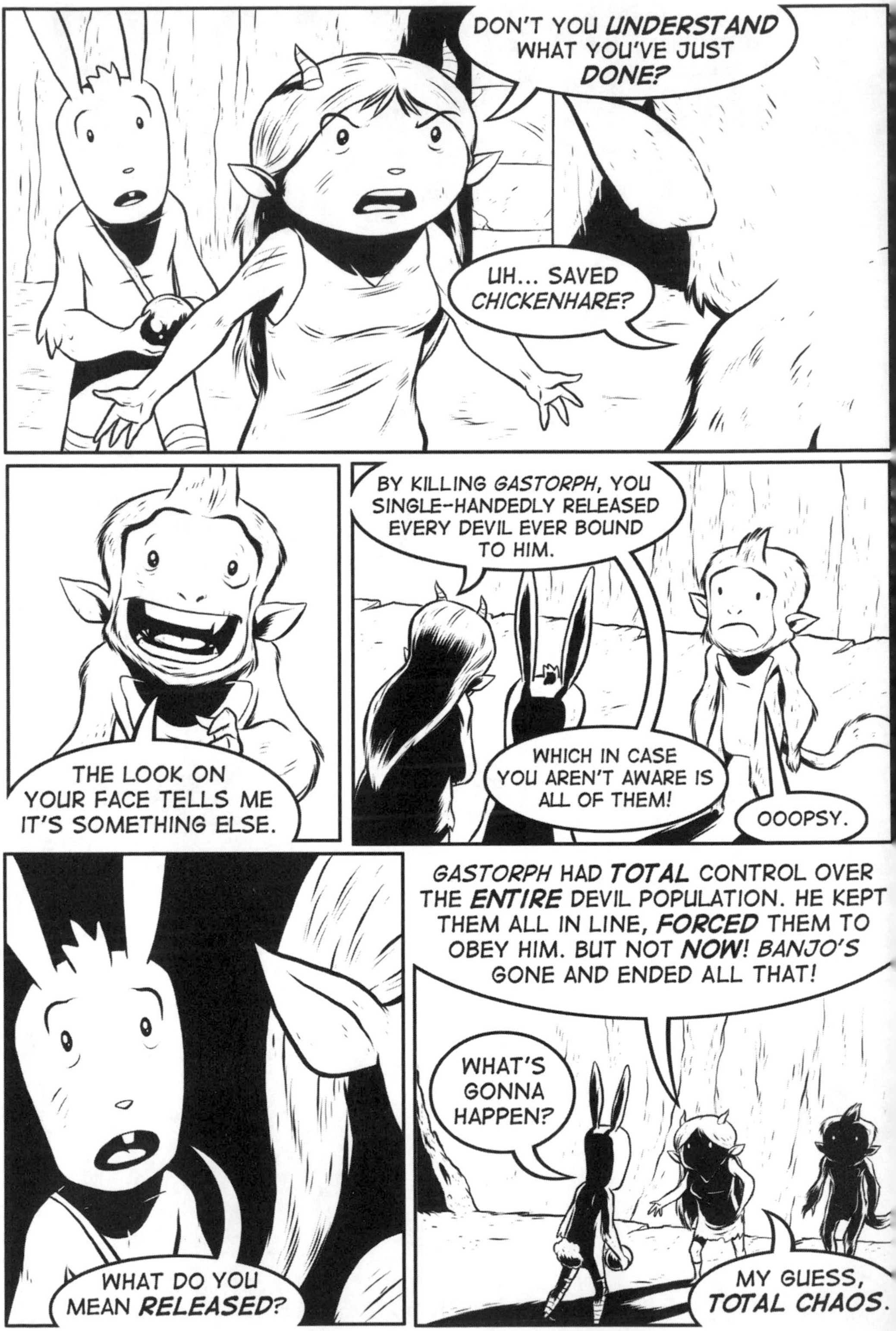
DON'T YOU *UNDERSTAND* WHAT YOU'VE JUST *DONE?*
UH... SAVED *CHICKENHARE?*
THE LOOK ON YOUR FACE TELLS ME IT'S SOMETHING ELSE.
BY KILLING *GASTORPH*, YOU SINGLE-HANDEDLY RELEASED EVERY DEVIL EVER BOUND TO HIM.
WHICH IN CASE YOU AREN'T AWARE IS ALL OF THEM!
OOOPSY.
WHAT DO YOU MEAN *RELEASED*?
GASTORPH HAD ***TOTAL*** CONTROL OVER THE ***ENTIRE*** DEVIL POPULATION. HE KEPT THEM ALL IN LINE, ***FORCED*** THEM TO OBEY HIM. BUT NOT ***NOW***! *BANJO'S* GONE AND ENDED ALL THAT!
WHAT'S GONNA HAPPEN?
MY GUESS, ***TOTAL CHAOS***.

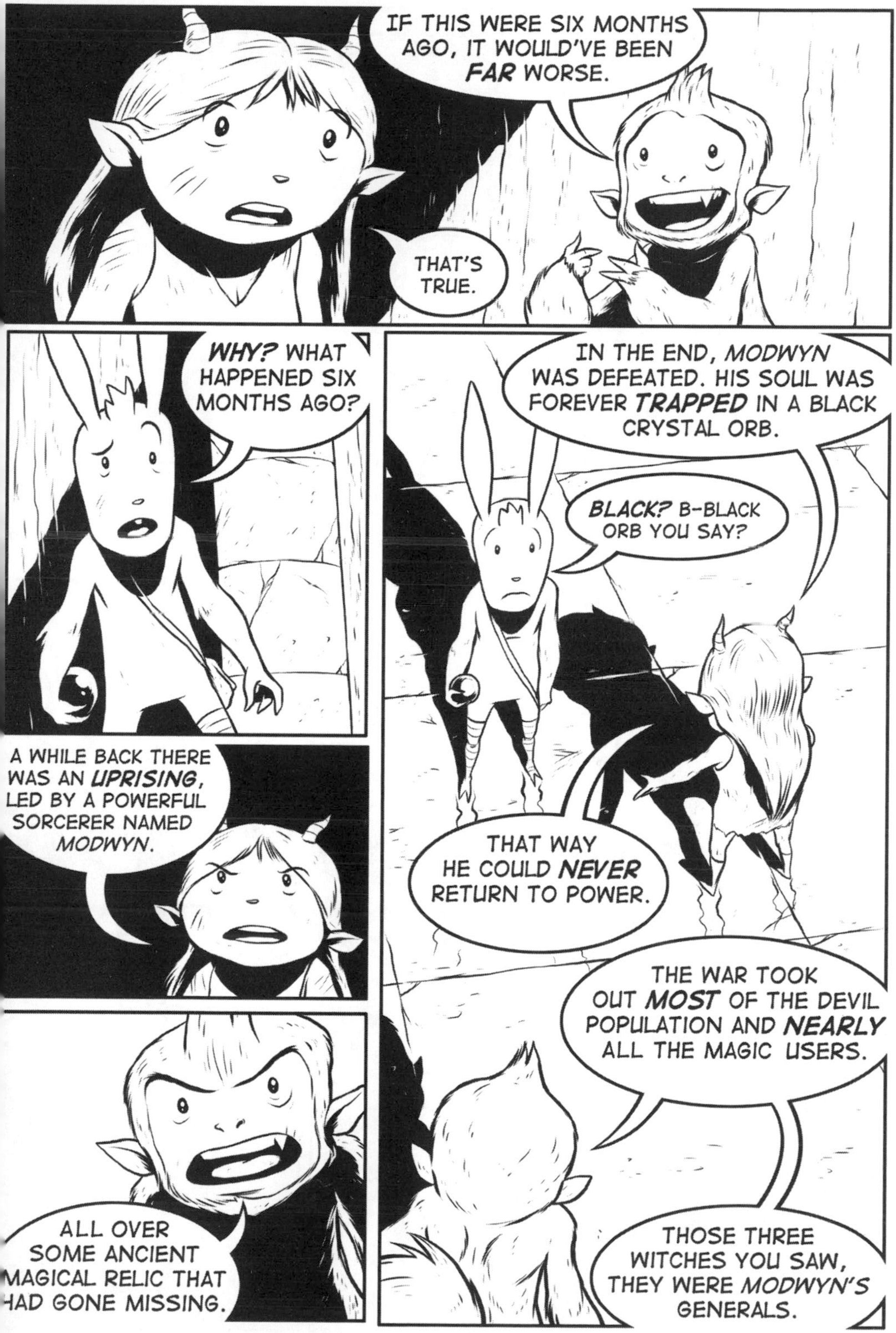
IF THIS WERE SIX MONTHS AGO, IT WOULD'VE BEEN FAR WORSE.
THAT'S TRUE.
WHY? WHAT HAPPENED SIX MONTHS AGO?
A WHILE BACK THERE WAS AN UPRISING, LED BY A POWERFUL SORCERER NAMED MODWYN.
ALL OVER SOME ANCIENT MAGICAL RELIC THAT HAD GONE MISSING.
IN THE END, MODWYN WAS DEFEATED. HIS SOUL WAS FOREVER TRAPPED IN A BLACK CRYSTAL ORB.
BLACK? B-BLACK ORB YOU SAY?
THAT WAY HE COULD NEVER RETURN TO POWER.
THE WAR TOOK OUT MOST OF THE DEVIL POPULATION AND NEARLY ALL THE MAGIC USERS.
THOSE THREE WITCHES YOU SAW, THEY WERE MODWYN'S GENERALS.

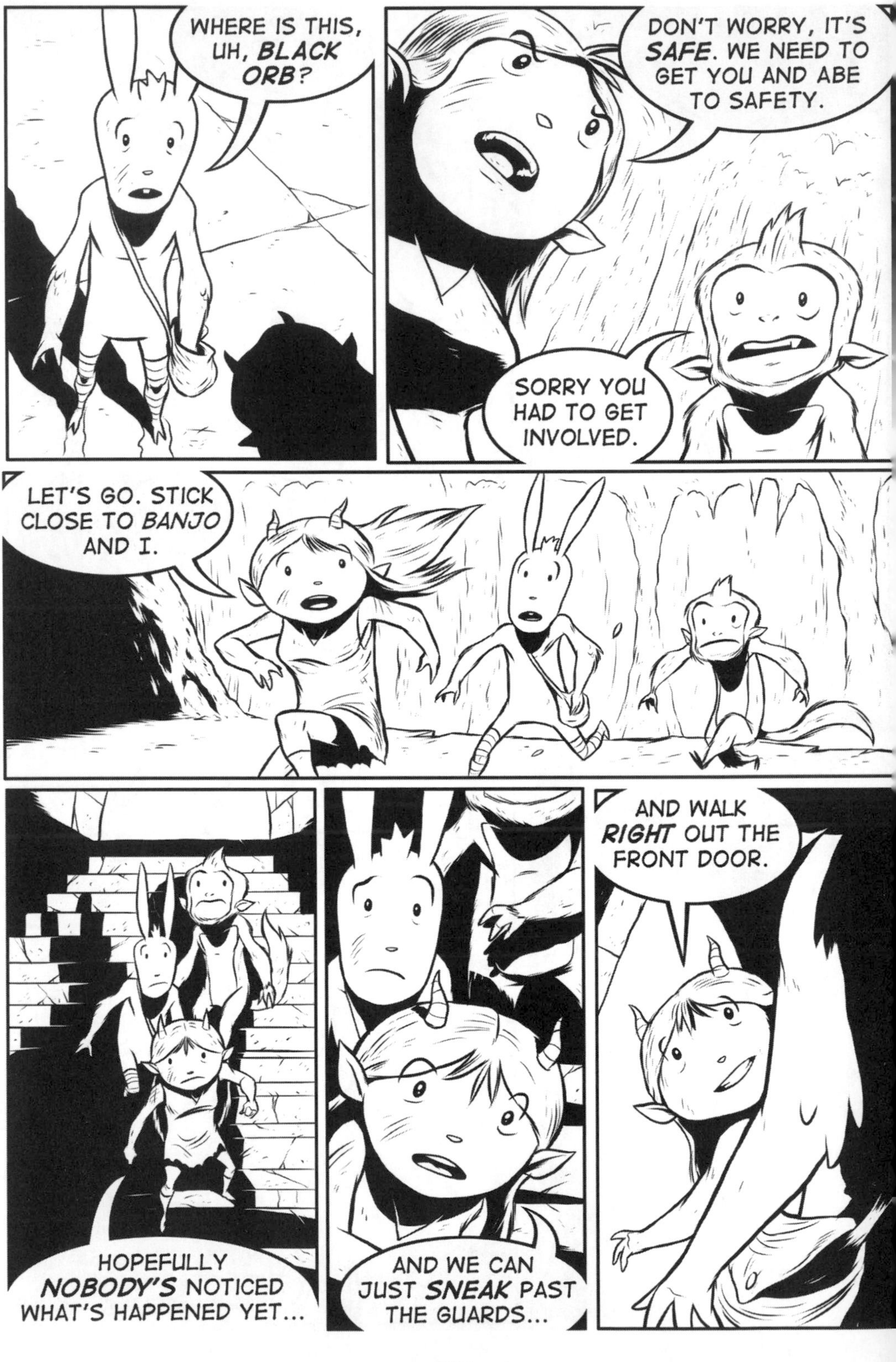
WHERE IS THIS, UH, *BLACK ORB*?
DON'T WORRY, IT'S *SAFE*. WE NEED TO GET YOU AND ABE TO SAFETY.
SORRY YOU HAD TO GET INVOLVED.
LET'S GO. STICK CLOSE TO *BANJO* AND I.
HOPEFULLY *NOBODY'S* NOTICED WHAT'S HAPPENED YET...
AND WE CAN JUST *SNEAK* PAST THE GUARDS...
AND WALK *RIGHT* OUT THE FRONT DOOR.

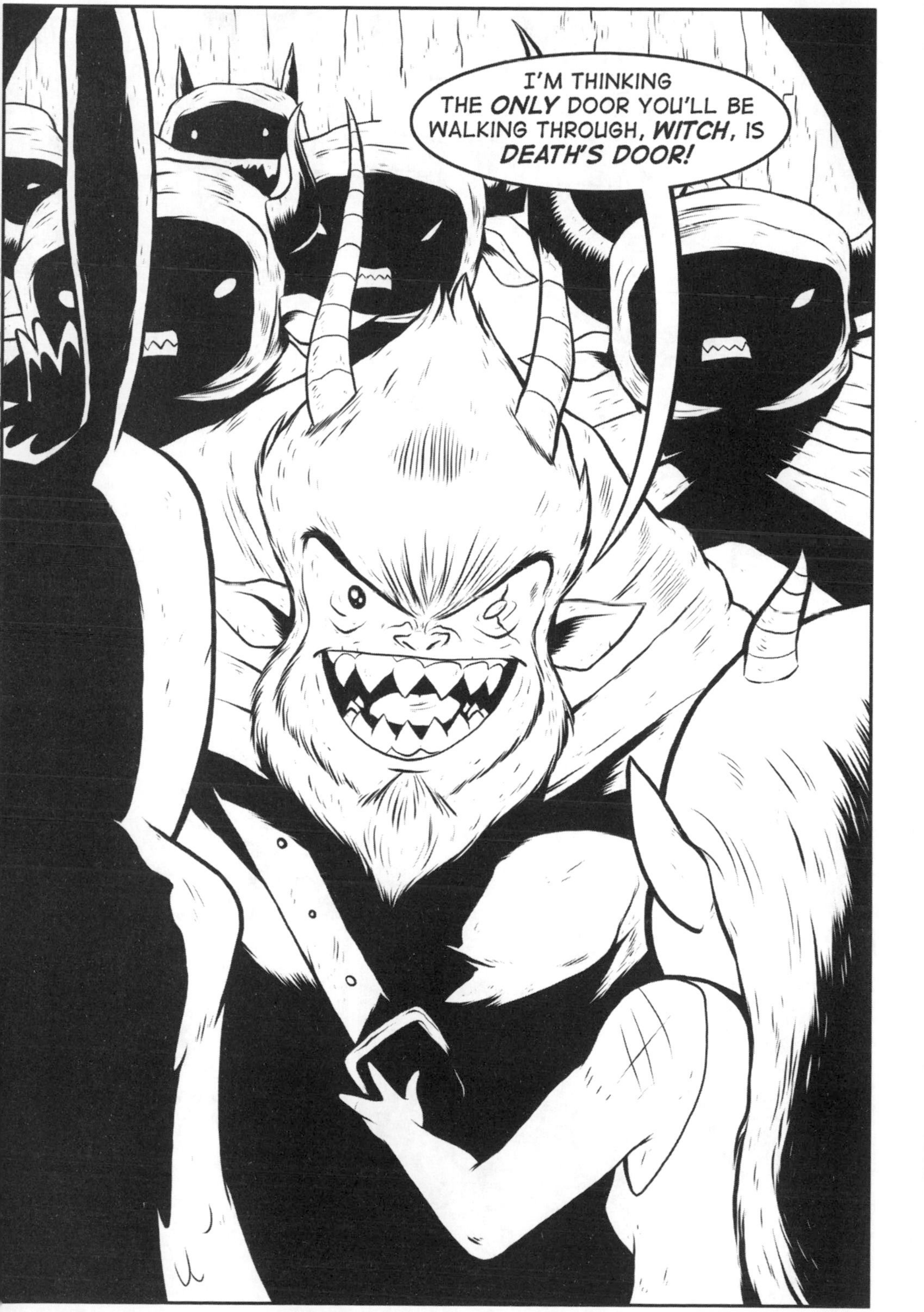
I'M THINKING THE ONLY DOOR YOU'LL BE WALKING THROUGH, WITCH, IS DEATH'S DOOR!

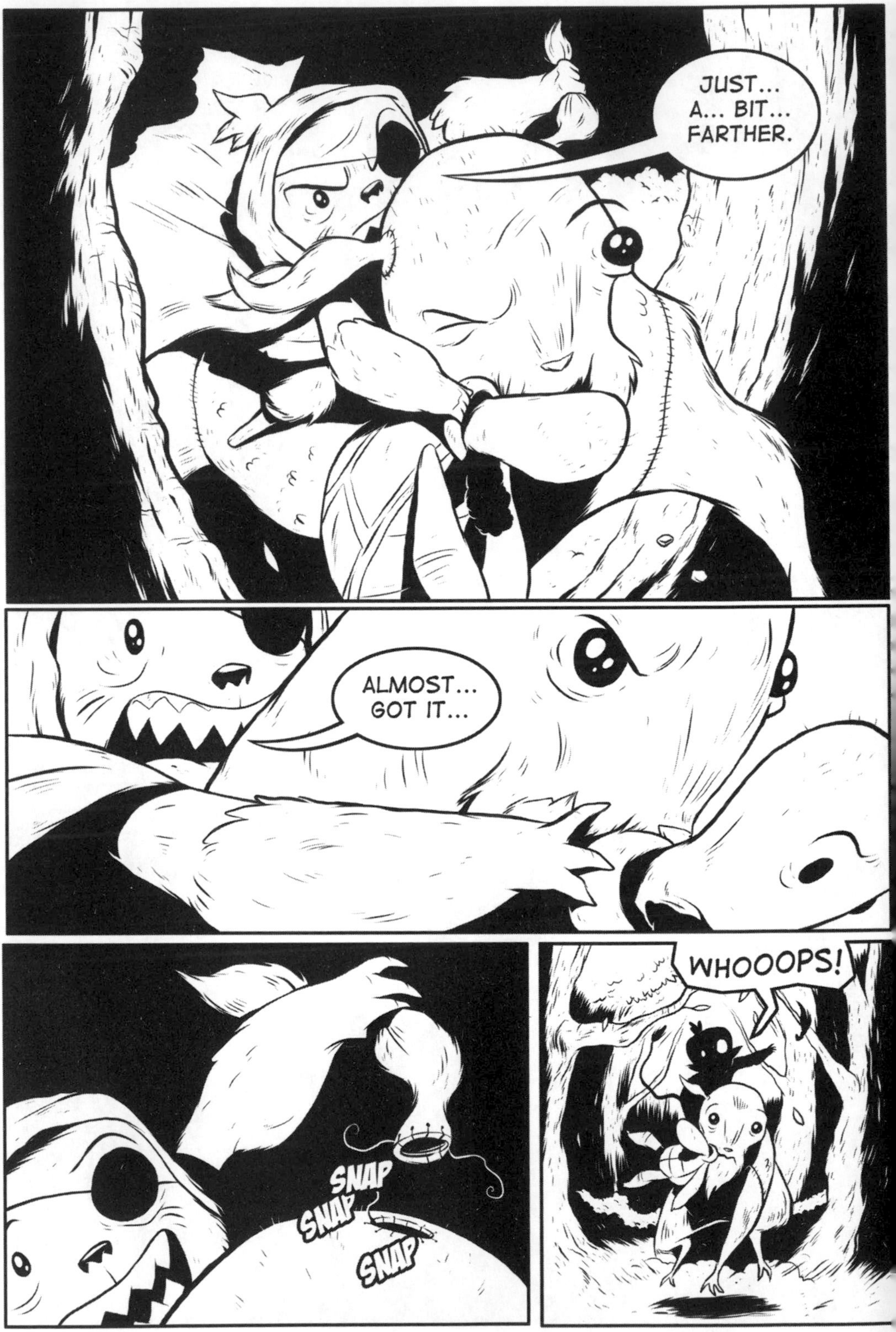
JUST... A... BIT... FARTHER.
ALMOST... GOT IT...
SNAP
SNAP
SNAP
WHOOOPS!

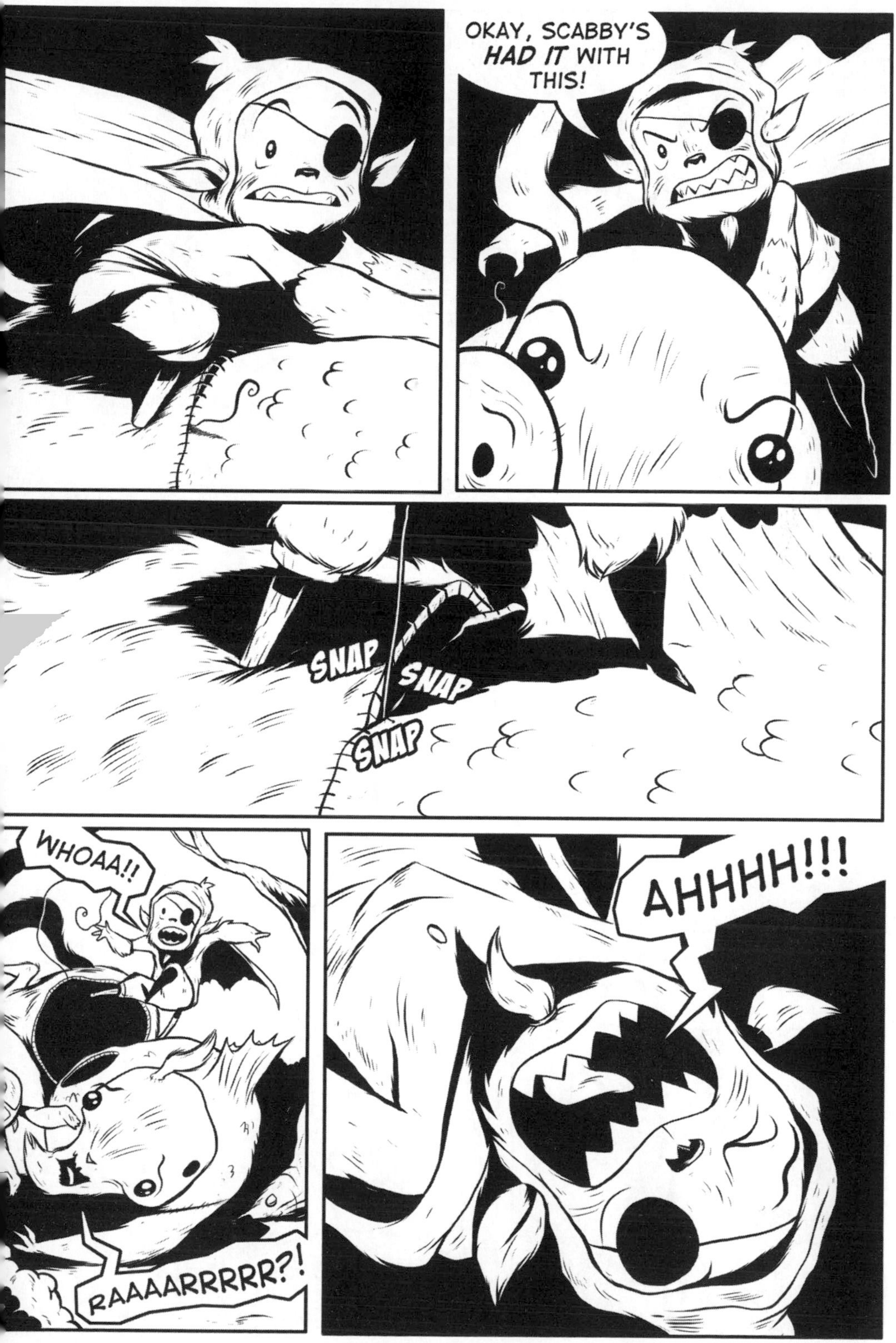
OKAY, SCABBY'S *HAD IT* WITH THIS!
SNAP
SNAP
SNAP
WHOAA!!
RAAAARRRRR?!
AHHHH!!!

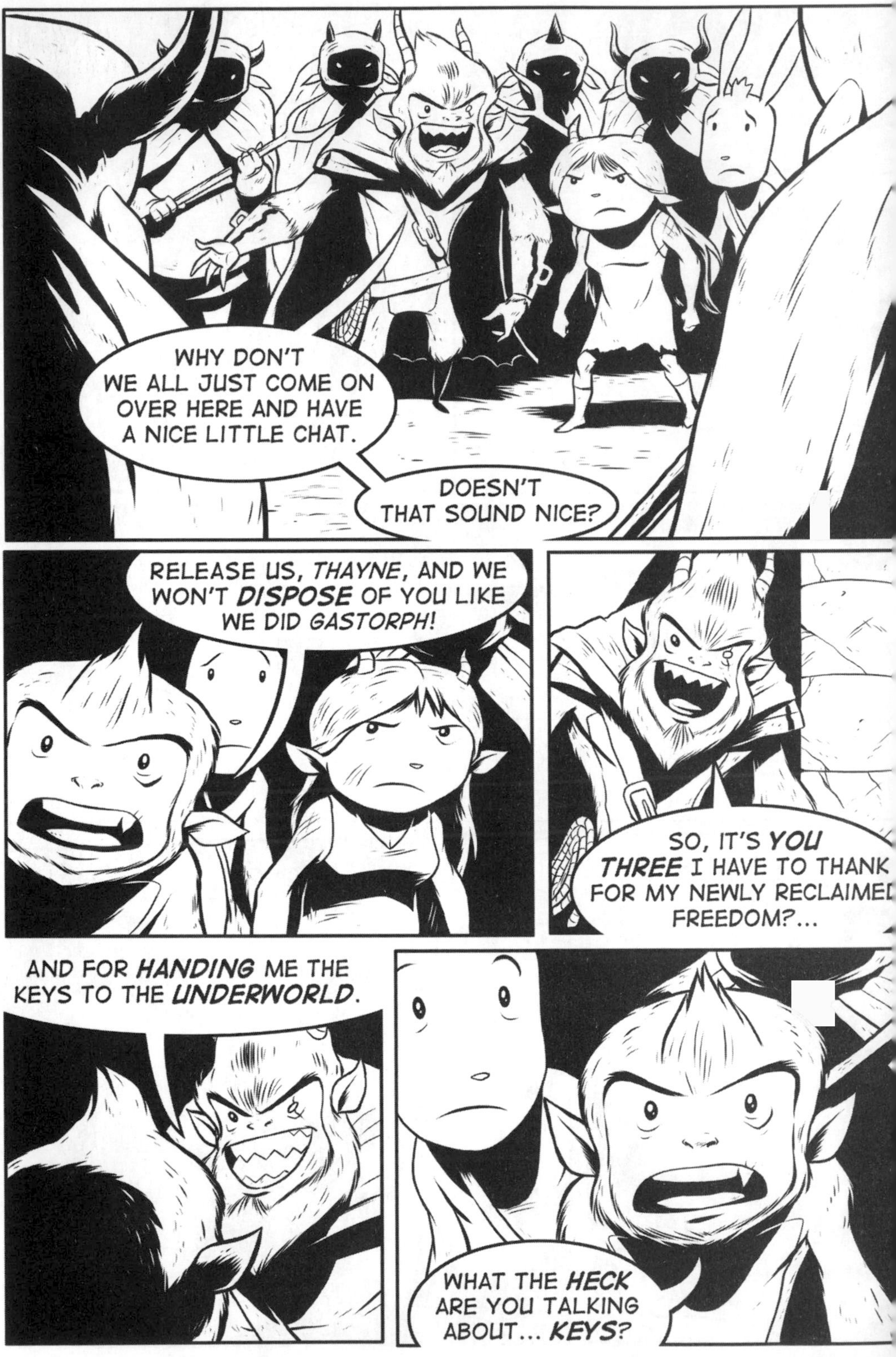
WHY DON'T WE ALL JUST COME ON OVER HERE AND HAVE A NICE LITTLE CHAT.
DOESN'T THAT SOUND NICE?
RELEASE US, THAYNE, AND WE WON'T DISPOSE OF YOU LIKE WE DID GASTORPH!
SO, IT'S YOU THREE I HAVE TO THANK FOR MY NEWLY RECLAIMED FREEDOM?...
AND FOR HANDING ME THE KEYS TO THE UNDERWORLD.
WHAT THE HECK ARE YOU TALKING ABOUT... KEYS?

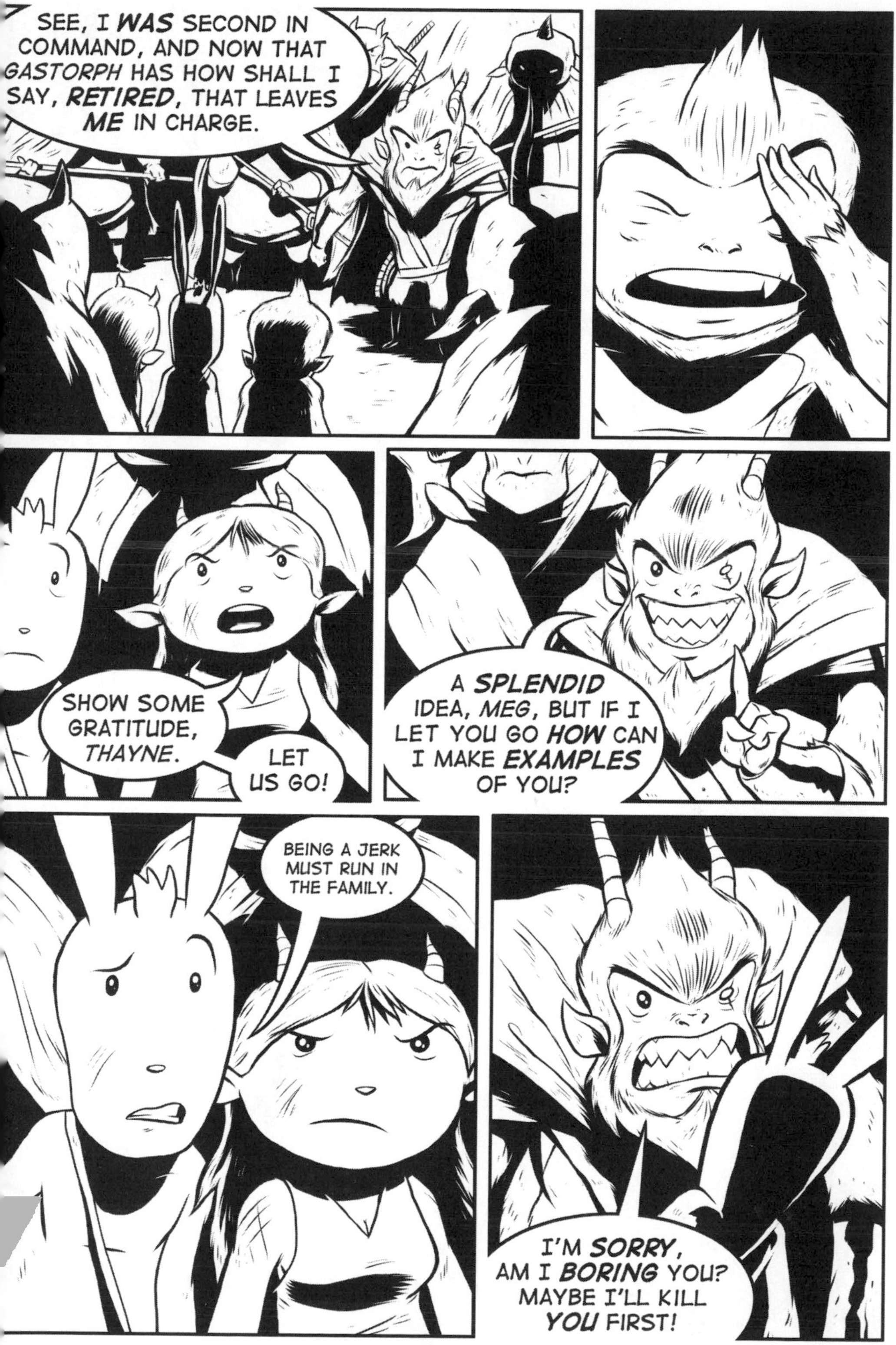
SEE, I WAS SECOND IN COMMAND, AND NOW THAT GASTORPH HAS HOW SHALL I SAY, RETIRED, THAT LEAVES ME IN CHARGE.
SHOW SOME GRATITUDE, THAYNE.
LET US GO!
A SPLENDID IDEA, MEG, BUT IF I LET YOU GO HOW CAN I MAKE EXAMPLES OF YOU?
BEING A JERK MUST RUN IN THE FAMILY.
I'M SORRY, AM I BORING YOU? MAYBE I'LL KILL YOU FIRST!

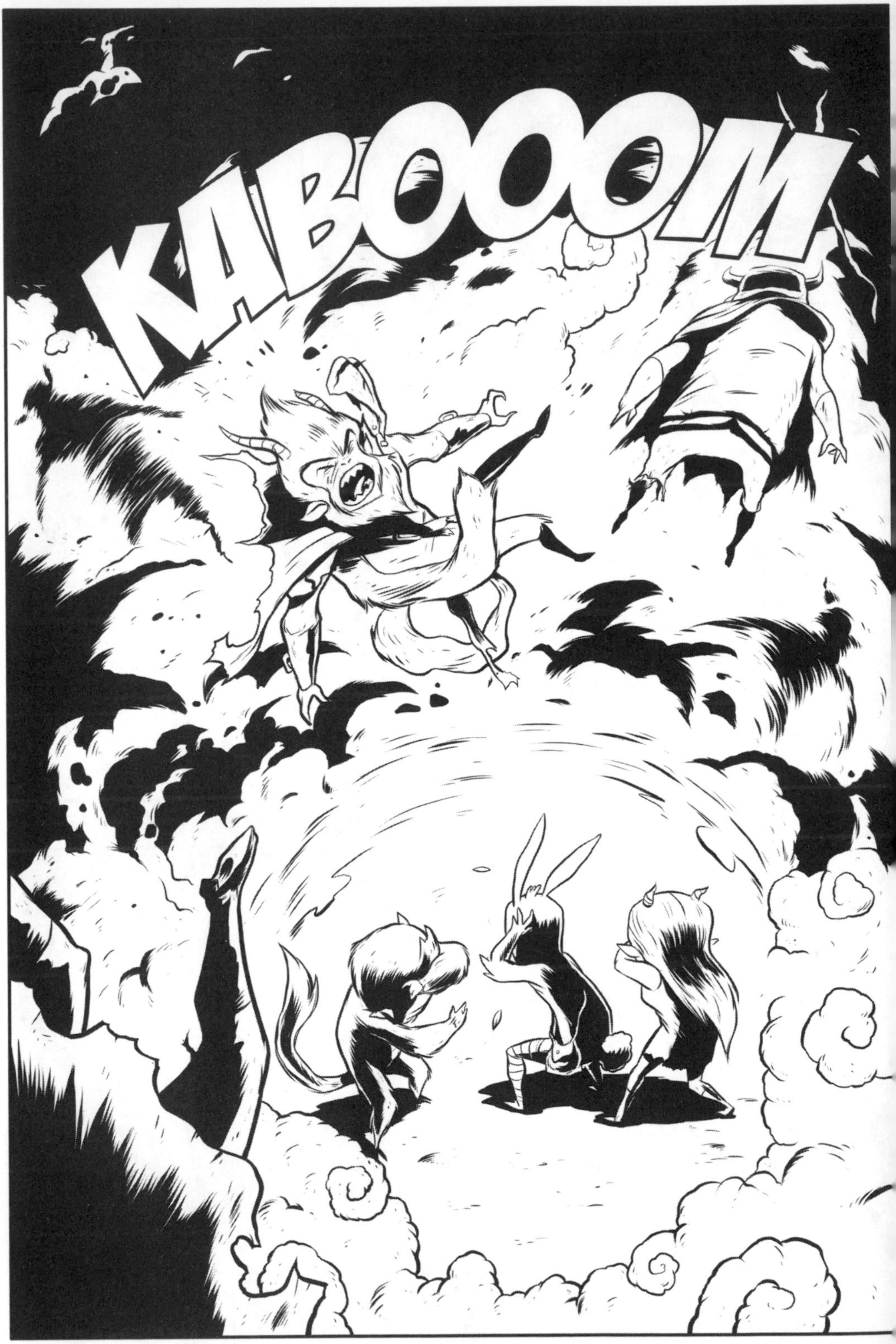
KABOOOM

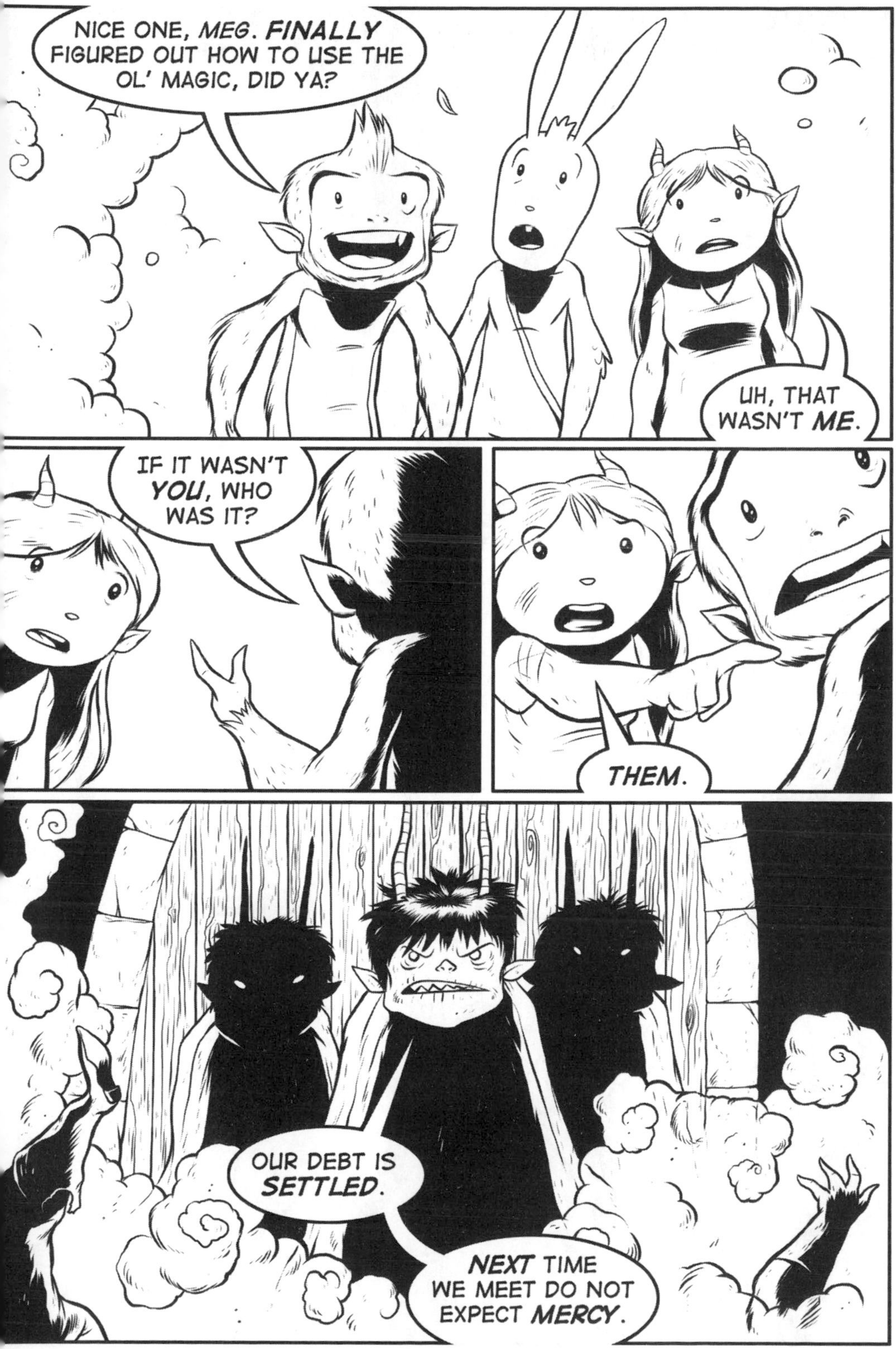
NICE ONE, MEG. FINALLY FIGURED OUT HOW TO USE THE OL' MAGIC, DID YA?
UH, THAT WASN'T ME.
IF IT WASN'T YOU, WHO WAS IT?
THEM.
OUR DEBT IS SETTLED.
NEXT TIME WE MEET DO NOT EXPECT MERCY.

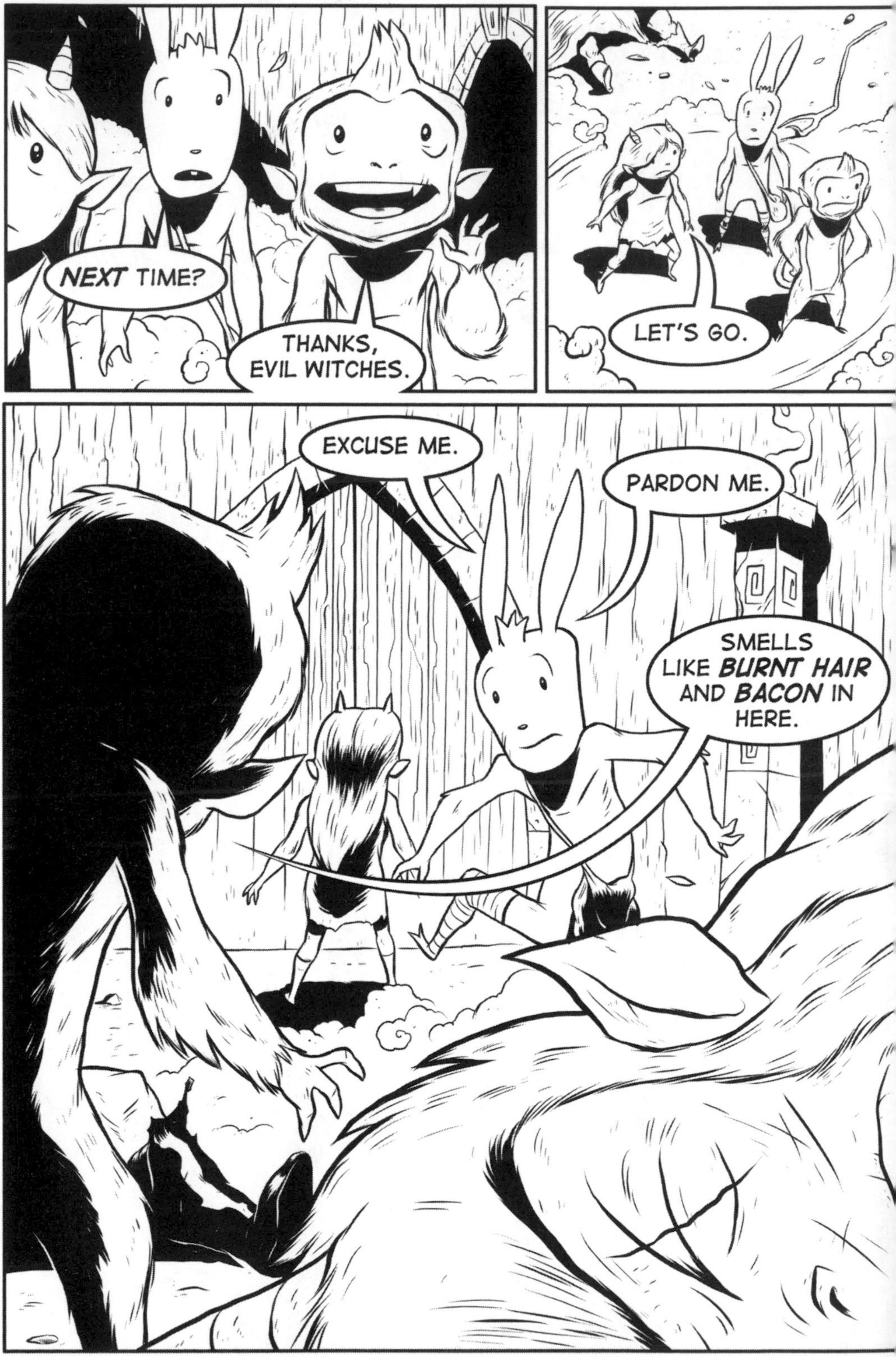
NEXT TIME?
THANKS, EVIL WITCHES.
LET'S GO.
EXCUSE ME.
PARDON ME.
SMELLS LIKE BURNT HAIR AND BACON IN HERE.

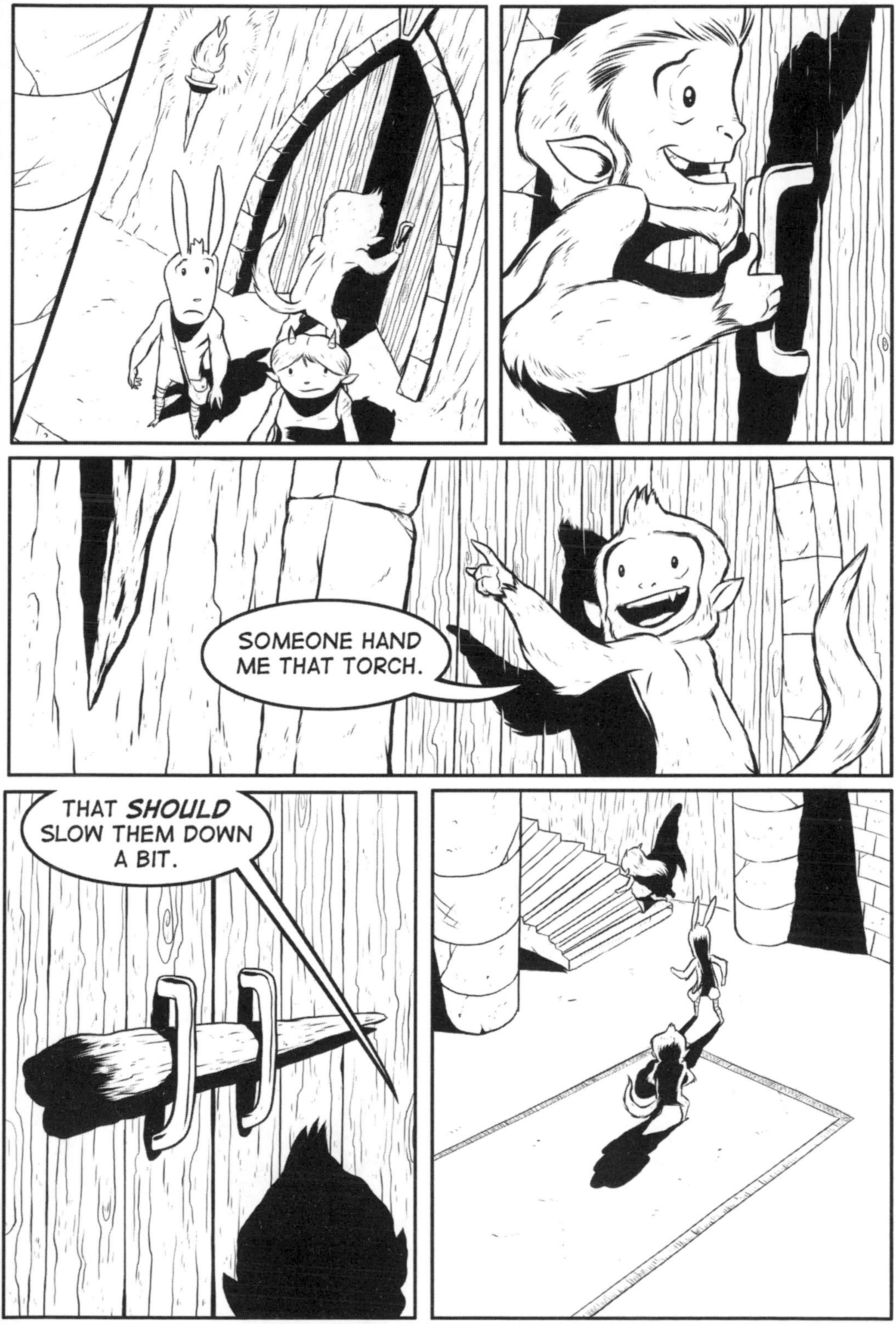
SOMEONE HAND ME THAT TORCH.
THAT *SHOULD* SLOW THEM DOWN A BIT.

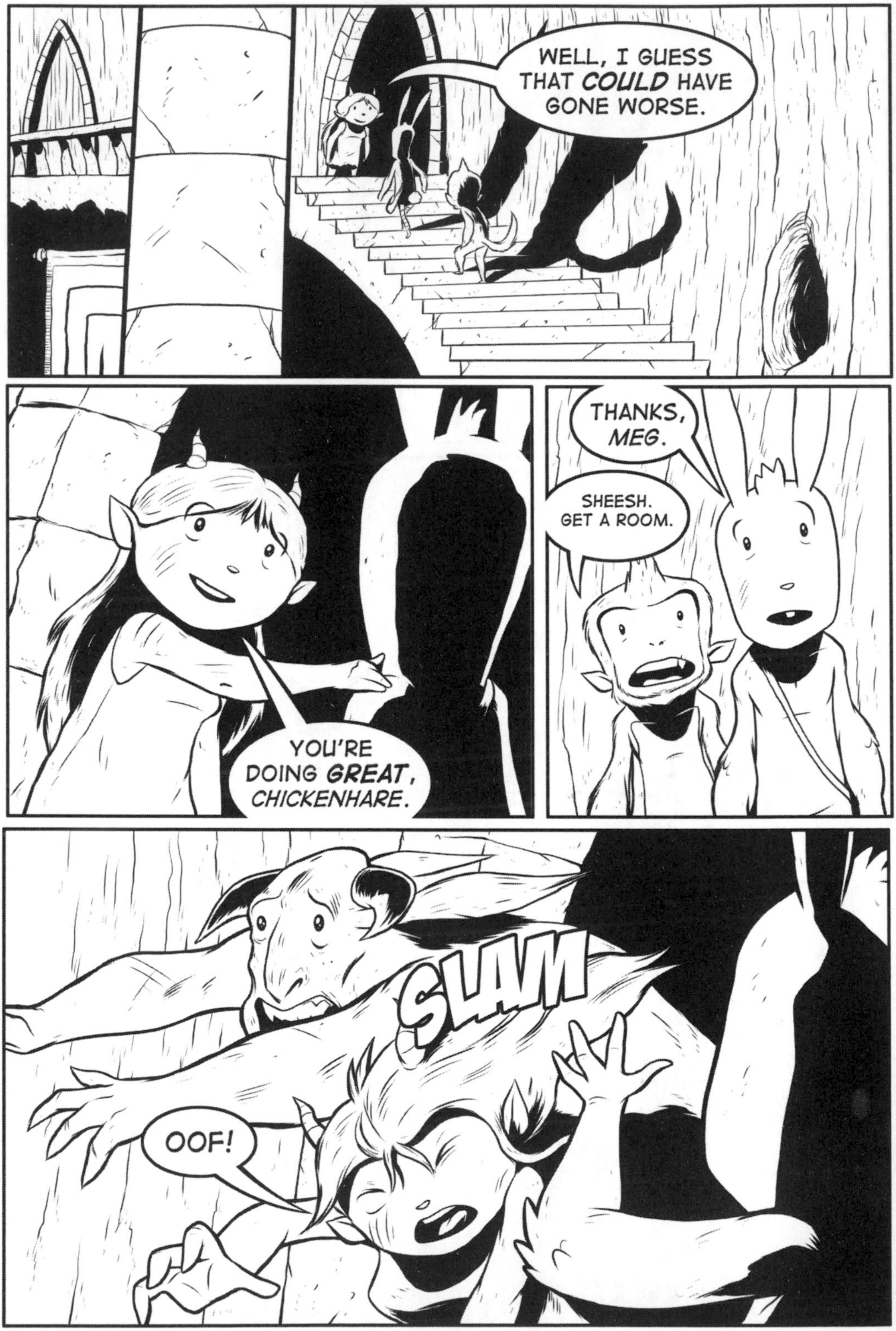
WELL, I GUESS THAT COULD HAVE GONE WORSE.
YOU'RE DOING GREAT, CHICKENHARE.
THANKS, MEG.
SHEESH. GET A ROOM.
SLAM
OOF!

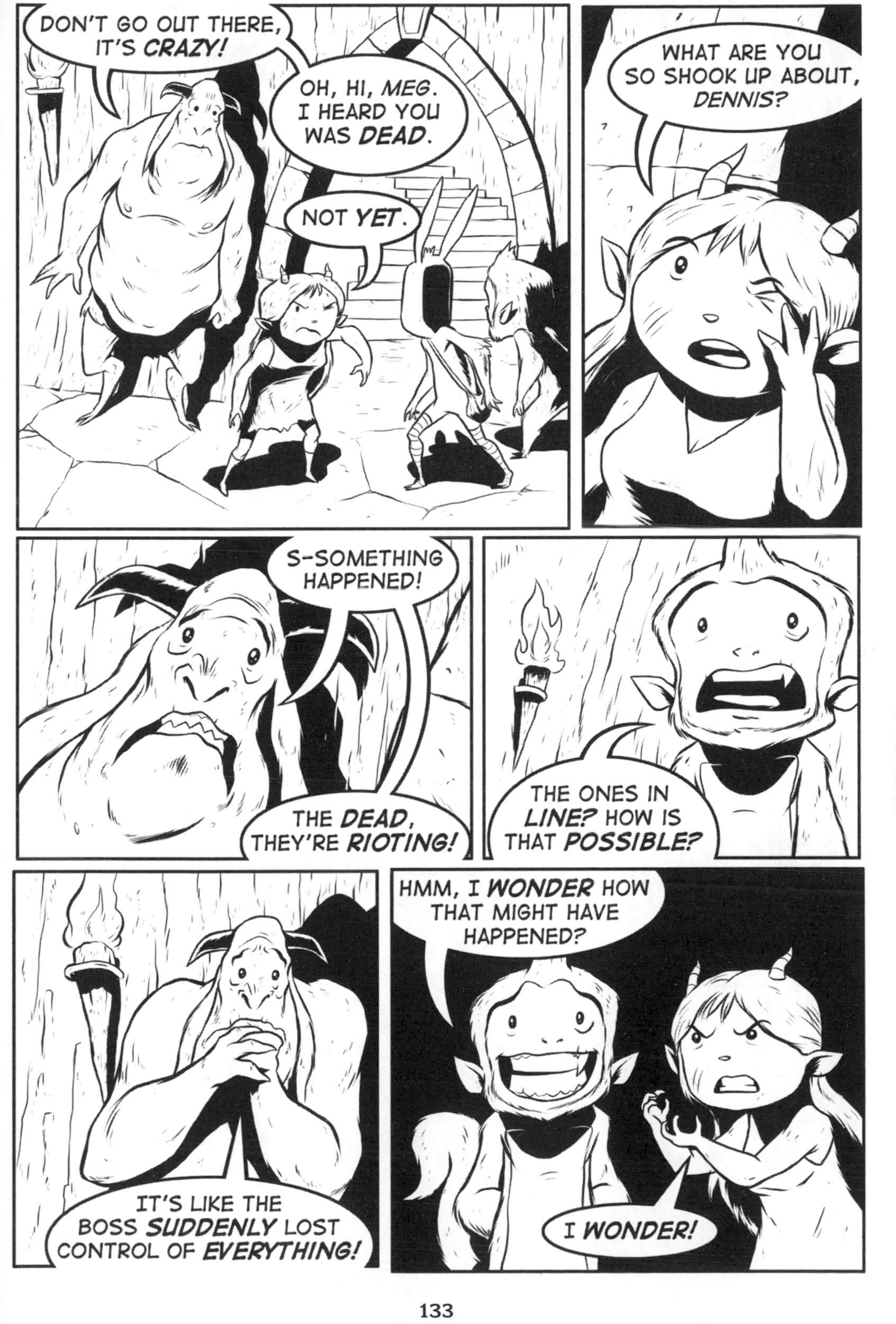
DON'T GO OUT THERE, IT'S CRAZY!
OH, HI, MEG. I HEARD YOU WAS DEAD.
NOT YET.
WHAT ARE YOU SO SHOOK UP ABOUT, DENNIS?
S-SOMETHING HAPPENED!
THE DEAD, THEY'RE RIOTING!
THE ONES IN LINE? HOW IS THAT POSSIBLE?
IT'S LIKE THE BOSS SUDDENLY LOST CONTROL OF EVERYTHING!
HMM, I WONDER HOW THAT MIGHT HAVE HAPPENED?
I WONDER!

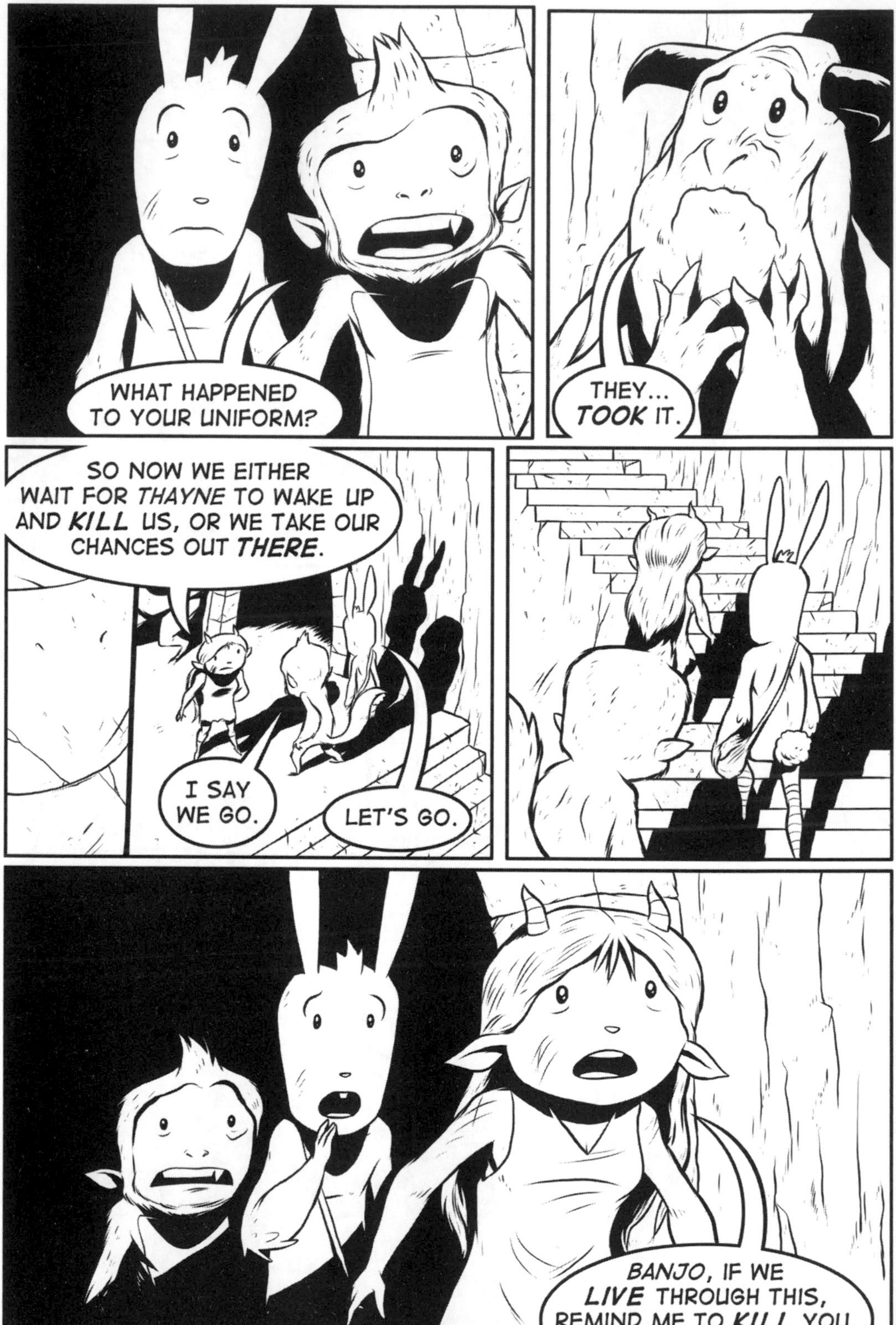
WHAT HAPPENED TO YOUR UNIFORM?
THEY... TOOK IT.
SO NOW WE EITHER WAIT FOR THAYNE TO WAKE UP AND KILL US, OR WE TAKE OUR CHANCES OUT THERE.
I SAY WE GO.
LET'S GO.
BANJO, IF WE LIVE THROUGH THIS, REMIND ME TO KILL YOU.

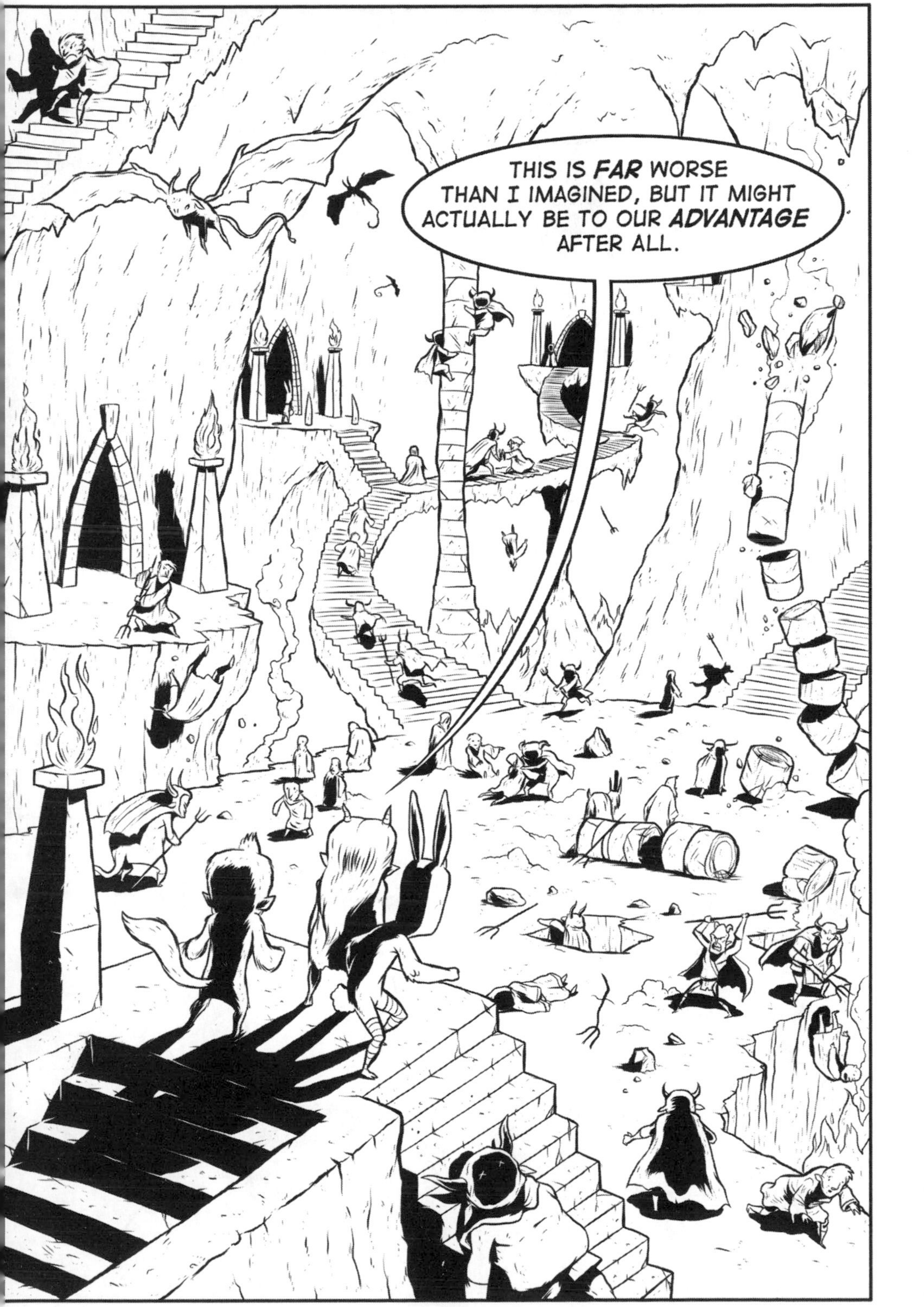
THIS IS FAR WORSE THAN I IMAGINED, BUT IT MIGHT ACTUALLY BE TO OUR ADVANTAGE AFTER ALL.

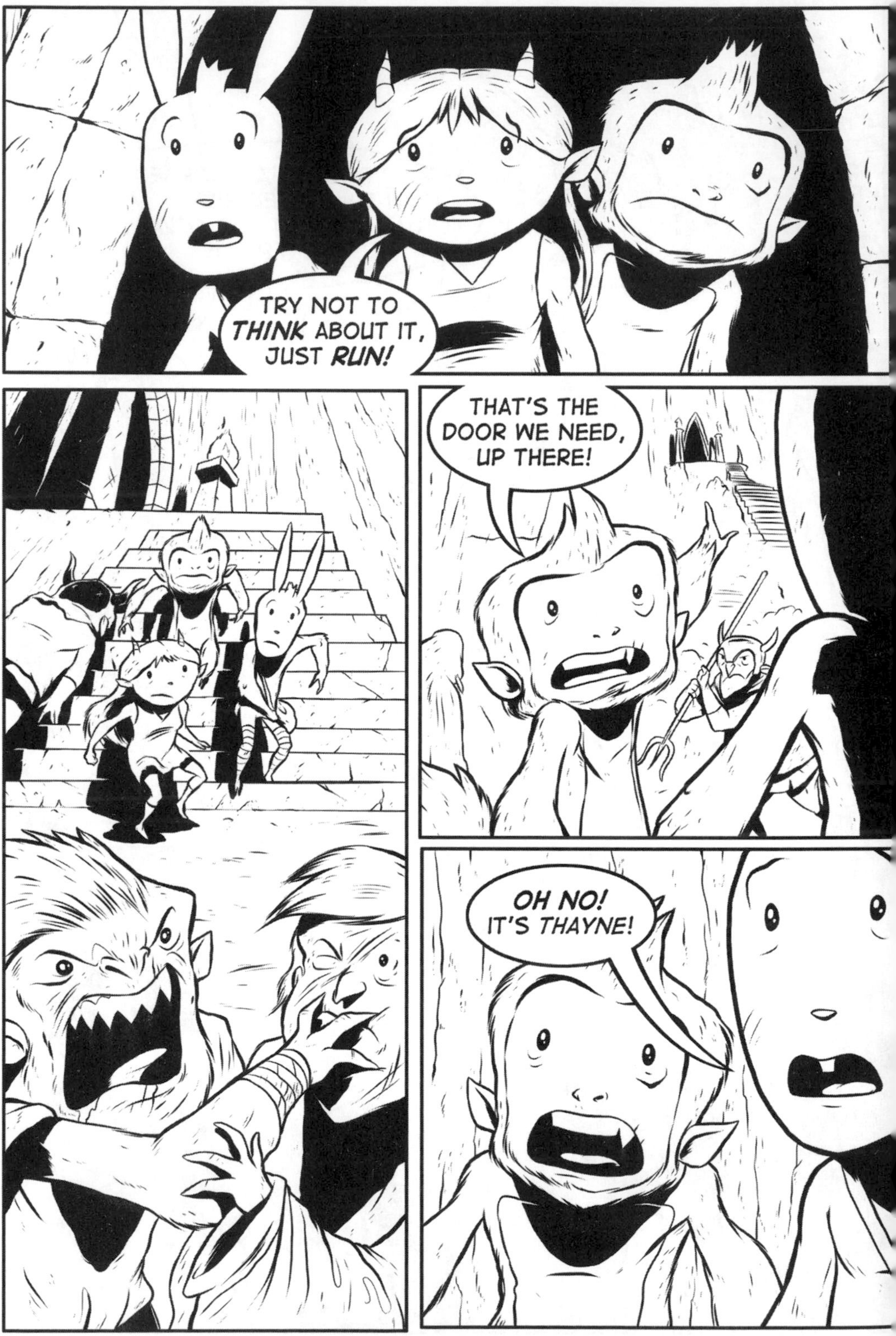
TRY NOT TO THINK ABOUT IT, JUST RUN!
THAT'S THE DOOR WE NEED, UP THERE!
OH NO! IT'S THAYNE!

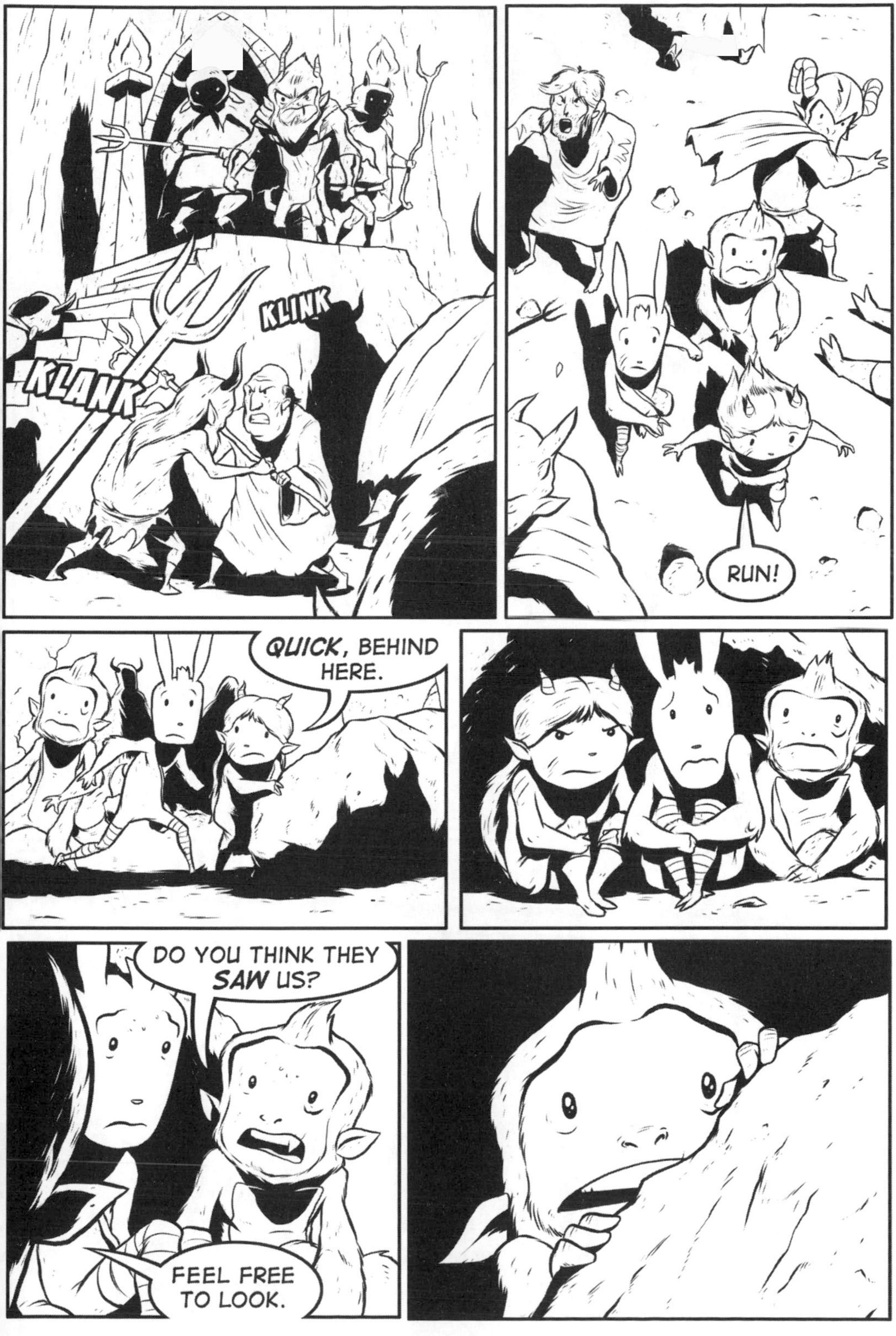
KLINK
KLANK
RUN!
QUICK, BEHIND HERE.
DO YOU THINK THEY SAW US?
FEEL FREE TO LOOK.

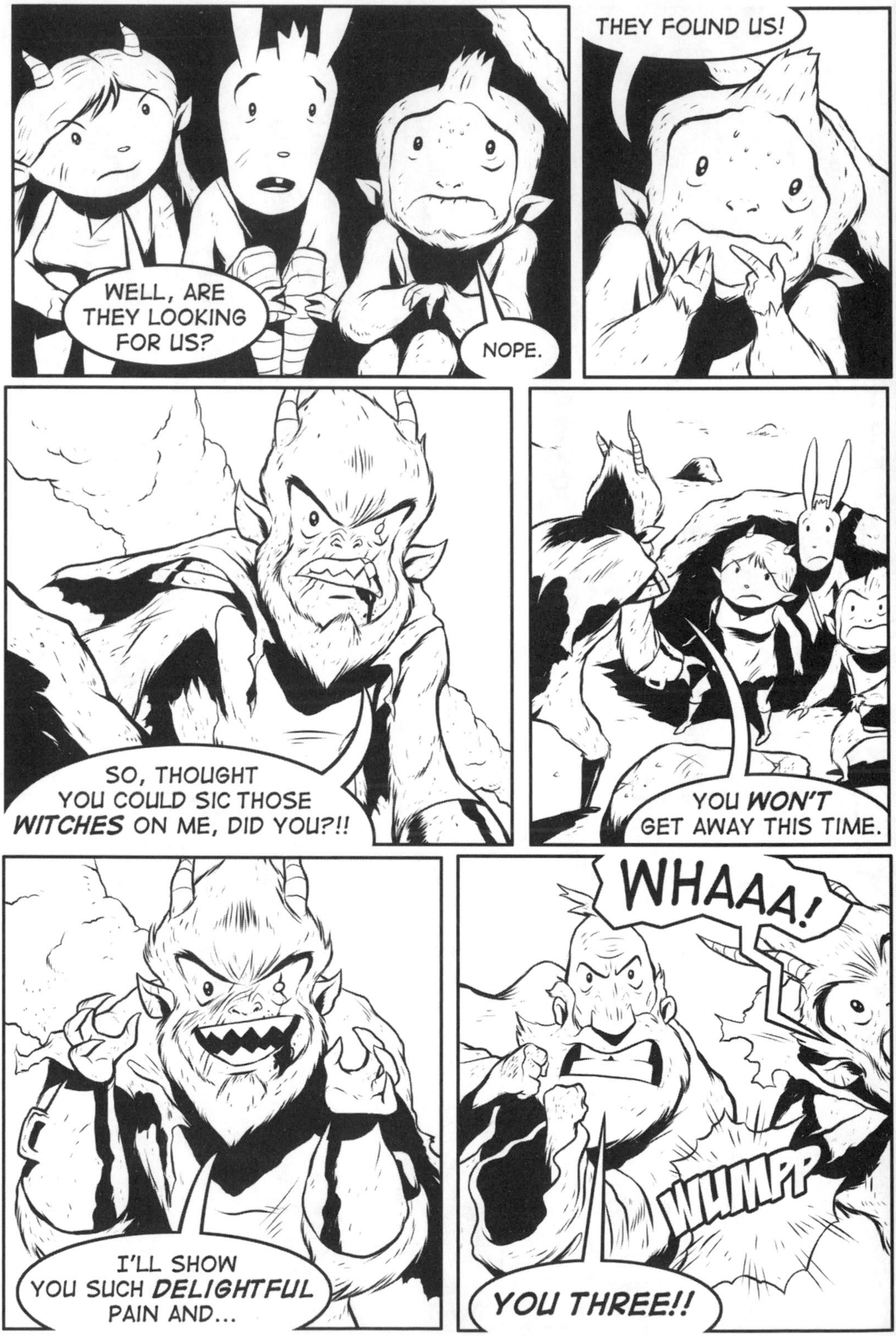
WELL, ARE THEY LOOKING FOR US?
NOPE.
THEY FOUND US!
SO, THOUGHT YOU COULD SIC THOSE *WITCHES* ON ME, DID YOU?!!
YOU *WON'T* GET AWAY THIS TIME.
I'LL SHOW YOU SUCH *DELIGHTFUL* PAIN AND...
WHAAA!
WUMPP
YOU THREE!!

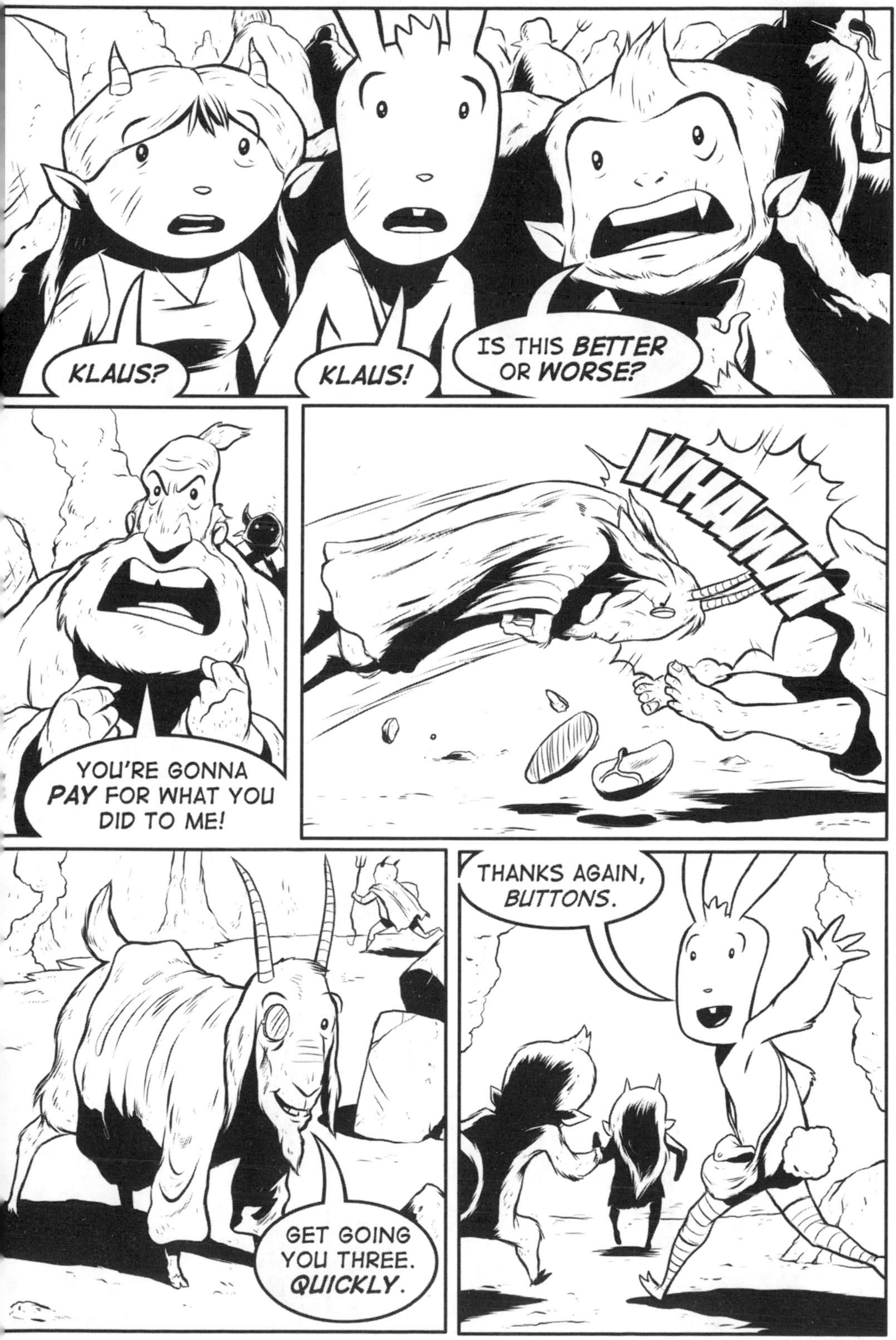
KLAUS?
KLAUS!
IS THIS BETTER OR WORSE?
YOU'RE GONNA PAY FOR WHAT YOU DID TO ME!
WHAM!
GET GOING YOU THREE. QUICKLY.
THANKS AGAIN, BUTTONS.

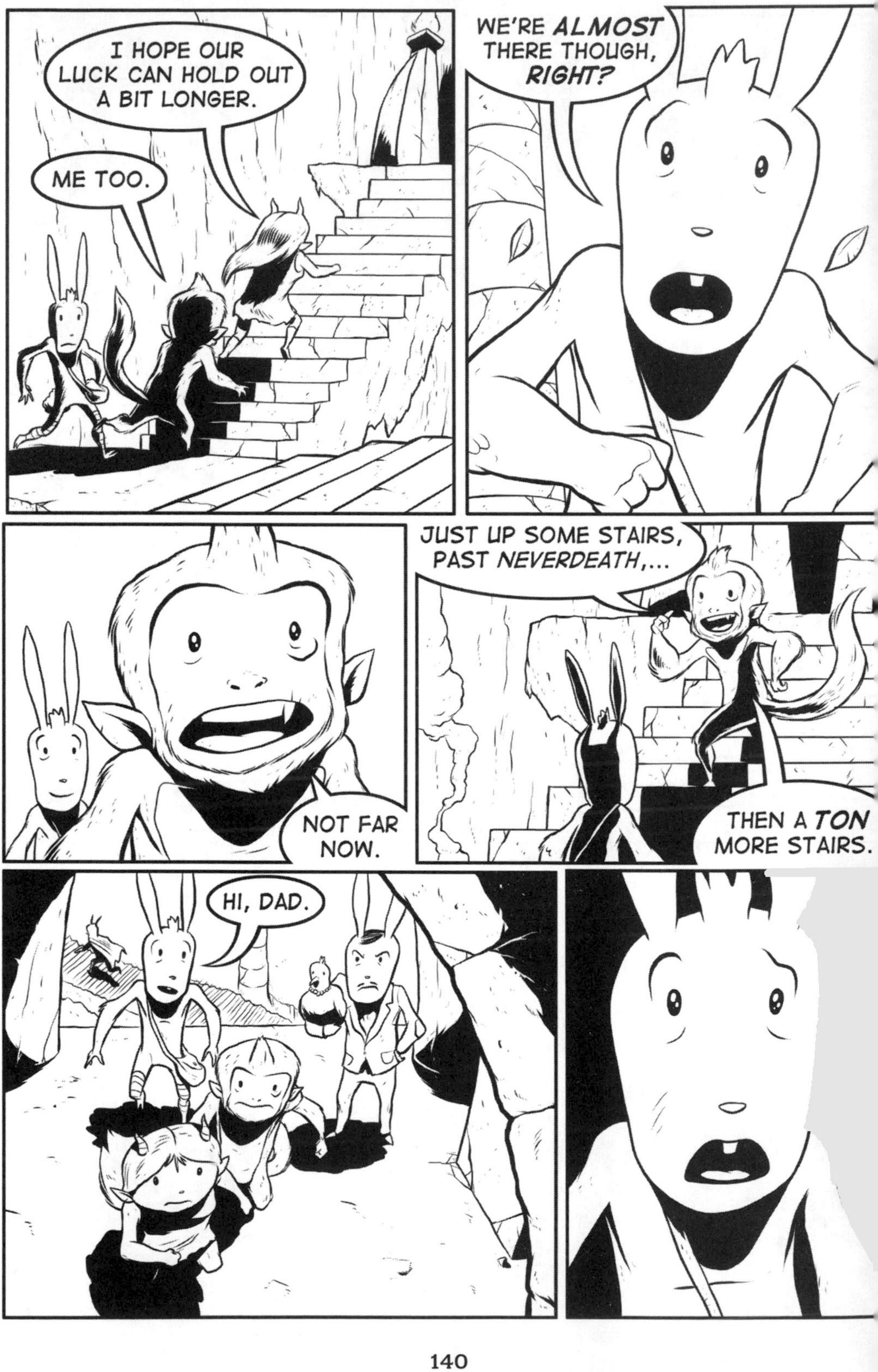

I HOPE OUR LUCK CAN HOLD OUT A BIT LONGER.
ME TOO.
WE'RE *ALMOST* THERE THOUGH, *RIGHT?*
NOT FAR NOW.
JUST UP SOME STAIRS, PAST *NEVERDEATH*,...
THEN A *TON* MORE STAIRS.
HI, DAD.

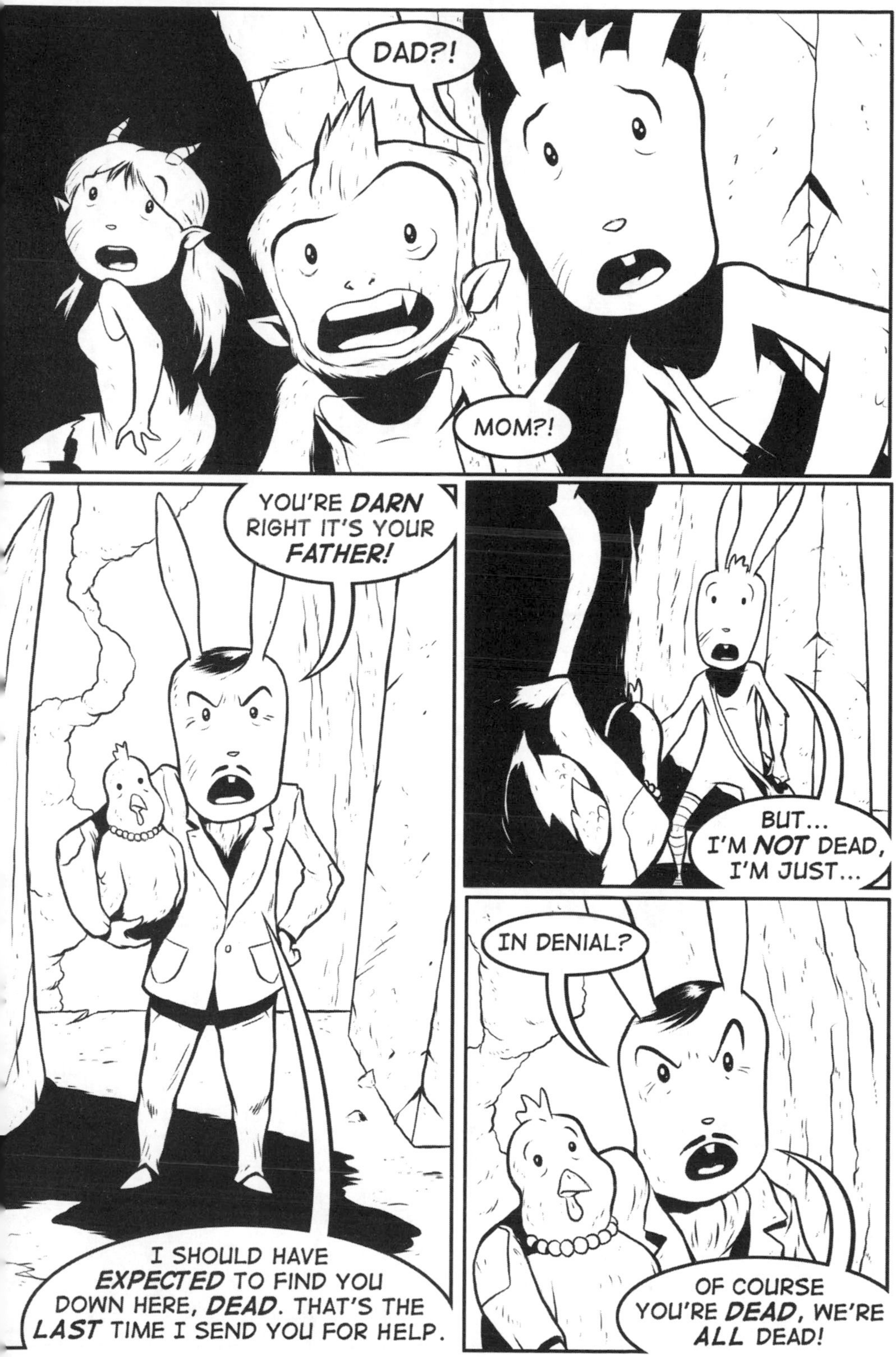
DAD?!
MOM?!
YOU'RE DARN RIGHT IT'S YOUR FATHER!
I SHOULD HAVE EXPECTED TO FIND YOU DOWN HERE, DEAD. THAT'S THE LAST TIME I SEND YOU FOR HELP.
BUT... I'M NOT DEAD, I'M JUST...
IN DENIAL?
OF COURSE YOU'RE DEAD, WE'RE ALL DEAD!

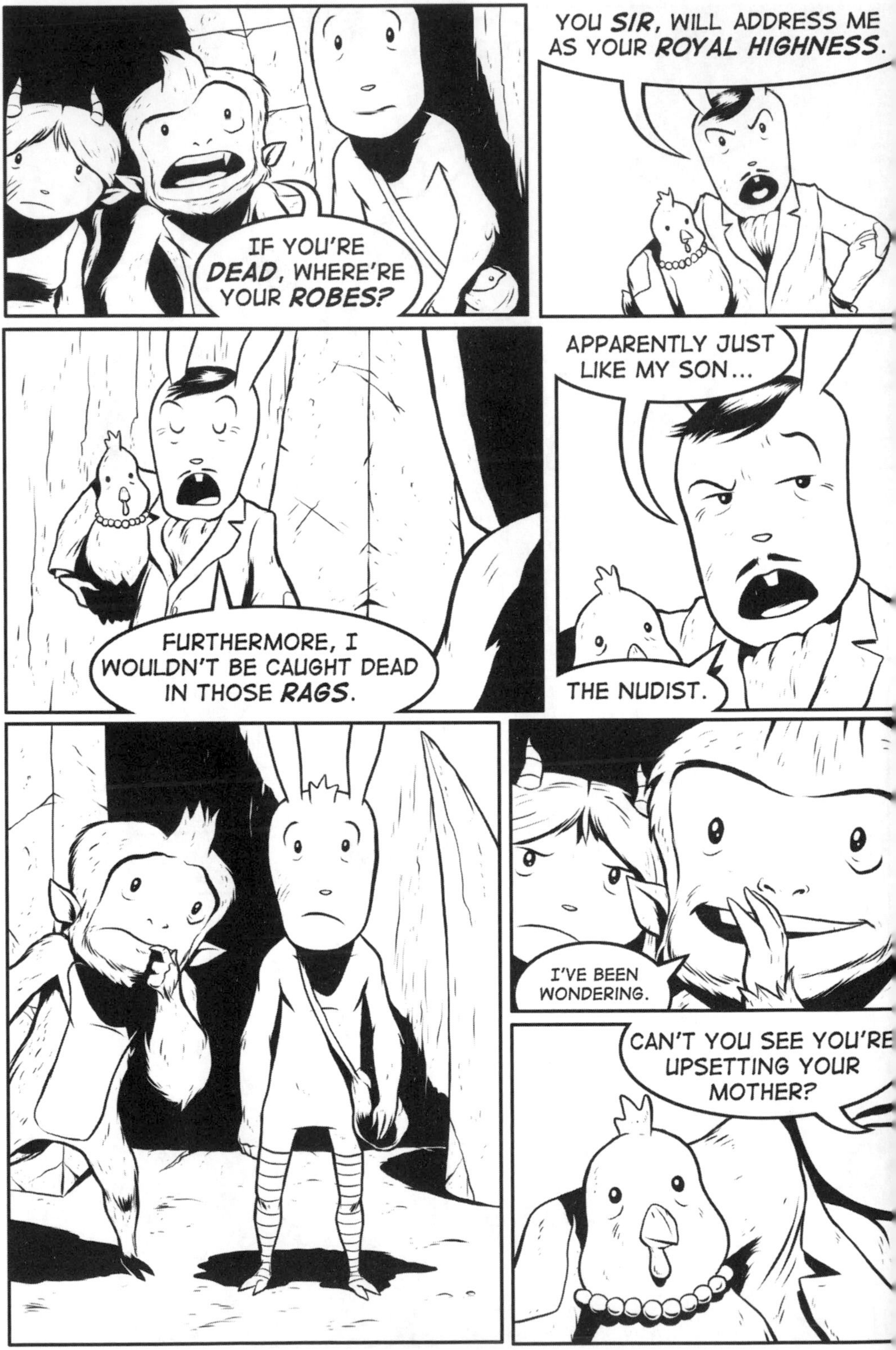
IF YOU'RE DEAD, WHERE'RE YOUR ROBES?
YOU SIR, WILL ADDRESS ME AS YOUR ROYAL HIGHNESS.
FURTHERMORE, I WOULDN'T BE CAUGHT DEAD IN THOSE RAGS.
APPARENTLY JUST LIKE MY SON...
THE NUDIST.
I'VE BEEN WONDERING.
CAN'T YOU SEE YOU'RE UPSETTING YOUR MOTHER?

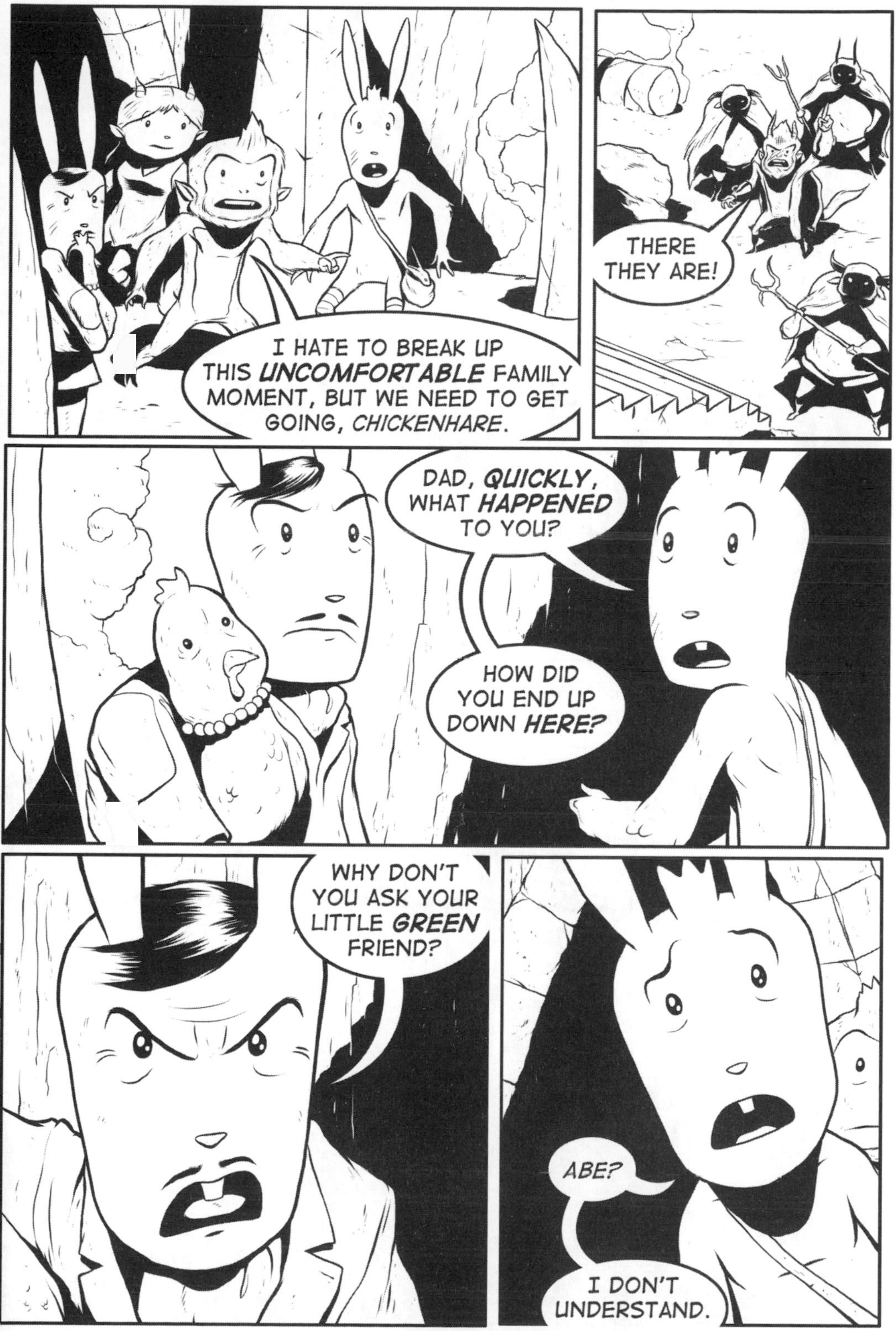
I HATE TO BREAK UP THIS *UNCOMFORTABLE* FAMILY MOMENT, BUT WE NEED TO GET GOING, *CHICKENHARE*.
THERE THEY ARE!
DAD, *QUICKLY*, WHAT *HAPPENED* TO YOU?
HOW DID YOU END UP DOWN *HERE?*
WHY DON'T YOU ASK YOUR LITTLE *GREEN* FRIEND?
ABE?
I DON'T UNDERSTAND.

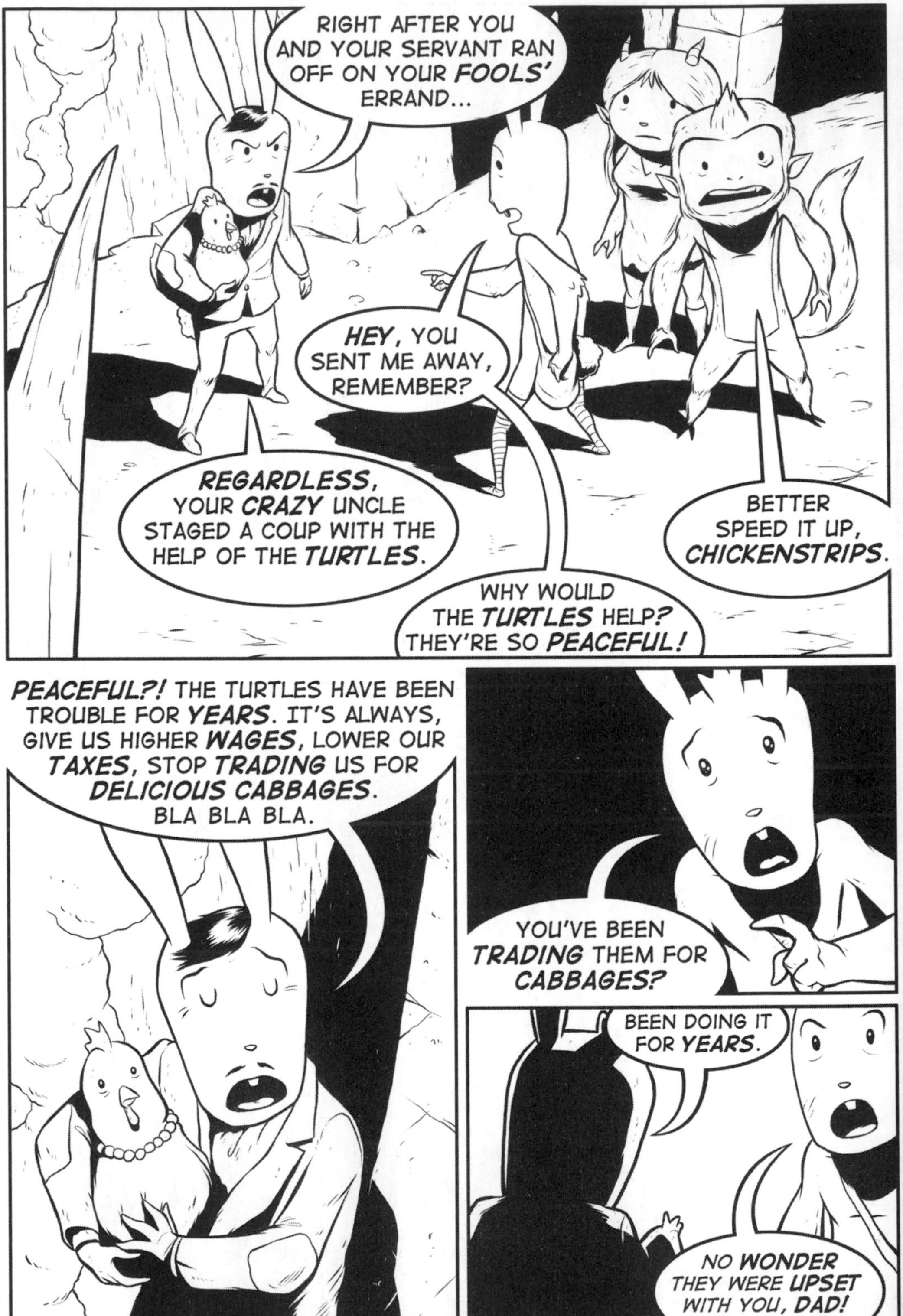
RIGHT AFTER YOU AND YOUR SERVANT RAN OFF ON YOUR FOOLS' ERRAND...
HEY, YOU SENT ME AWAY, REMEMBER?
REGARDLESS, YOUR CRAZY UNCLE STAGED A COUP WITH THE HELP OF THE TURTLES.
WHY WOULD THE TURTLES HELP? THEY'RE SO PEACEFUL!
BETTER SPEED IT UP, CHICKENSTRIPS.
PEACEFUL?! THE TURTLES HAVE BEEN TROUBLE FOR YEARS. IT'S ALWAYS, GIVE US HIGHER WAGES, LOWER OUR TAXES, STOP TRADING US FOR DELICIOUS CABBAGES. BLA BLA BLA.
YOU'VE BEEN TRADING THEM FOR CABBAGES?
BEEN DOING IT FOR YEARS.
NO WONDER THEY WERE UPSET WITH YOU, DAD!

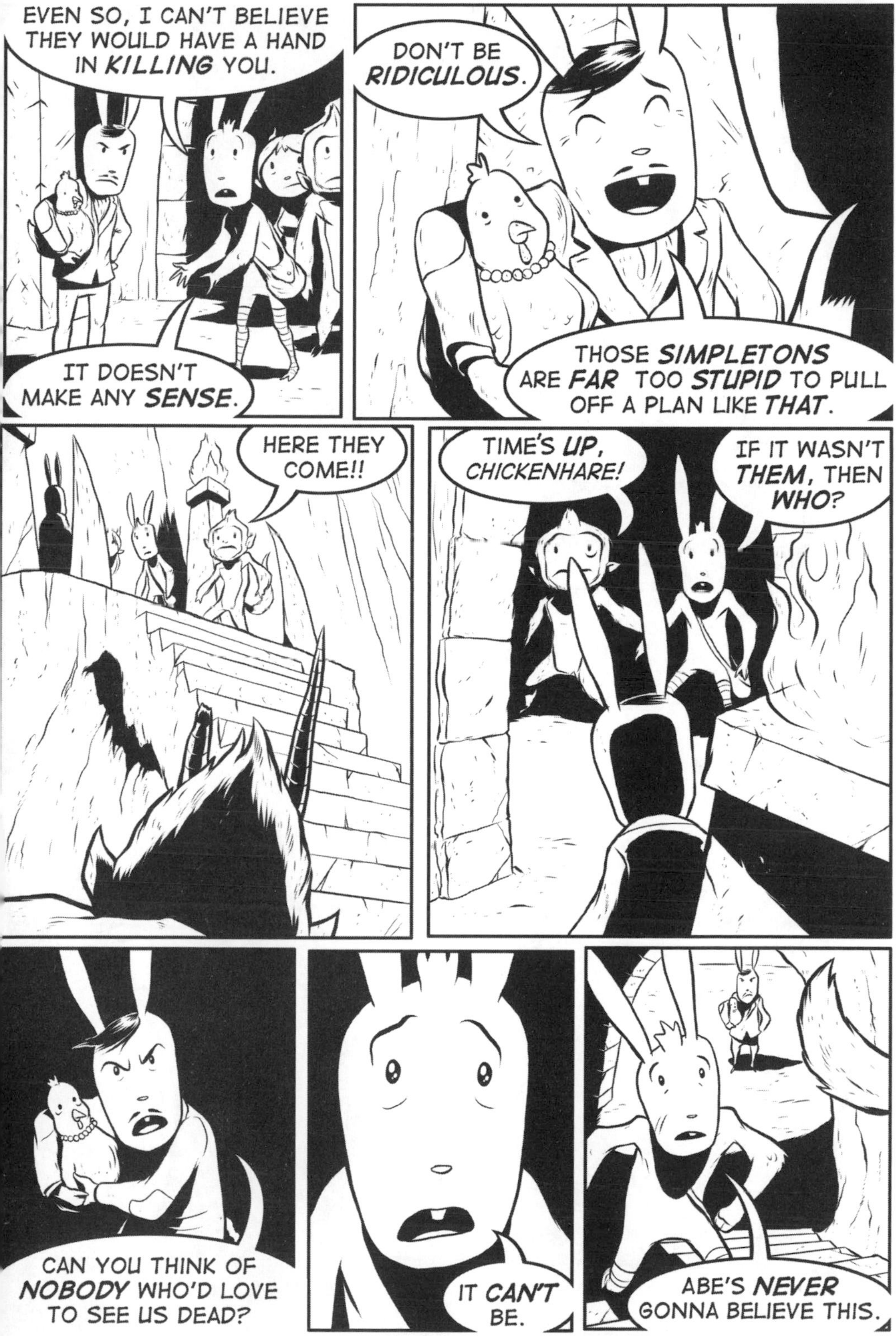
EVEN SO, I CAN'T BELIEVE THEY WOULD HAVE A HAND IN *KILLING* YOU.
IT DOESN'T MAKE ANY *SENSE*.
DON'T BE *RIDICULOUS*.
THOSE *SIMPLETONS* ARE *FAR* TOO *STUPID* TO PULL OFF A PLAN LIKE *THAT*.
HERE THEY COME!!
TIME'S *UP*, CHICKENHARE!
IF IT WASN'T *THEM*, THEN *WHO*?
CAN YOU THINK OF *NOBODY* WHO'D LOVE TO SEE US DEAD?
IT *CAN'T* BE.
ABE'S *NEVER* GONNA BELIEVE THIS.

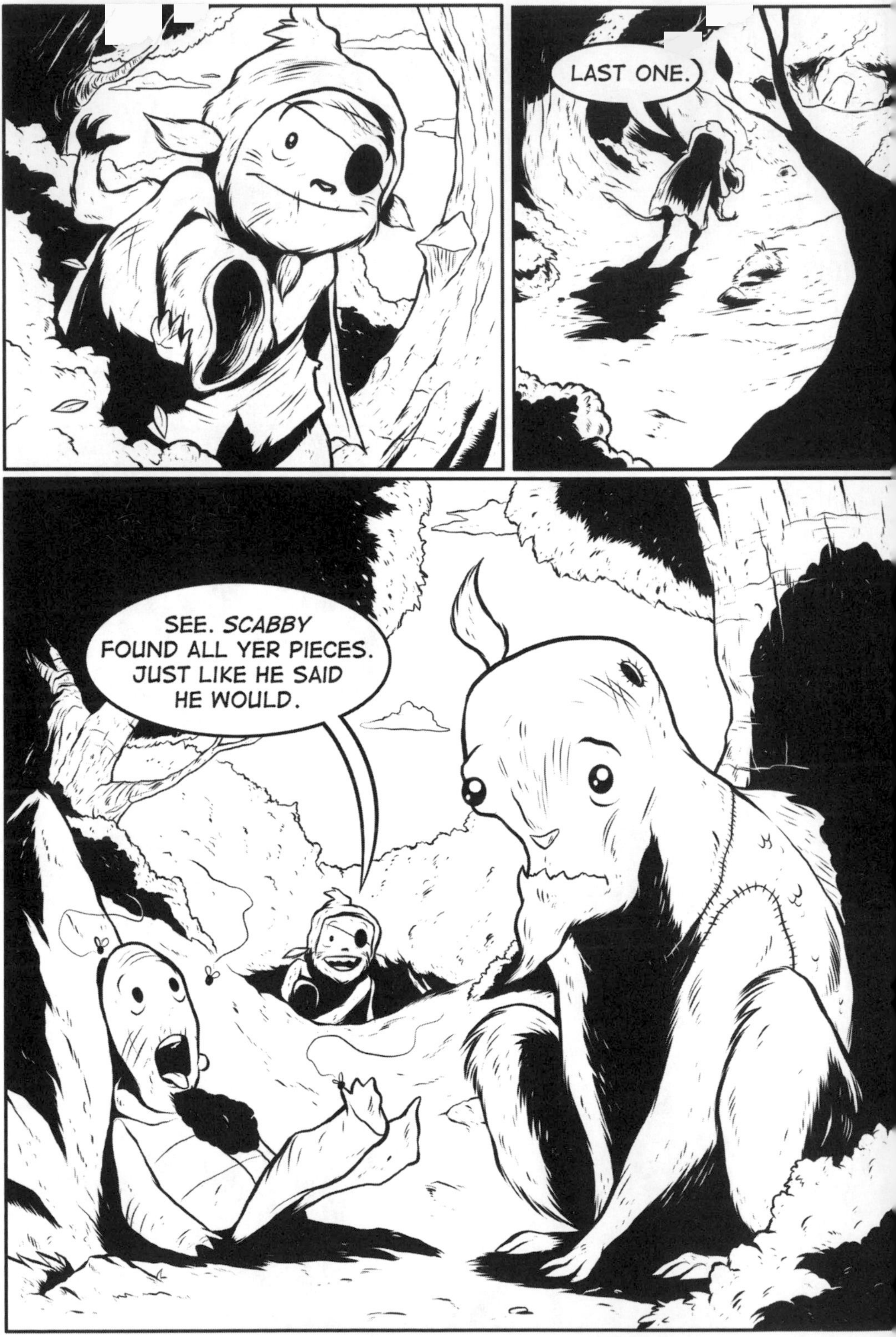
LAST ONE.
SEE. *SCABBY* FOUND ALL YER PIECES. JUST LIKE HE SAID HE WOULD.

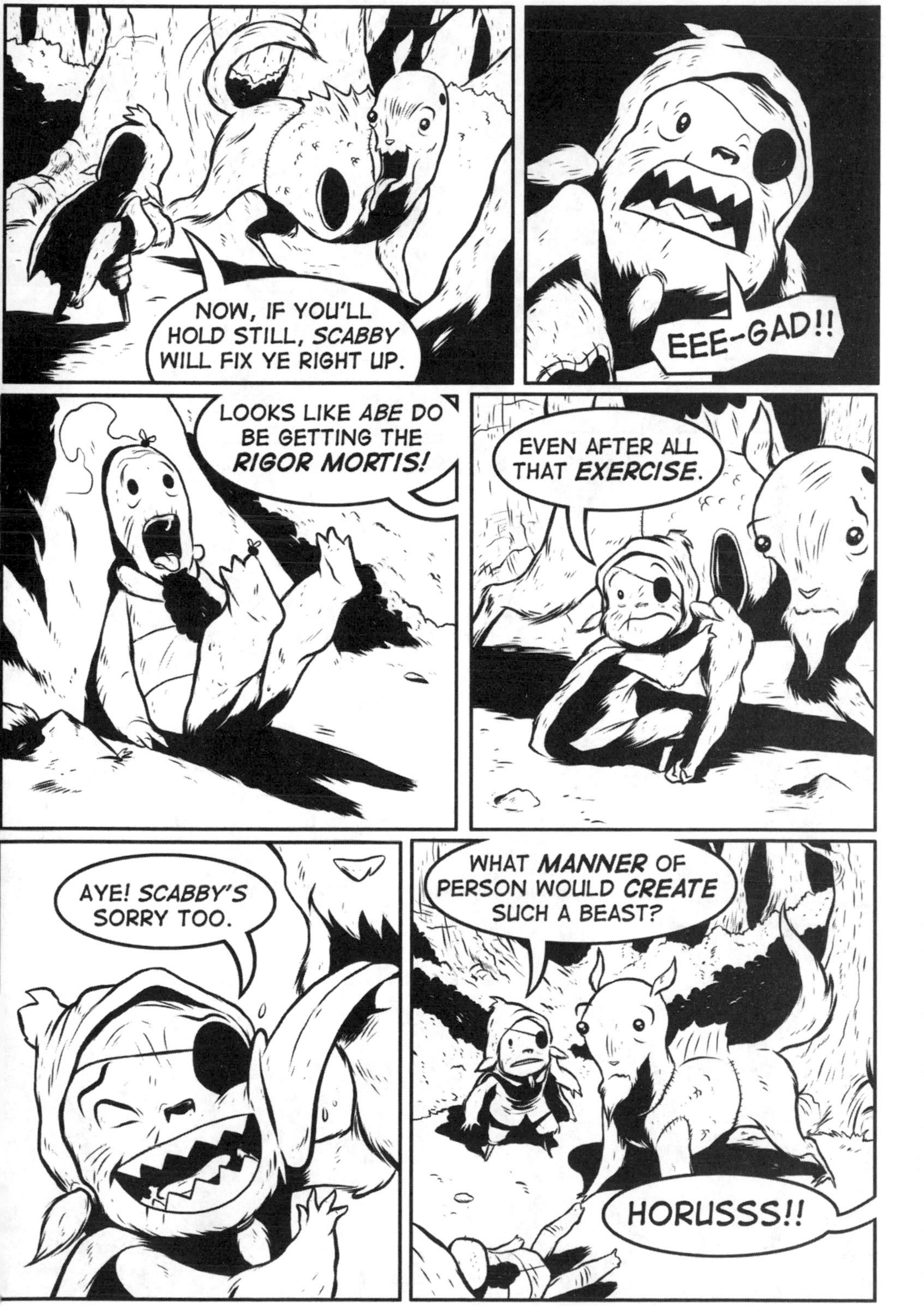
NOW, IF YOU'LL HOLD STILL, SCABBY WILL FIX YE RIGHT UP.
EEE-GAD!!
LOOKS LIKE ABE DO BE GETTING THE RIGOR MORTIS!
EVEN AFTER ALL THAT EXERCISE.
AYE! SCABBY'S SORRY TOO.
WHAT MANNER OF PERSON WOULD CREATE SUCH A BEAST?
HORUSSS!!

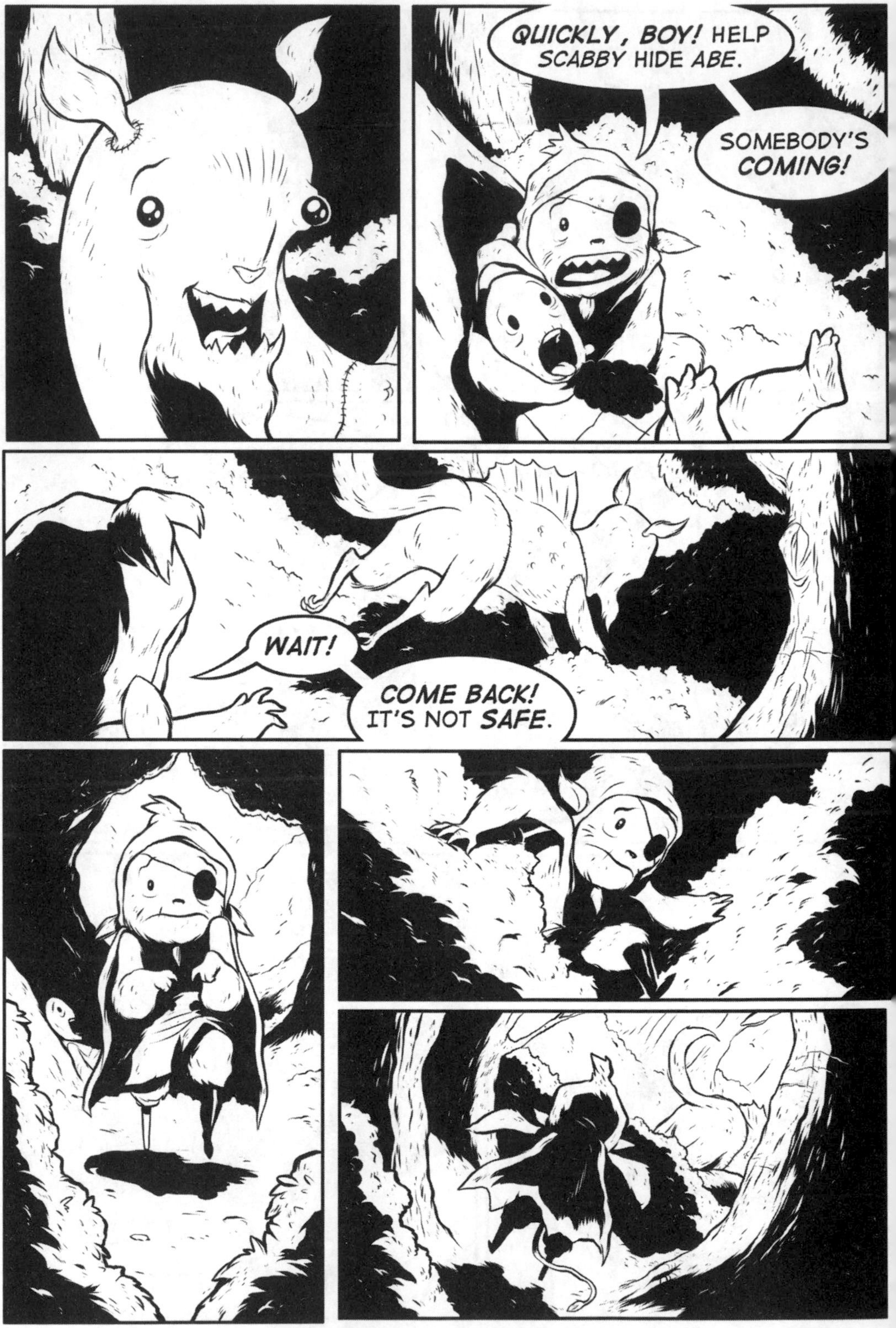
QUICKLY, BOY! HELP SCABBY HIDE ABE.
SOMEBODY'S COMING!
WAIT!
COME BACK! IT'S NOT SAFE.

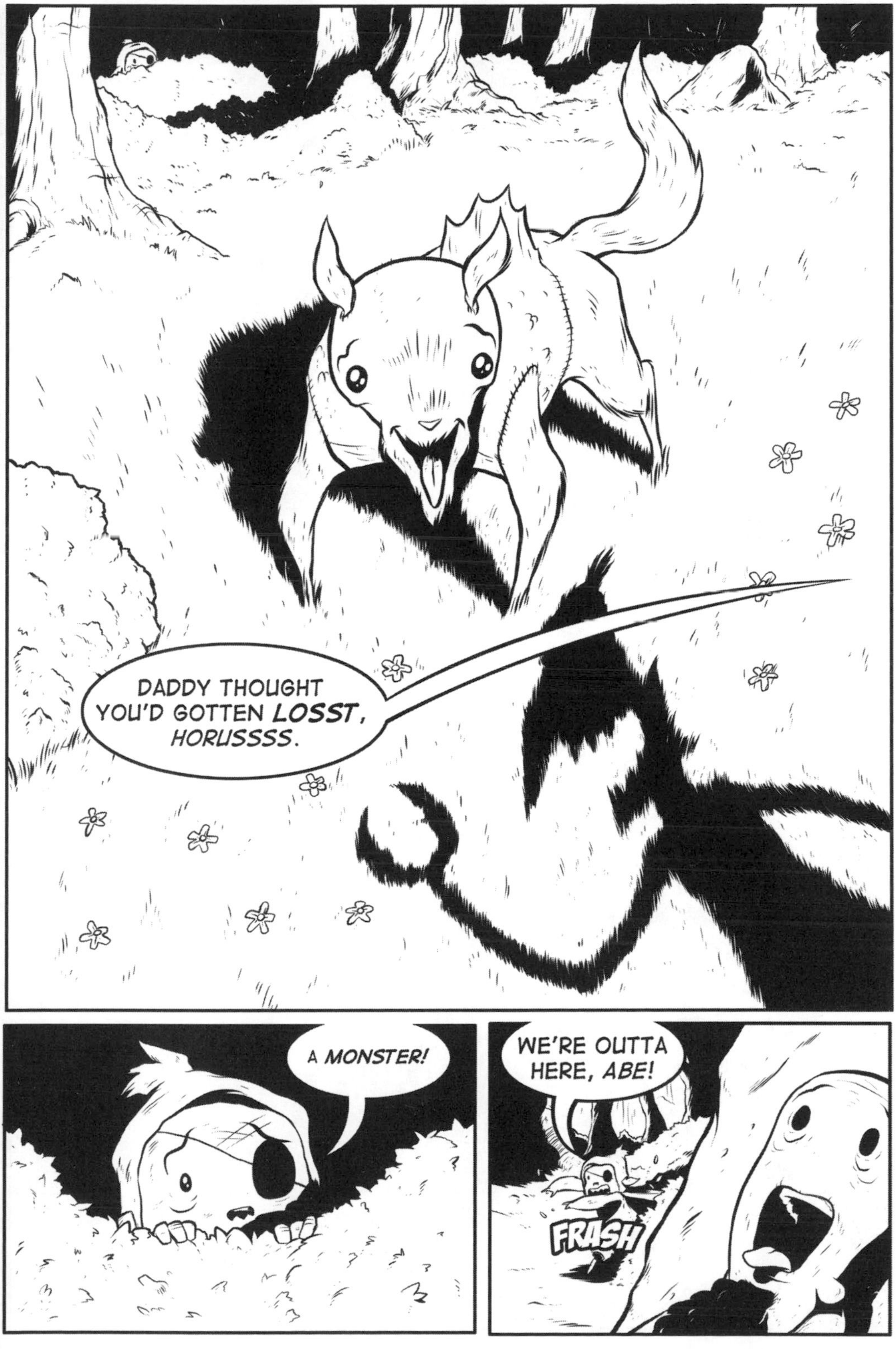
DADDY THOUGHT YOU'D GOTTEN *LOSST*, *HORUSSSS*.
A *MONSTER!*
WE'RE OUTTA HERE, *ABE!*
FRASH

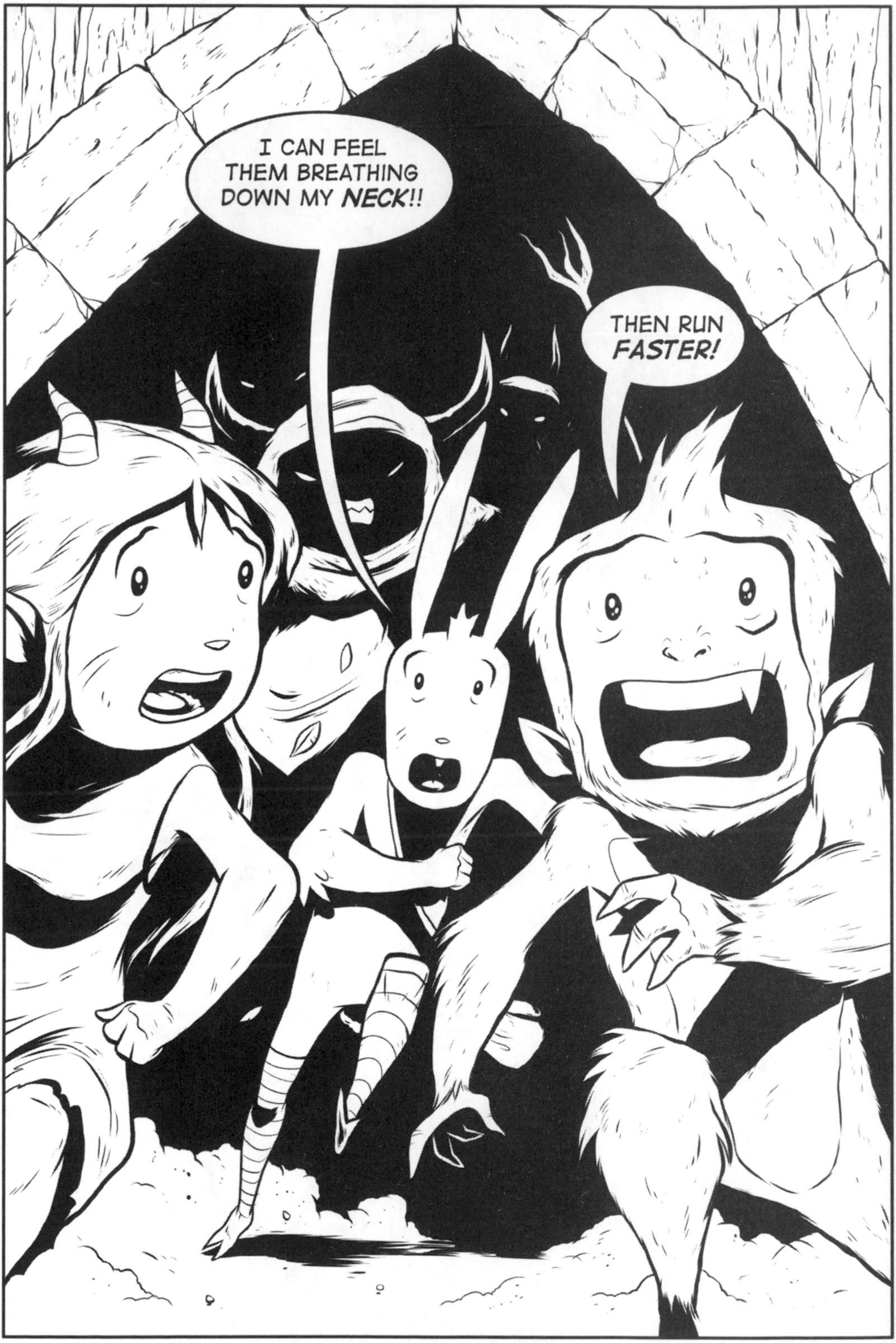
I CAN FEEL THEM BREATHING DOWN MY NECK!!
THEN RUN FASTER!

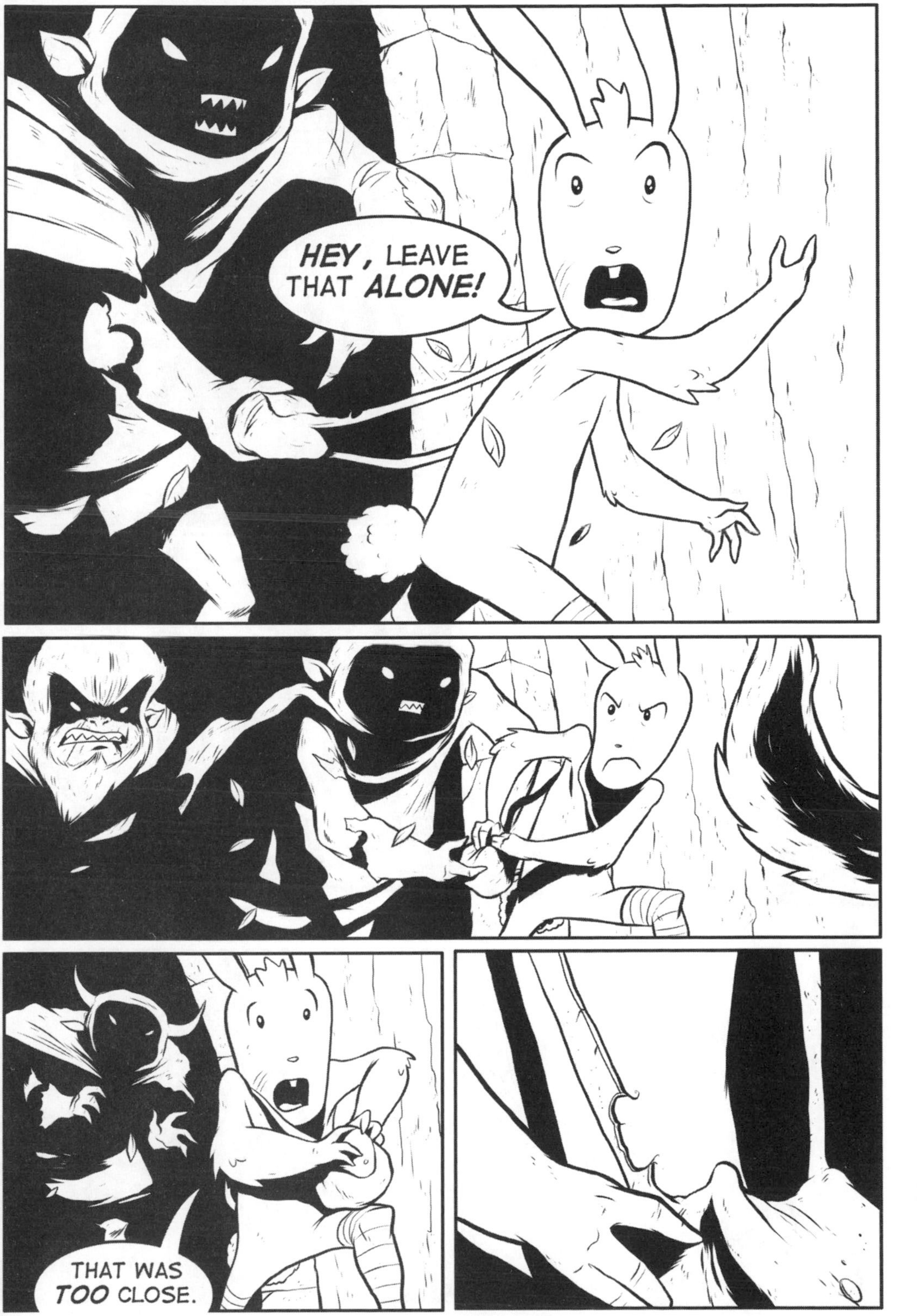
HEY, LEAVE THAT ALONE!
THAT WAS TOO CLOSE.

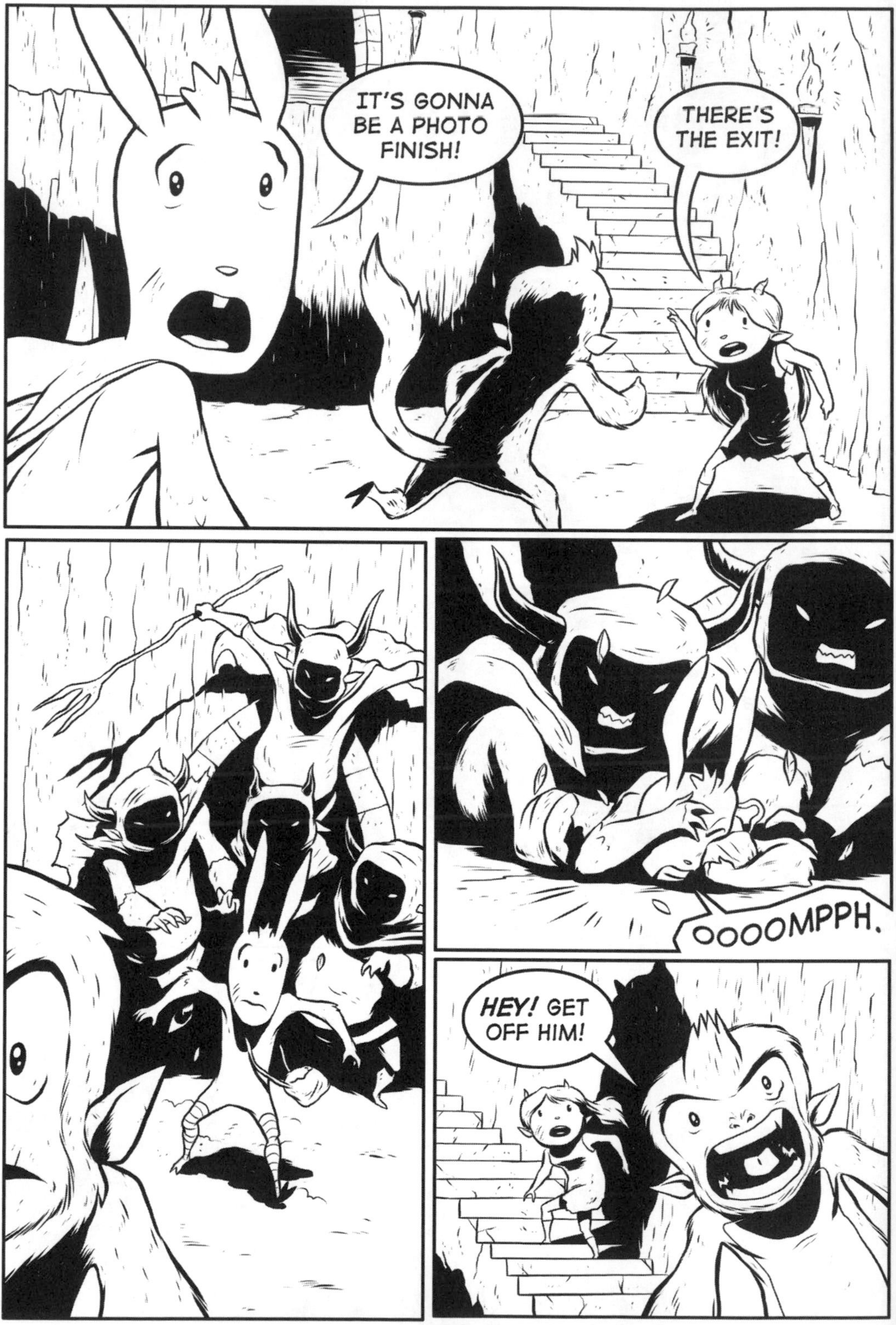
IT'S GONNA BE A PHOTO FINISH!
THERE'S THE EXIT!
OOOOMPPH.
HEY! GET OFF HIM!

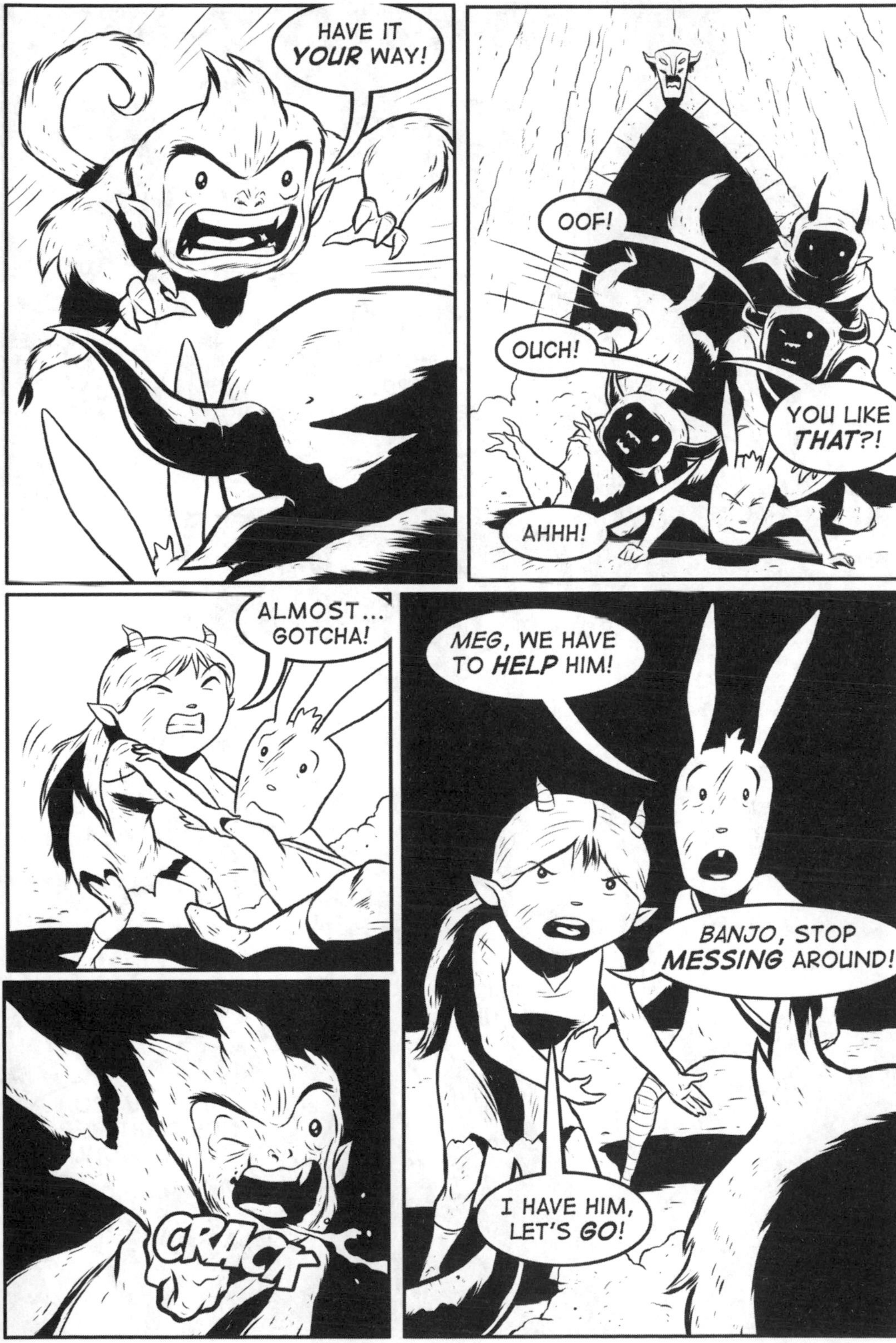
HAVE IT YOUR WAY!
OOF!
OUCH!
YOU LIKE THAT?!
AHHH!
ALMOST... GOTCHA!
MEG, WE HAVE TO HELP HIM!
BANJO, STOP MESSING AROUND!
CRACK
I HAVE HIM, LET'S GO!

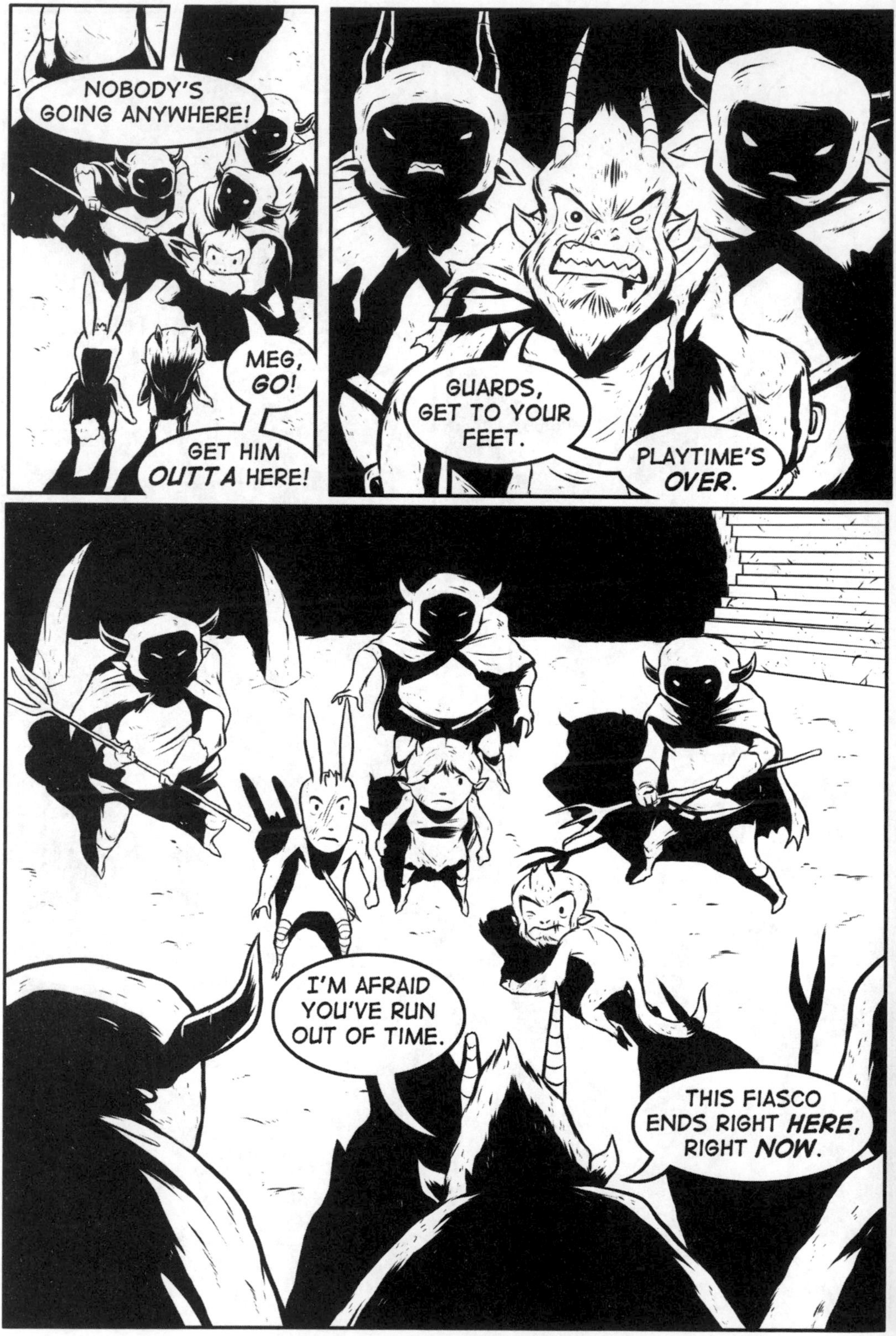
NOBODY'S GOING ANYWHERE!
MEG, GO!
GET HIM OUTTA HERE!
GUARDS, GET TO YOUR FEET.
PLAYTIME'S OVER.
I'M AFRAID YOU'VE RUN OUT OF TIME.
THIS FIASCO ENDS RIGHT HERE, RIGHT NOW.

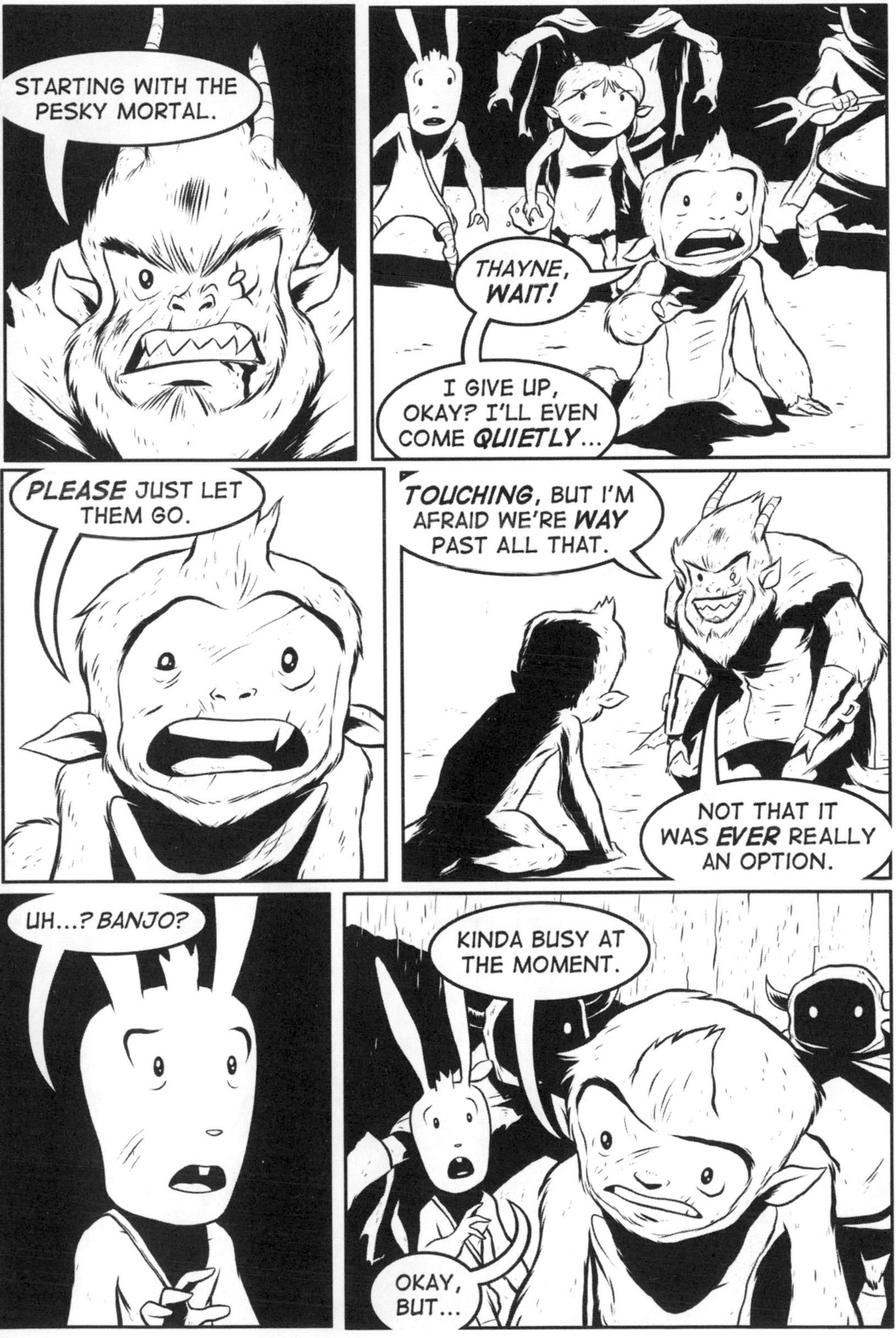
STARTING WITH THE PESKY MORTAL.
THAYNE, WAIT!
I GIVE UP, OKAY? I'LL EVEN COME QUIETLY...
PLEASE JUST LET THEM GO.
TOUCHING, BUT I'M AFRAID WE'RE WAY PAST ALL THAT.
NOT THAT IT WAS EVER REALLY AN OPTION.
UH...? BANJO?
KINDA BUSY AT THE MOMENT.
OKAY, BUT...

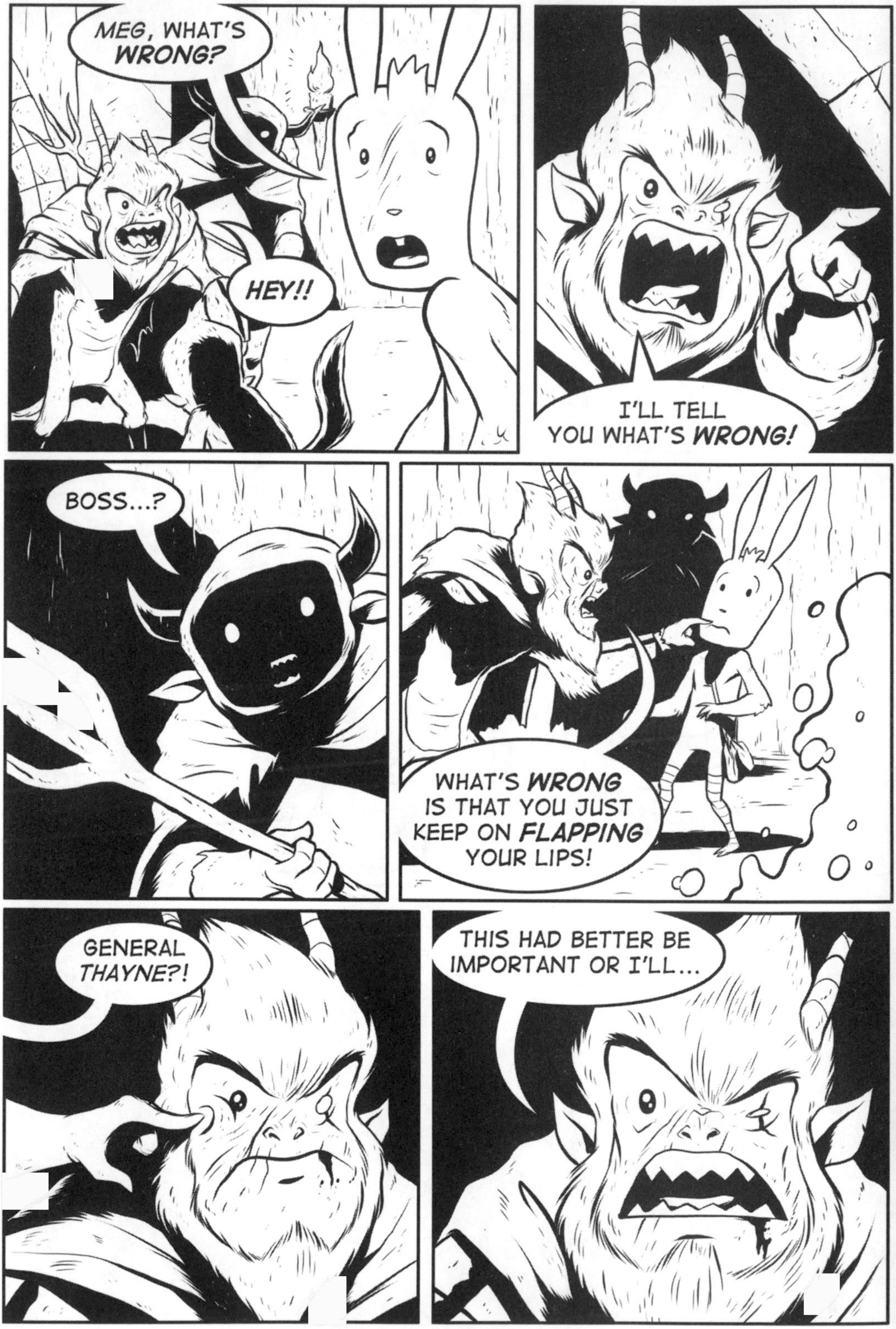
MEG, WHAT'S WRONG?
HEY!!
I'LL TELL YOU WHAT'S WRONG!
BOSS...?
WHAT'S WRONG IS THAT YOU JUST KEEP ON FLAPPING YOUR LIPS!
GENERAL THAYNE?!
THIS HAD BETTER BE IMPORTANT OR I'LL...

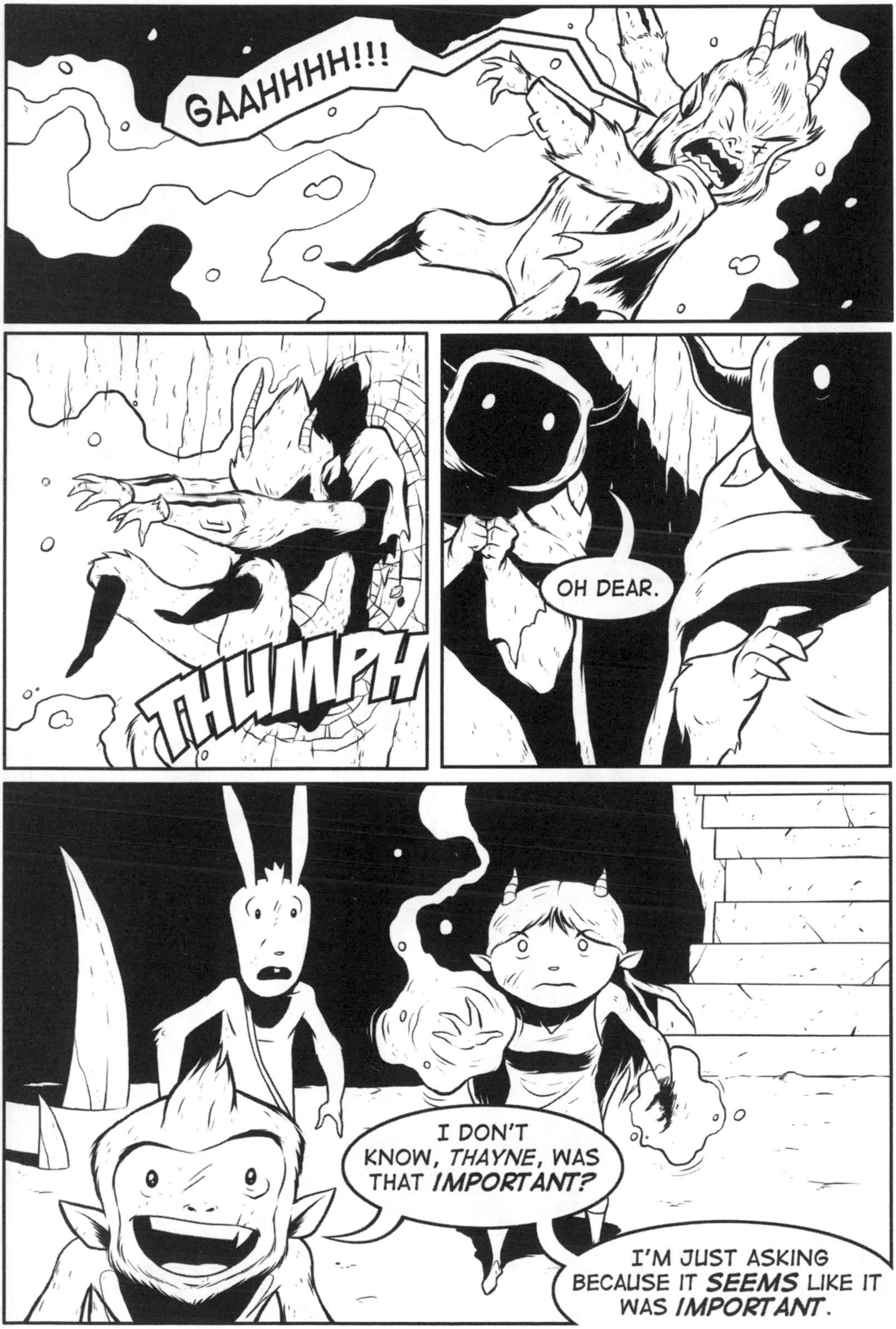
GAAHHHH!!!
THUMPH
OH DEAR.
I DON'T KNOW, *THAYNE*, WAS THAT ***IMPORTANT?***
I'M JUST ASKING BECAUSE IT ***SEEMS*** LIKE IT WAS ***IMPORTANT***.

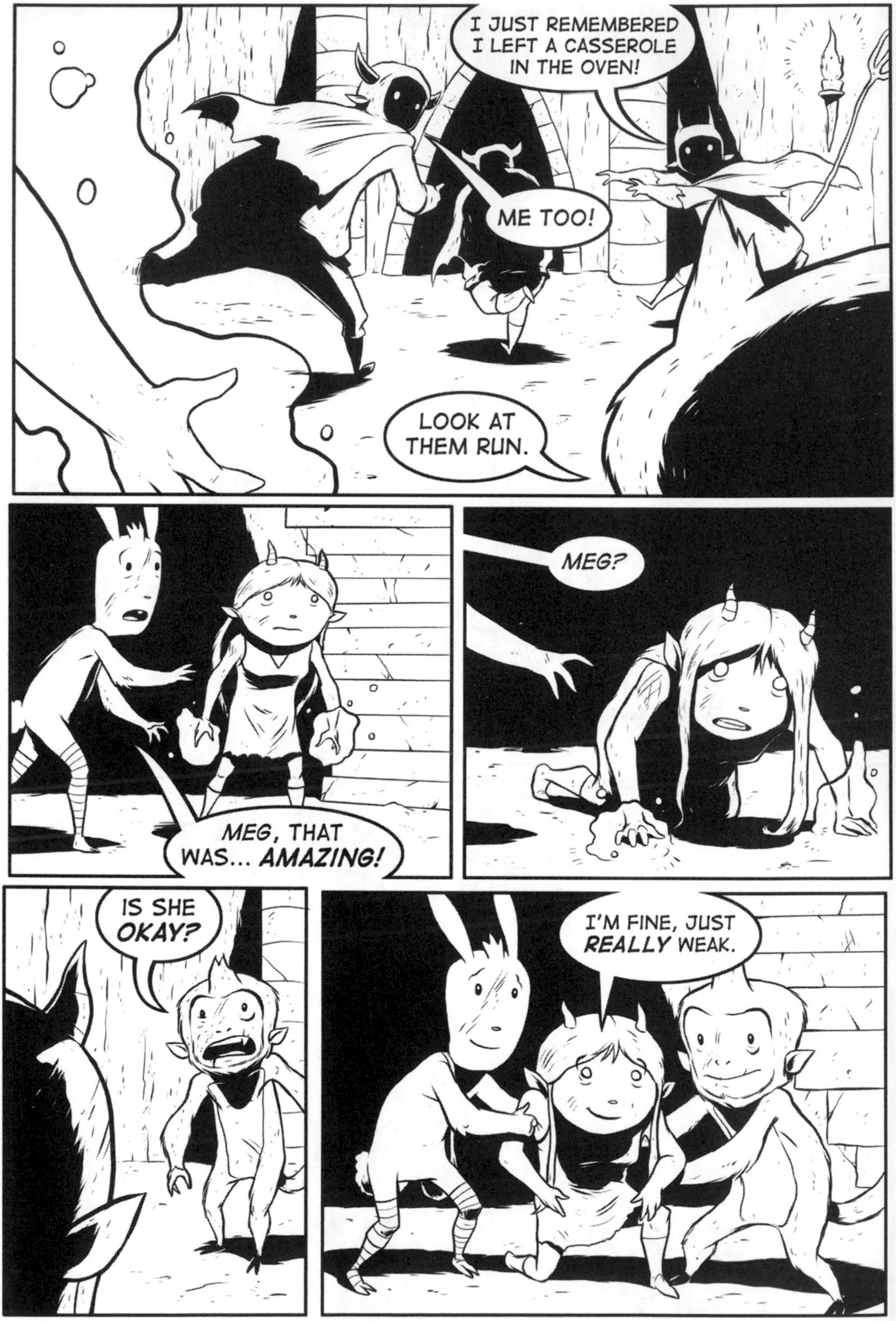
I JUST REMEMBERED I LEFT A CASSEROLE IN THE OVEN!
ME TOO!
LOOK AT THEM RUN.
MEG, THAT WAS... AMAZING!
MEG?
IS SHE OKAY?
I'M FINE, JUST REALLY WEAK.

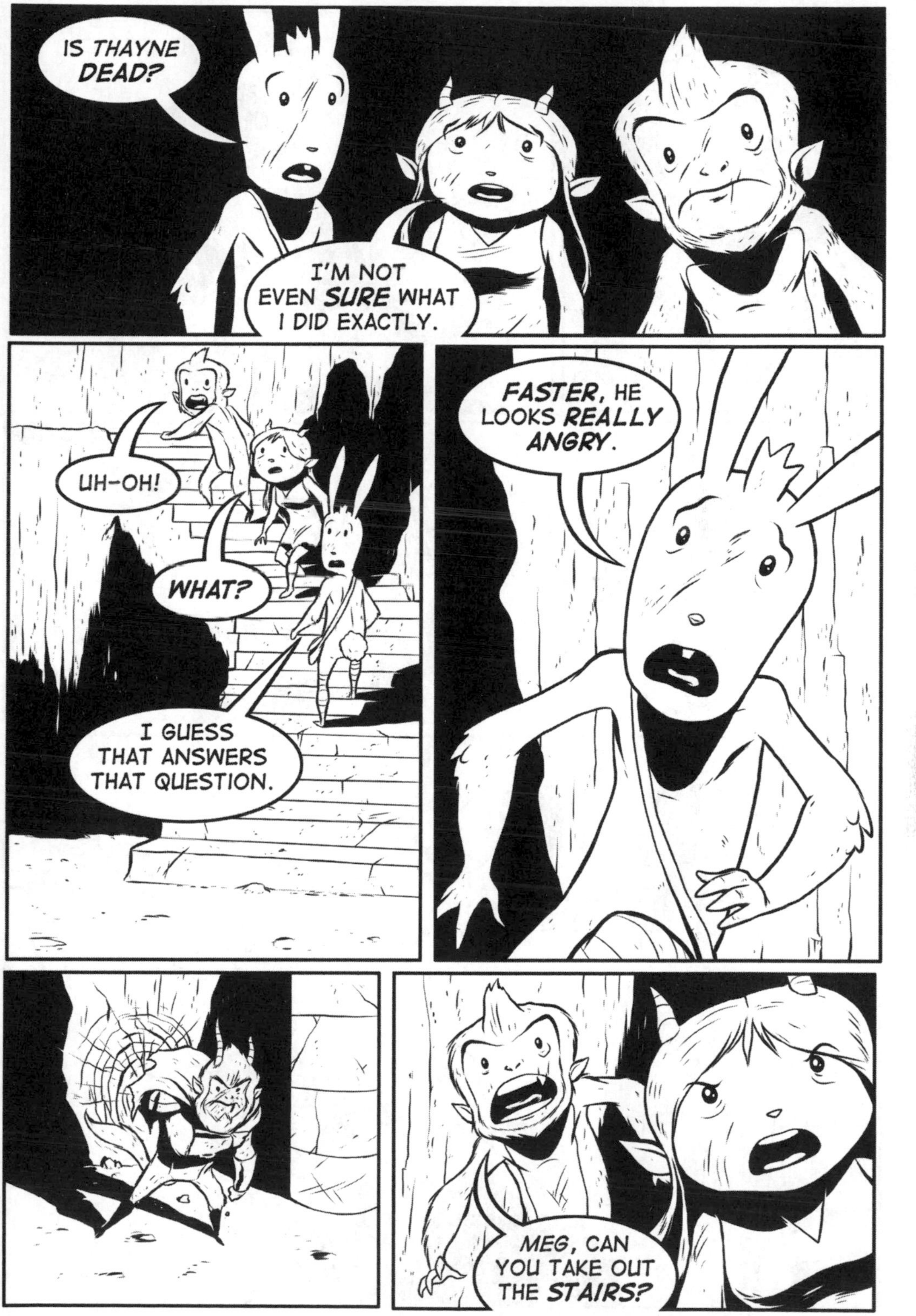
IS THAYNE DEAD?
I'M NOT EVEN SURE WHAT I DID EXACTLY.
UH-OH!
WHAT?
I GUESS THAT ANSWERS THAT QUESTION.
FASTER, HE LOOKS REALLY ANGRY.
MEG, CAN YOU TAKE OUT THE STAIRS?

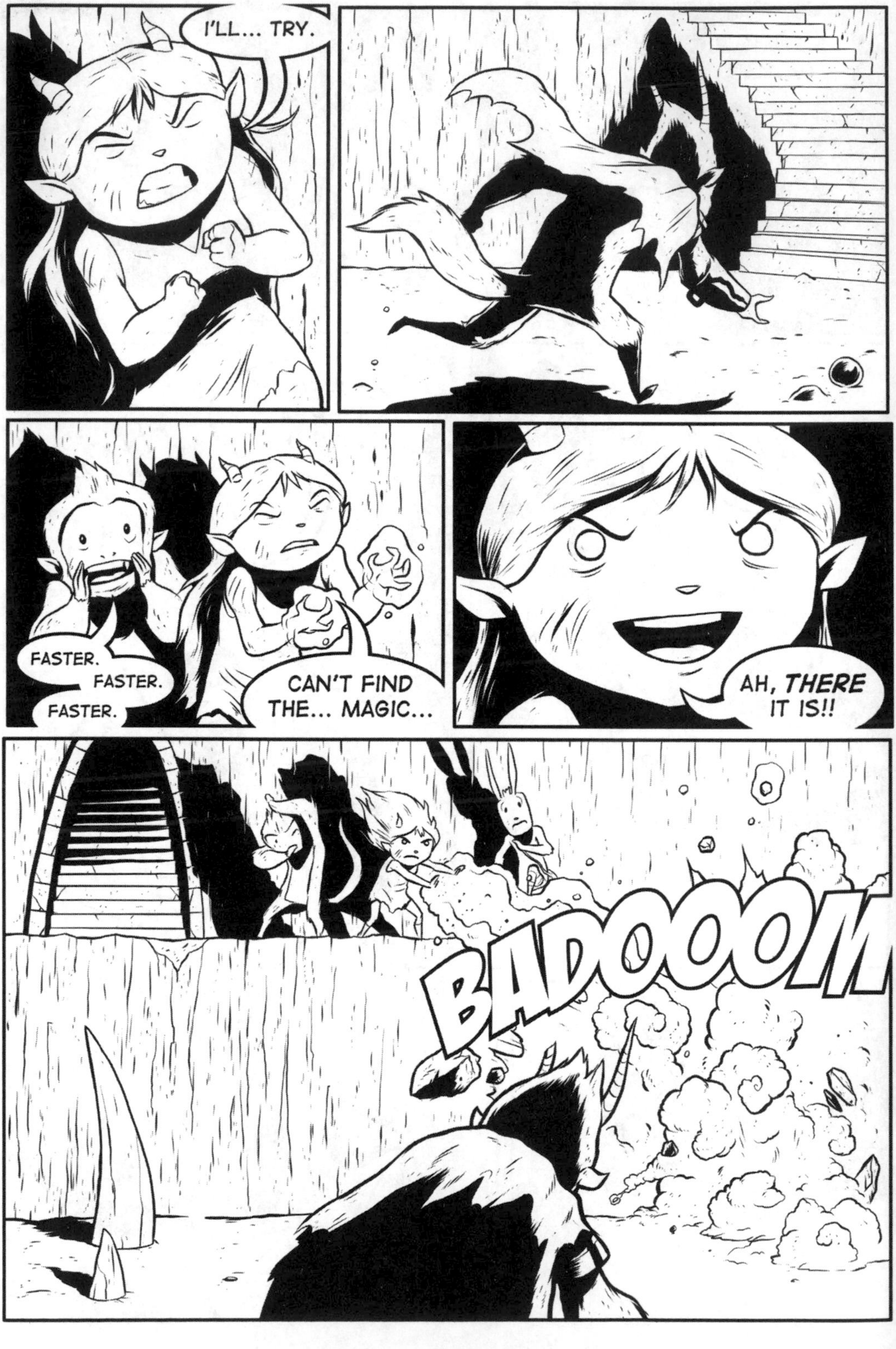
I'LL... TRY.
FASTER.
FASTER.
FASTER.
CAN'T FIND THE... MAGIC...
AH, *THERE* IT IS!!
BADOOOM

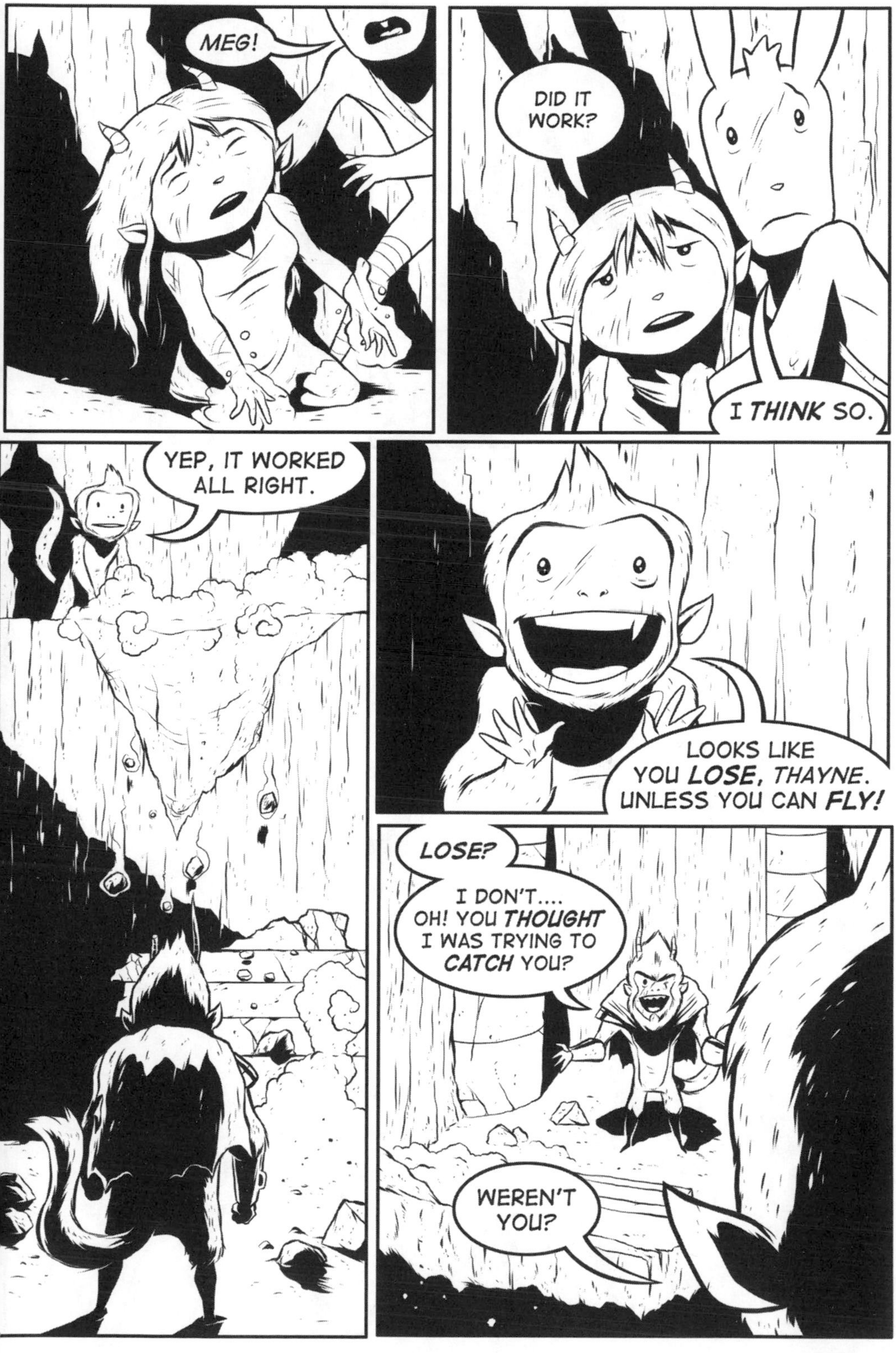

MEG!
DID IT WORK?
I THINK SO.
YEP, IT WORKED ALL RIGHT.
LOOKS LIKE YOU LOSE, THAYNE. UNLESS YOU CAN FLY!
LOSE?
I DON'T.... OH! YOU THOUGHT I WAS TRYING TO CATCH YOU?
WEREN'T YOU?

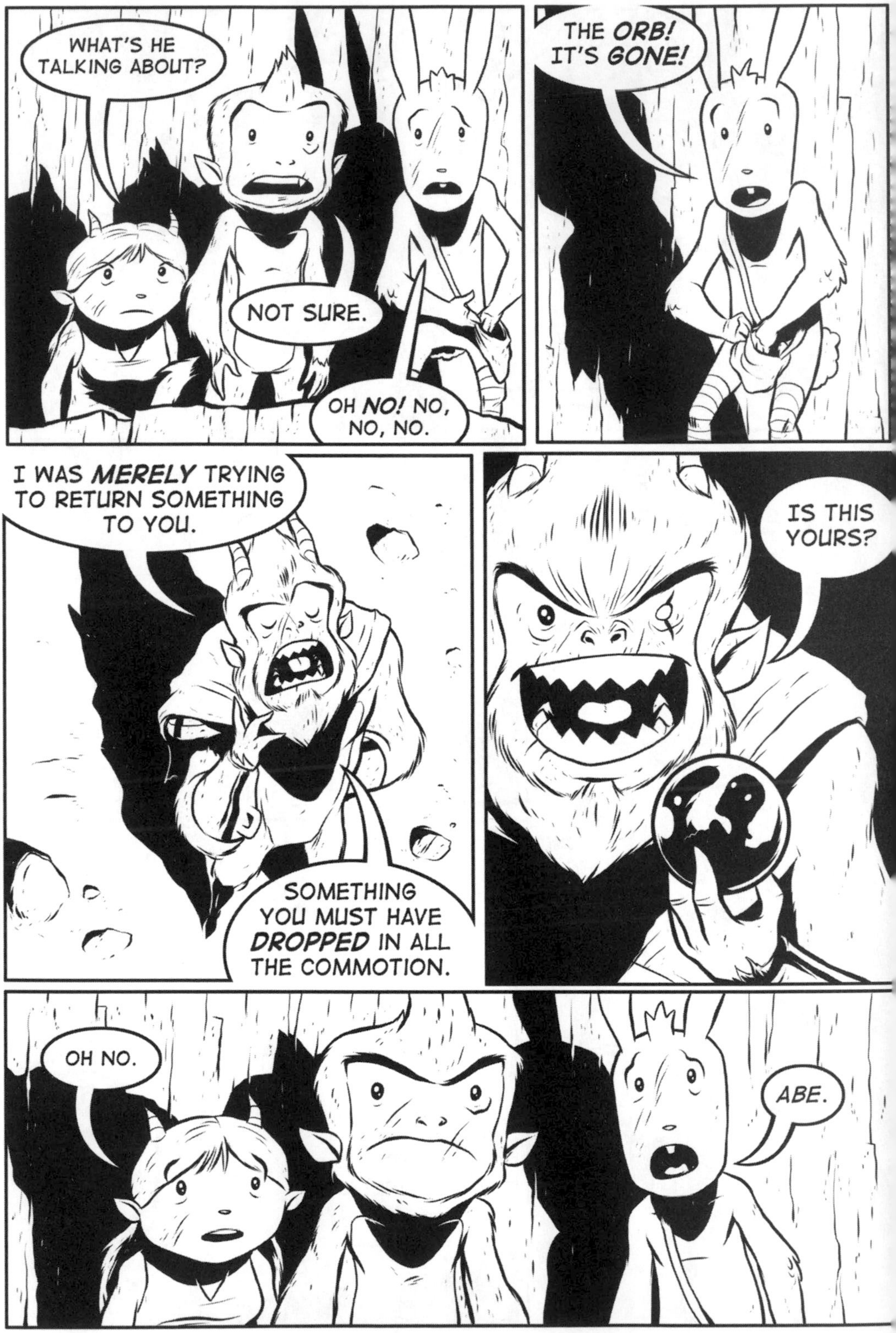

WHAT'S HE TALKING ABOUT?
NOT SURE.
OH *NO!* NO, NO, NO.
THE *ORB!* IT'S *GONE!*
I WAS *MERELY* TRYING TO RETURN SOMETHING TO YOU.
SOMETHING YOU MUST HAVE *DROPPED* IN ALL THE COMMOTION.
IS THIS YOURS?
OH NO.
ABE.

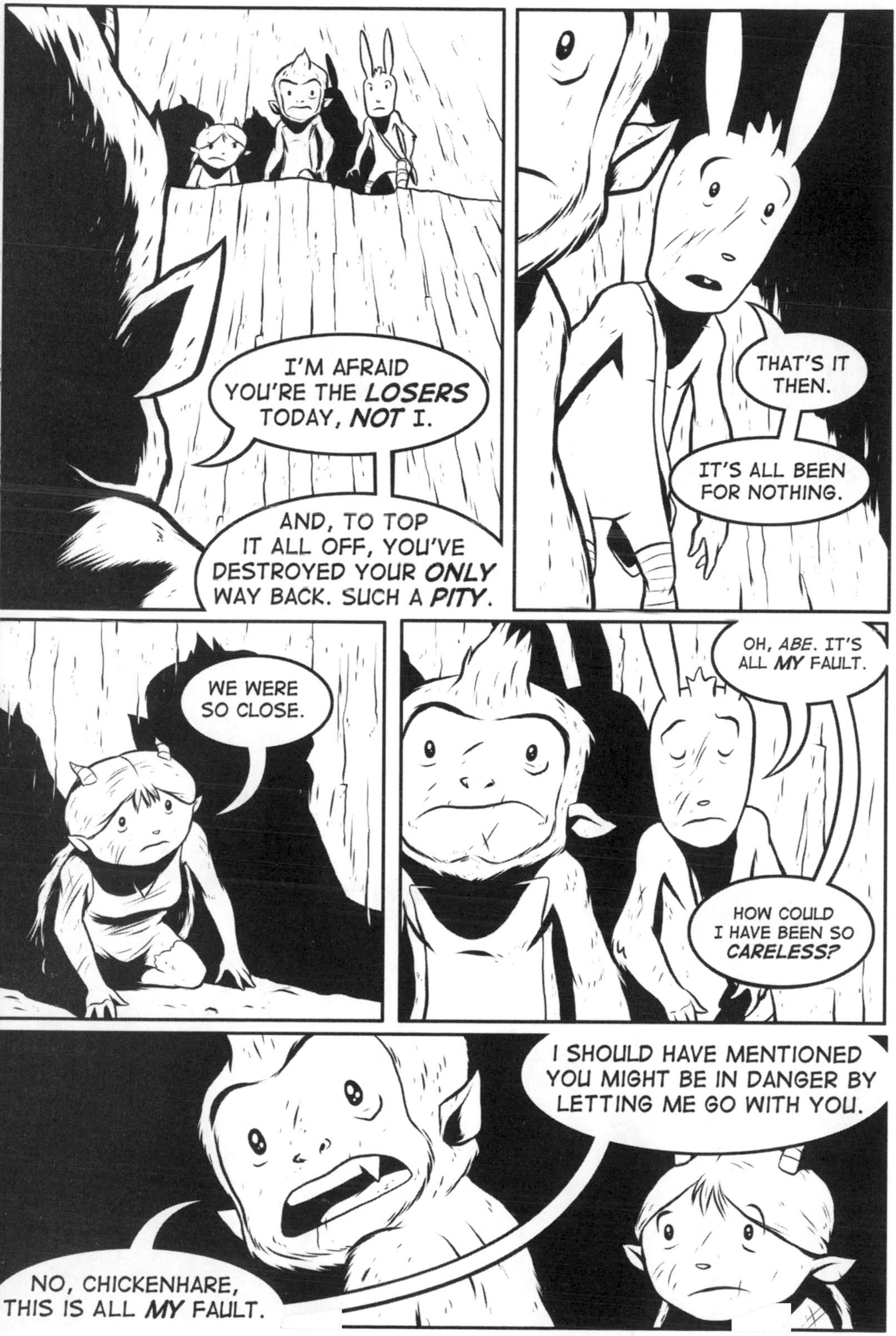
I'M AFRAID YOU'RE THE *LOSERS* TODAY, *NOT* I.
AND, TO TOP IT ALL OFF, YOU'VE DESTROYED YOUR *ONLY* WAY BACK. SUCH A *PITY*.
THAT'S IT THEN.
IT'S ALL BEEN FOR NOTHING.
WE WERE SO CLOSE.
OH, *ABE*. IT'S ALL *MY* FAULT.
HOW COULD I HAVE BEEN SO *CARELESS?*
I SHOULD HAVE MENTIONED YOU MIGHT BE IN DANGER BY LETTING ME GO WITH YOU.
NO, CHICKENHARE, THIS IS ALL *MY* FAULT.

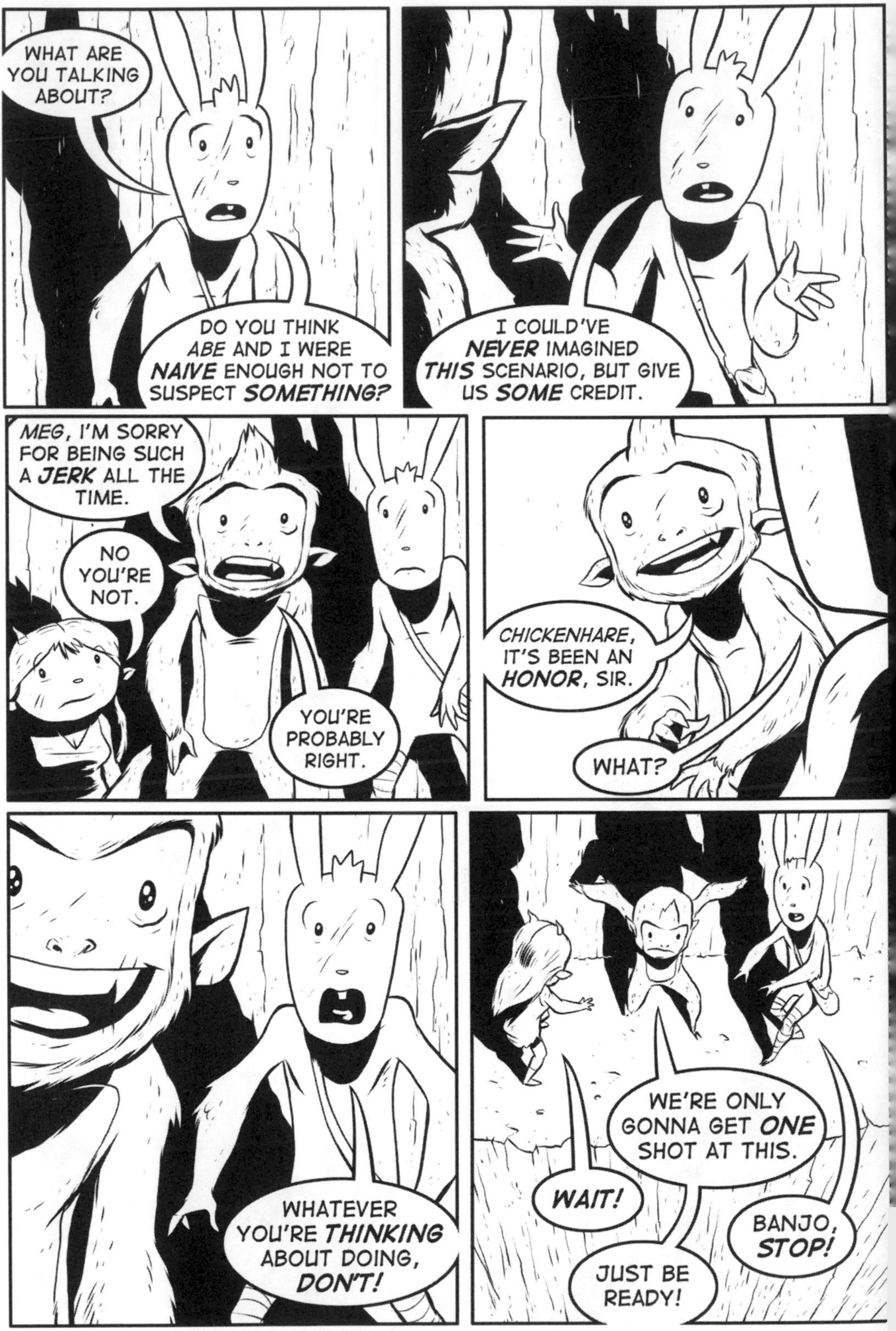
WHAT ARE YOU TALKING ABOUT?
DO YOU THINK *ABE* AND I WERE ***NAIVE*** ENOUGH NOT TO SUSPECT ***SOMETHING?***
I COULD'VE ***NEVER*** IMAGINED ***THIS*** SCENARIO, BUT GIVE US ***SOME*** CREDIT.
MEG, I'M SORRY FOR BEING SUCH A ***JERK*** ALL THE TIME.
NO YOU'RE NOT.
YOU'RE PROBABLY RIGHT.
CHICKENHARE, IT'S BEEN AN ***HONOR***, SIR.
WHAT?
WHATEVER YOU'RE ***THINKING*** ABOUT DOING, ***DON'T!***
WE'RE ONLY GONNA GET ***ONE*** SHOT AT THIS.
WAIT!
JUST BE READY!
BANJO, ***STOP!***

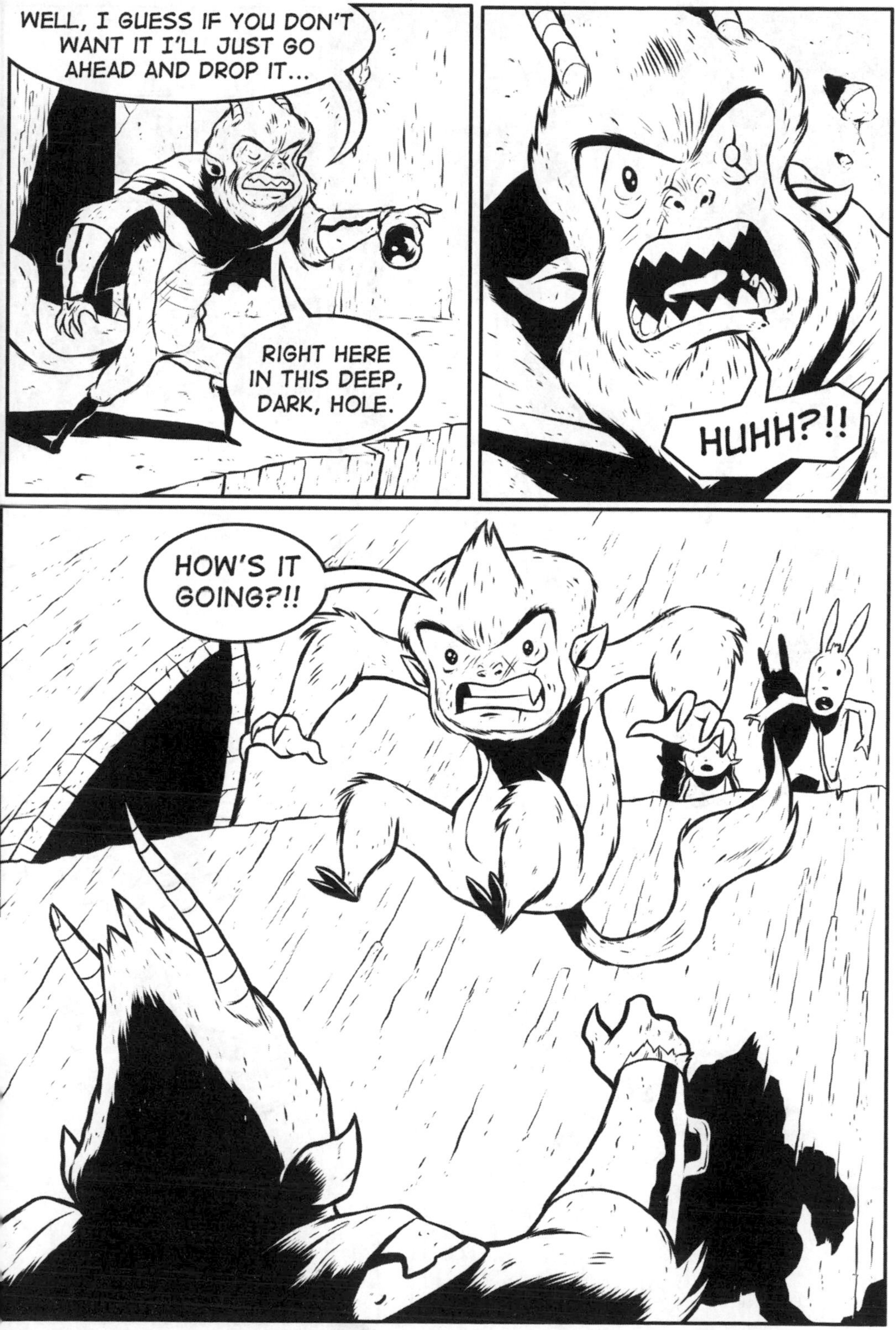
WELL, I GUESS IF YOU DON'T WANT IT I'LL JUST GO AHEAD AND DROP IT...
RIGHT HERE IN THIS DEEP, DARK, HOLE.
HUHH?!!
HOW'S IT GOING?!!

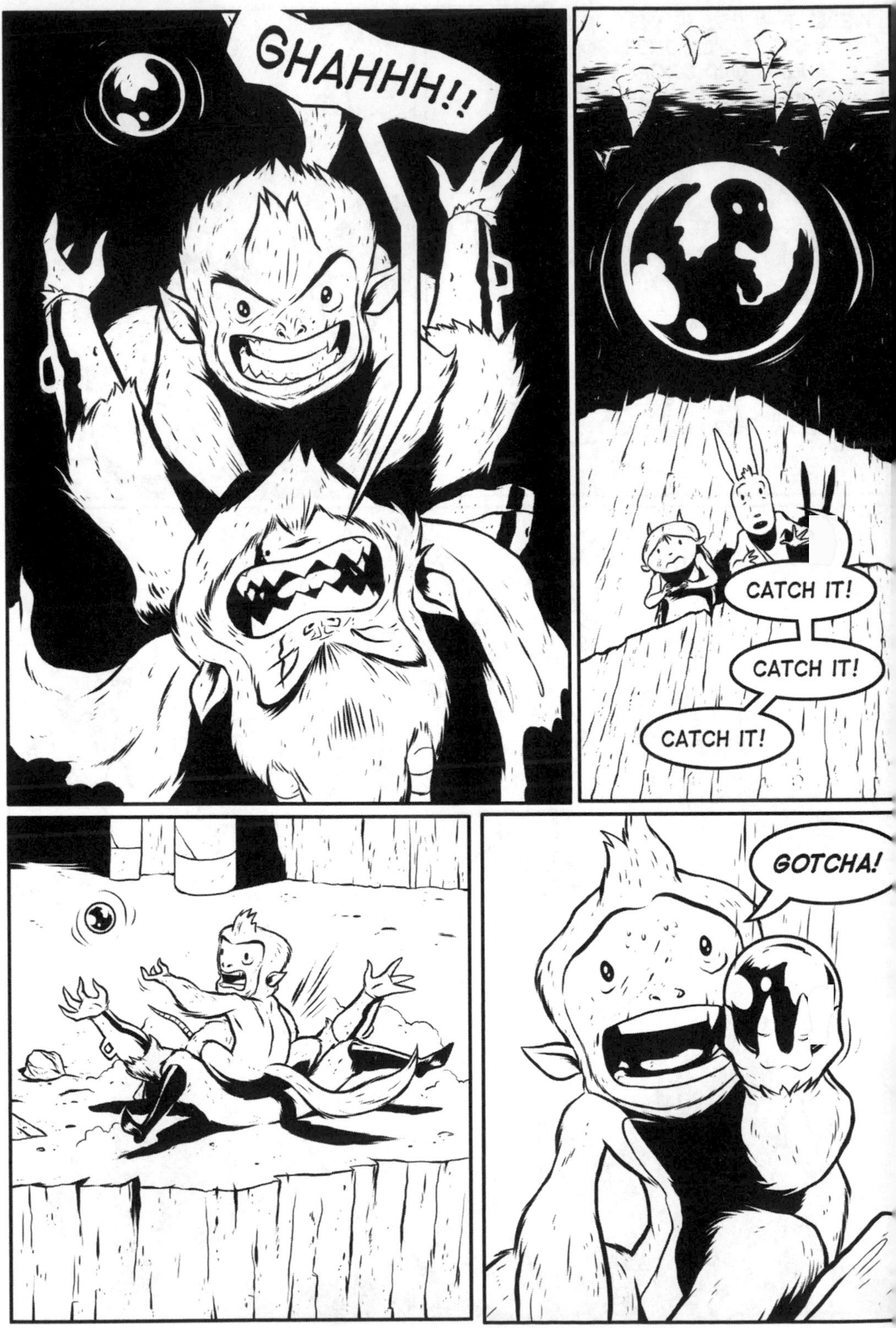
GHAHHH!!
CATCH IT!
CATCH IT!
CATCH IT!
GOTCHA!

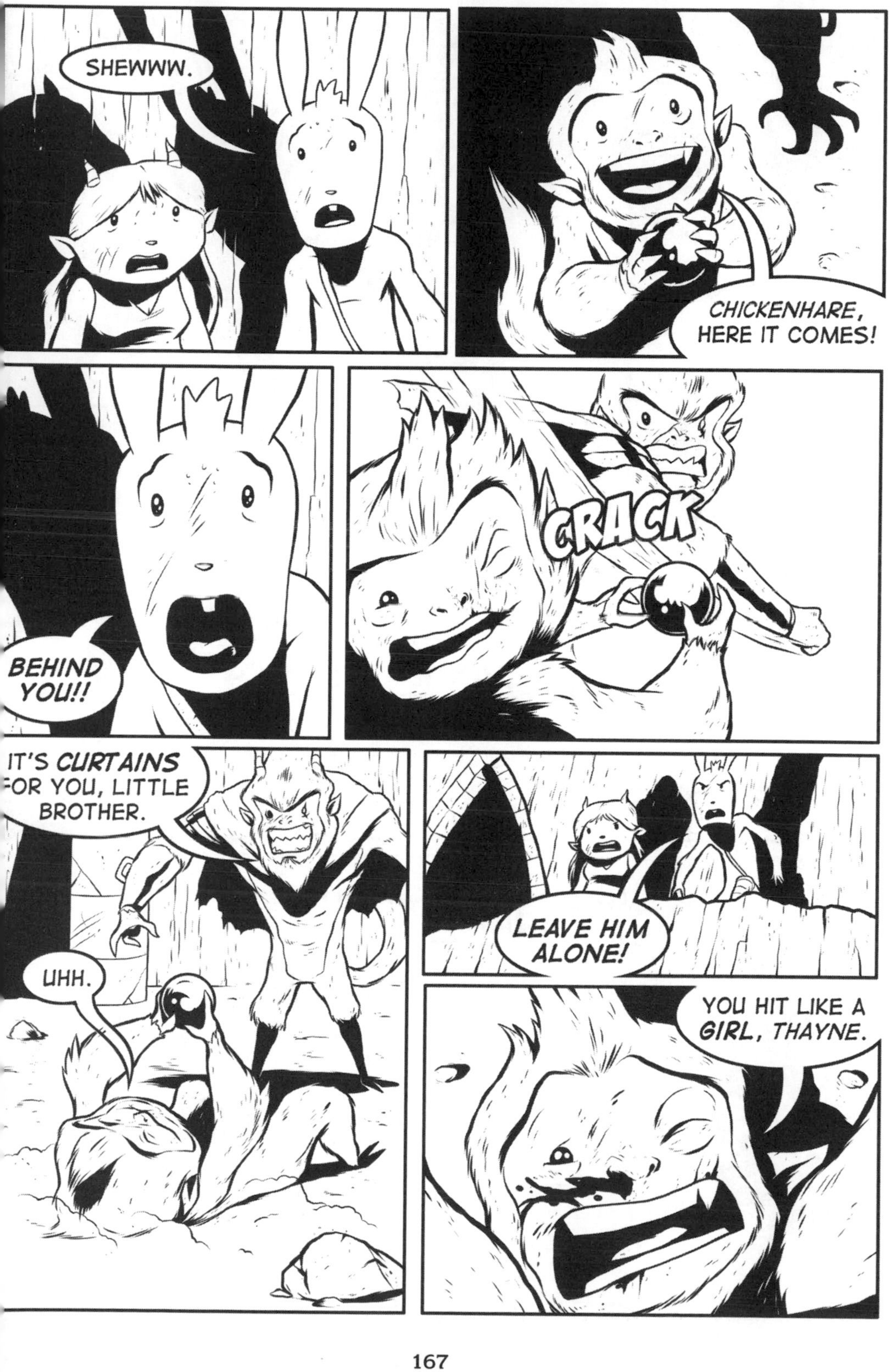
SHEWWW.
CHICKENHARE, HERE IT COMES!
BEHIND YOU!!
CRACK
IT'S CURTAINS FOR YOU, LITTLE BROTHER.
UHH.
LEAVE HIM ALONE!
YOU HIT LIKE A GIRL, THAYNE.

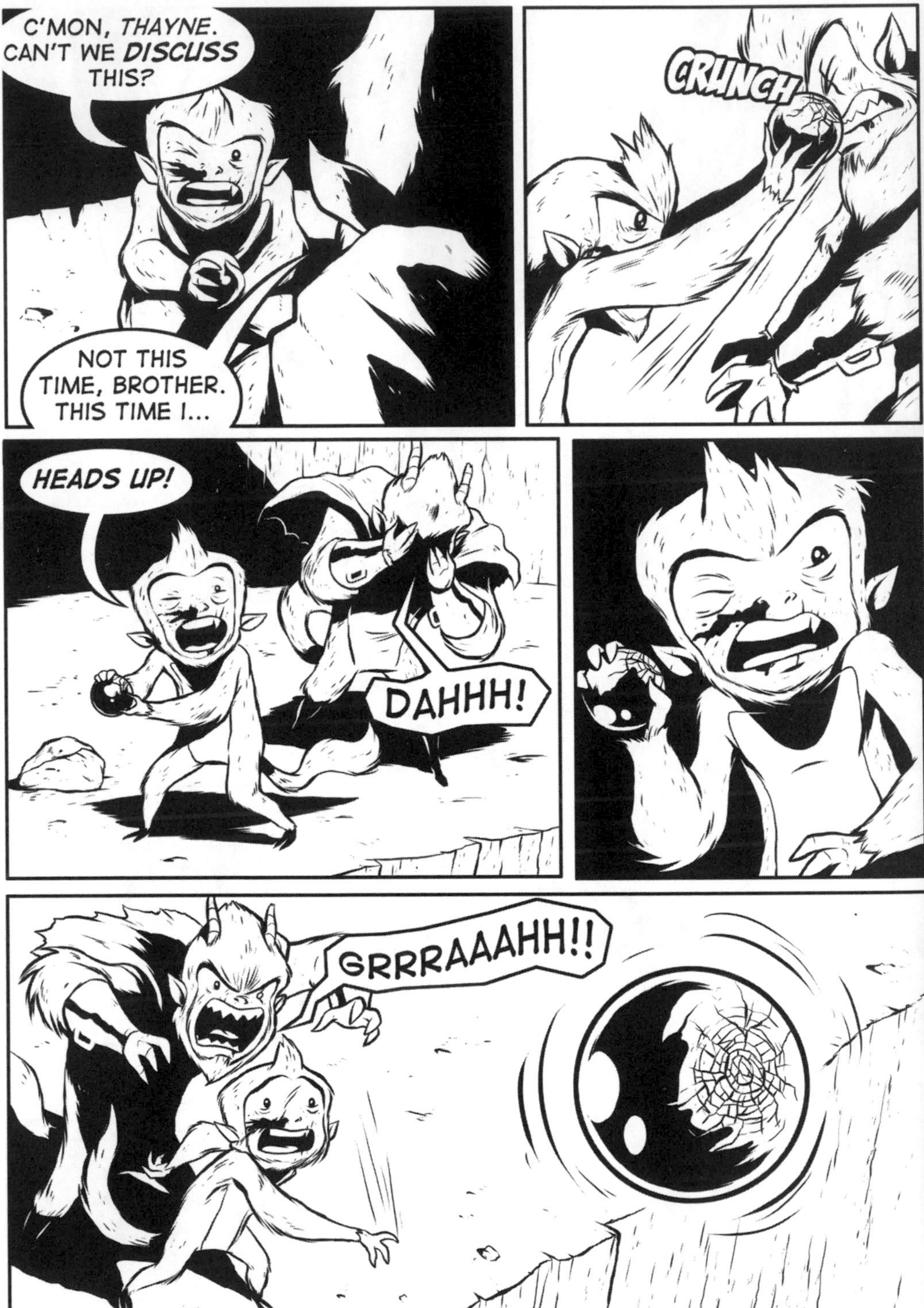
C'MON, *THAYNE*. CAN'T WE ***DISCUSS*** THIS?
NOT THIS TIME, BROTHER. THIS TIME I...
CRUNCH
HEADS UP!
DAHHH!
GRRRAAAHH!!

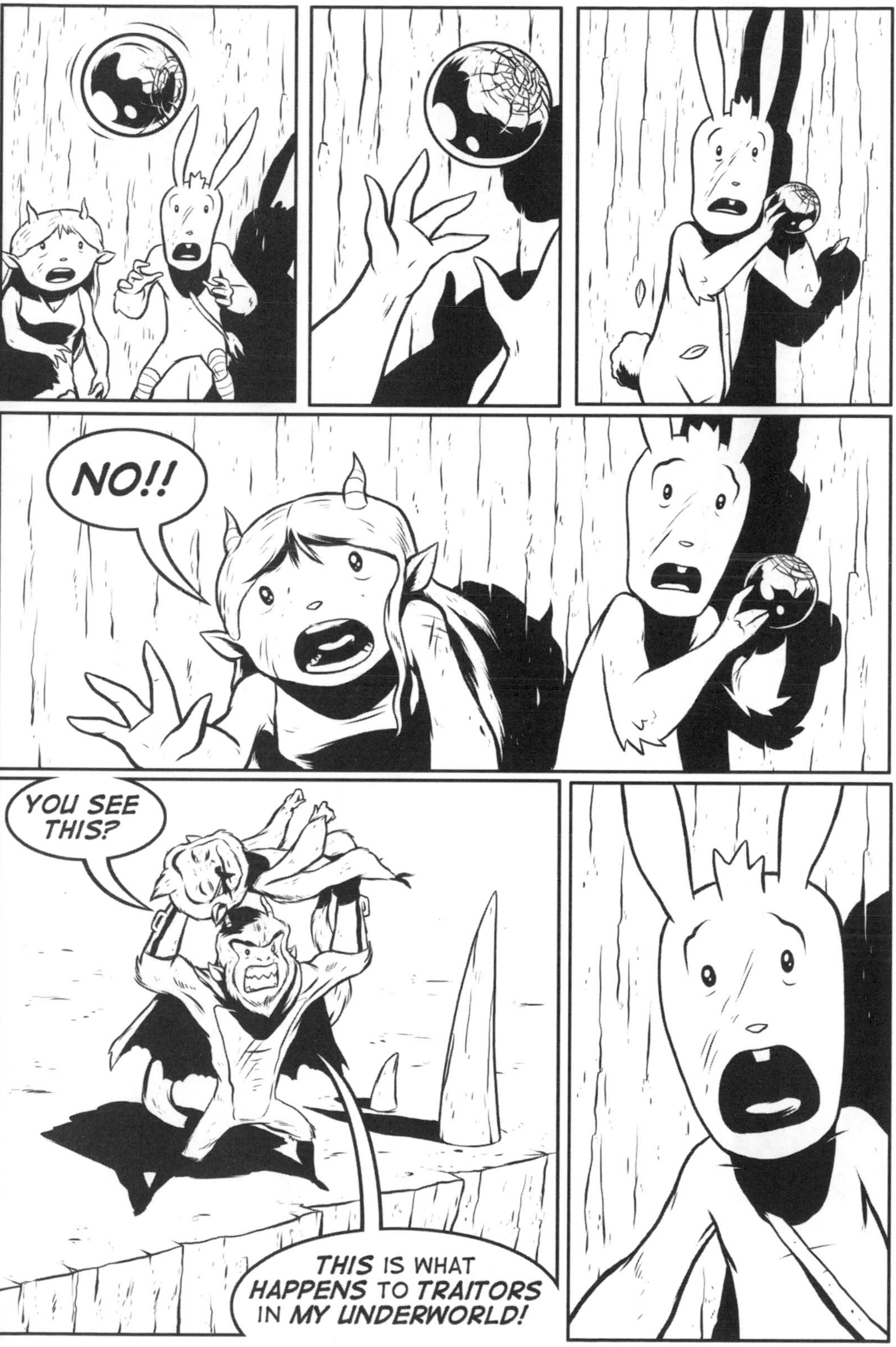
NO!!
YOU SEE THIS?
THIS IS WHAT HAPPENS TO TRAITORS IN MY UNDERWORLD!

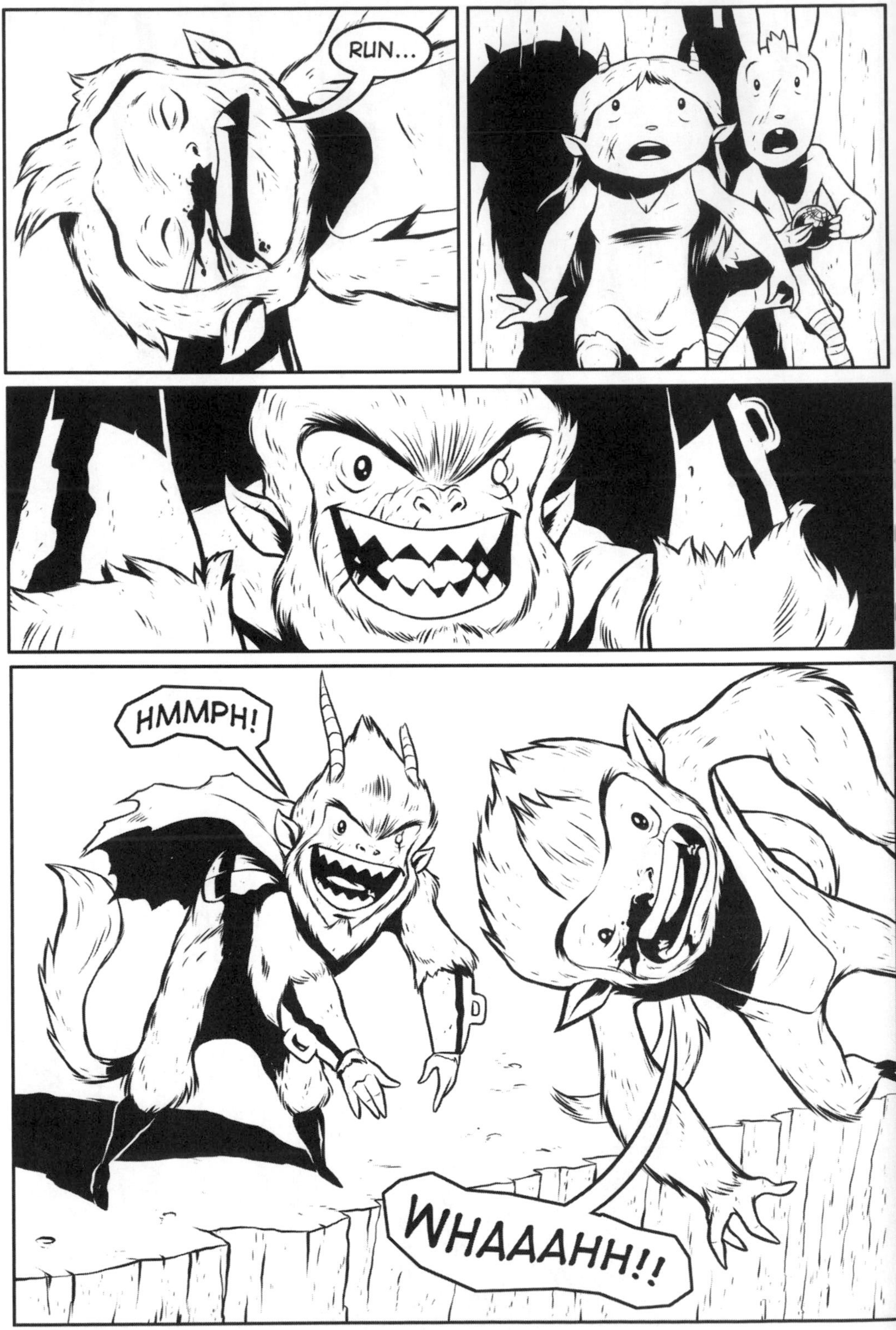
RUN...
HMMPH!
WHAAAHH!!

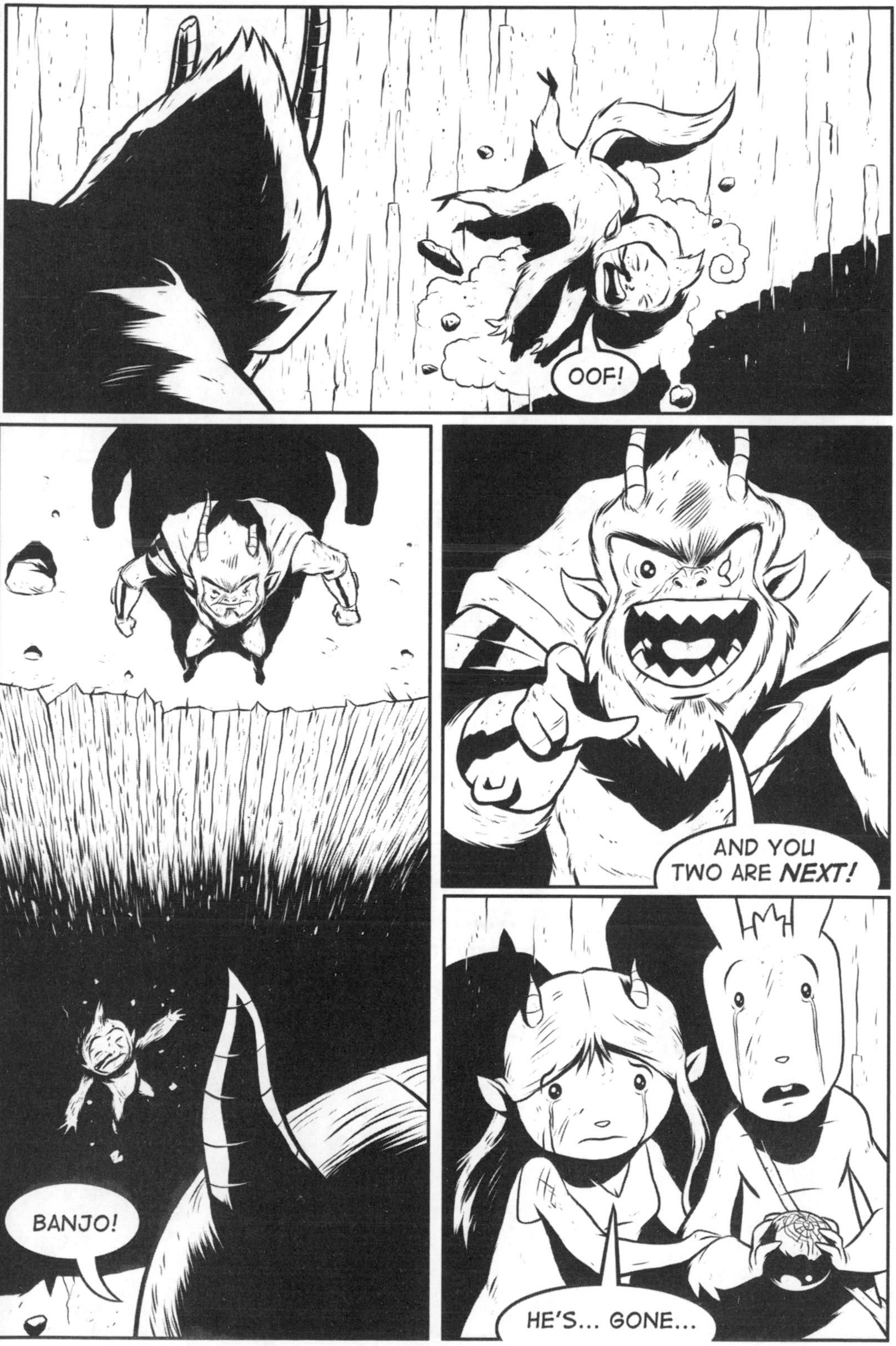
OOF!
AND YOU TWO ARE *NEXT!*
BANJO!
HE'S... GONE...

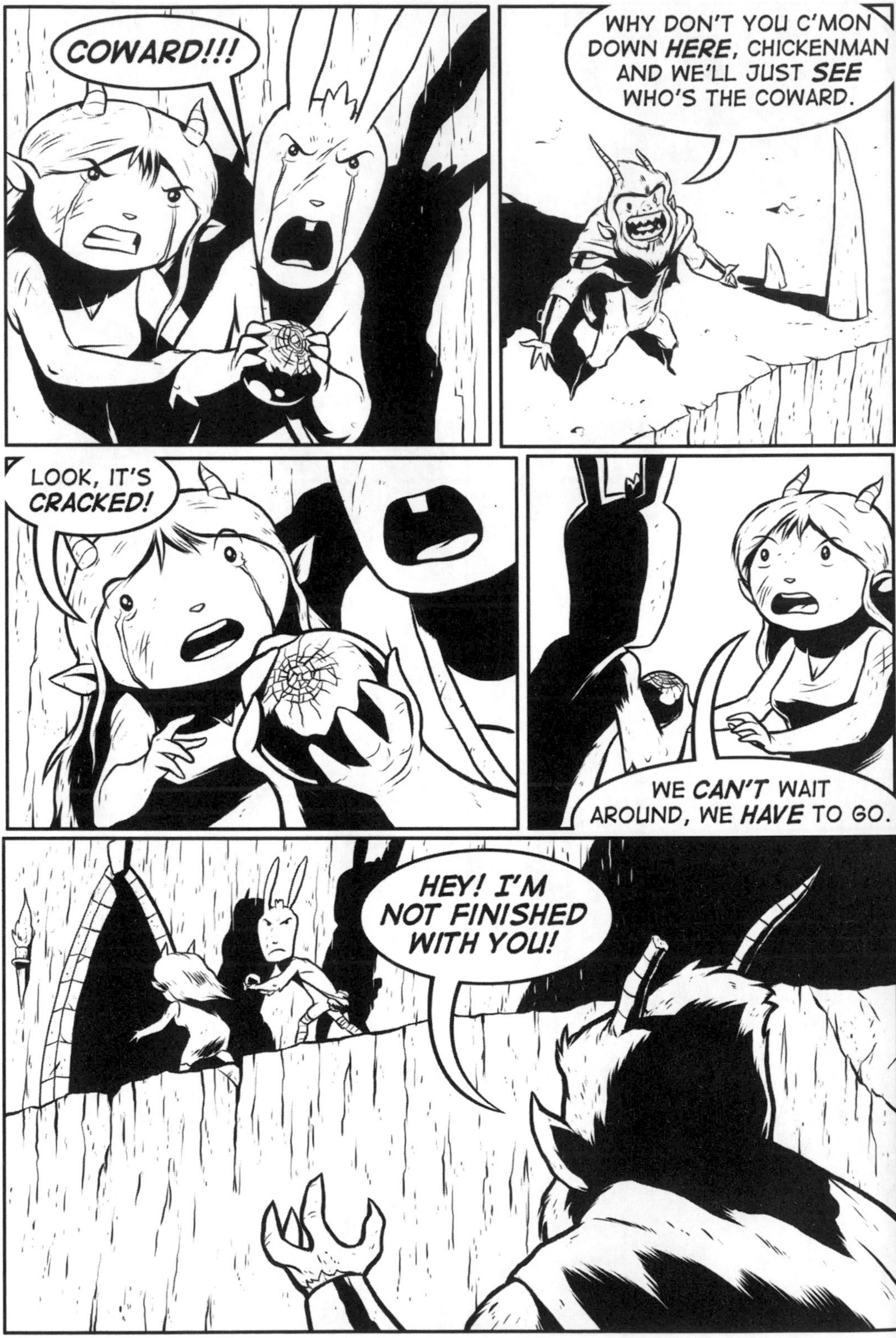
COWARD!!!
WHY DON'T YOU C'MON DOWN HERE, CHICKENMAN AND WE'LL JUST SEE WHO'S THE COWARD.
LOOK, IT'S CRACKED!
WE CAN'T WAIT AROUND, WE HAVE TO GO.
HEY! I'M NOT FINISHED WITH YOU!

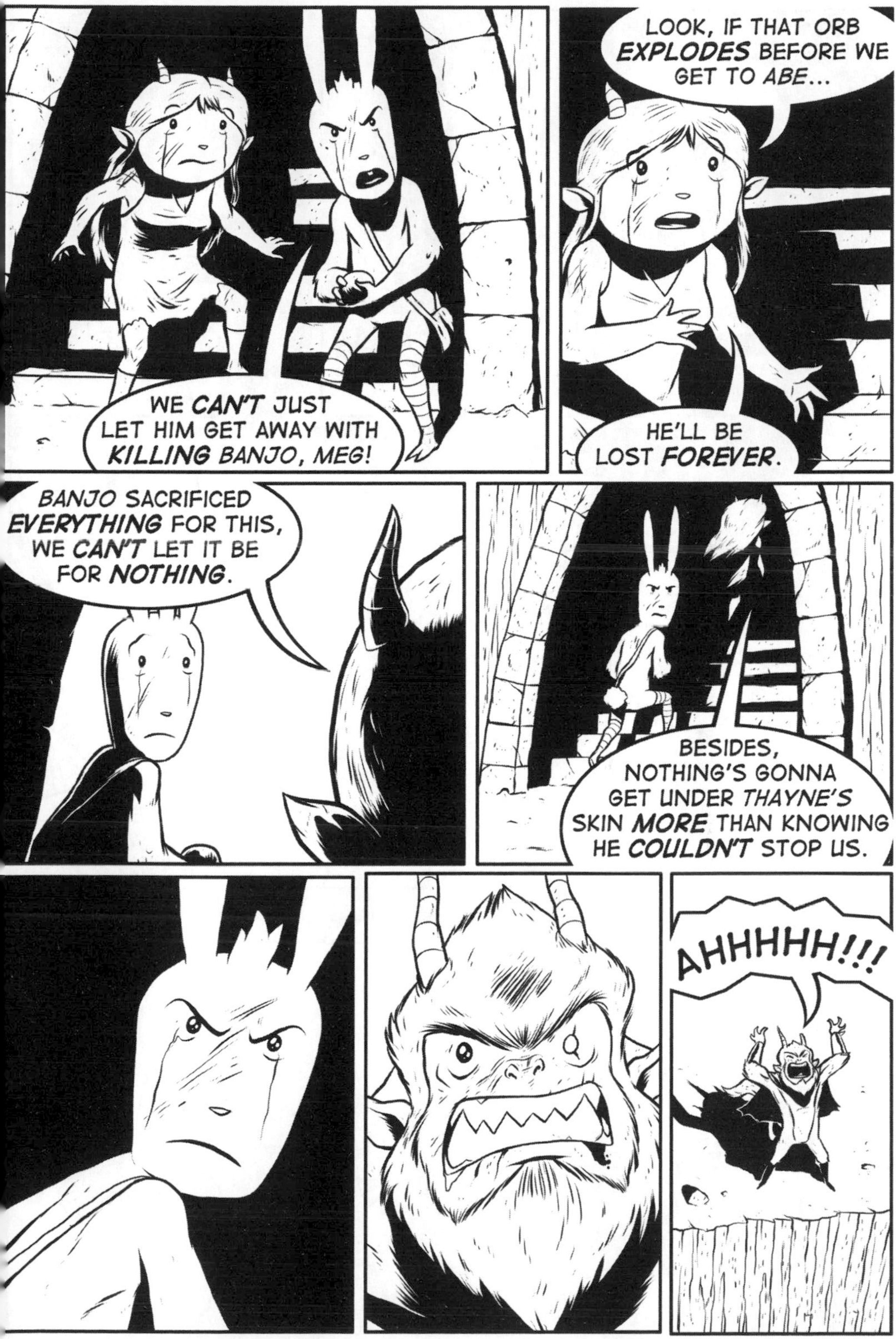
WE CAN'T JUST LET HIM GET AWAY WITH KILLING BANJO, MEG!
LOOK, IF THAT ORB EXPLODES BEFORE WE GET TO ABE...
HE'LL BE LOST FOREVER.
BANJO SACRIFICED EVERYTHING FOR THIS, WE CAN'T LET IT BE FOR NOTHING.
BESIDES, NOTHING'S GONNA GET UNDER THAYNE'S SKIN MORE THAN KNOWING HE COULDN'T STOP US.
AHHHHH!!!

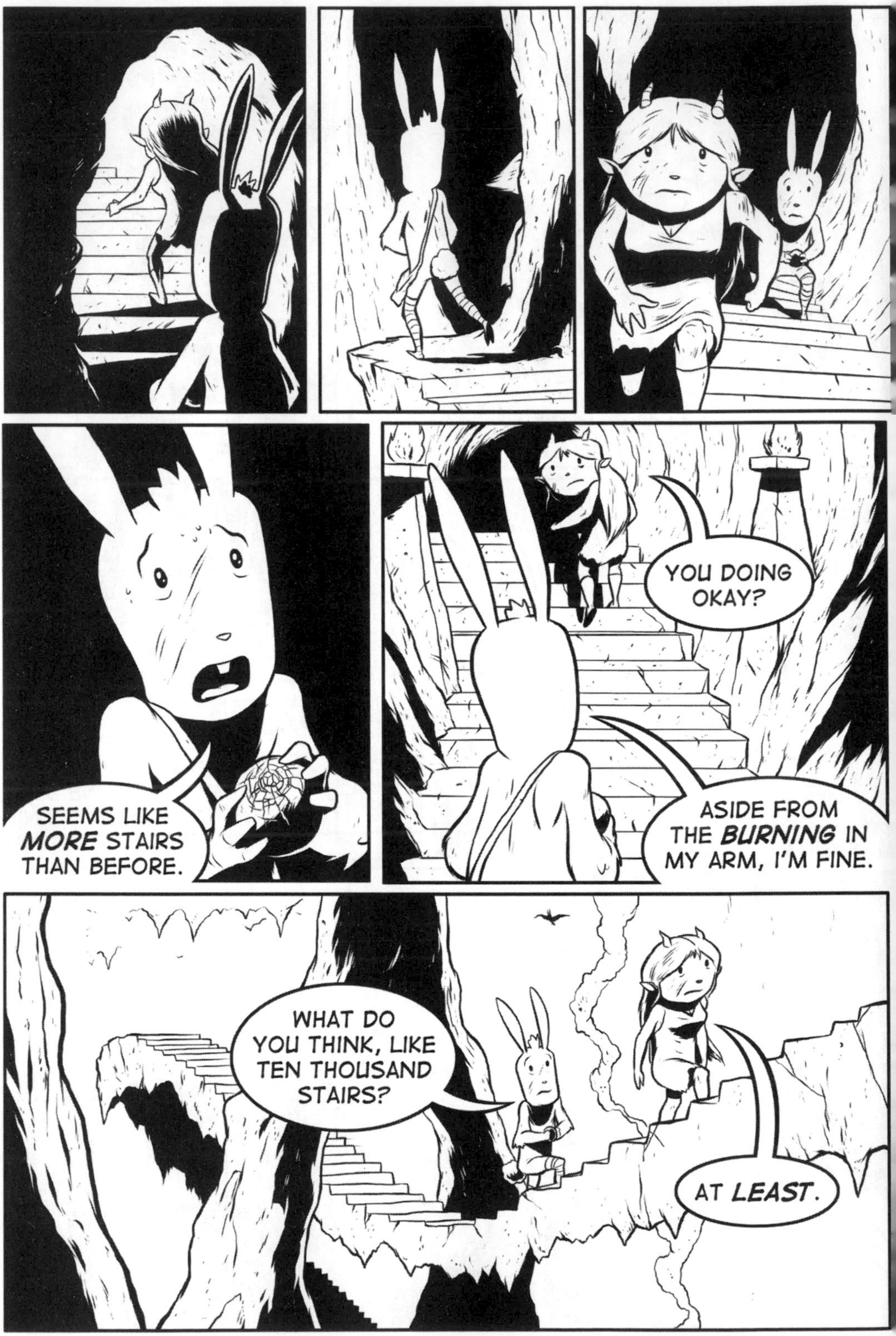

SEEMS LIKE *MORE* STAIRS THAN BEFORE.
YOU DOING OKAY?
ASIDE FROM THE *BURNING* IN MY ARM, I'M FINE.
WHAT DO YOU THINK, LIKE TEN THOUSAND STAIRS?
AT *LEAST*.

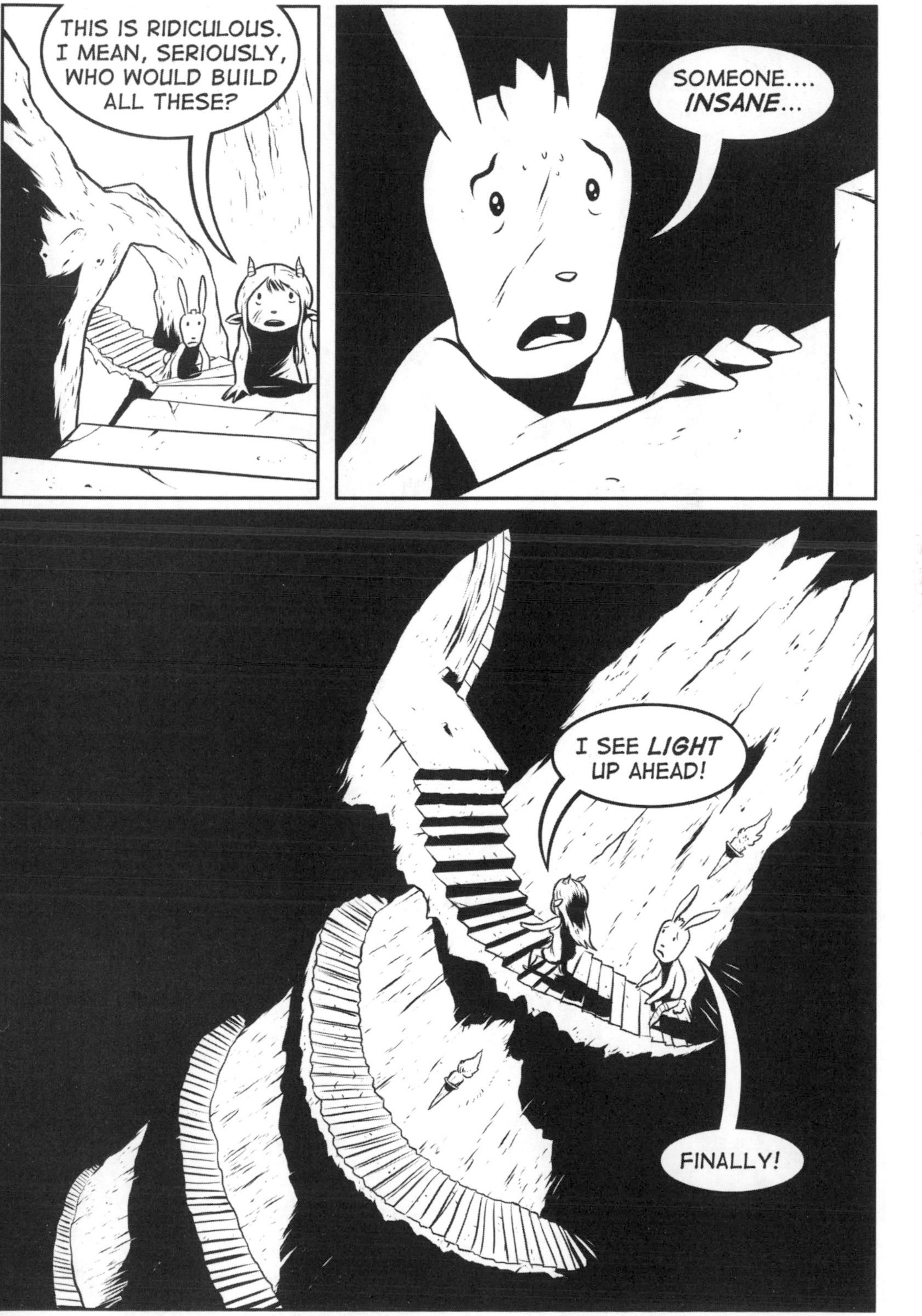
THIS IS RIDICULOUS. I MEAN, SERIOUSLY, WHO WOULD BUILD ALL THESE?
SOMEONE.... INSANE...
I SEE LIGHT UP AHEAD!
FINALLY!

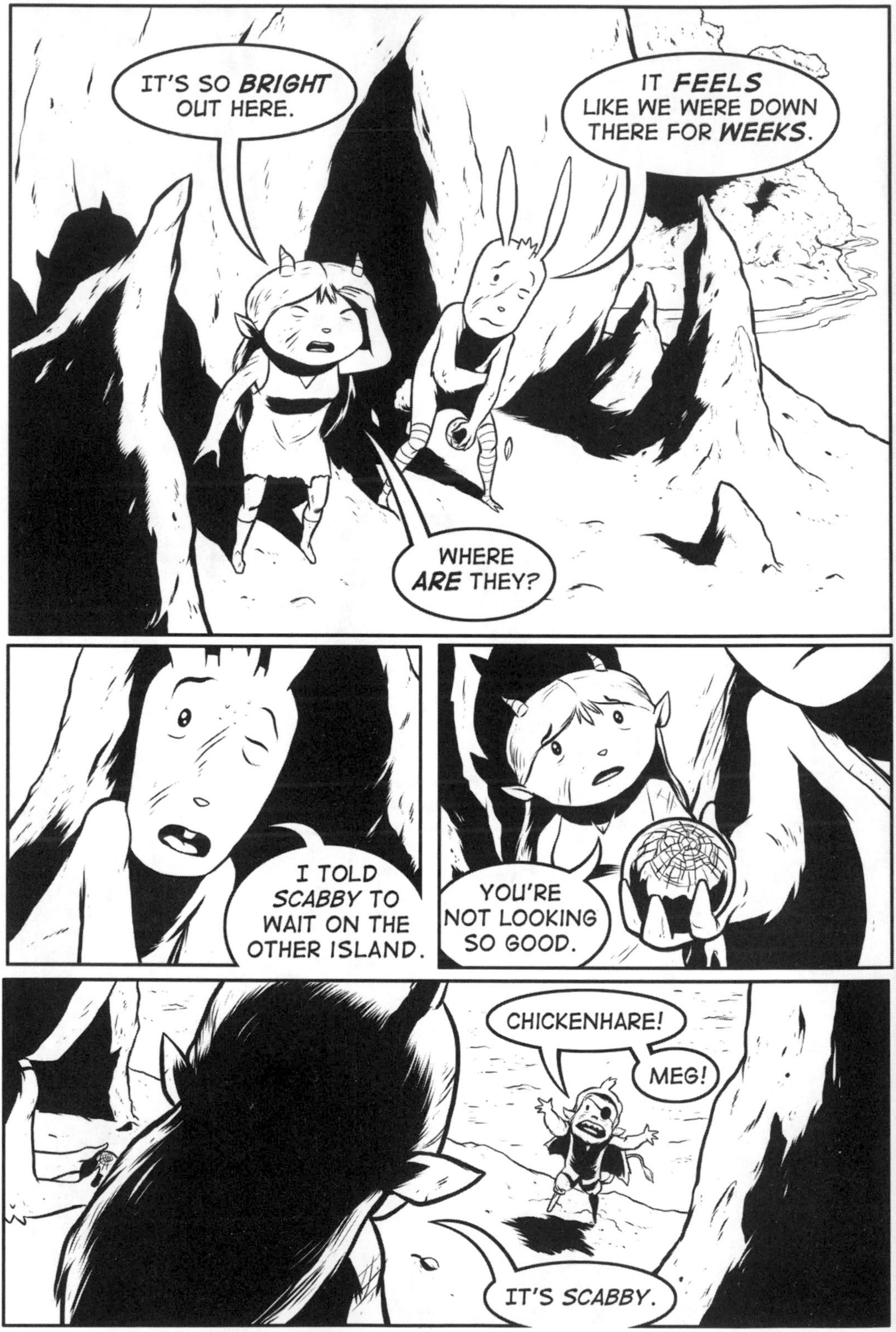

IT'S SO BRIGHT OUT HERE.
IT FEELS LIKE WE WERE DOWN THERE FOR WEEKS.
WHERE ARE THEY?
I TOLD SCABBY TO WAIT ON THE OTHER ISLAND.
YOU'RE NOT LOOKING SO GOOD.
CHICKENHARE!
MEG!
IT'S SCABBY.

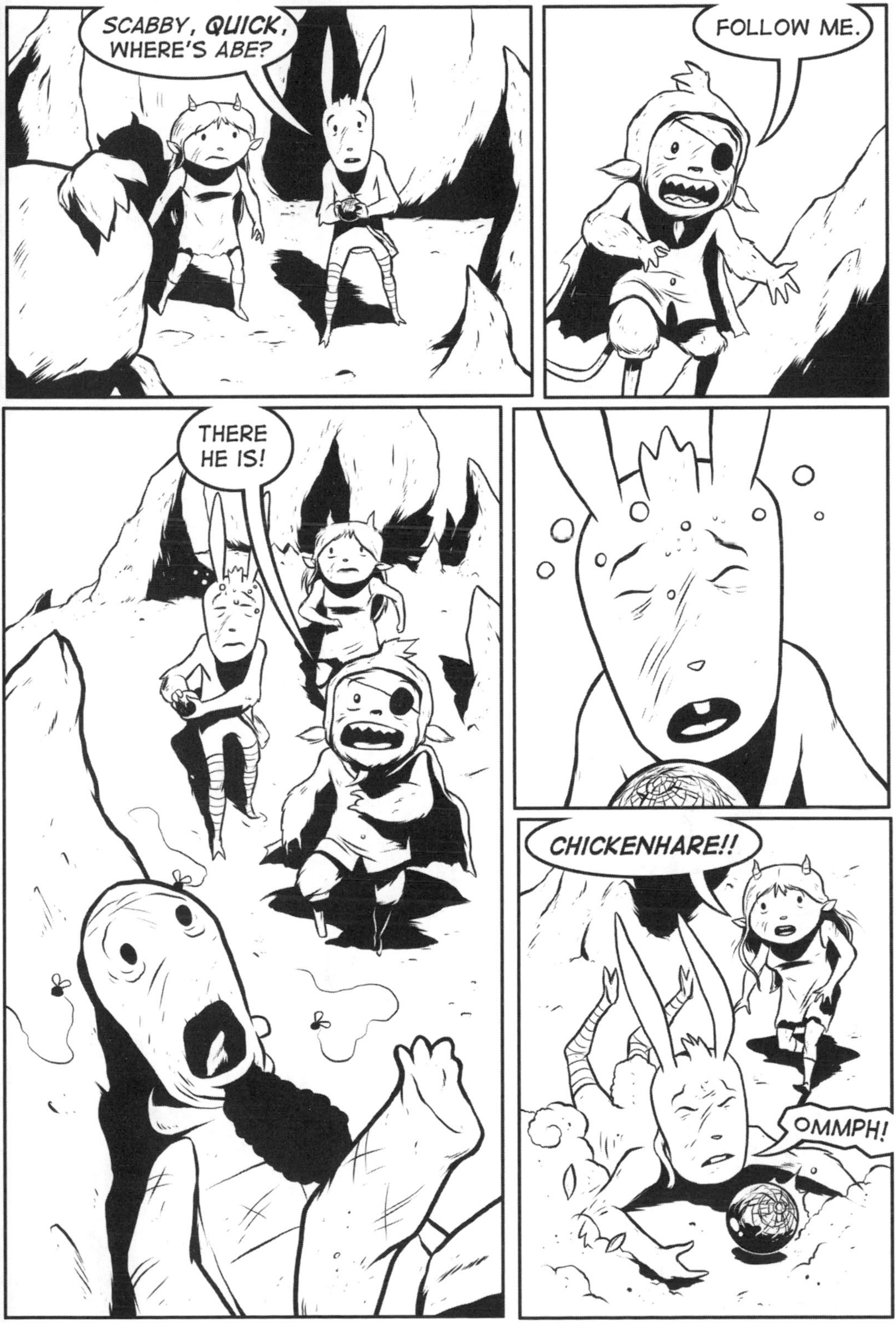
SCABBY, QUICK, WHERE'S ABE?
FOLLOW ME.
THERE HE IS!
CHICKENHARE!!
OMMPH!

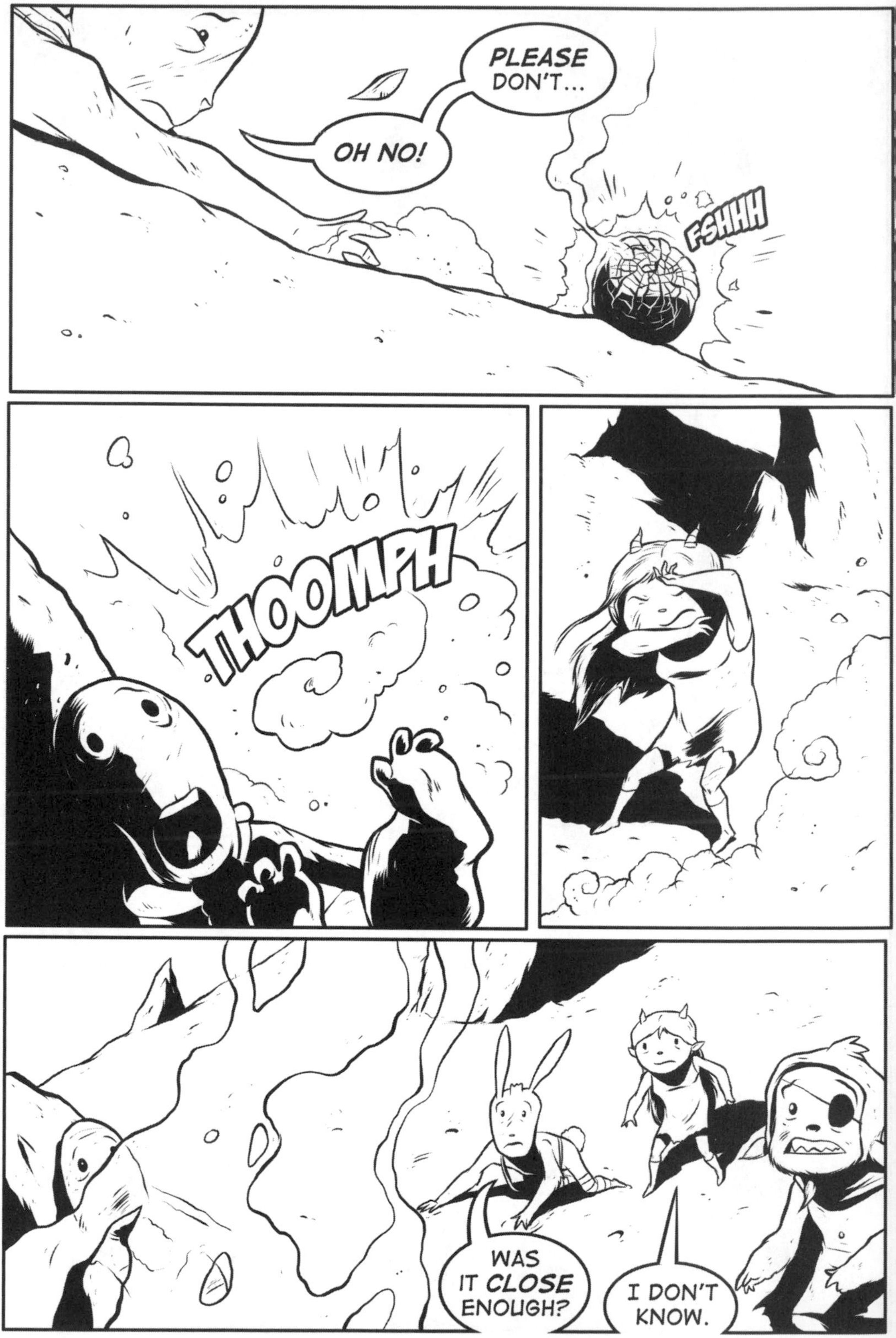
PLEASE DON'T...
OH NO!
FSHHH
THOOMPH
WAS IT CLOSE ENOUGH?
I DON'T KNOW.

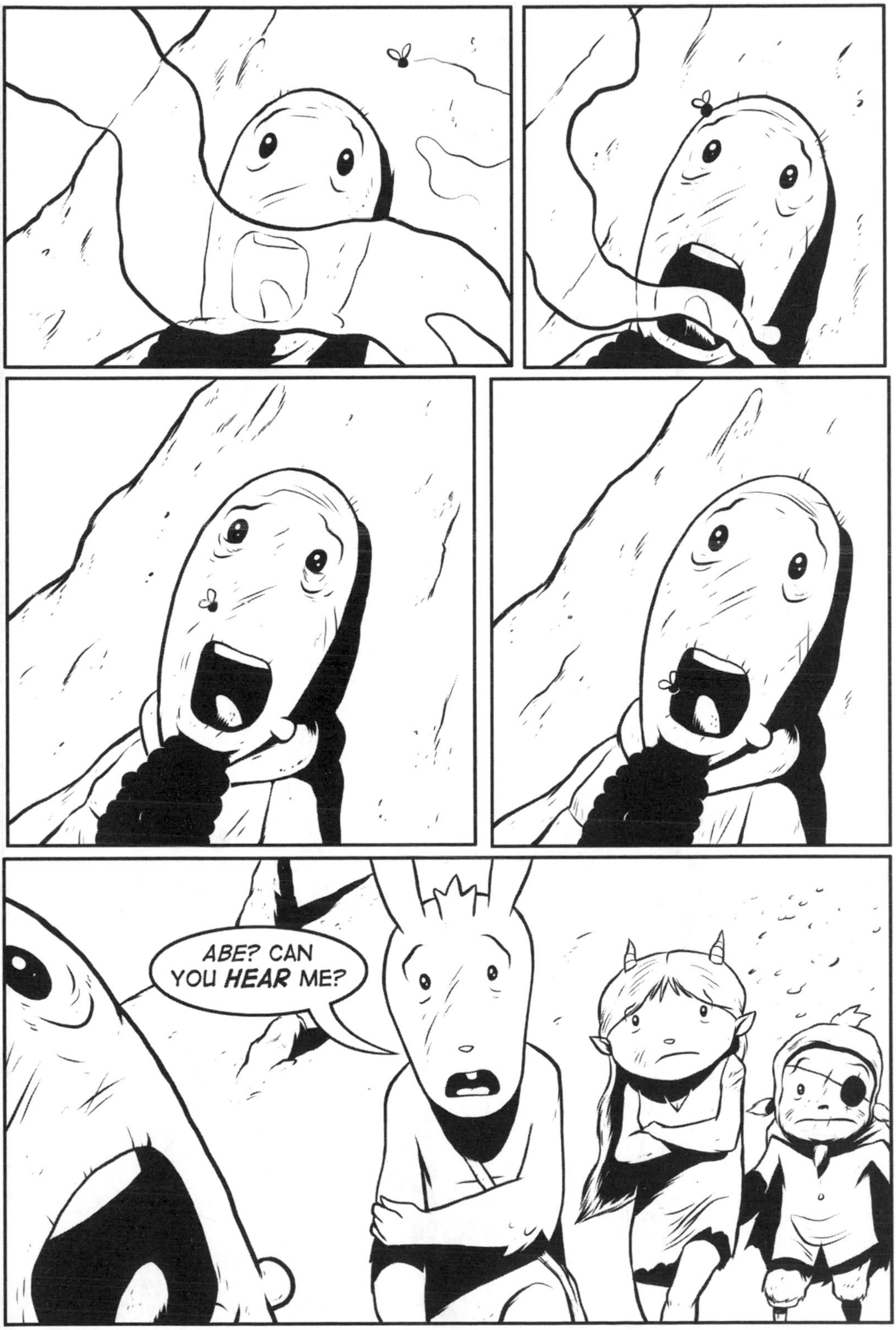
ABE? CAN YOU HEAR ME?

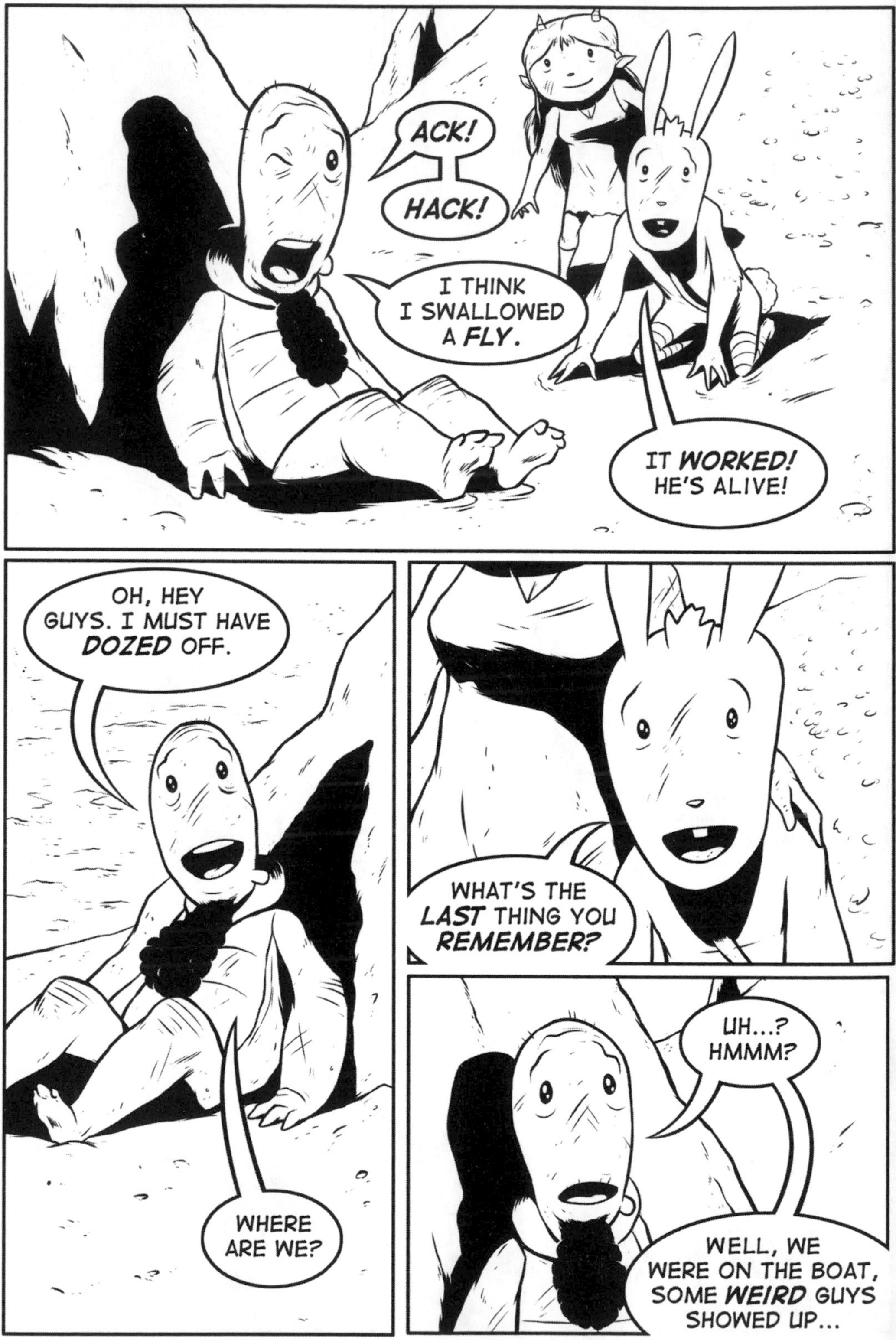
ACK!
HACK!
I THINK I SWALLOWED A FLY.
IT WORKED! HE'S ALIVE!
OH, HEY GUYS. I MUST HAVE DOZED OFF.
WHERE ARE WE?
WHAT'S THE LAST THING YOU REMEMBER?
UH...? HMMM?
WELL, WE WERE ON THE BOAT, SOME WEIRD GUYS SHOWED UP...

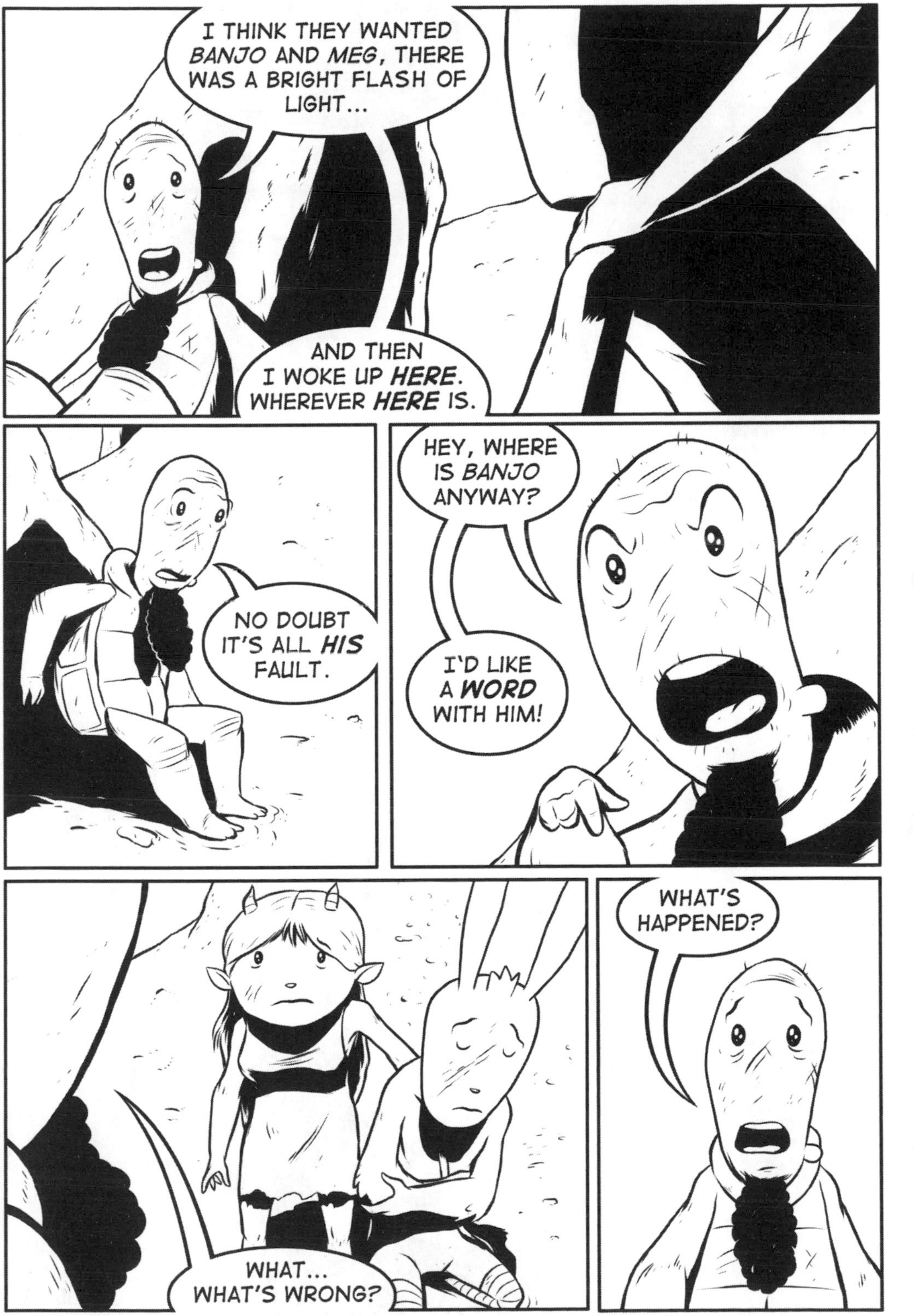
I THINK THEY WANTED BANJO AND MEG, THERE WAS A BRIGHT FLASH OF LIGHT...
AND THEN I WOKE UP HERE. WHEREVER HERE IS.
NO DOUBT IT'S ALL HIS FAULT.
HEY, WHERE IS BANJO ANYWAY?
I'D LIKE A WORD WITH HIM!
WHAT... WHAT'S WRONG?
WHAT'S HAPPENED?

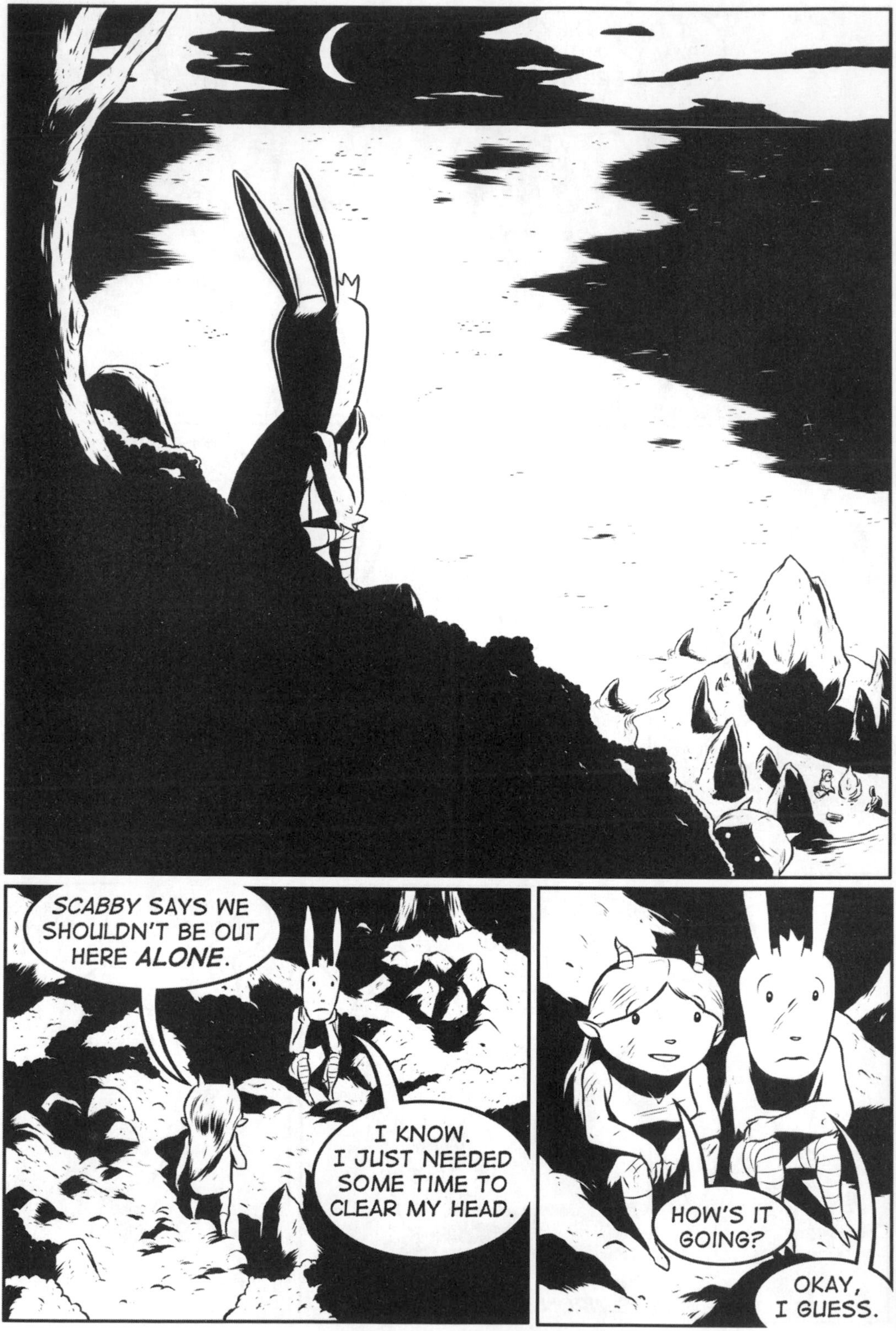
SCABBY SAYS WE SHOULDN'T BE OUT HERE ALONE.
I KNOW. I JUST NEEDED SOME TIME TO CLEAR MY HEAD.
HOW'S IT GOING?
OKAY, I GUESS.

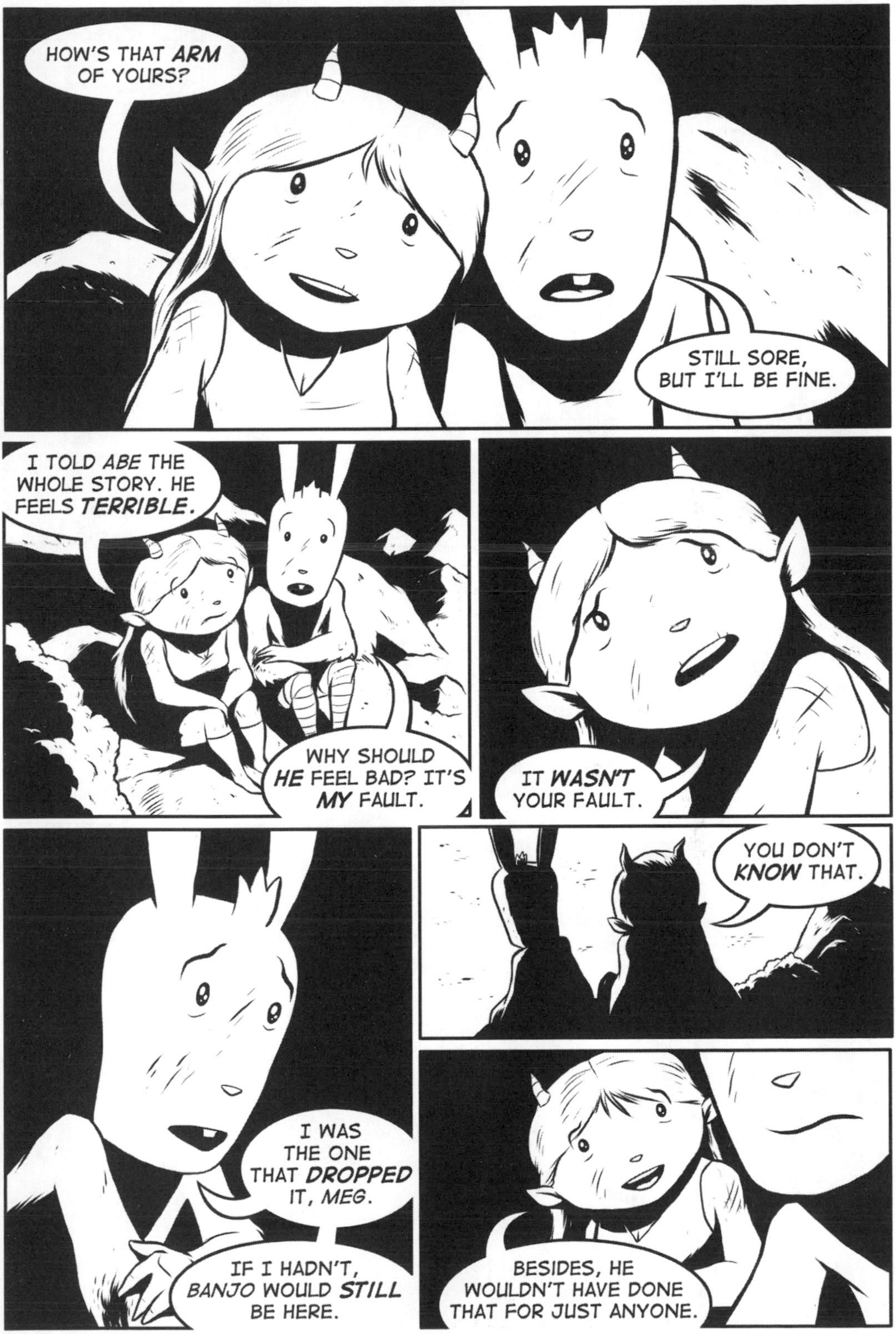
HOW'S THAT ARM OF YOURS?
STILL SORE, BUT I'LL BE FINE.
I TOLD ABE THE WHOLE STORY. HE FEELS TERRIBLE.
WHY SHOULD HE FEEL BAD? IT'S MY FAULT.
IT WASN'T YOUR FAULT.
I WAS THE ONE THAT DROPPED IT, MEG.
IF I HADN'T, BANJO WOULD STILL BE HERE.
YOU DON'T KNOW THAT.
BESIDES, HE WOULDN'T HAVE DONE THAT FOR JUST ANYONE.

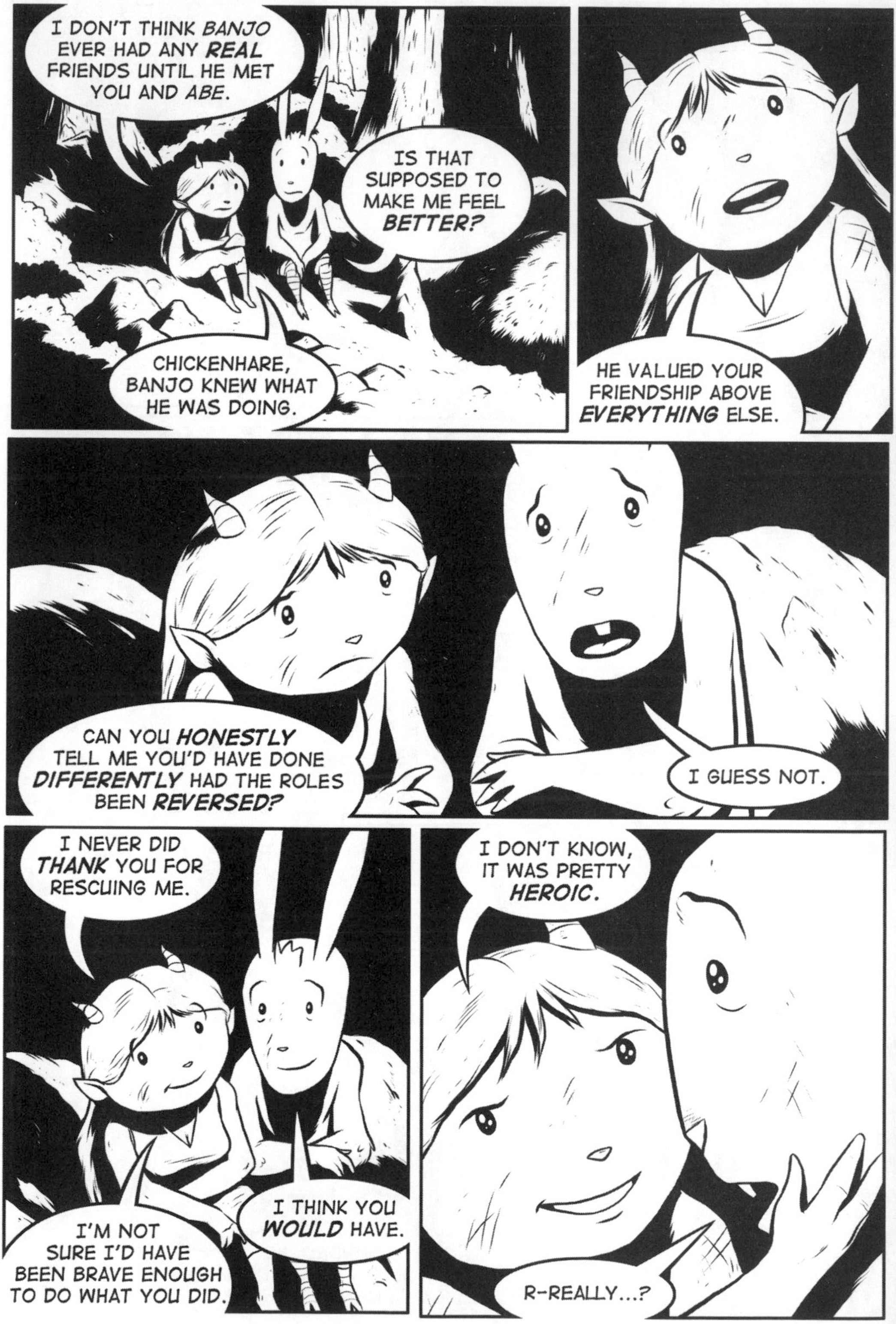
I DON'T THINK *BANJO* EVER HAD ANY ***REAL*** FRIENDS UNTIL HE MET YOU AND *ABE*.
IS THAT SUPPOSED TO MAKE ME FEEL ***BETTER?***
CHICKENHARE, BANJO KNEW WHAT HE WAS DOING.
HE VALUED YOUR FRIENDSHIP ABOVE ***EVERYTHING*** ELSE.
CAN YOU ***HONESTLY*** TELL ME YOU'D HAVE DONE ***DIFFERENTLY*** HAD THE ROLES BEEN ***REVERSED?***
I GUESS NOT.
I NEVER DID ***THANK*** YOU FOR RESCUING ME.
I'M NOT SURE I'D HAVE BEEN BRAVE ENOUGH TO DO WHAT YOU DID.
I THINK YOU ***WOULD*** HAVE.
I DON'T KNOW, IT WAS PRETTY ***HEROIC***.
R-REALLY...?

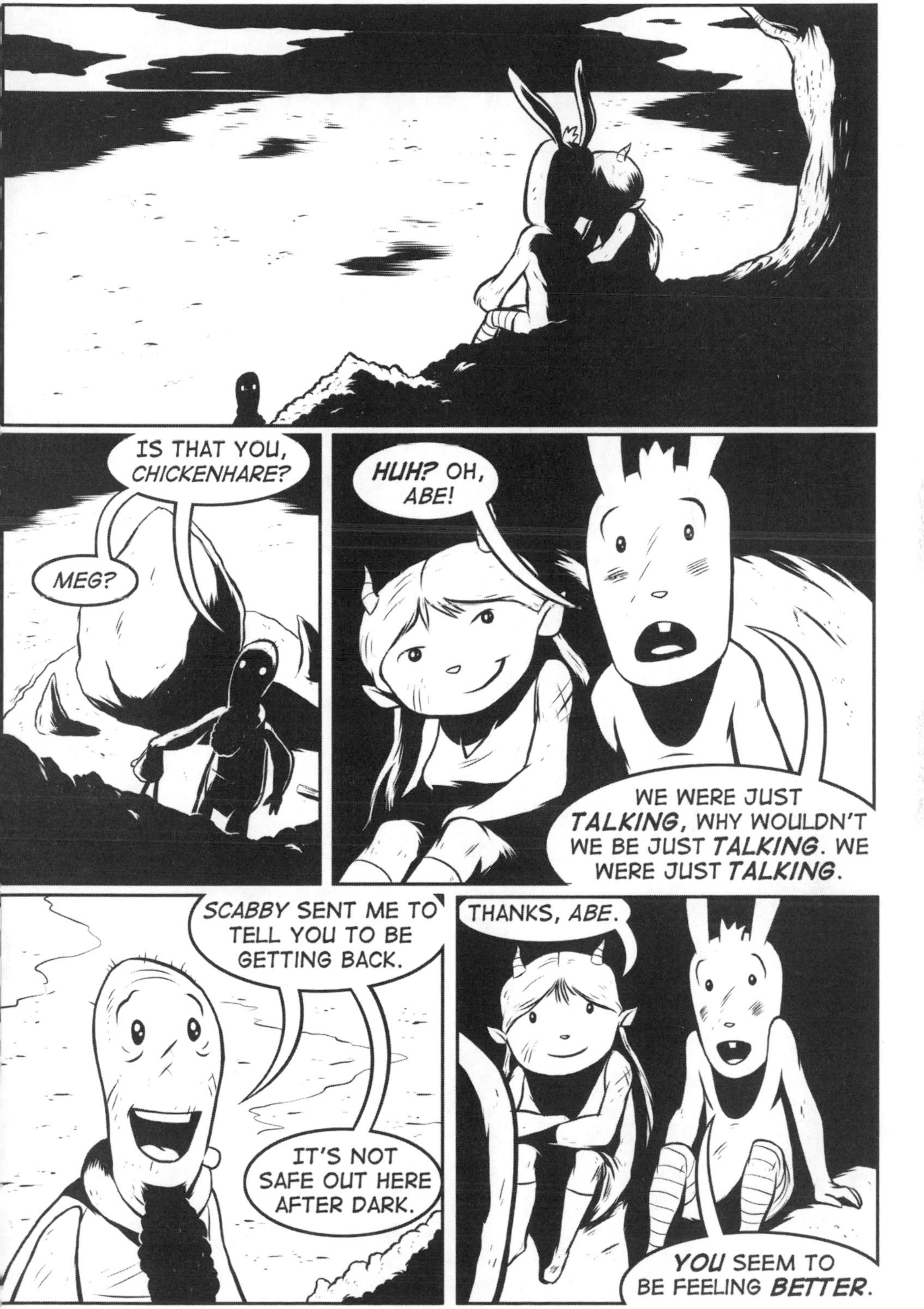

IS THAT YOU, CHICKENHARE?
MEG?
HUH? OH, ABE!
WE WERE JUST TALKING, WHY WOULDN'T WE BE JUST TALKING. WE WERE JUST TALKING.
SCABBY SENT ME TO TELL YOU TO BE GETTING BACK.
IT'S NOT SAFE OUT HERE AFTER DARK.
THANKS, ABE.
YOU SEEM TO BE FEELING BETTER.

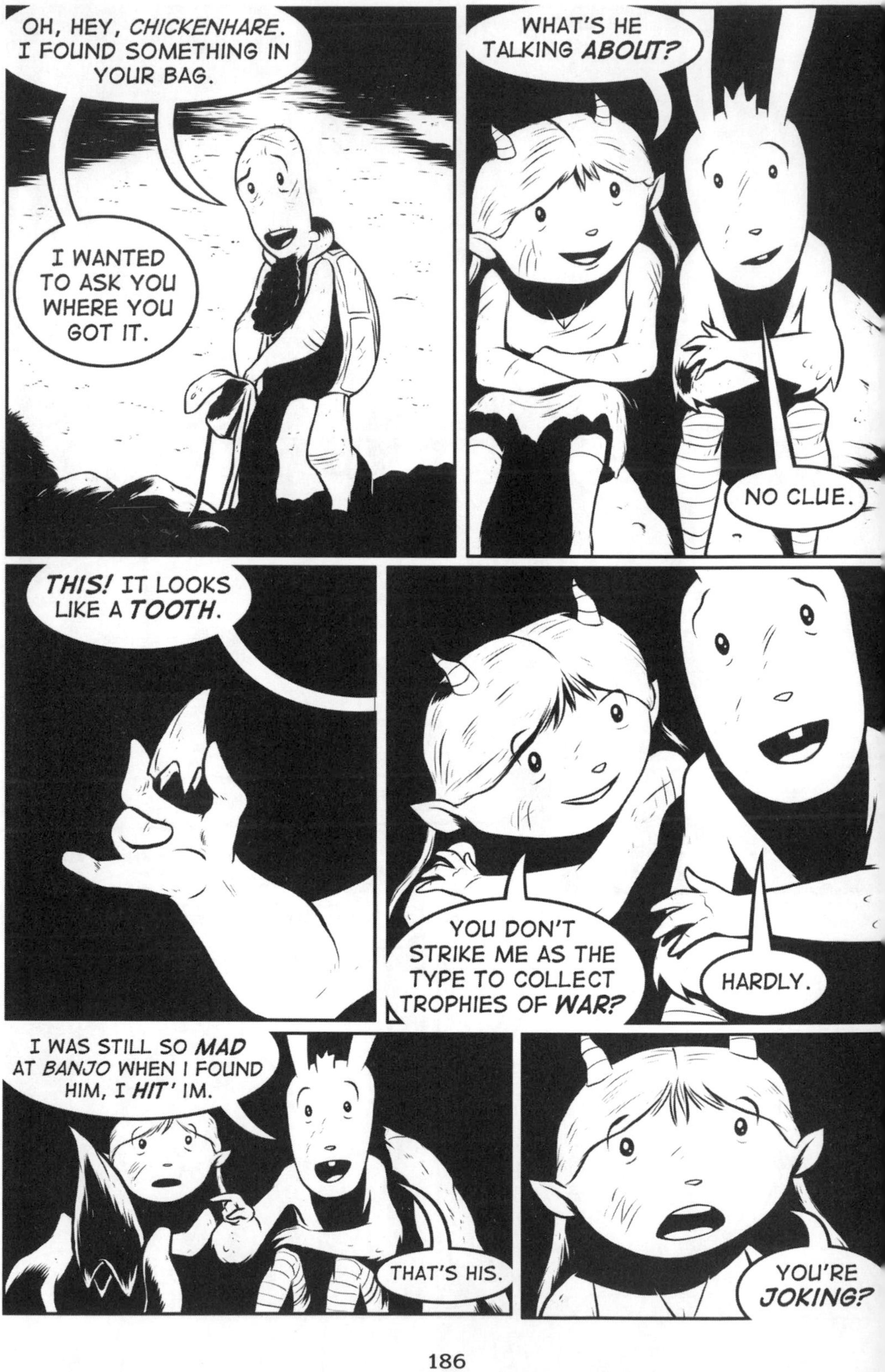
OH, HEY, *CHICKENHARE*. I FOUND SOMETHING IN YOUR BAG.
I WANTED TO ASK YOU WHERE YOU GOT IT.
WHAT'S HE TALKING *ABOUT?*
NO CLUE.
THIS! IT LOOKS LIKE A *TOOTH*.
YOU DON'T STRIKE ME AS THE TYPE TO COLLECT TROPHIES OF *WAR?*
HARDLY.
I WAS STILL SO *MAD* AT *BANJO* WHEN I FOUND HIM, I *HIT*' IM.
THAT'S HIS.
YOU'RE *JOKING?*

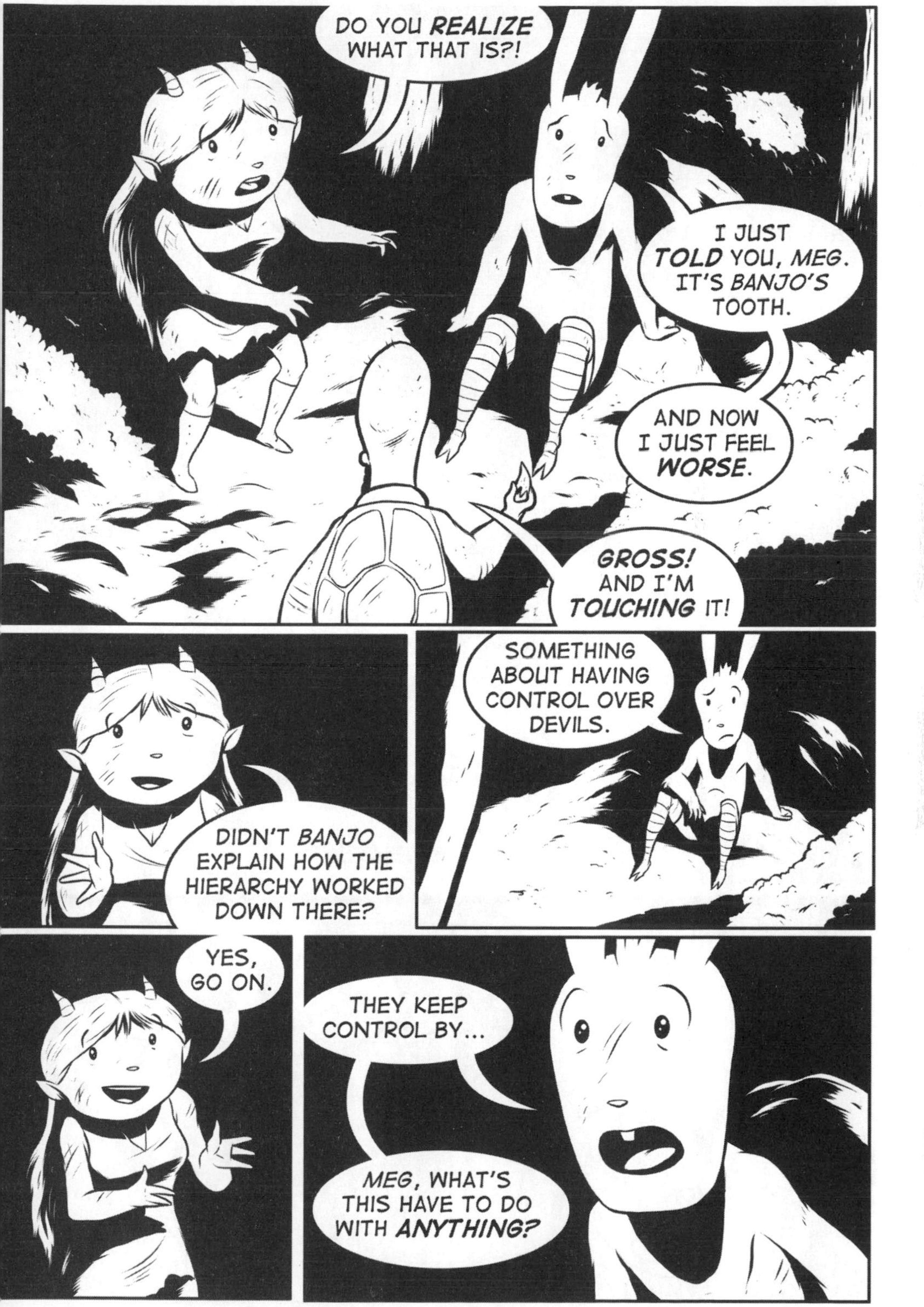
DO YOU REALIZE WHAT THAT IS?!
I JUST TOLD YOU, MEG. IT'S BANJO'S TOOTH.
AND NOW I JUST FEEL WORSE.
GROSS! AND I'M TOUCHING IT!
SOMETHING ABOUT HAVING CONTROL OVER DEVILS.
DIDN'T BANJO EXPLAIN HOW THE HIERARCHY WORKED DOWN THERE?
YES, GO ON.
THEY KEEP CONTROL BY...
MEG, WHAT'S THIS HAVE TO DO WITH ANYTHING?

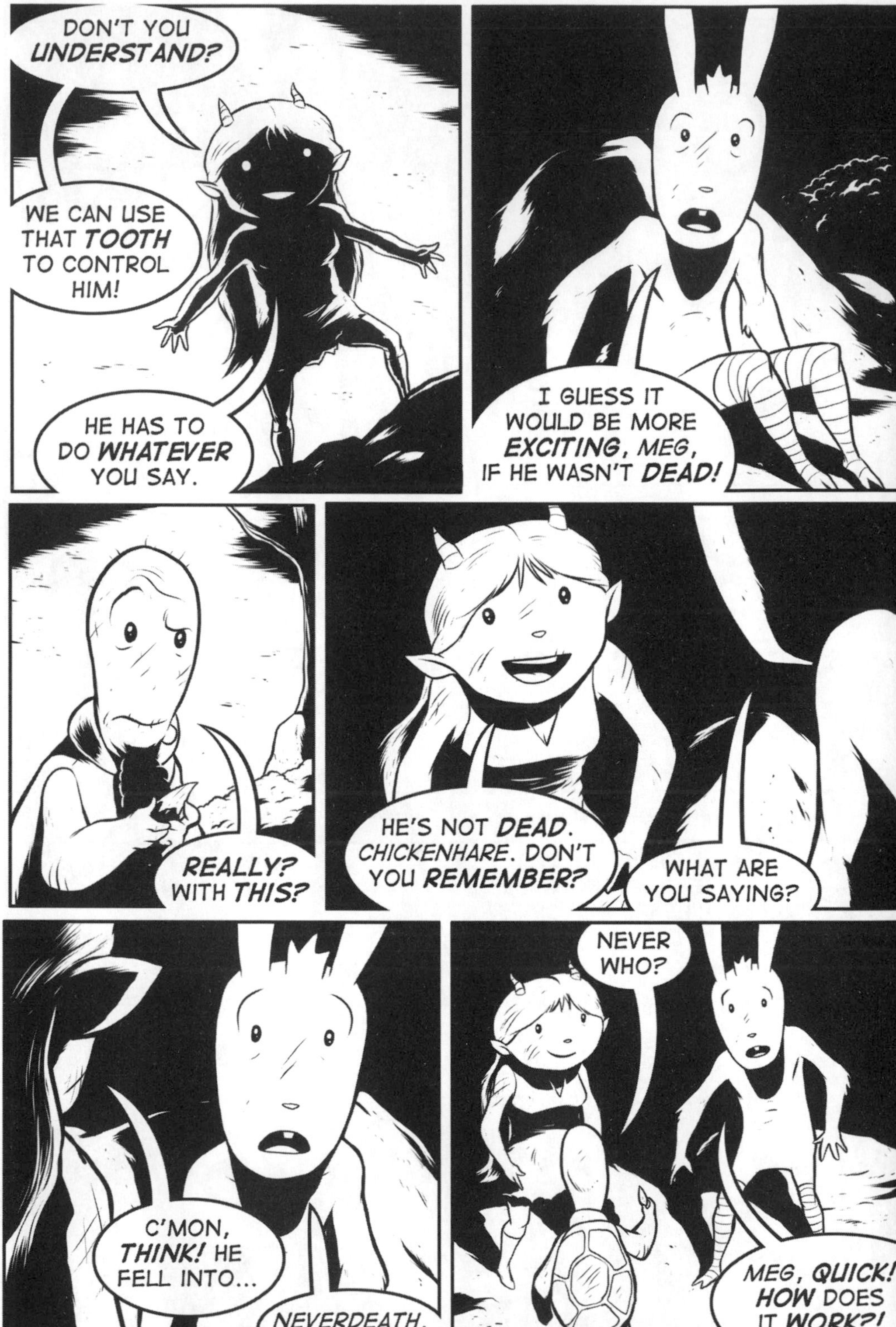
DON'T YOU UNDERSTAND?
WE CAN USE THAT TOOTH TO CONTROL HIM!
HE HAS TO DO WHATEVER YOU SAY.
I GUESS IT WOULD BE MORE EXCITING, MEG, IF HE WASN'T DEAD!
REALLY? WITH THIS?
HE'S NOT DEAD. CHICKENHARE. DON'T YOU REMEMBER?
WHAT ARE YOU SAYING?
C'MON, THINK! HE FELL INTO...
NEVERDEATH.
NEVER WHO?
MEG, QUICK! HOW DOES IT WORK?!

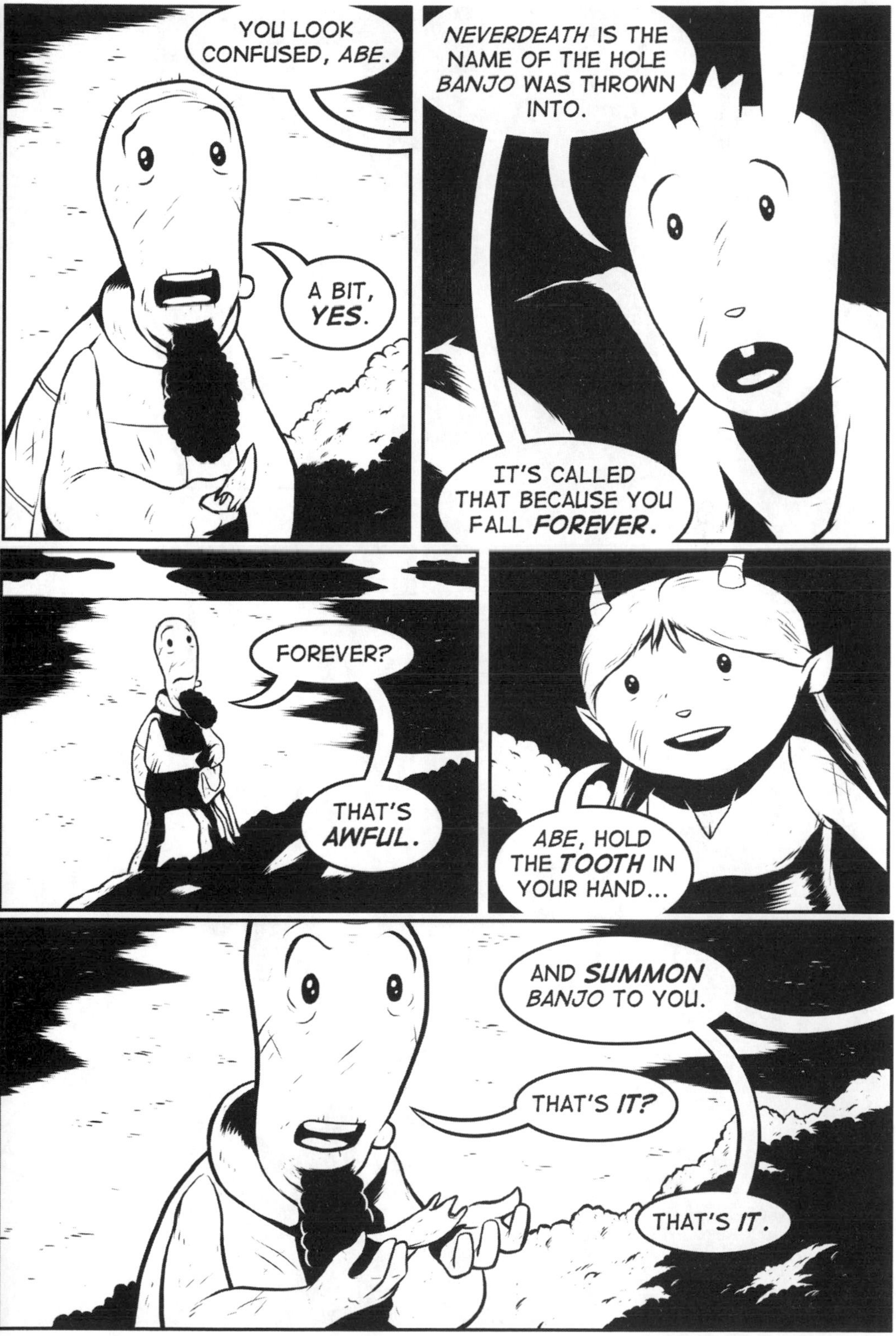
YOU LOOK CONFUSED, *ABE*.
A BIT, ***YES***.
NEVERDEATH IS THE NAME OF THE HOLE *BANJO* WAS THROWN INTO.
IT'S CALLED THAT BECAUSE YOU FALL ***FOREVER***.
FOREVER?
THAT'S ***AWFUL***.
ABE, HOLD THE ***TOOTH*** IN YOUR HAND...
AND ***SUMMON*** *BANJO* TO YOU.
THAT'S *IT?*
THAT'S *IT*.

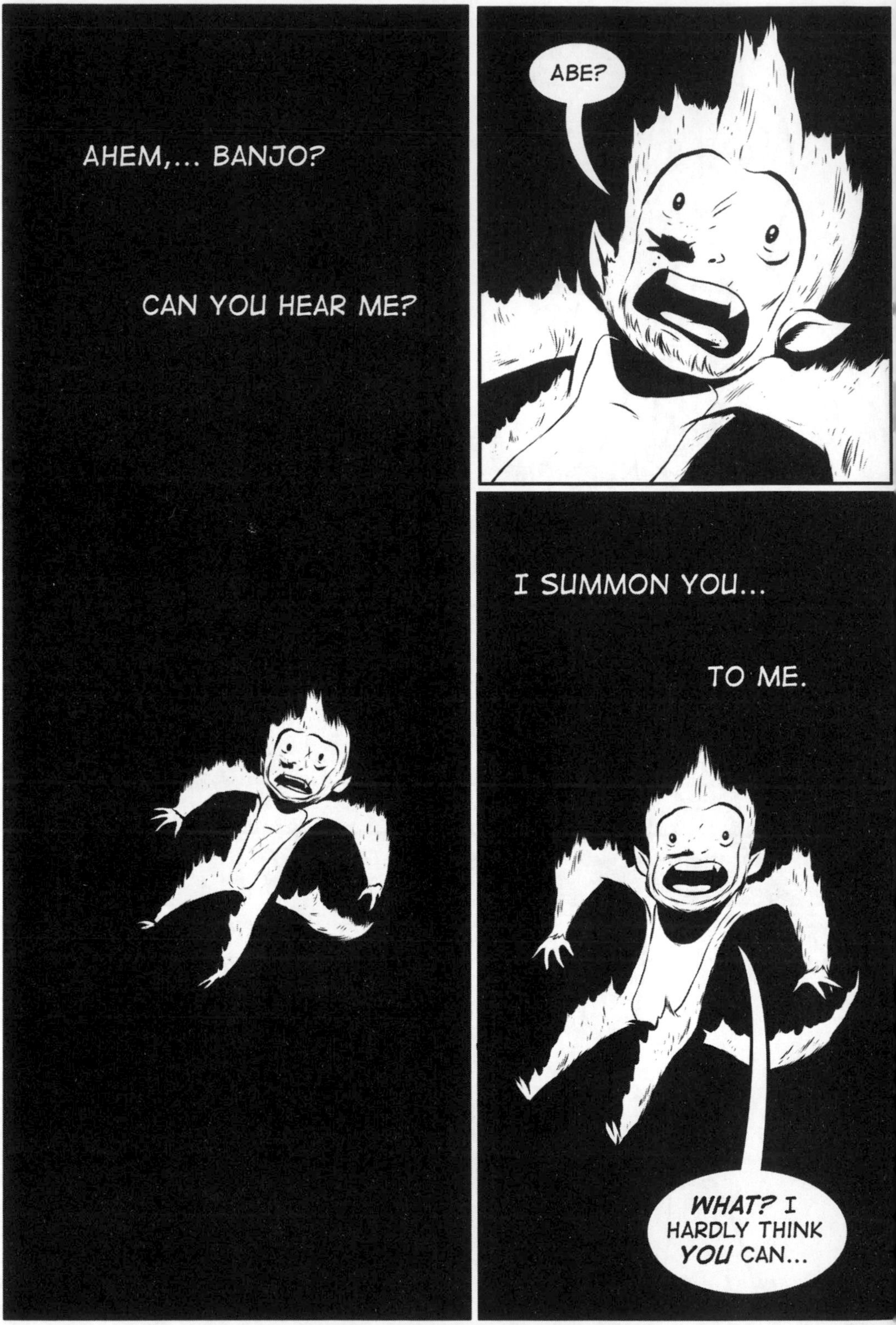
AHEM,... BANJO?
CAN YOU HEAR ME?
ABE?
I SUMMON YOU...
TO ME.
WHAT? I HARDLY THINK YOU CAN...

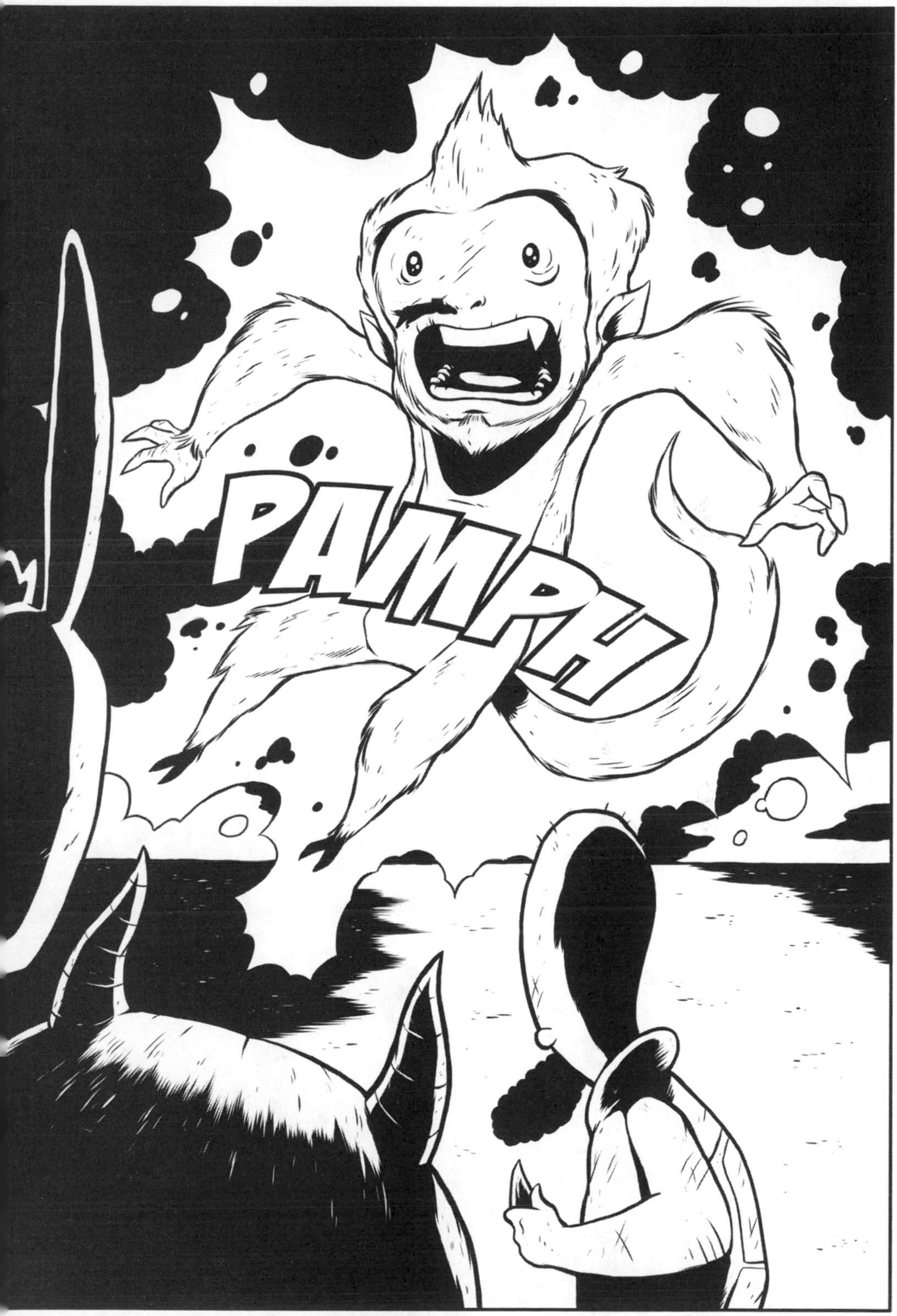
PAMPH

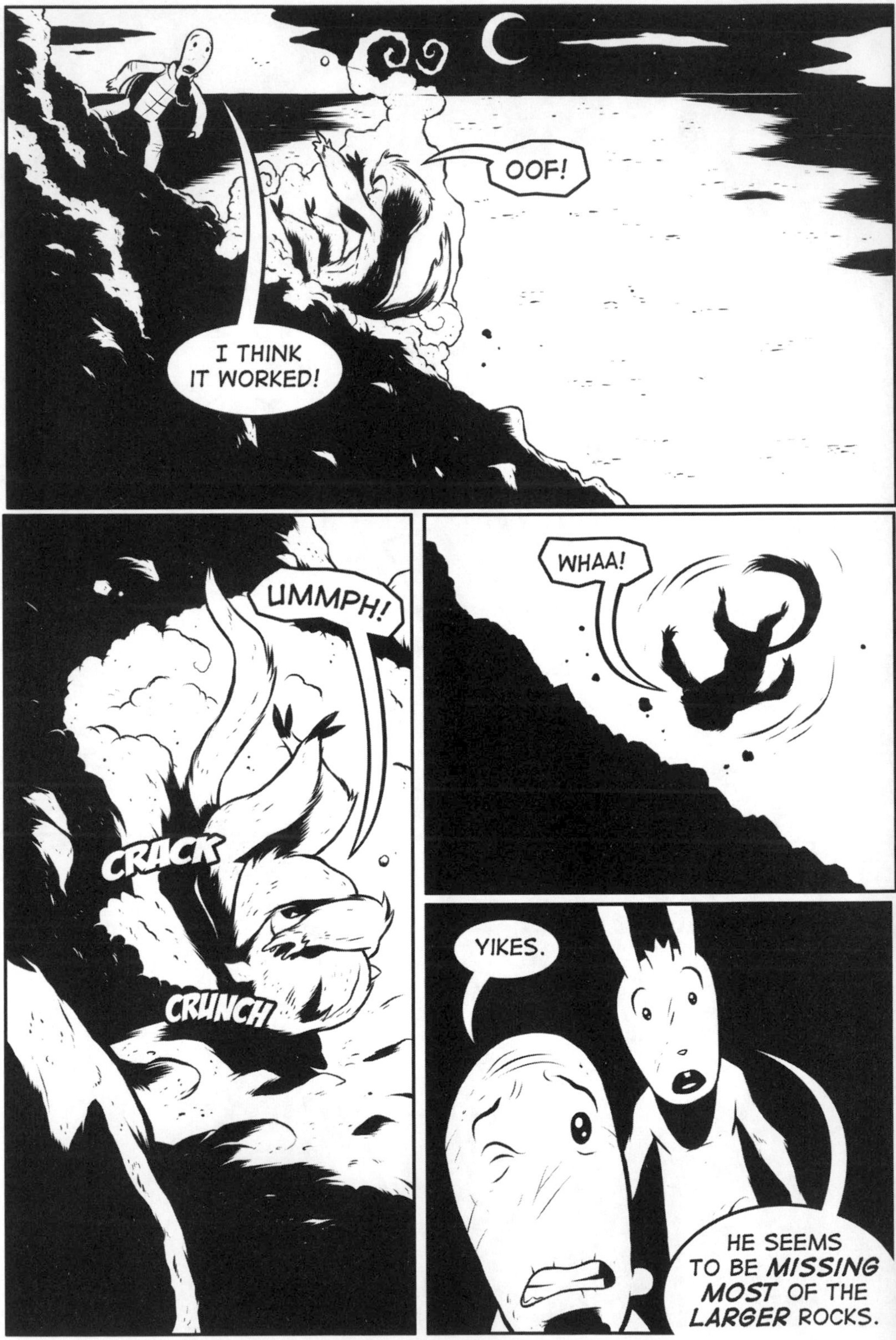
OOF!
I THINK IT WORKED!
UMMPH!
CRACK
CRUNCH
WHAA!
YIKES.
HE SEEMS TO BE MISSING MOST OF THE LARGER ROCKS.

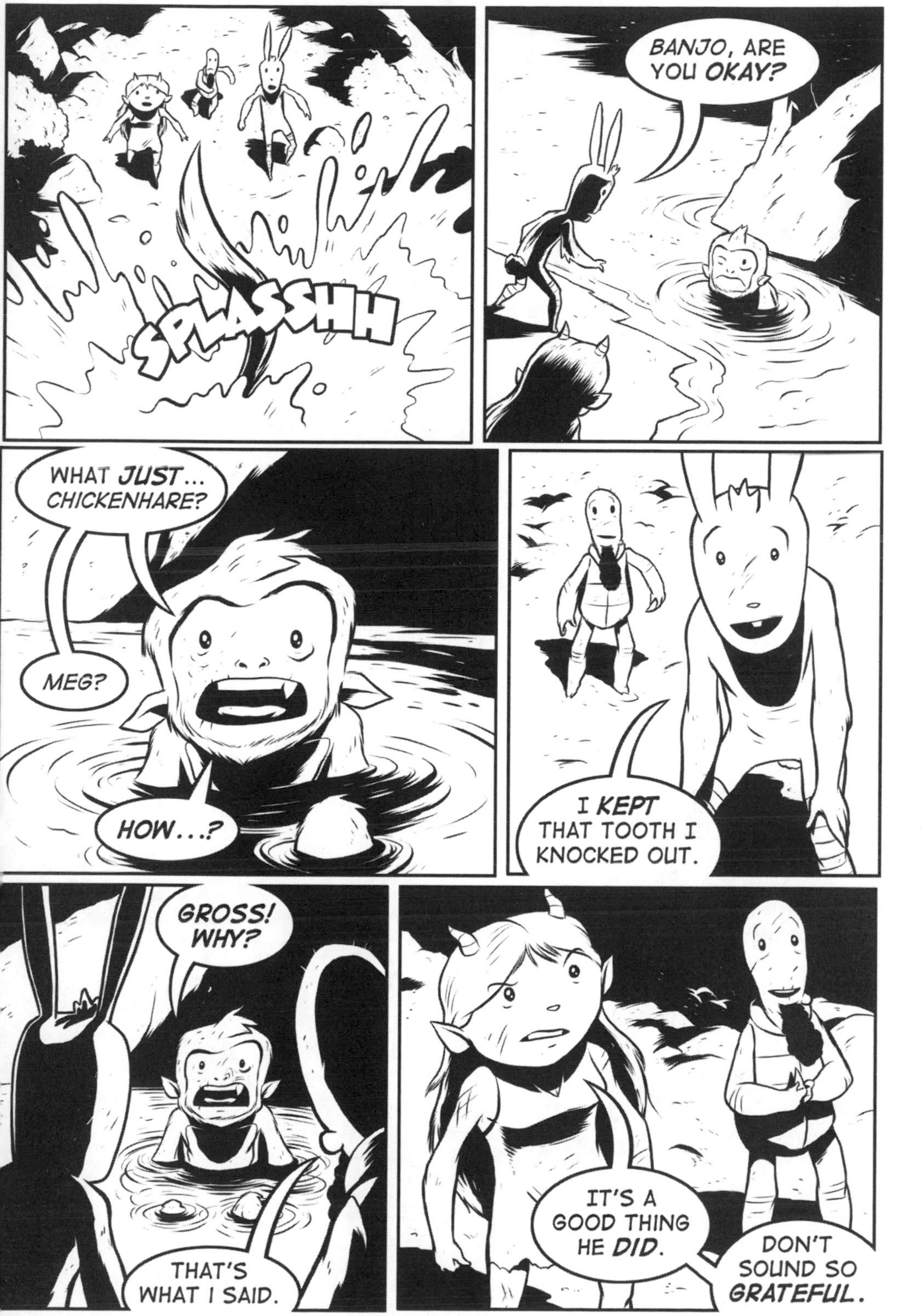
SPLASSHH
BANJO, ARE YOU OKAY?
WHAT JUST... CHICKENHARE?
MEG?
HOW...?
I KEPT THAT TOOTH I KNOCKED OUT.
GROSS! WHY?
THAT'S WHAT I SAID.
IT'S A GOOD THING HE DID.
DON'T SOUND SO GRATEFUL.

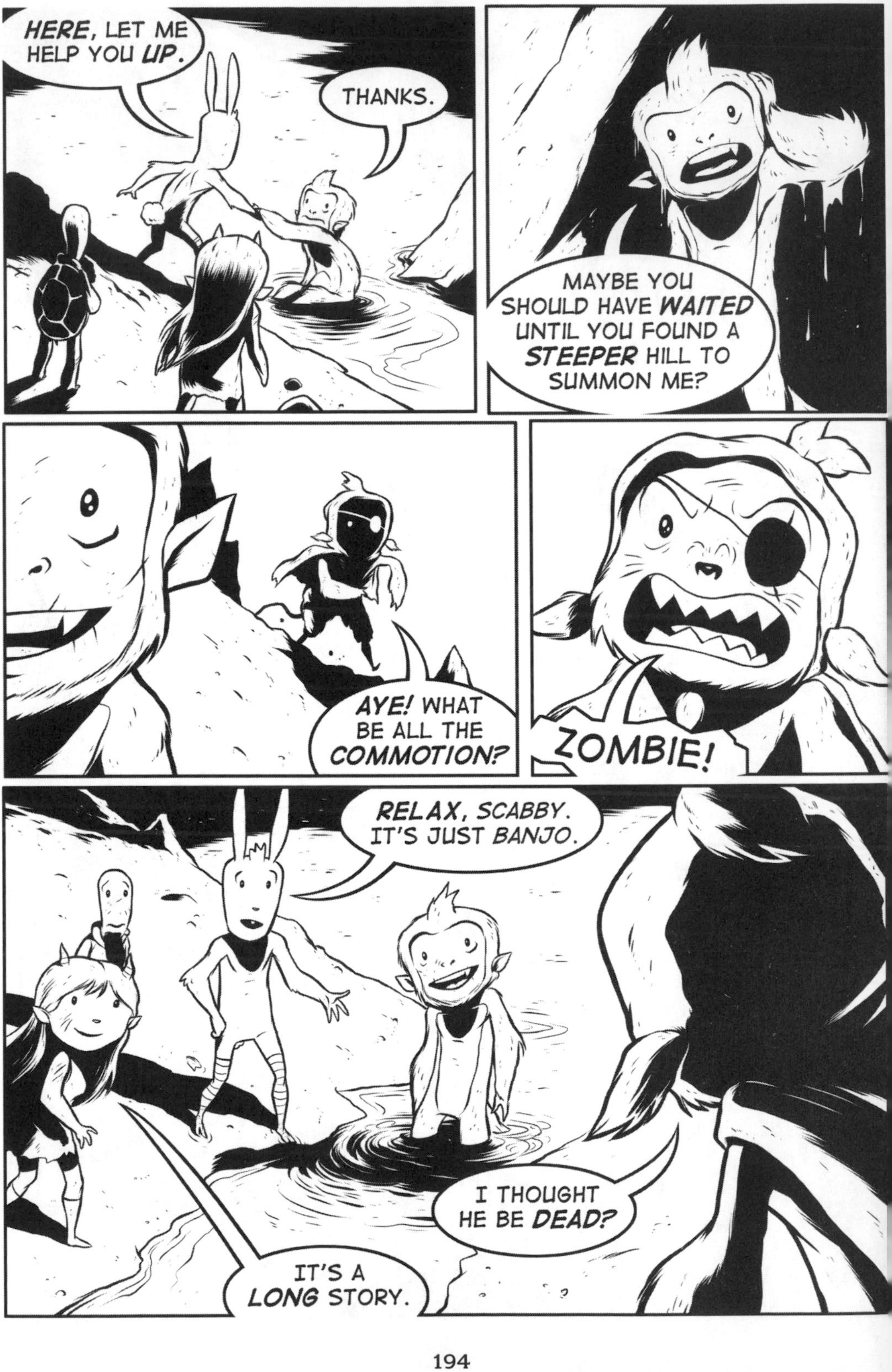
HERE, LET ME HELP YOU UP.
THANKS.
MAYBE YOU SHOULD HAVE WAITED UNTIL YOU FOUND A STEEPER HILL TO SUMMON ME?
AYE! WHAT BE ALL THE COMMOTION?
ZOMBIE!
RELAX, SCABBY. IT'S JUST BANJO.
I THOUGHT HE BE DEAD?
IT'S A LONG STORY.

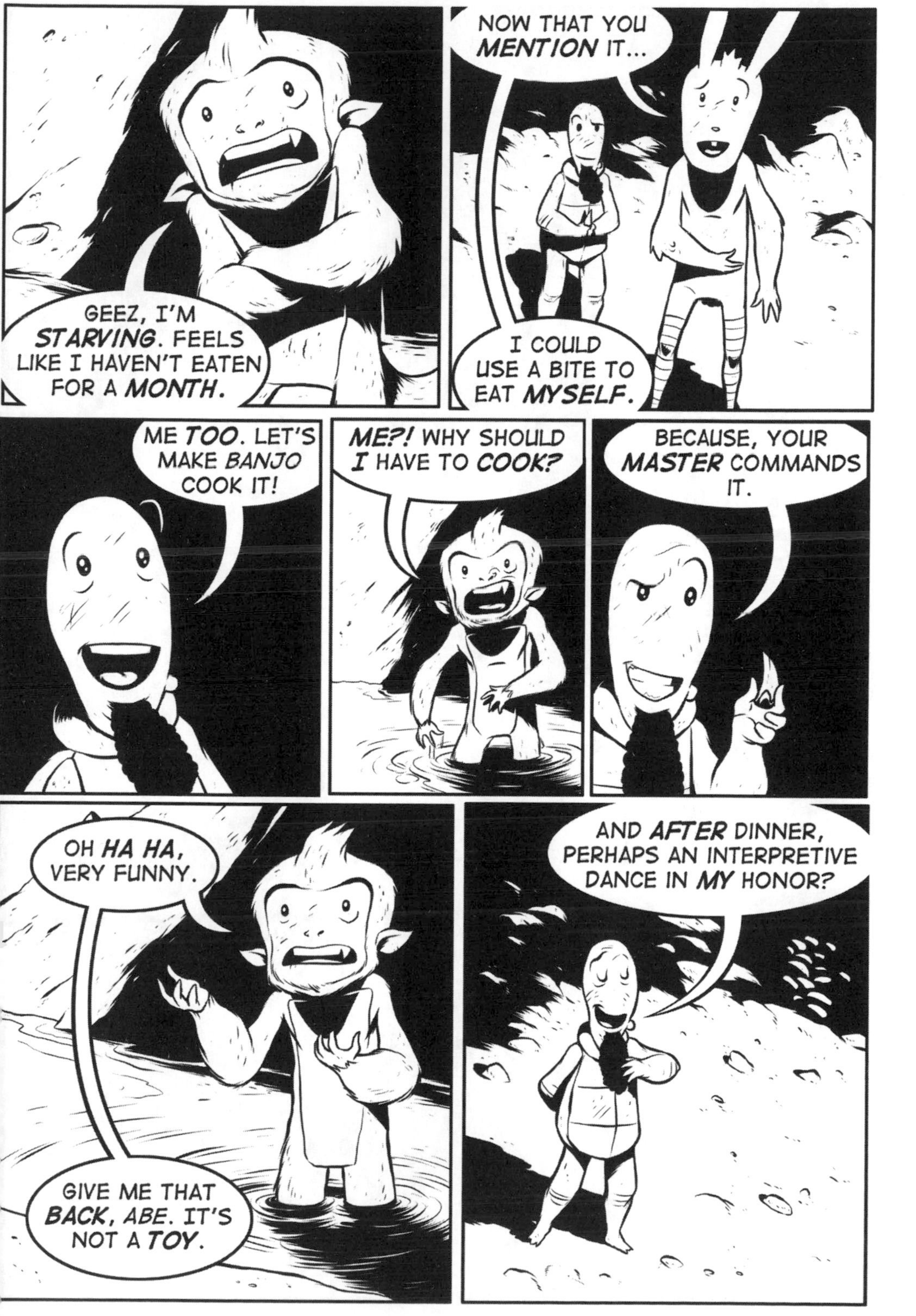
GEEZ, I'M STARVING. FEELS LIKE I HAVEN'T EATEN FOR A MONTH.
NOW THAT YOU MENTION IT...
I COULD USE A BITE TO EAT MYSELF.
ME TOO. LET'S MAKE BANJO COOK IT!
ME?! WHY SHOULD I HAVE TO COOK?
BECAUSE, YOUR MASTER COMMANDS IT.
OH HA HA, VERY FUNNY.
GIVE ME THAT BACK, ABE. IT'S NOT A TOY.
AND AFTER DINNER, PERHAPS AN INTERPRETIVE DANCE IN MY HONOR?

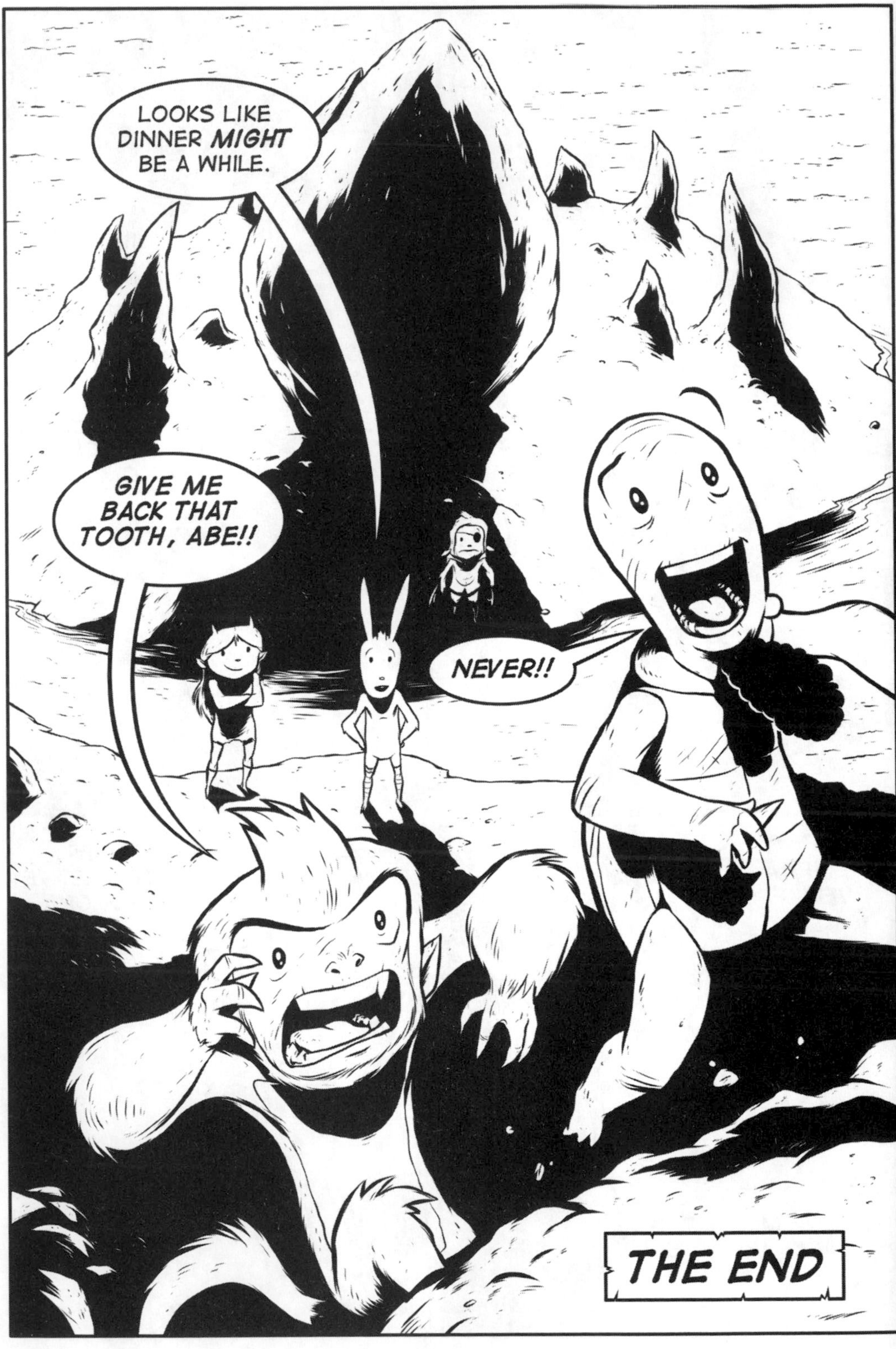
LOOKS LIKE DINNER *MIGHT* BE A WHILE.
GIVE ME BACK THAT TOOTH, ABE!!
NEVER!!
THE END

JUST A TINY BIT MORE...

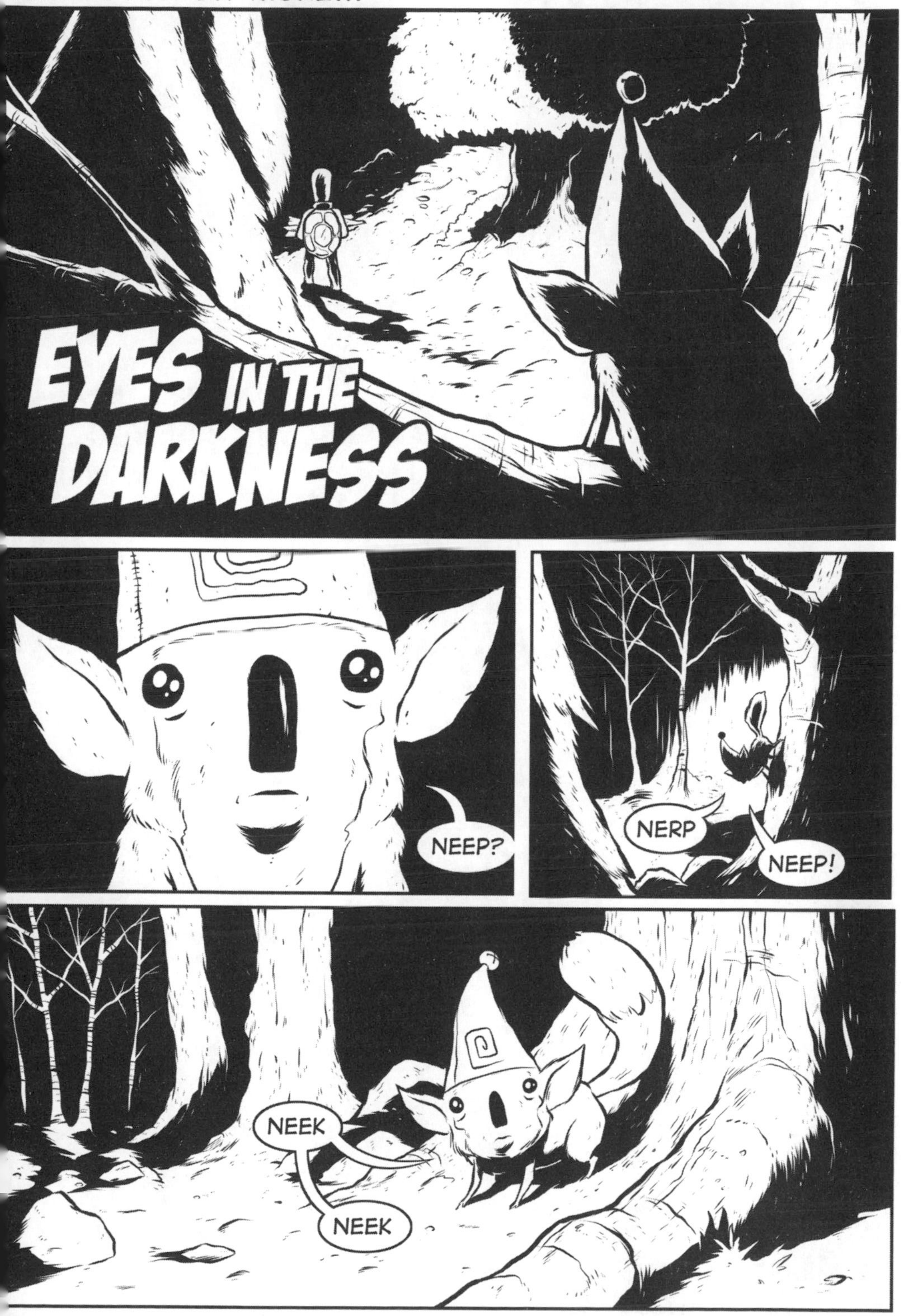
EYES IN THE DARKNESS
NEEP?
NERP
NEEP!
NEEK
NEEK

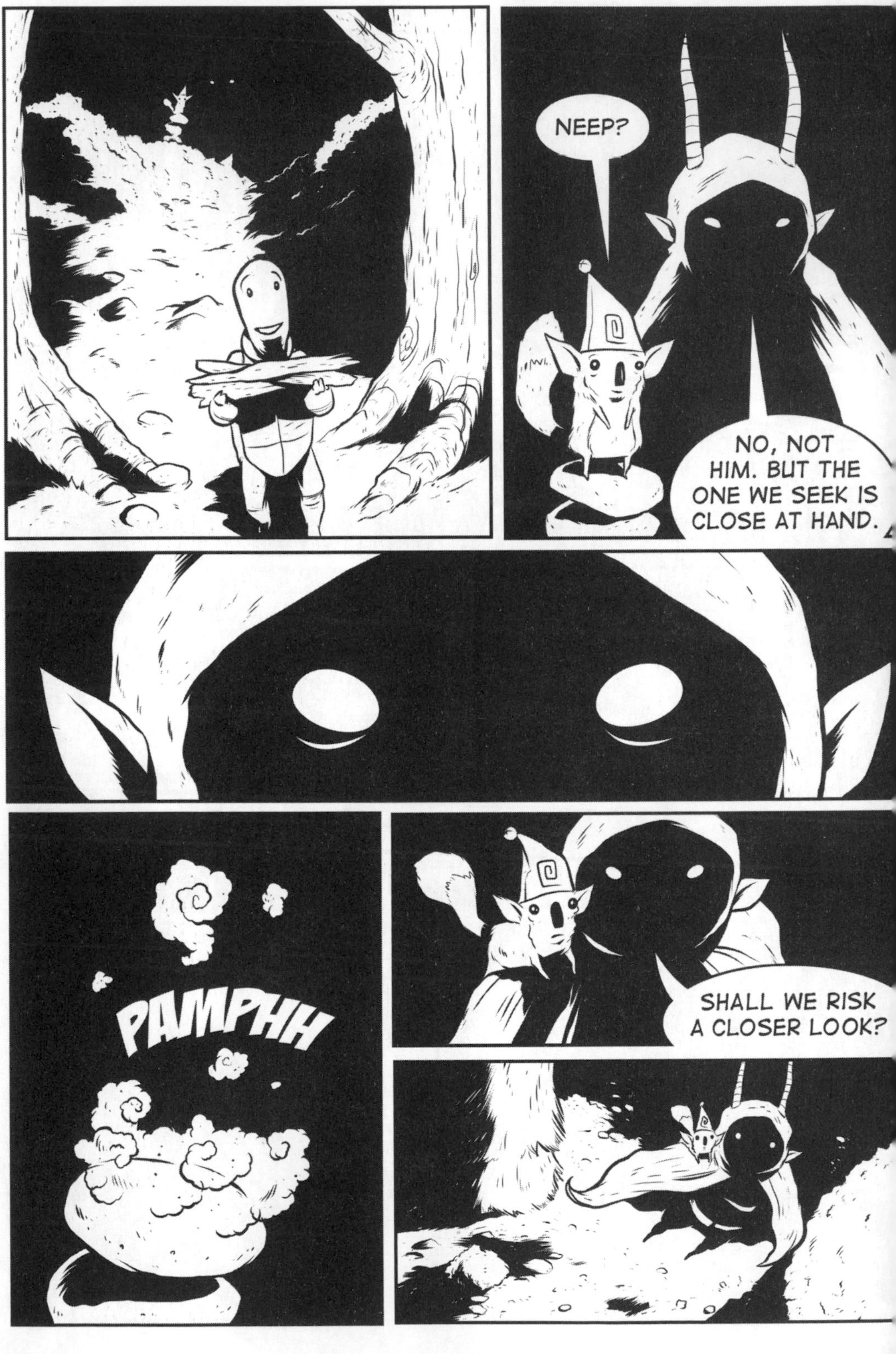
NEEP?
NO, NOT HIM. BUT THE ONE WE SEEK IS CLOSE AT HAND.
PAMPHH
SHALL WE RISK A CLOSER LOOK?

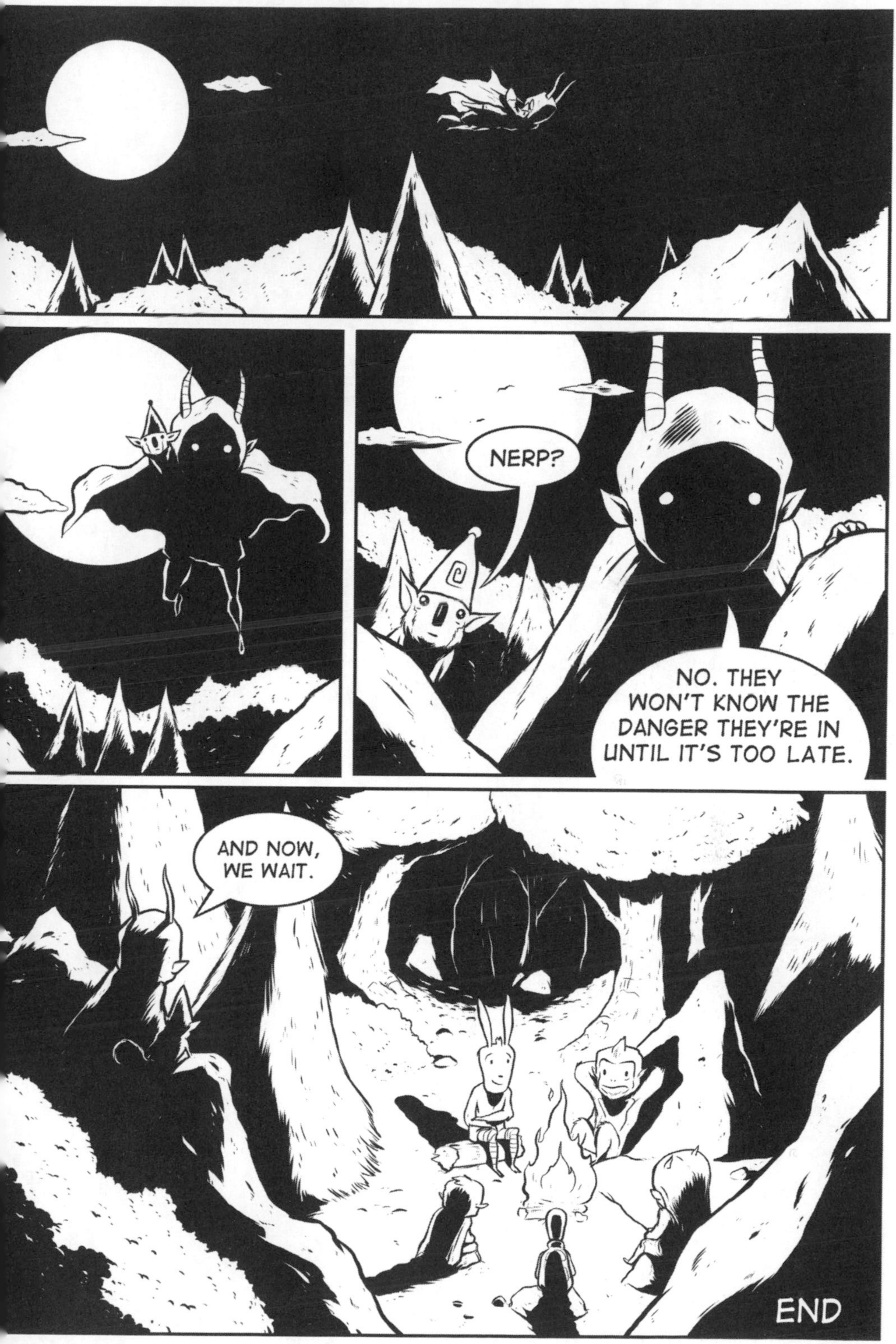
NERP?
NO. THEY WON'T KNOW THE DANGER THEY'RE IN UNTIL IT'S TOO LATE.
AND NOW, WE WAIT.
END

What do you get when you cross a chicken with a hare?

The funniest, most exciting all-ages graphic novel of ALL TIME!

Night is falling on the frozen landscape as Chickenhare and his turtle friend Abe find themselves on their way to be sold to Klaus—an insane taxidermist with a penchant for unique animals and enough emotional baggage to go on a very long vacation!

With the help of two mysterious new companions (not to mention a very friendly, very dead goat!), Chickenhare and Abe might be able to escape, but . . . where? Right into the lair of the deadly cave-dwelling critters known as the Shromph! . . . er, Shromps? Shromphses? Never mind! Just get ready for some fun!

Chickenhare: The House of Klaus
ISBN 978-1-59307-574-3
$9.95